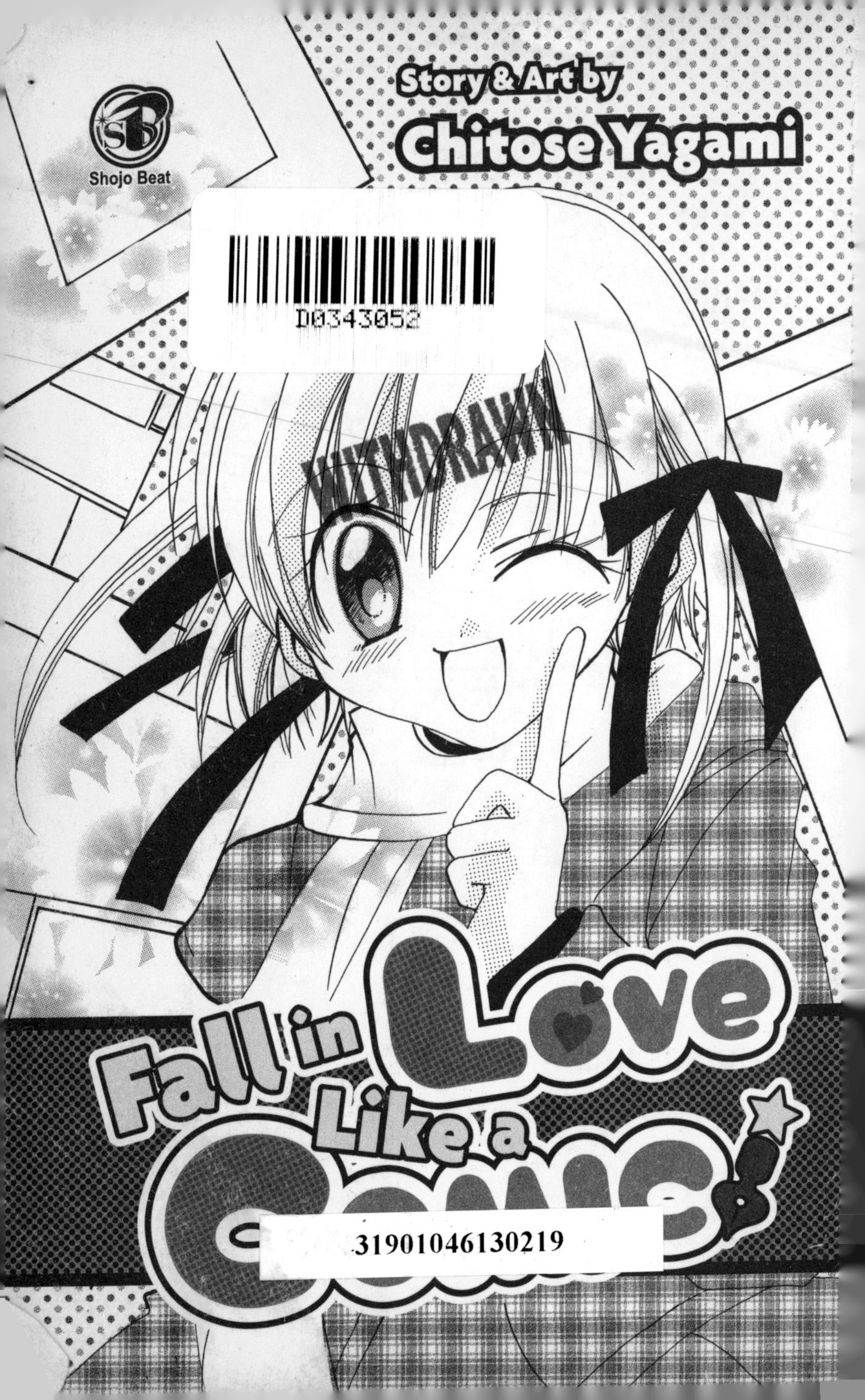
Shojo Beat
Story & Art by
Chitose Yagami
Fall in Love
Like a

Fall in Love Like a Comic!

CHITOSE YAGAMI

Contents

Vol. 1

INK

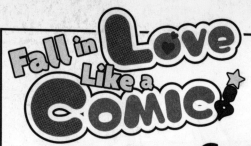

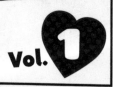

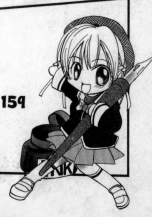

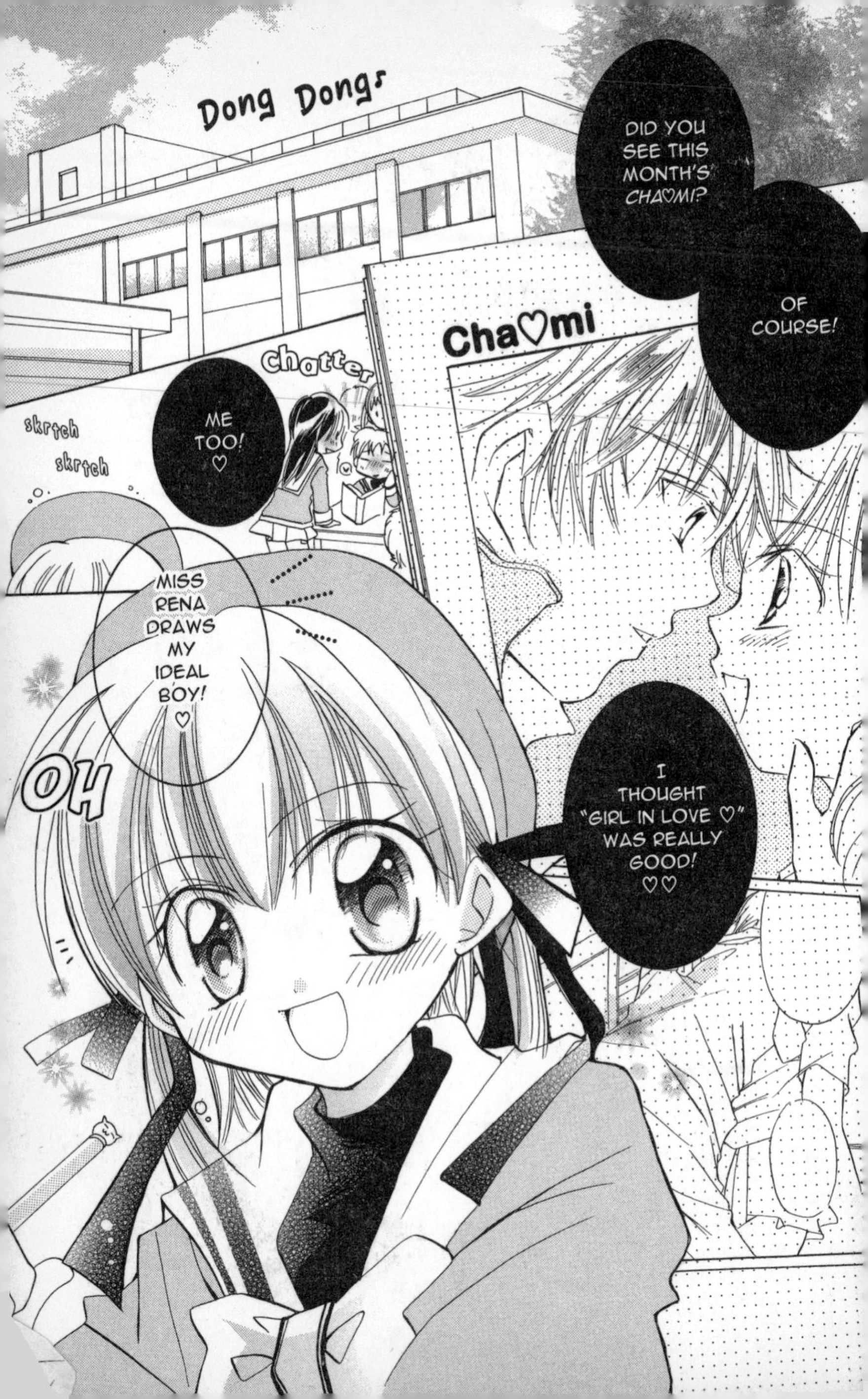
Dong Dong
DID YOU SEE THIS MONTH'S CHA♡MI?
OF COURSE!
Cha♡mi
chatter
ME TOO! ♡
skrtch skrtch
MISS RENA DRAWS MY IDEAL BOY! ♡
I THOUGHT "GIRL IN LOVE ♡" WAS REALLY GOOD! ♡♡
OH

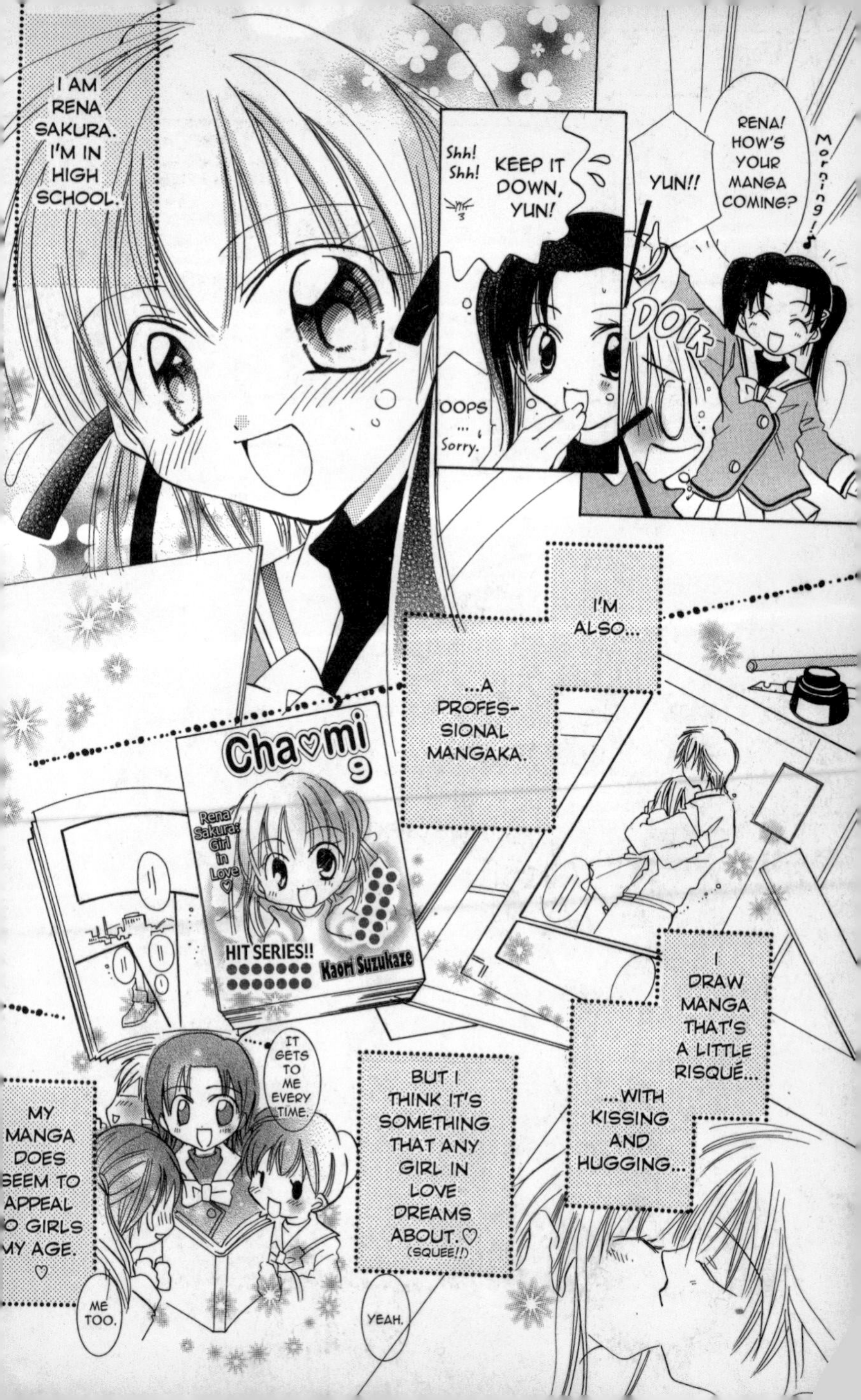
Morning!♪
RENA! HOW'S YOUR MANGA COMING?
DOIK
YUN!!
Shh! Shh!
KEEP IT DOWN, YUN!
OOPS... Sorry.
I AM RENA SAKURA. I'M IN HIGH SCHOOL.
I'M ALSO...
...A PROFESSIONAL MANGAKA.
Cha♡mi
9
Rena Sakura: Girl in Love♡
HIT SERIES!!
Kaori Suzukaze
I DRAW MANGA THAT'S A LITTLE RISQUÉ...
...WITH KISSING AND HUGGING...
BUT I THINK IT'S SOMETHING THAT ANY GIRL IN LOVE DREAMS ABOUT.♡
(SQUEE!!)
YEAH.
IT GETS TO ME EVERY TIME.
MY MANGA DOES SEEM TO APPEAL TO GIRLS MY AGE.♡
ME TOO.

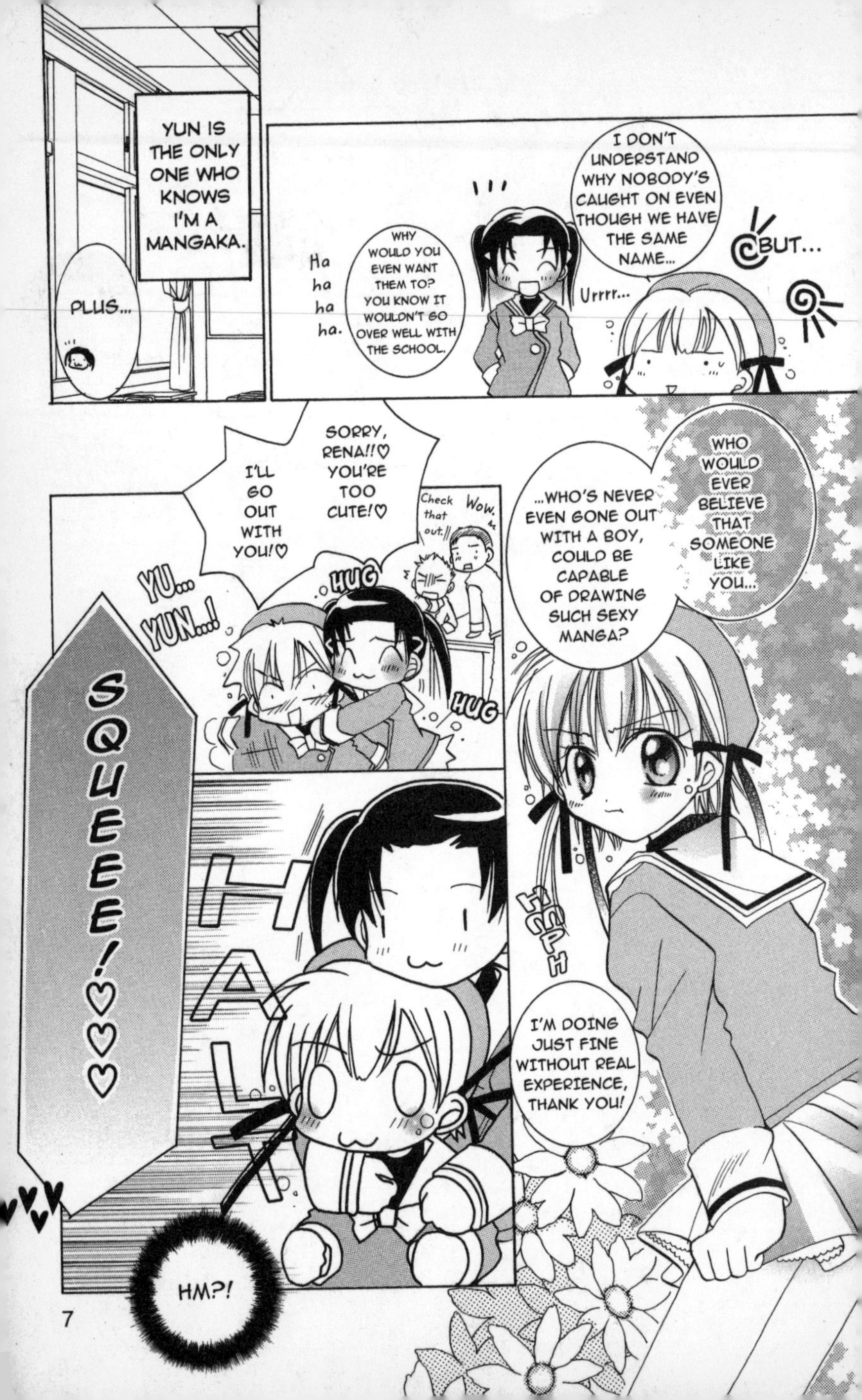
I DON'T UNDERSTAND WHY NOBODY'S CAUGHT ON EVEN THOUGH WE HAVE THE SAME NAME...
BUT...
Urrrr...
WHY WOULD YOU EVEN WANT THEM TO? YOU KNOW IT WOULDN'T GO OVER WELL WITH THE SCHOOL.
Ha ha ha ha.
YUN IS THE ONLY ONE WHO KNOWS I'M A MANGAKA.
PLUS...
WHO WOULD EVER BELIEVE THAT SOMEONE LIKE YOU...
...WHO'S NEVER EVEN GONE OUT WITH A BOY, COULD BE CAPABLE OF DRAWING SUCH SEXY MANGA?
HMPH
I'M DOING JUST FINE WITHOUT REAL EXPERIENCE, THANK YOU!
SORRY, RENA!!♡ YOU'RE TOO CUTE!♡
I'LL GO OUT WITH YOU!♡
Wow.
Check that out.
HUG
HUG
YU... YUN...!
SQUEEE!♡♡♡
HM?!

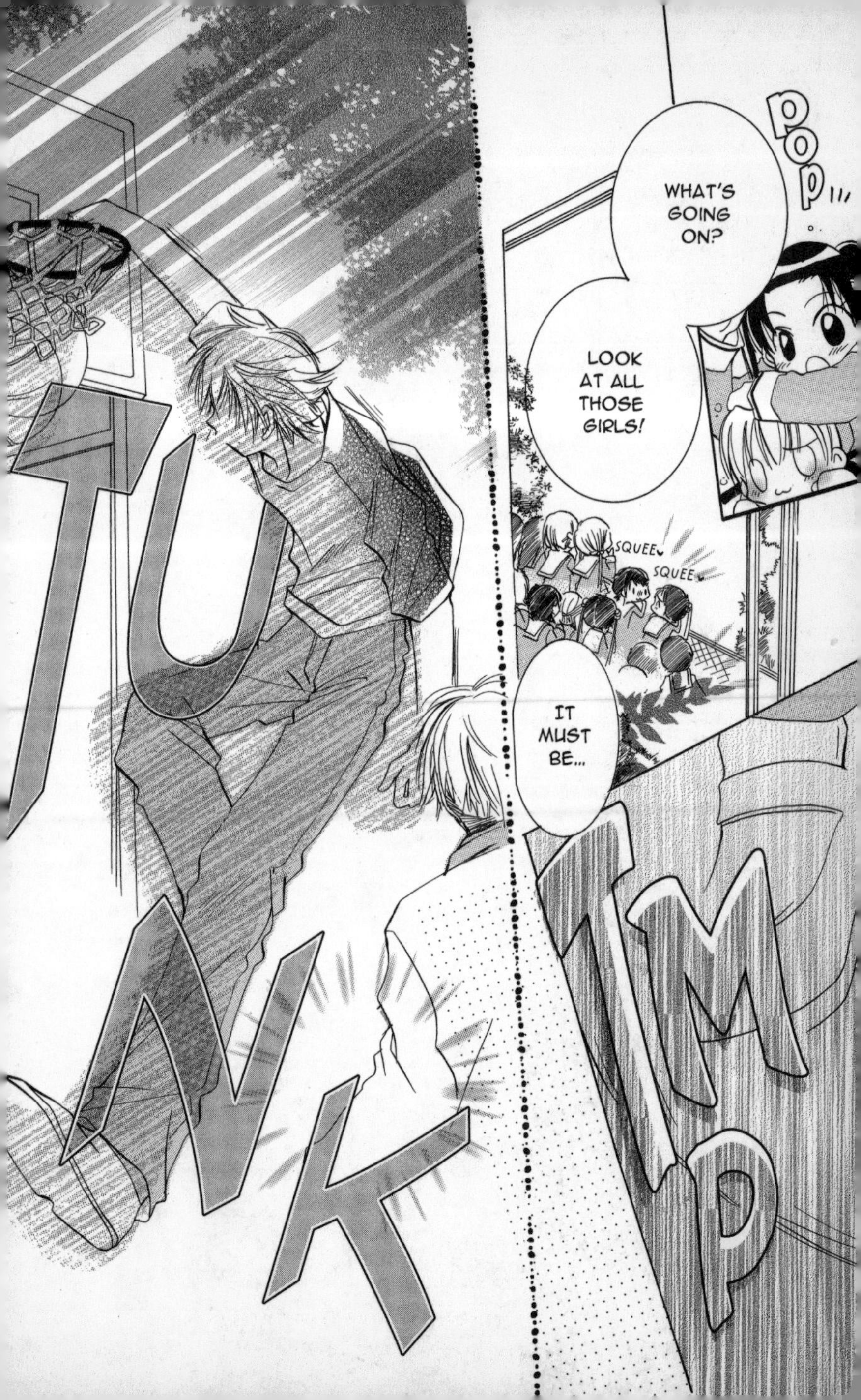
pop
WHAT'S GOING ON?
LOOK AT ALL THOSE GIRLS!
SQUEE
SQUEE
IT MUST BE...
TMP
TUNK

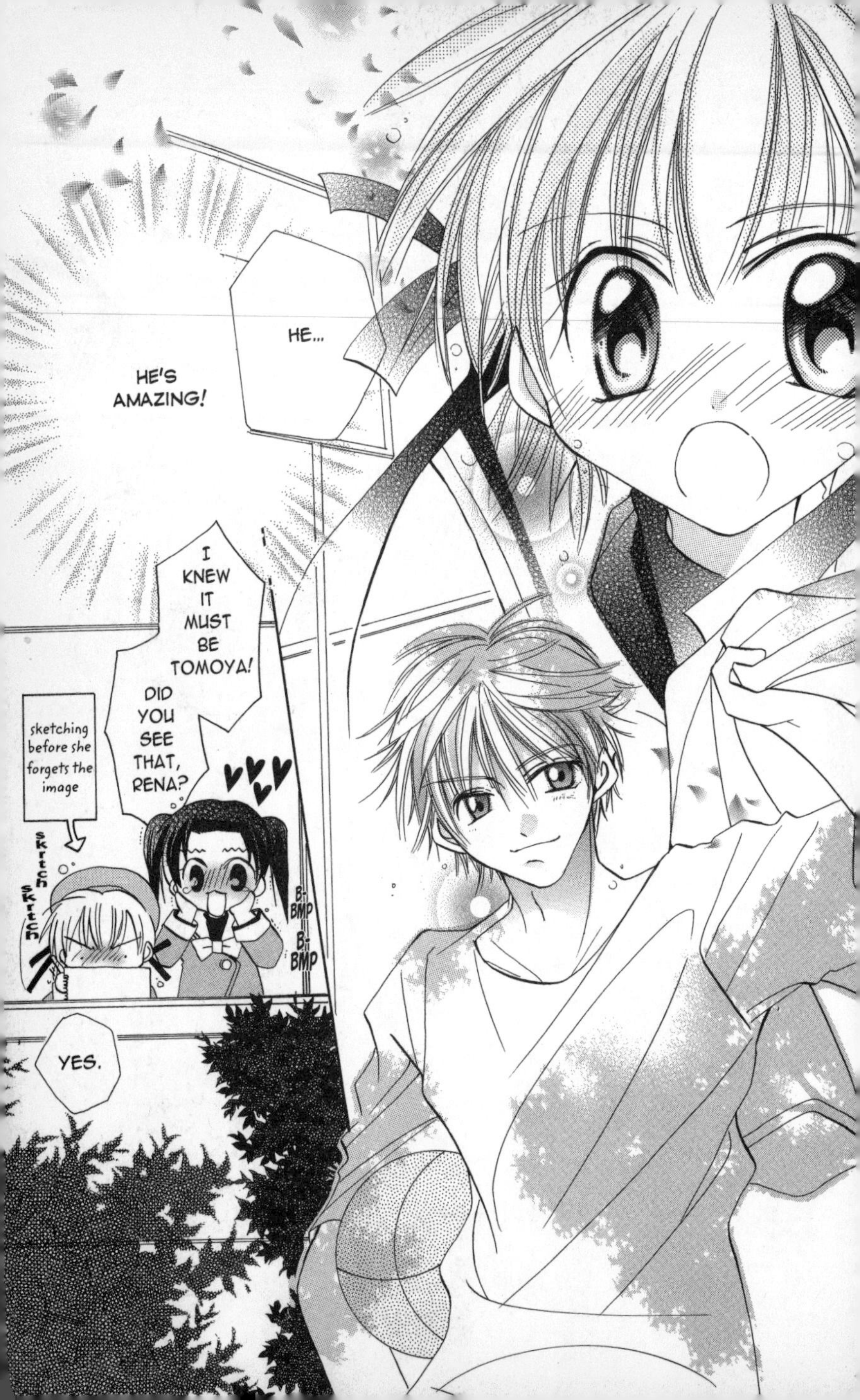
HE...
HE'S AMAZING!
I KNEW IT MUST BE TOMOYA!
DID YOU SEE THAT, RENA?
B-BMP B-BMP
sketching before she forgets the image
SKRITCH SKRITCH
YES.

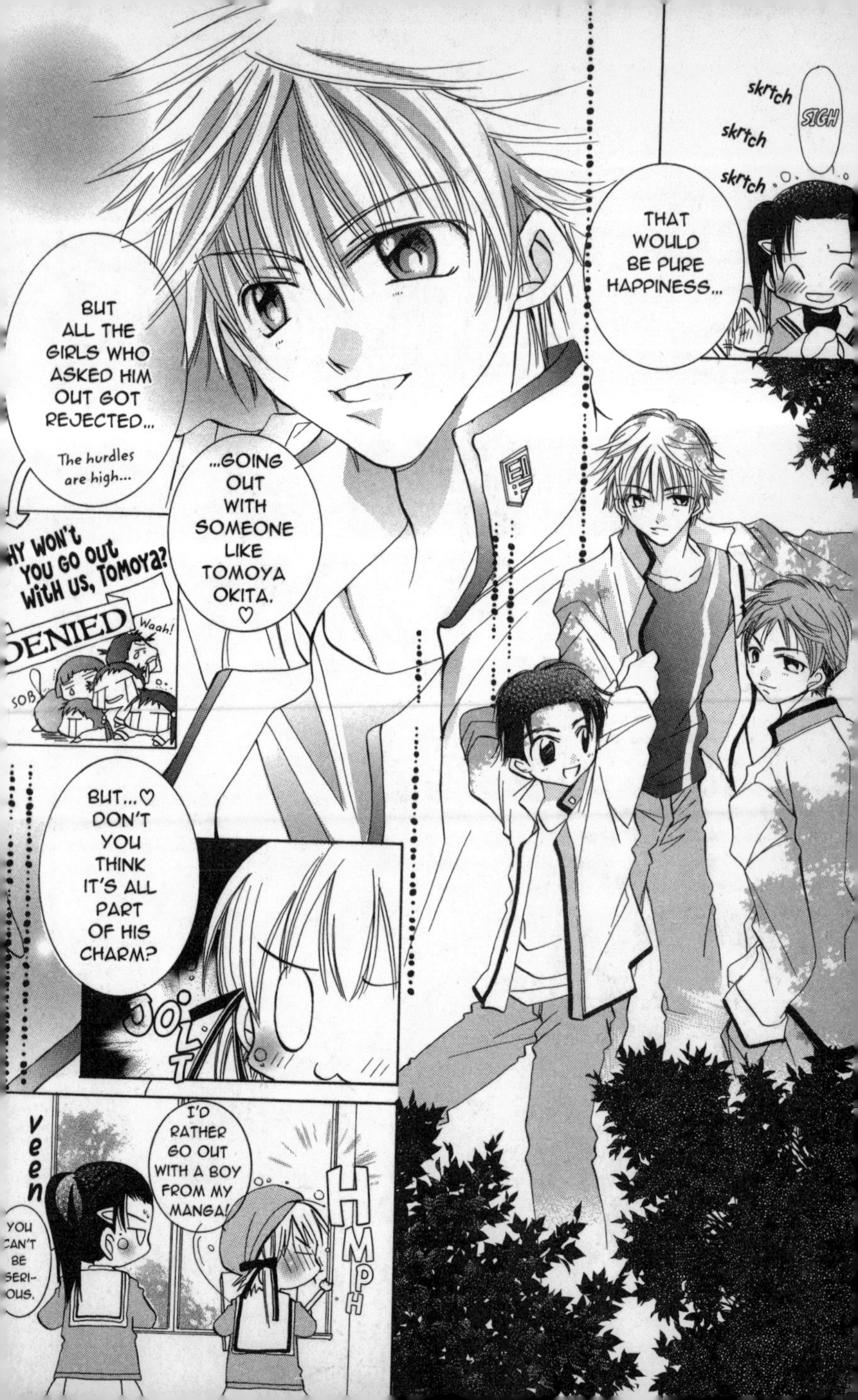
skrtch
SIGH
skrtch
skrtch
THAT WOULD BE PURE HAPPINESS...
...GOING OUT WITH SOMEONE LIKE TOMOYA OKITA. ♡
BUT ALL THE GIRLS WHO ASKED HIM OUT GOT REJECTED...
The hurdles are high...
HY WON'T YOU GO OUT WITH US, TOMOYA?
DENIED
Waah!
SOB
BUT...♡ DON'T YOU THINK IT'S ALL PART OF HIS CHARM?
JOLT
I'D RATHER GO OUT WITH A BOY FROM MY MANGA!
HMPH
Veen
YOU CAN'T BE SERI-OUS.

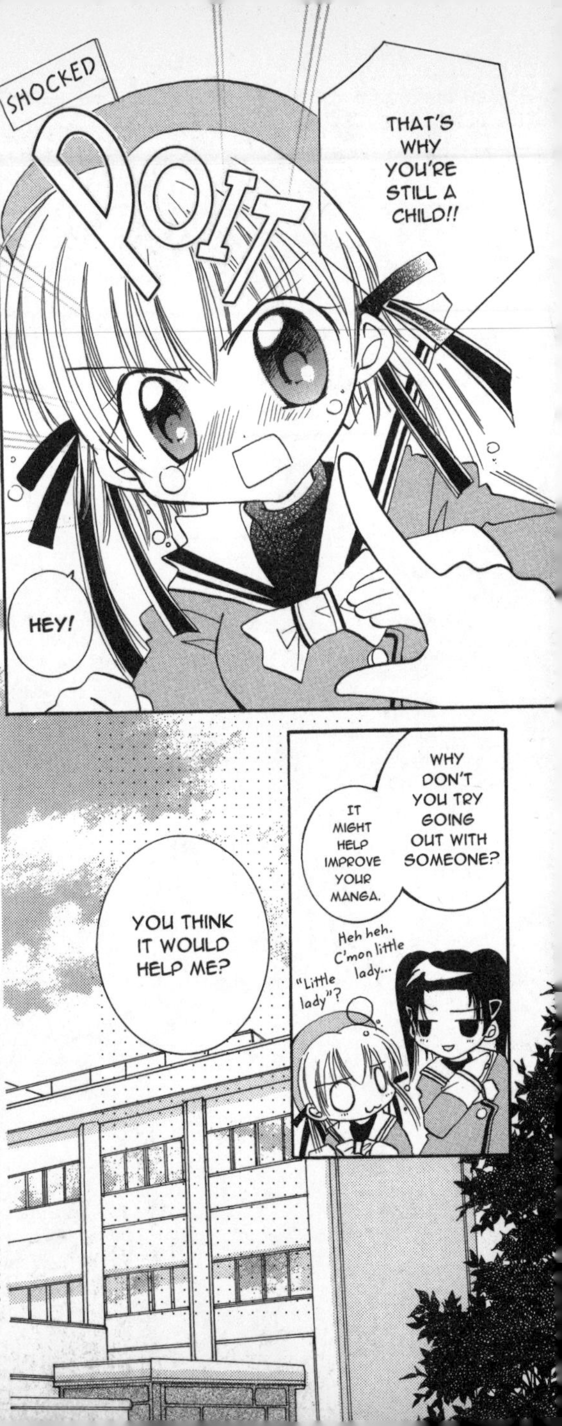
SHOCKED
POIT
THAT'S WHY YOU'RE STILL A CHILD!!
HEY!
WHY DON'T YOU TRY GOING OUT WITH SOMEONE?
IT MIGHT HELP IMPROVE YOUR MANGA.
Heh heh. C'mon little lady...
"Little lady"?
YOU THINK IT WOULD HELP ME?

Greetings!

Hello. I'm Chitose Yagami.

This is officially my second manga, and it's quite a bit longer than what I've done before--help me!!

Fall in Love like a Comic is the first manga I've had published in Ciao magazine. Time goes by so quickly...

I was encouraged by the many letters I received during its publication. Thank you so much! I feel badly that I haven't been able to respond to all your letters, but I hope to do so when I have a little more time.

Thank you again!

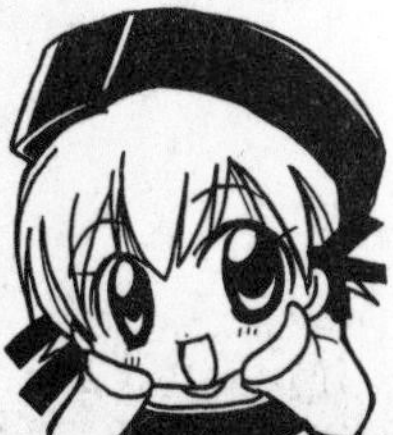
INK

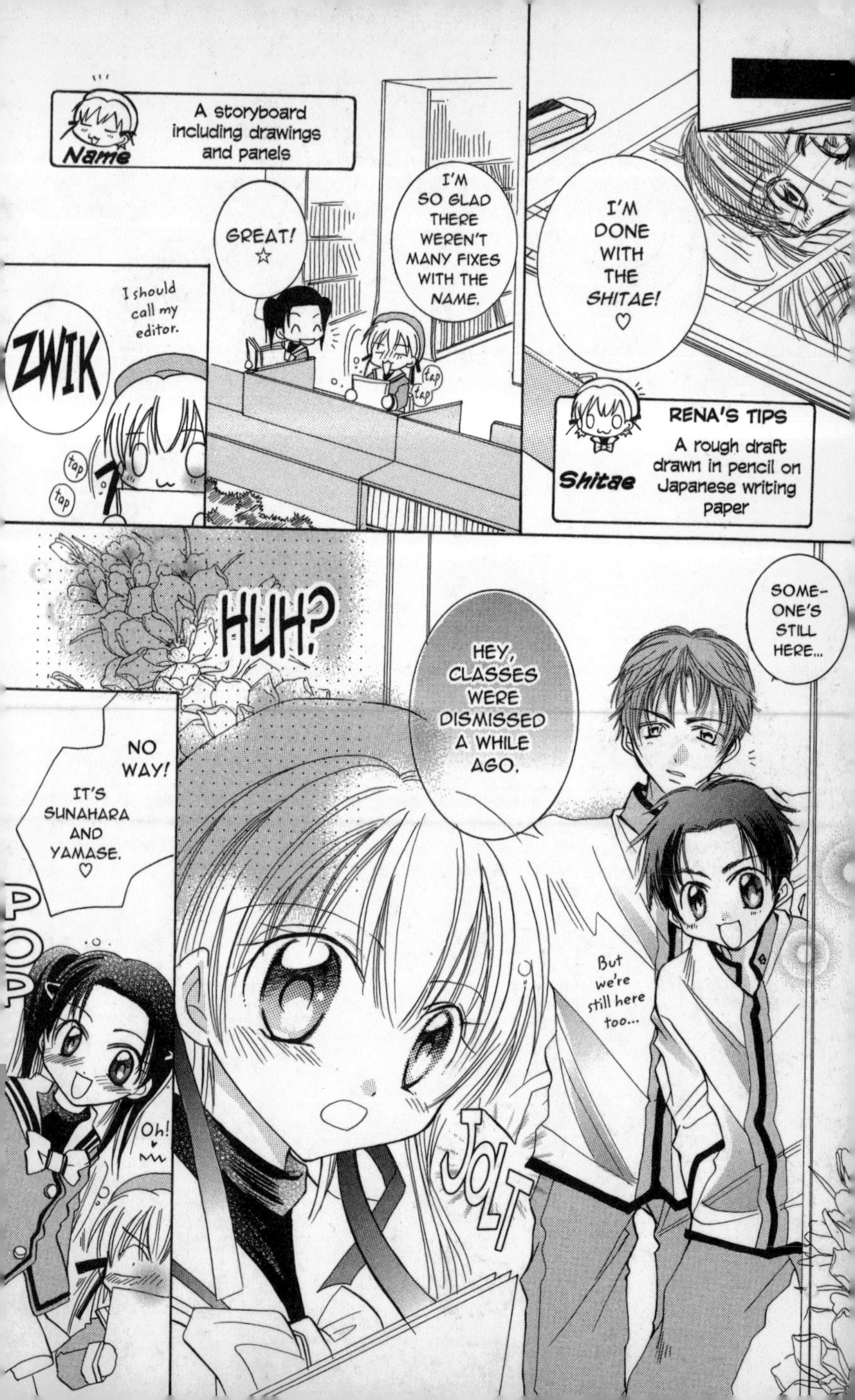
I'M DONE WITH THE SHITAE! ♡
RENA'S TIPS
Shitae
A rough draft drawn in pencil on Japanese writing paper
I'M SO GLAD THERE WEREN'T MANY FIXES WITH THE NAME.
GREAT! ☆
Name
A storyboard including drawings and panels
tap tap
I should call my editor.
ZWIK
tap
tap
SOME-ONE'S STILL HERE...
HEY, CLASSES WERE DISMISSED A WHILE AGO.
HUH?
But we're still here too...
JOLT
NO WAY!
IT'S SUNAHARA AND YAMASE. ♡
POP
Oh!

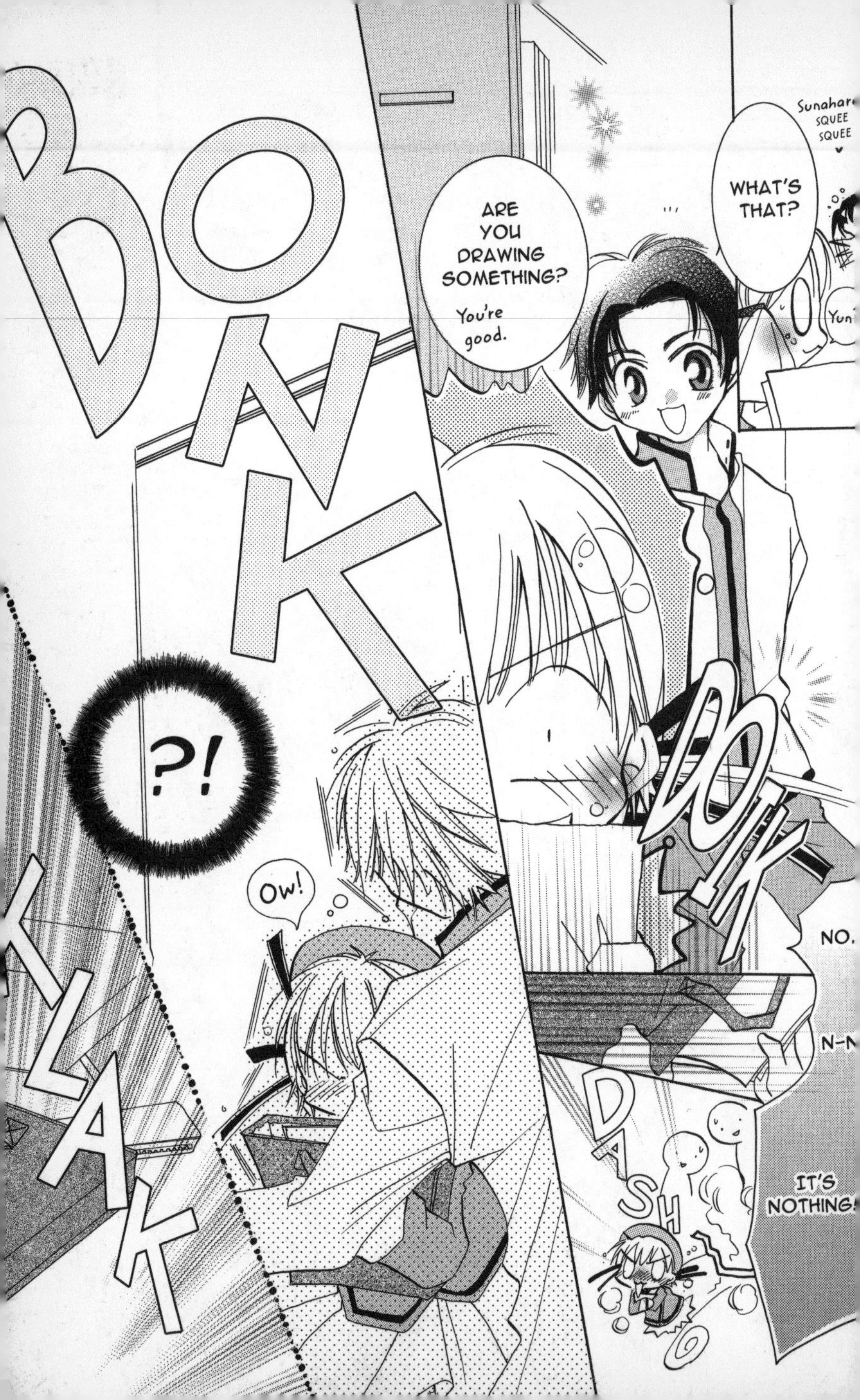

Sunahar
SQUEE SQUEE
WHAT'S THAT?
Yun
ARE YOU DRAWING SOMETHING?
You're good.
BONK
DOINK
?!
Ow!
NO.
N-N
IT'S NOTHING
DASH
KLLAK

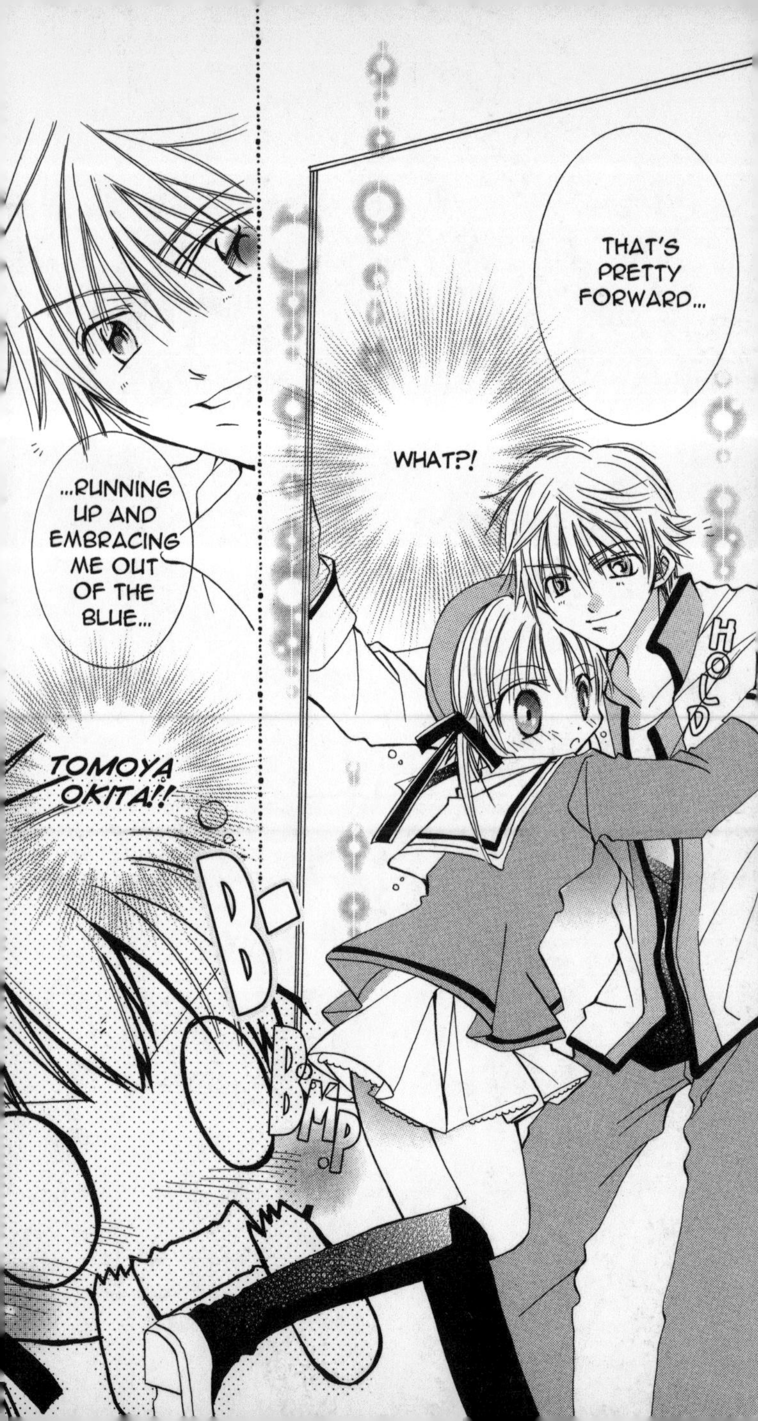
THAT'S PRETTY FORWARD...
WHAT?!
HOLD
...RUNNING UP AND EMBRACING ME OUT OF THE BLUE...
TOMOYA OKITA!!
B-

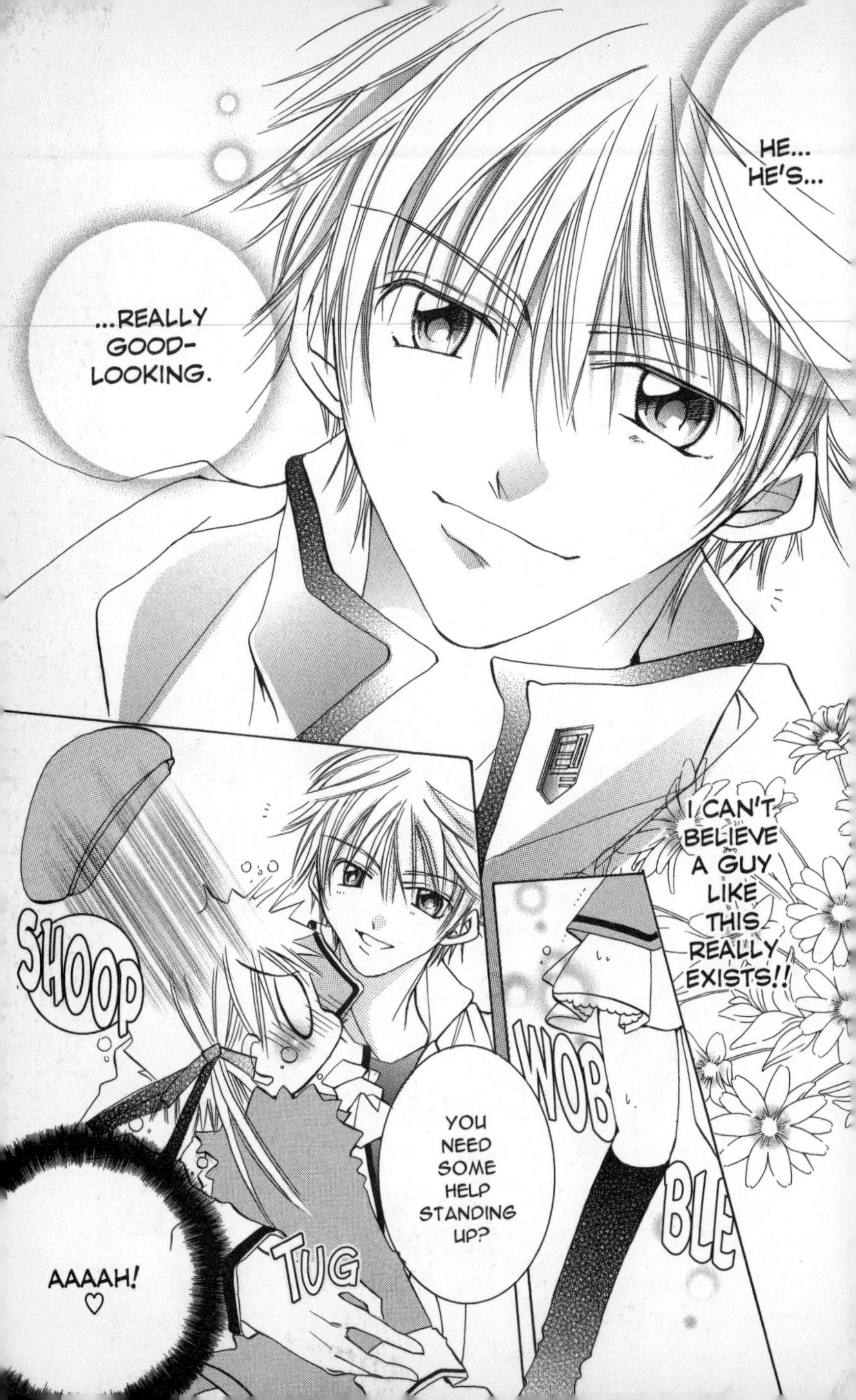

HE... HE'S...
...REALLY GOOD-LOOKING.
I CAN'T BELIEVE A GUY LIKE THIS REALLY EXISTS!!
WOBBLE
SHOOP
YOU NEED SOME HELP STANDING UP?
TUG
AAAAH! ♡

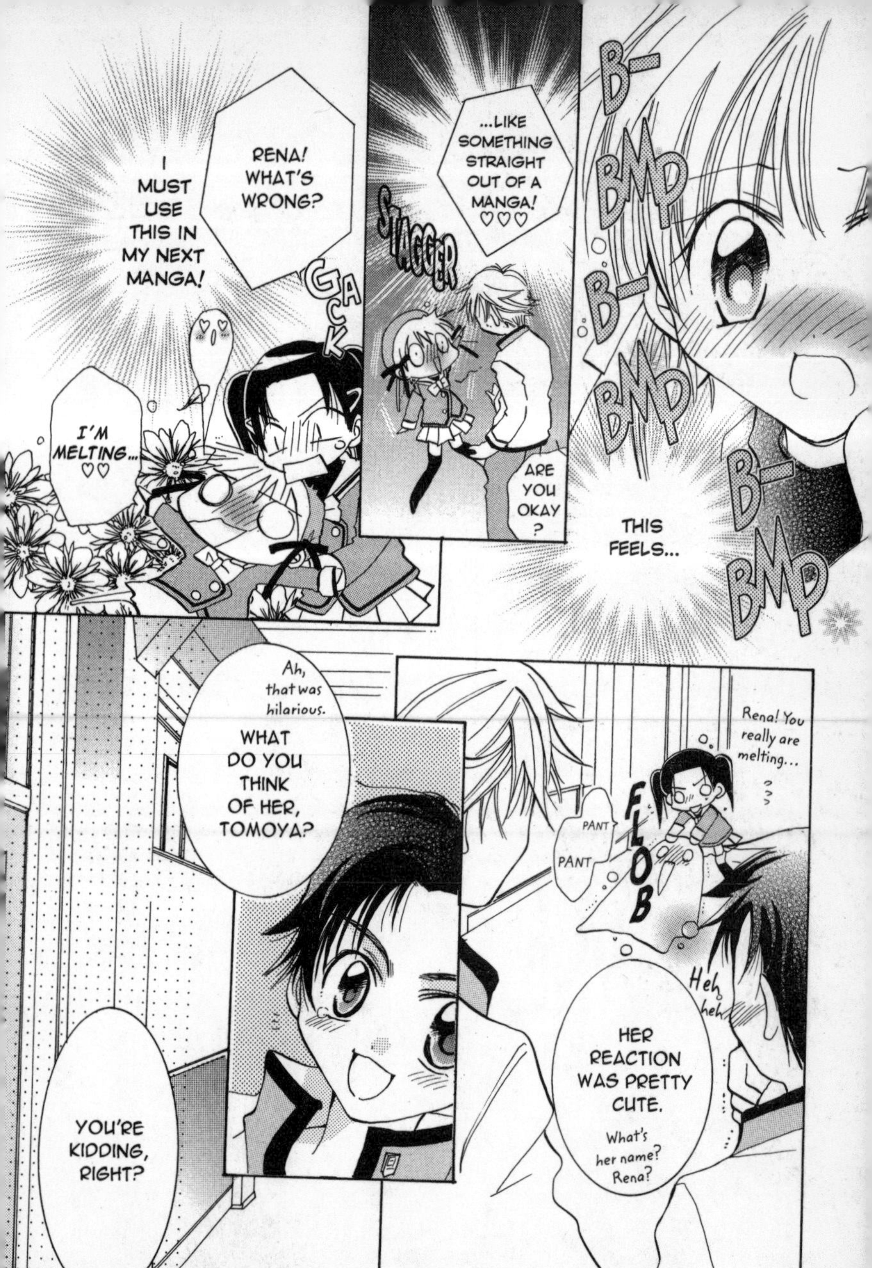
B-BMP
B-BMP
B-BMP
B-BMP
THIS FEELS...
...LIKE SOMETHING STRAIGHT OUT OF A MANGA! ♡♡♡
STAGGER
ARE YOU OKAY?
RENA! WHAT'S WRONG?
I MUST USE THIS IN MY NEXT MANGA!
GACK
I'M MELTING... ♡♡
Rena! You really are melting...
??
PANT
PANT
FLOB
Heh heh
HER REACTION WAS PRETTY CUTE.
What's her name? Rena?
Ah, that was hilarious.
WHAT DO YOU THINK OF HER, TOMOYA?
YOU'RE KIDDING, RIGHT?

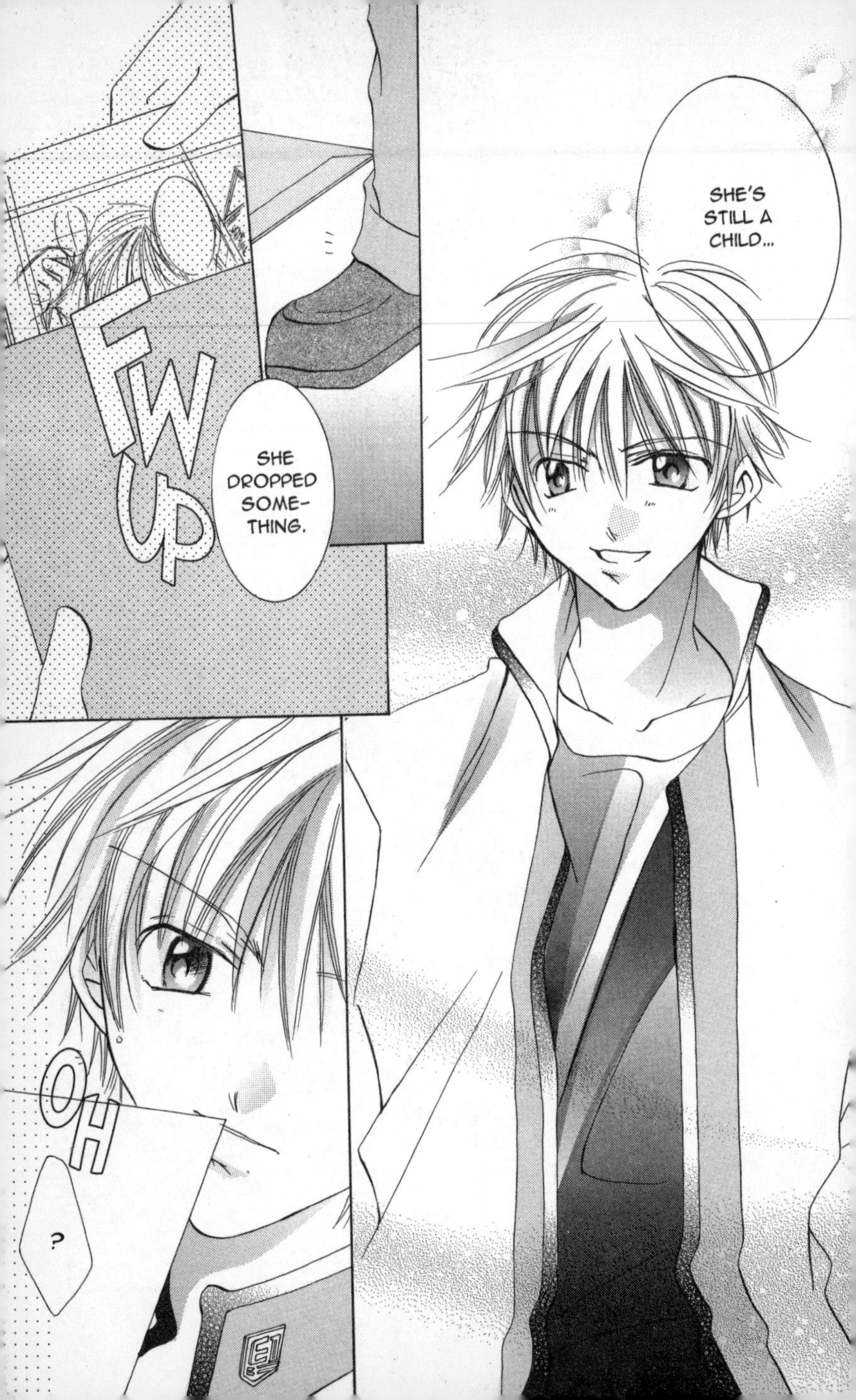
SHE'S STILL A CHILD...
SHE DROPPED SOMETHING.
FWUP
OH
?

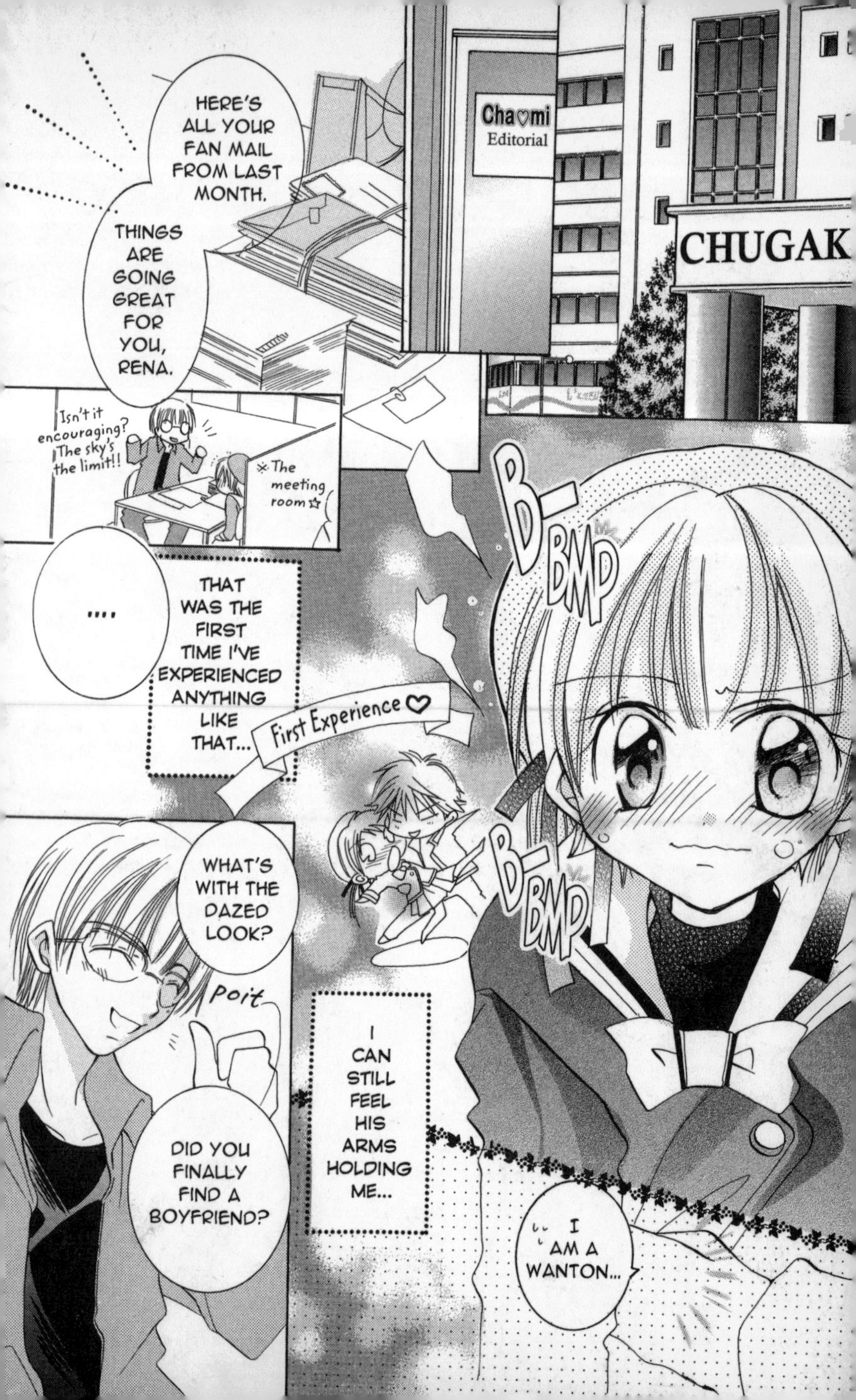
Cha♡mi Editorial
CHUGAK
HERE'S ALL YOUR FAN MAIL FROM LAST MONTH.
THINGS ARE GOING GREAT FOR YOU, RENA.
※The meeting room☆
Isn't it encouraging? The sky's the limit!!
B-BMP
B-BMP
....
THAT WAS THE FIRST TIME I'VE EXPERIENCED ANYTHING LIKE THAT...
First Experience♡
WHAT'S WITH THE DAZED LOOK?
Poit
DID YOU FINALLY FIND A BOYFRIEND?
I CAN STILL FEEL HIS ARMS HOLDING ME...
I AM A WANTON...

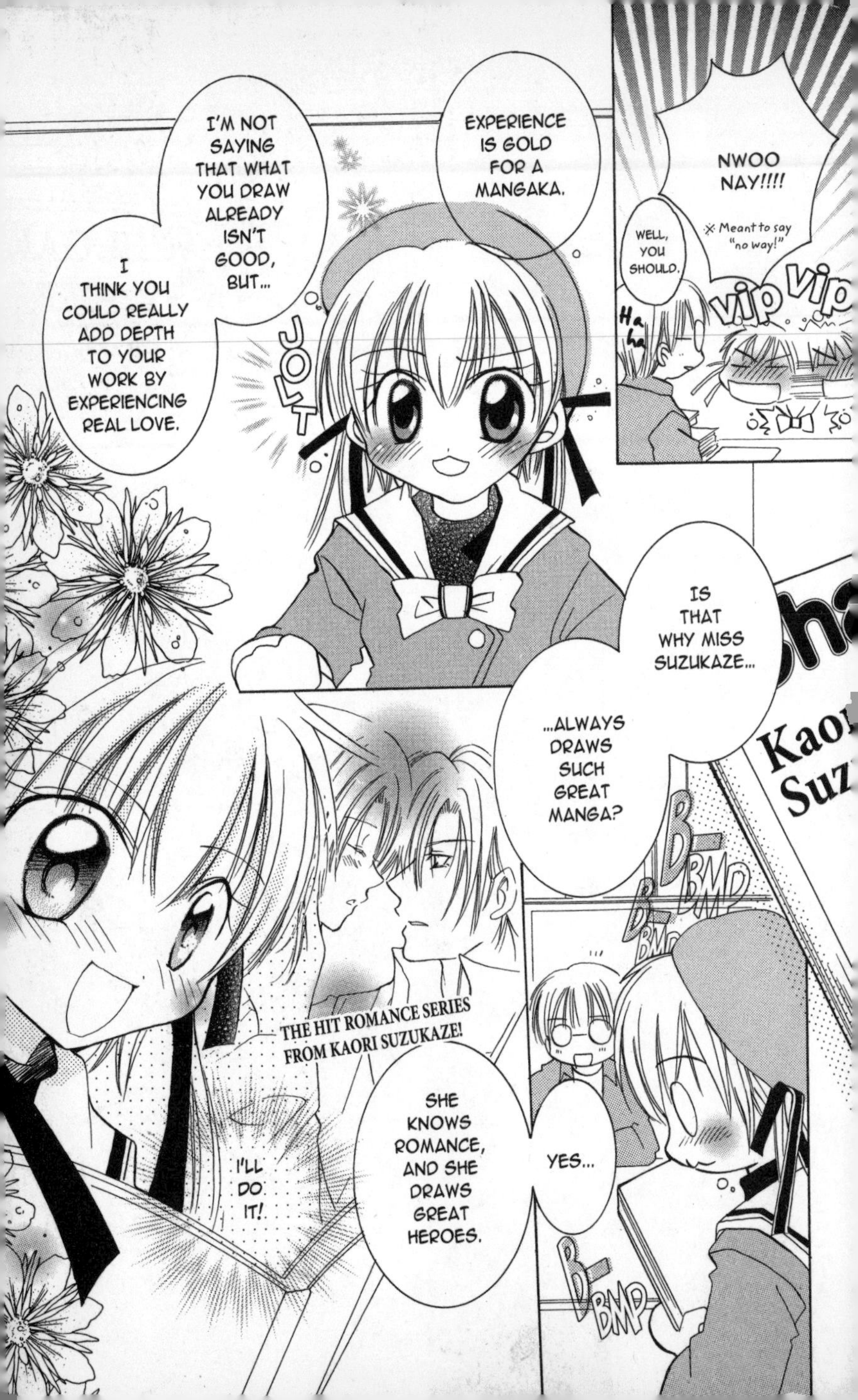
NWOO NAY!!!!
※ Meant to say "no way!"
WELL, YOU SHOULD.
Ha ha
vip vip
EXPERIENCE IS GOLD FOR A MANGAKA.
I'M NOT SAYING THAT WHAT YOU DRAW ALREADY ISN'T GOOD, BUT...
I THINK YOU COULD REALLY ADD DEPTH TO YOUR WORK BY EXPERIENCING REAL LOVE.
JOLT
IS THAT WHY MISS SUZUKAZE...
...ALWAYS DRAWS SUCH GREAT MANGA?
Kaori Suz
B-BMP
B-BMP
YES...
SHE KNOWS ROMANCE, AND SHE DRAWS GREAT HEROES.
B-BMP
THE HIT ROMANCE SERIES FROM KAORI SUZUKAZE!
I'LL DO IT!

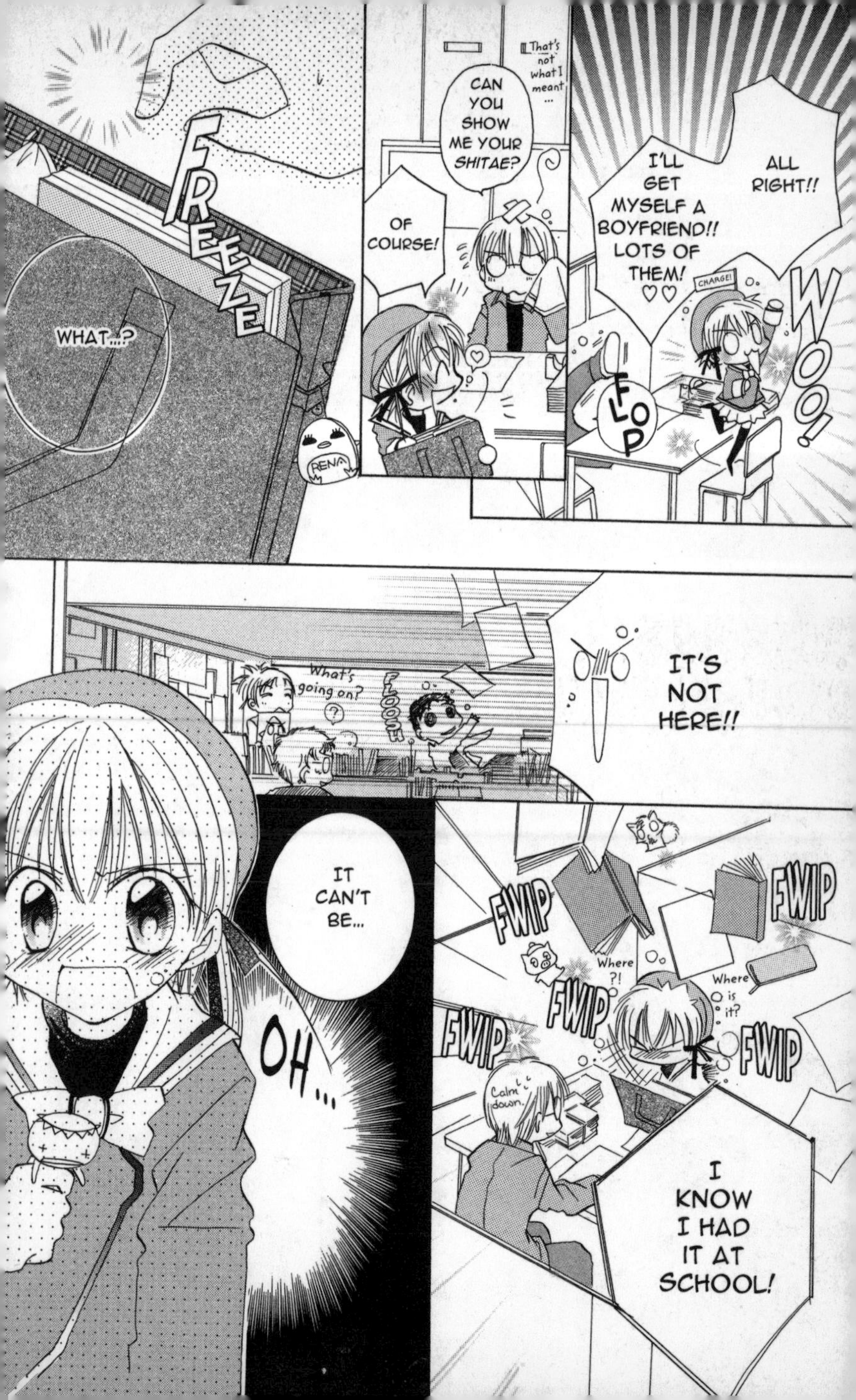
ALL RIGHT!!
I'LL GET MYSELF A BOYFRIEND!! LOTS OF THEM! ♡♡
CHARGE!
WOO!
FLOP
CAN YOU SHOW ME YOUR SHITAE?
That's not what I meant...
OF COURSE!
FREEZE
WHAT...?
RENA
IT'S NOT HERE!!
What's going on?
FLOOSH
FWIP
FWIP
Where is it?
Where?!
FWIP
FWIP
FWIP
Calm down.
I KNOW I HAD IT AT SCHOOL!
IT CAN'T BE...
OH...

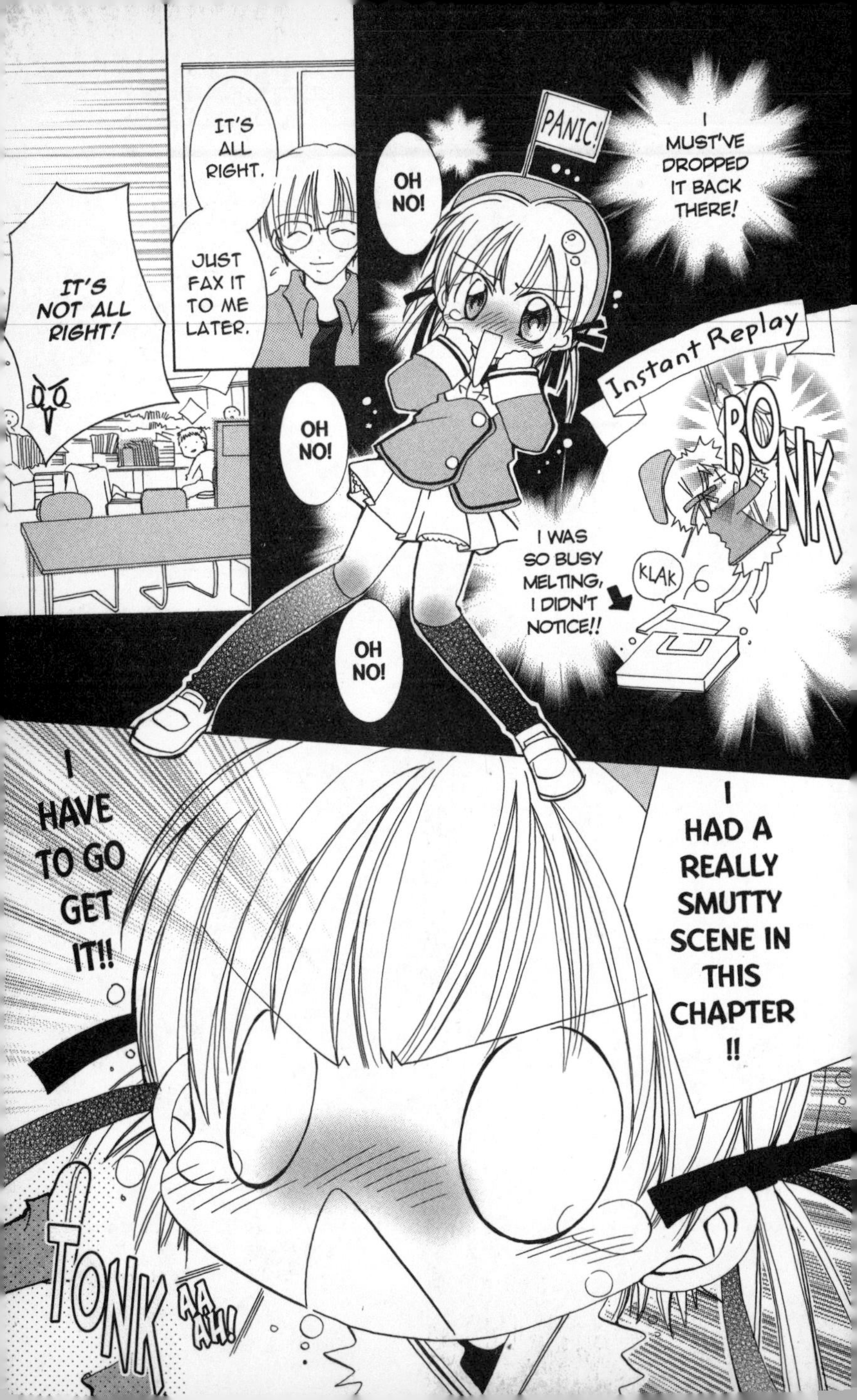
PANIC!
I MUST'VE DROPPED IT BACK THERE!
OH NO!
Instant Replay
BONK
KLAK
I WAS SO BUSY MELTING, I DIDN'T NOTICE!!
OH NO!
OH NO!
IT'S ALL RIGHT.
JUST FAX IT TO ME LATER.
IT'S NOT ALL RIGHT!
I HAD A REALLY SMUTTY SCENE IN THIS CHAPTER!!
I HAVE TO GO GET IT!!
TONK
AAAH!

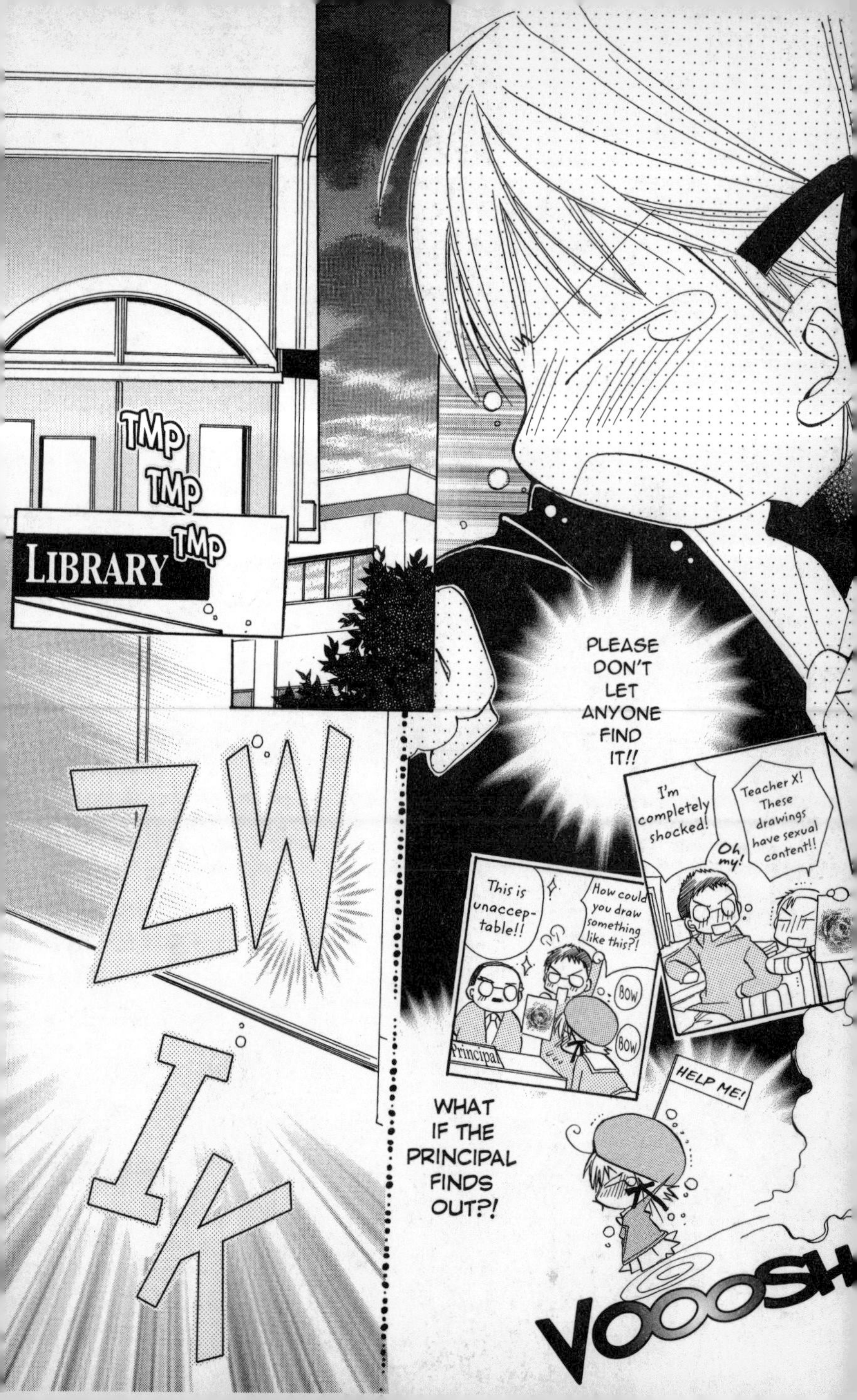

PLEASE DON'T LET ANYONE FIND IT!!
Teacher X! These drawings have sexual content!!
I'm completely shocked!
Oh my!
How could you draw something like this?!
This is unaccep-table!!
BOW
BOW
Principal
HELP ME!
WHAT IF THE PRINCIPAL FINDS OUT?!
VOOOSH
TMP
TMP
TMP
LIBRARY
ZWIK

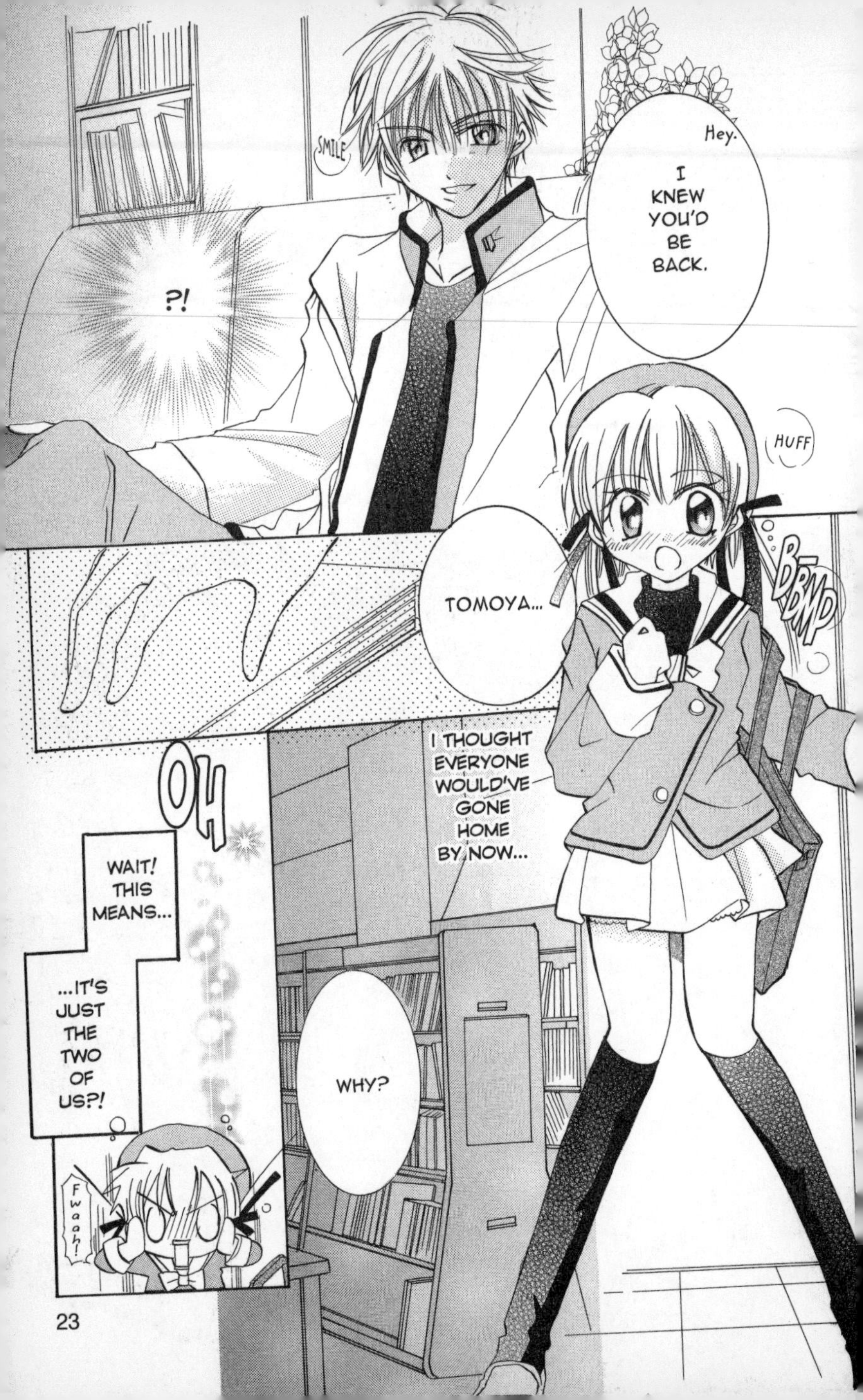
Hey.
I KNEW YOU'D BE BACK.
SMILE
?!
HUFF
B-BMP
TOMOYA...
I THOUGHT EVERYONE WOULD'VE GONE HOME BY NOW...
WHY?
OH
WAIT! THIS MEANS...
...IT'S JUST THE TWO OF US?!
Fwaah!

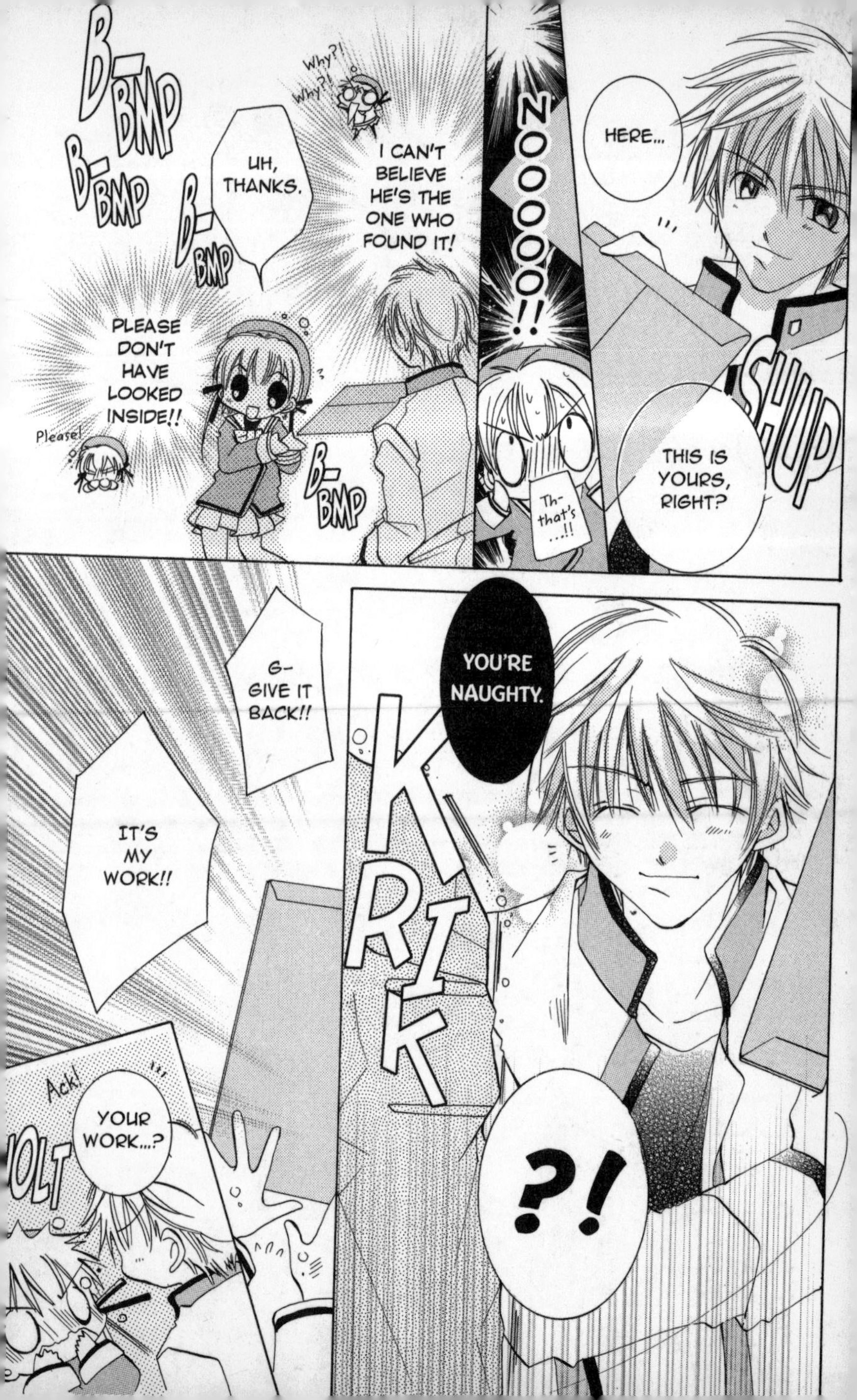
HERE...
THIS IS YOURS, RIGHT?
SHUP
NOOOOOO!!
Th-that's...!!
I CAN'T BELIEVE HE'S THE ONE WHO FOUND IT!
Why?! Why?!
UH, THANKS.
B-BMP
B-BMP
B-BMP
B-BMP
PLEASE DON'T HAVE LOOKED INSIDE!!
Please!
B-BMP
YOU'RE NAUGHTY.
KRIK
?!
G-GIVE IT BACK!!
IT'S MY WORK!!
YOUR WORK...?
Ack!
OLT

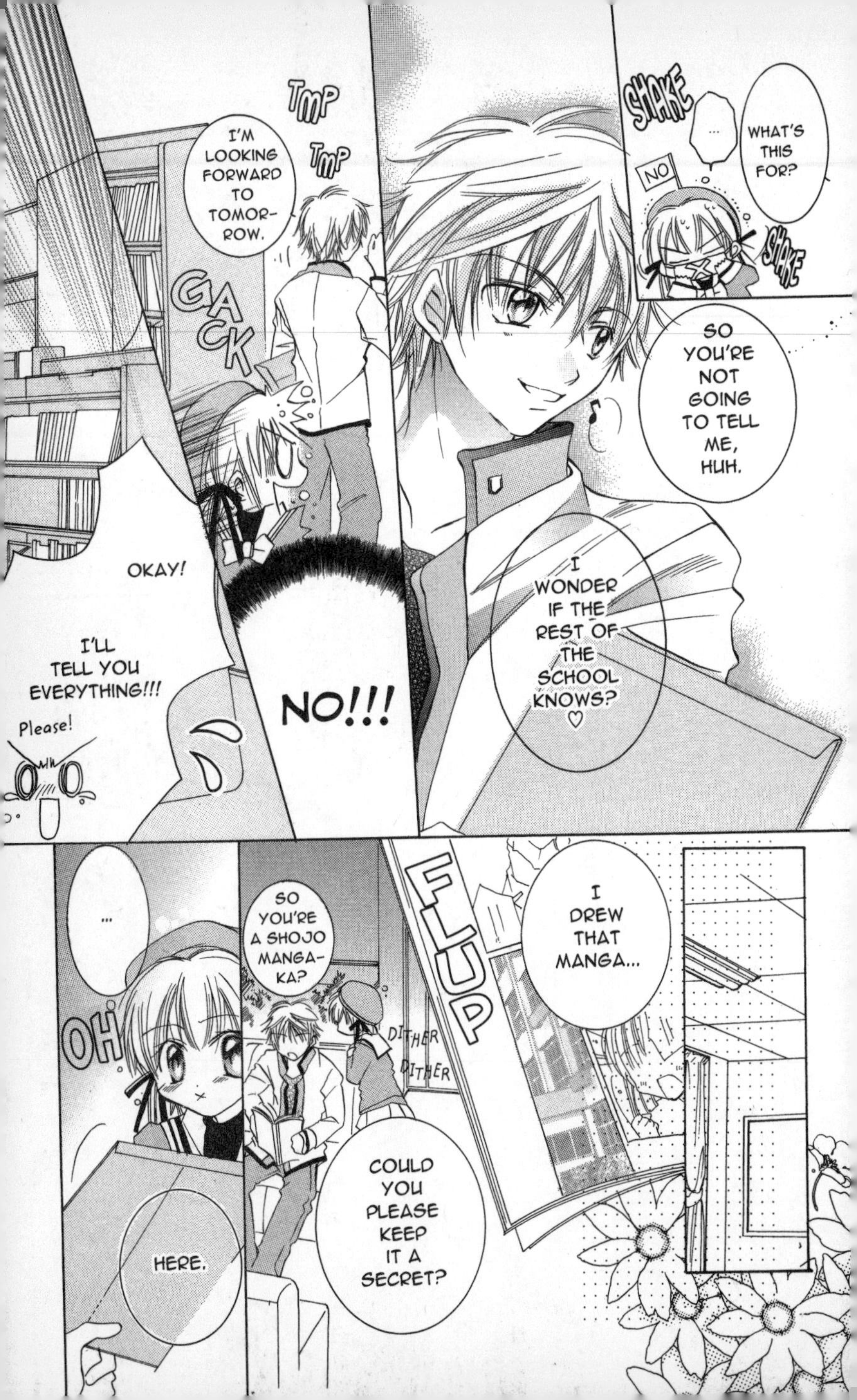
SHAKE
...
WHAT'S THIS FOR?
NO
SHAKE
SO YOU'RE NOT GOING TO TELL ME, HUH.
I WONDER IF THE REST OF THE SCHOOL KNOWS? ♡
TMP
TMP
I'M LOOKING FORWARD TO TOMORROW.
GACK
NO!!!
OKAY!
I'LL TELL YOU EVERYTHING!!!
Please!
I DREW THAT MANGA...
FLUP
SO YOU'RE A SHOJO MANGA-KA?
DITHER DITHER
COULD YOU PLEASE KEEP IT A SECRET?
...
OH
HERE.

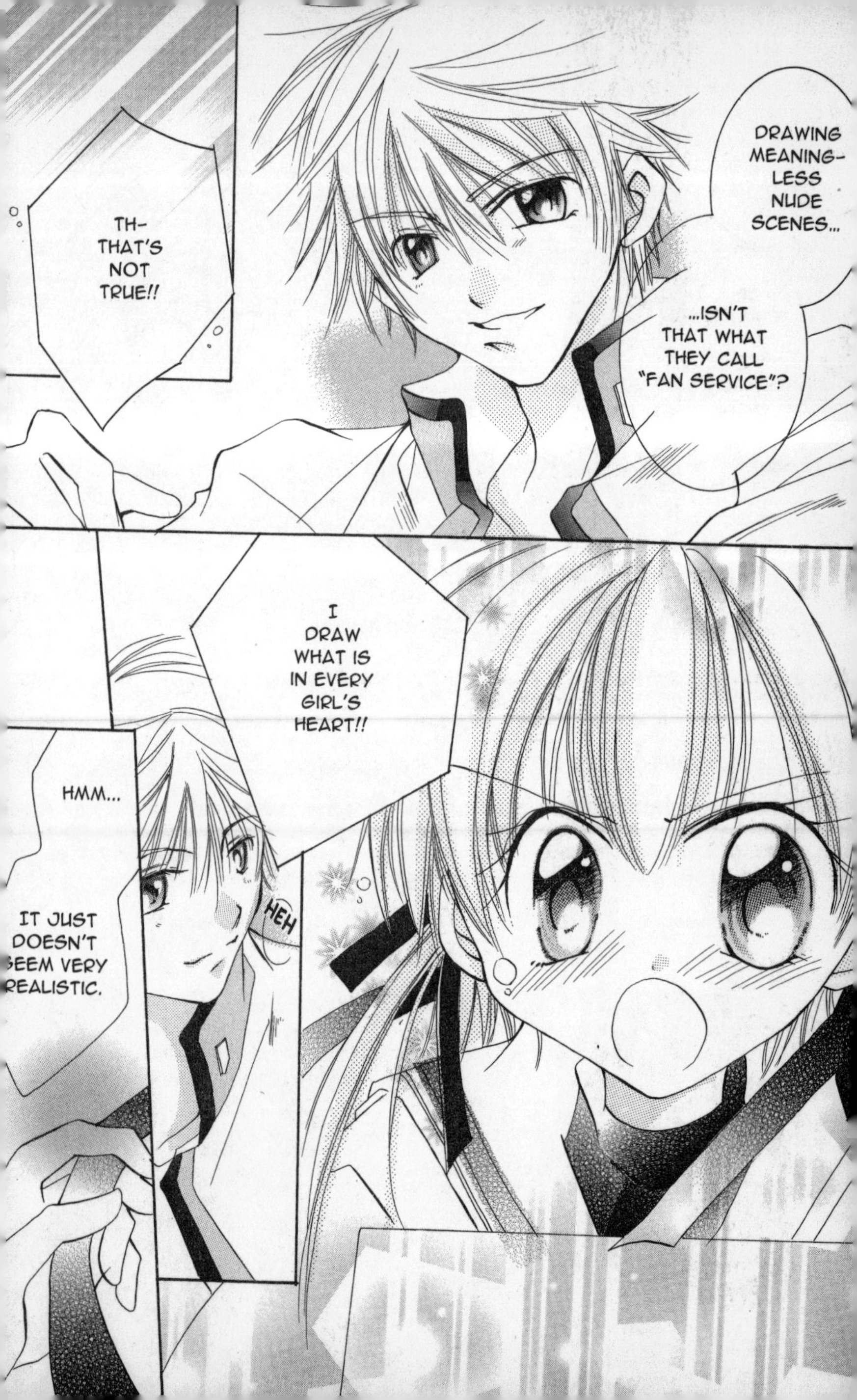
DRAWING MEANING-LESS NUDE SCENES...
...ISN'T THAT WHAT THEY CALL "FAN SERVICE"?
TH-THAT'S NOT TRUE!!
I DRAW WHAT IS IN EVERY GIRL'S HEART!!
HMM...
HEH
IT JUST DOESN'T SEEM VERY REALISTIC.

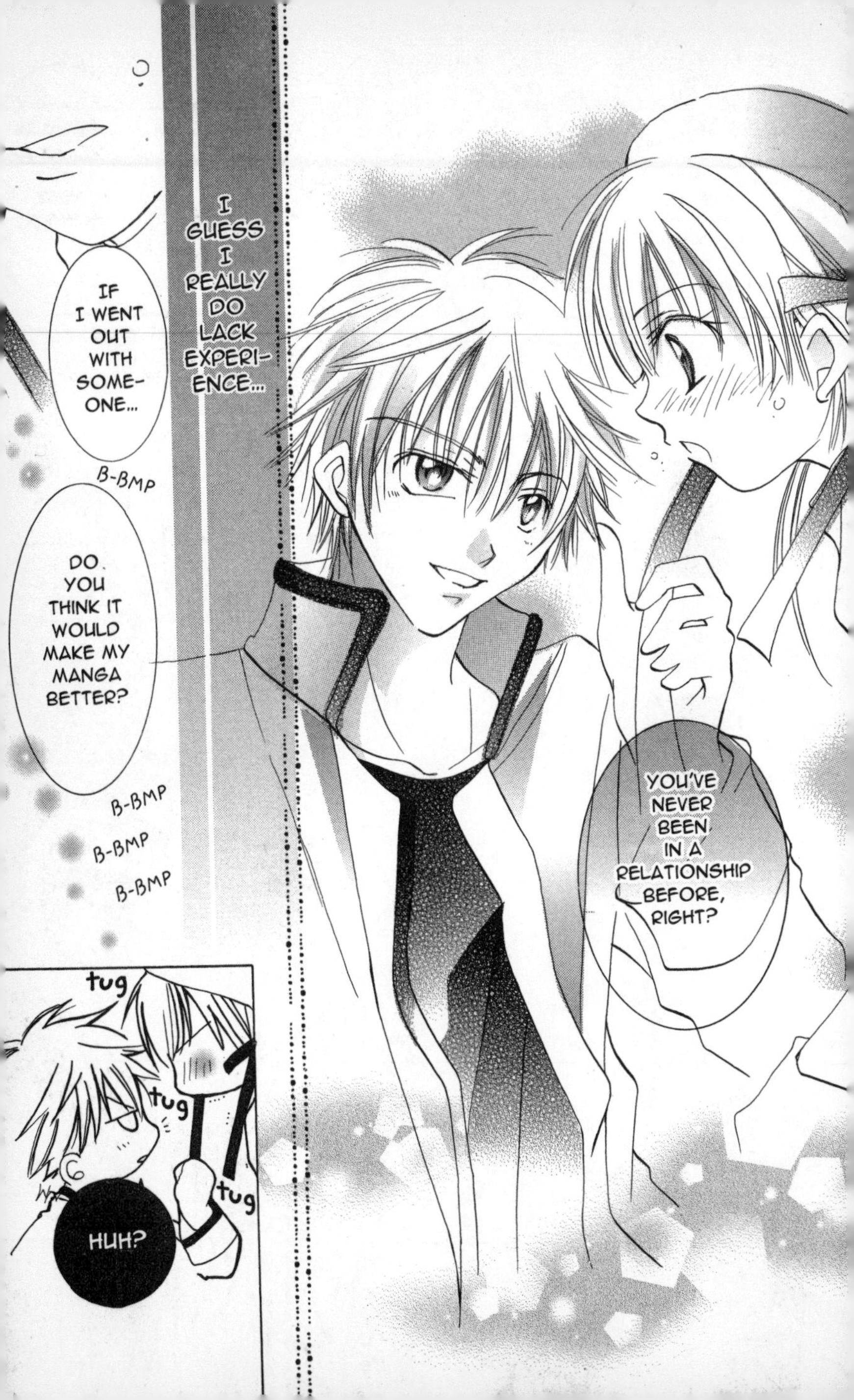
YOU'VE NEVER BEEN IN A RELATIONSHIP BEFORE, RIGHT?
I GUESS I REALLY DO LACK EXPERIENCE...
IF I WENT OUT WITH SOMEONE...
B-BMP
DO YOU THINK IT WOULD MAKE MY MANGA BETTER?
B-BMP
B-BMP
B-BMP
tug
tug
tug
HUH?

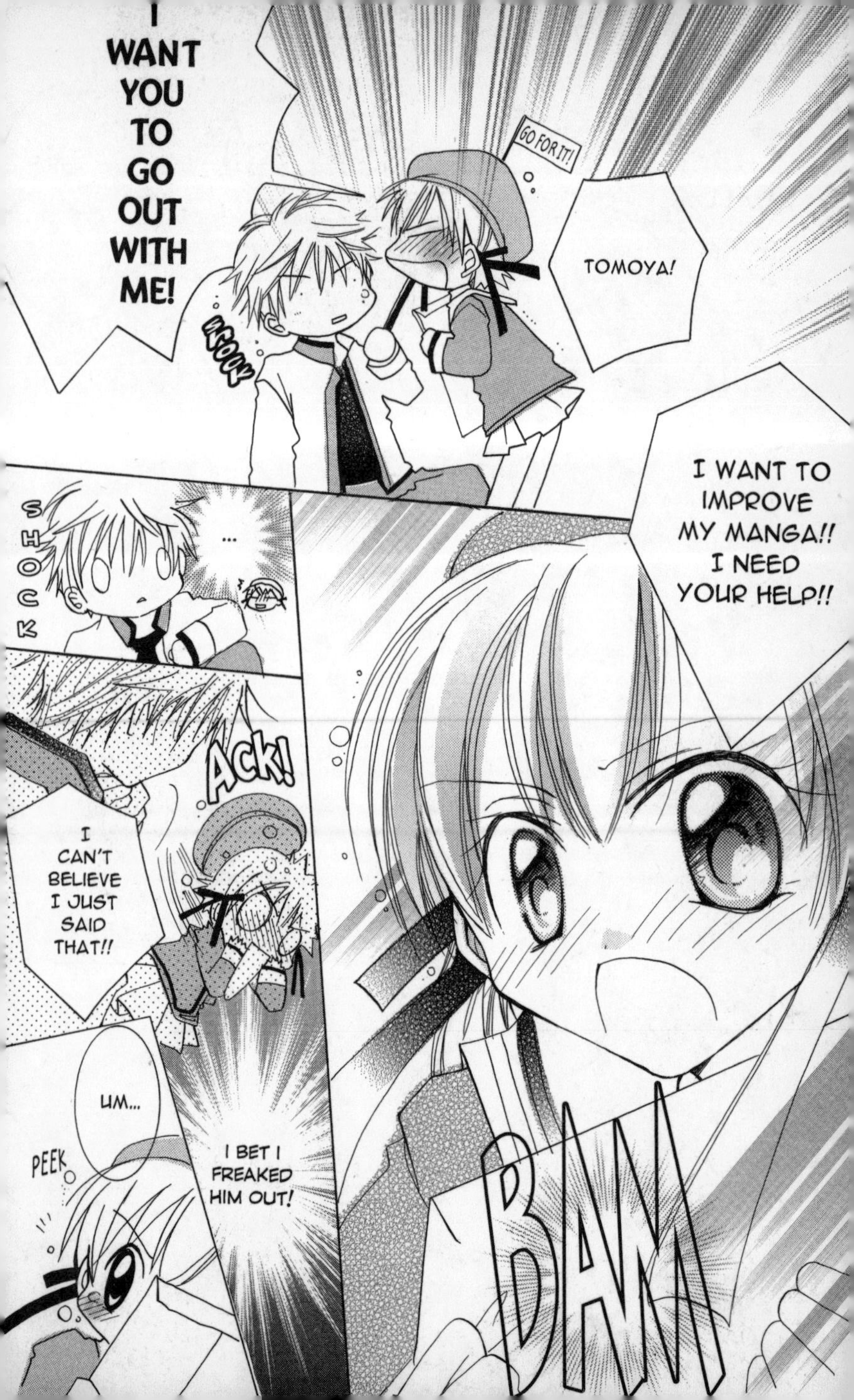
GO FOR IT!
TOMOYA!
I WANT YOU TO GO OUT WITH ME!
I WANT TO IMPROVE MY MANGA!! I NEED YOUR HELP!!
BAM
SHOCK
...
ACK!
I CAN'T BELIEVE I JUST SAID THAT!!
I BET I FREAKED HIM OUT!
UM...
PEEK

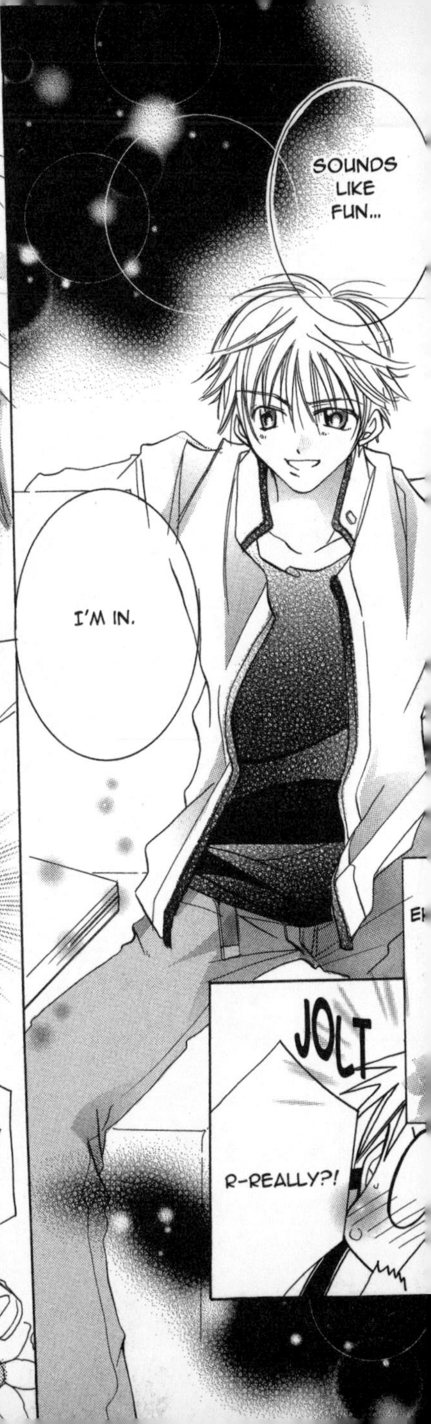
SOUNDS LIKE FUN...
I'M IN.
JOLT
R-REALLY?!
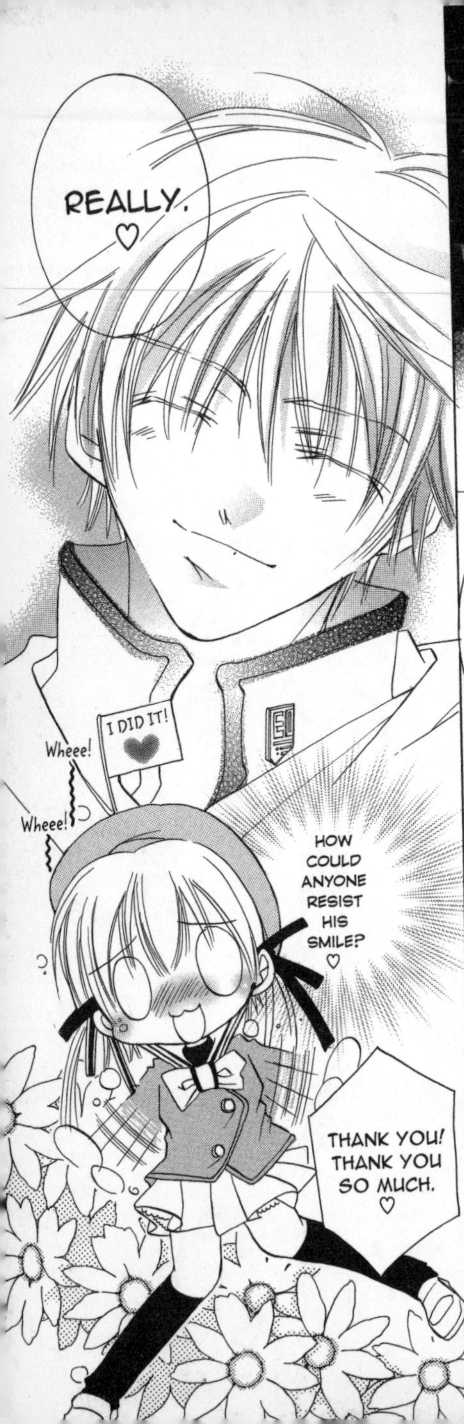
REALLY. ♡
I DID IT!
Wheee!
Wheee!
HOW COULD ANYONE RESIST HIS SMILE? ♡
THANK YOU! THANK YOU SO MUCH. ♡

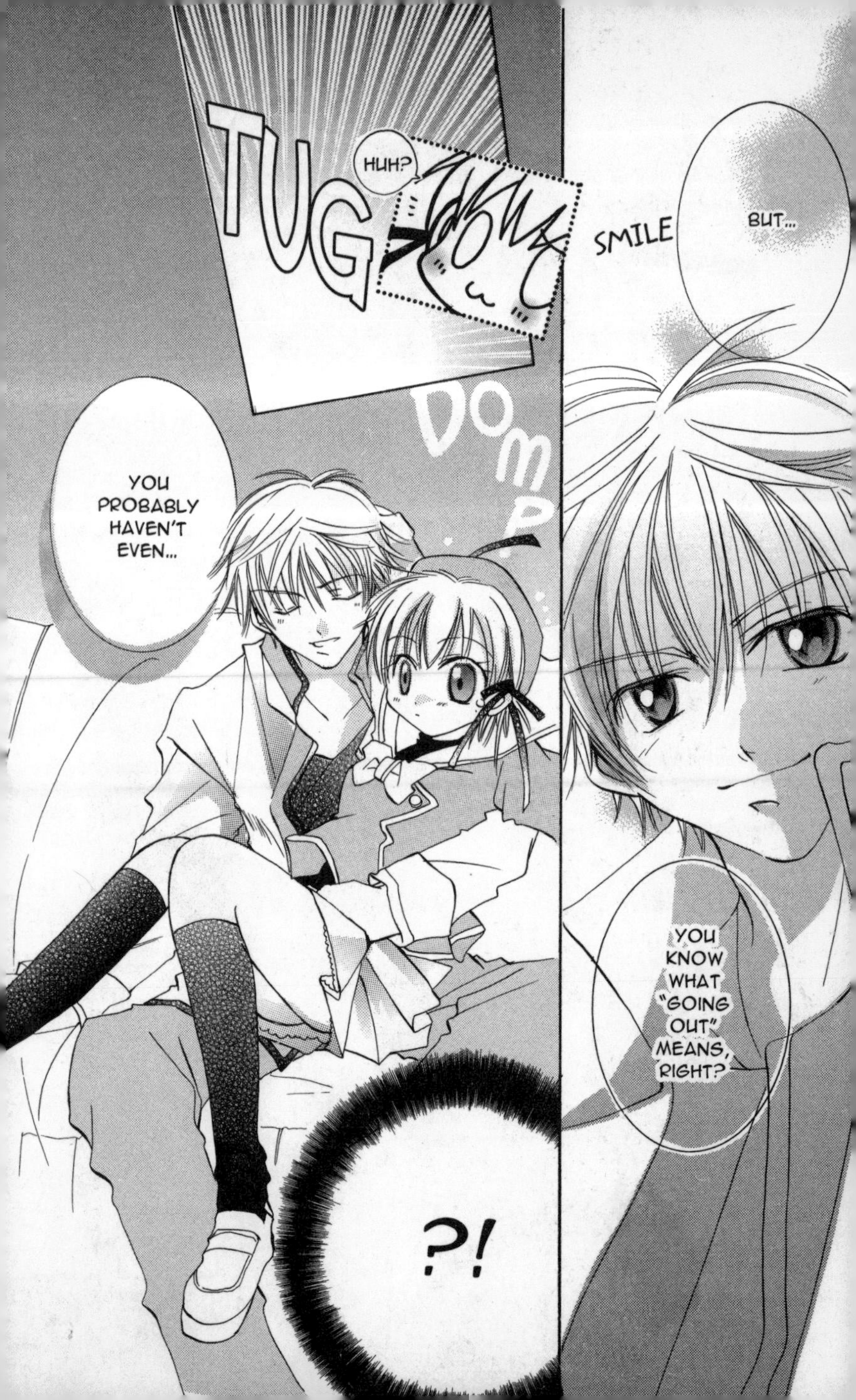
BUT...
SMILE
YOU KNOW WHAT "GOING OUT" MEANS, RIGHT?
HUH?
TUG
DOMP
YOU PROBABLY HAVEN'T EVEN...
?!

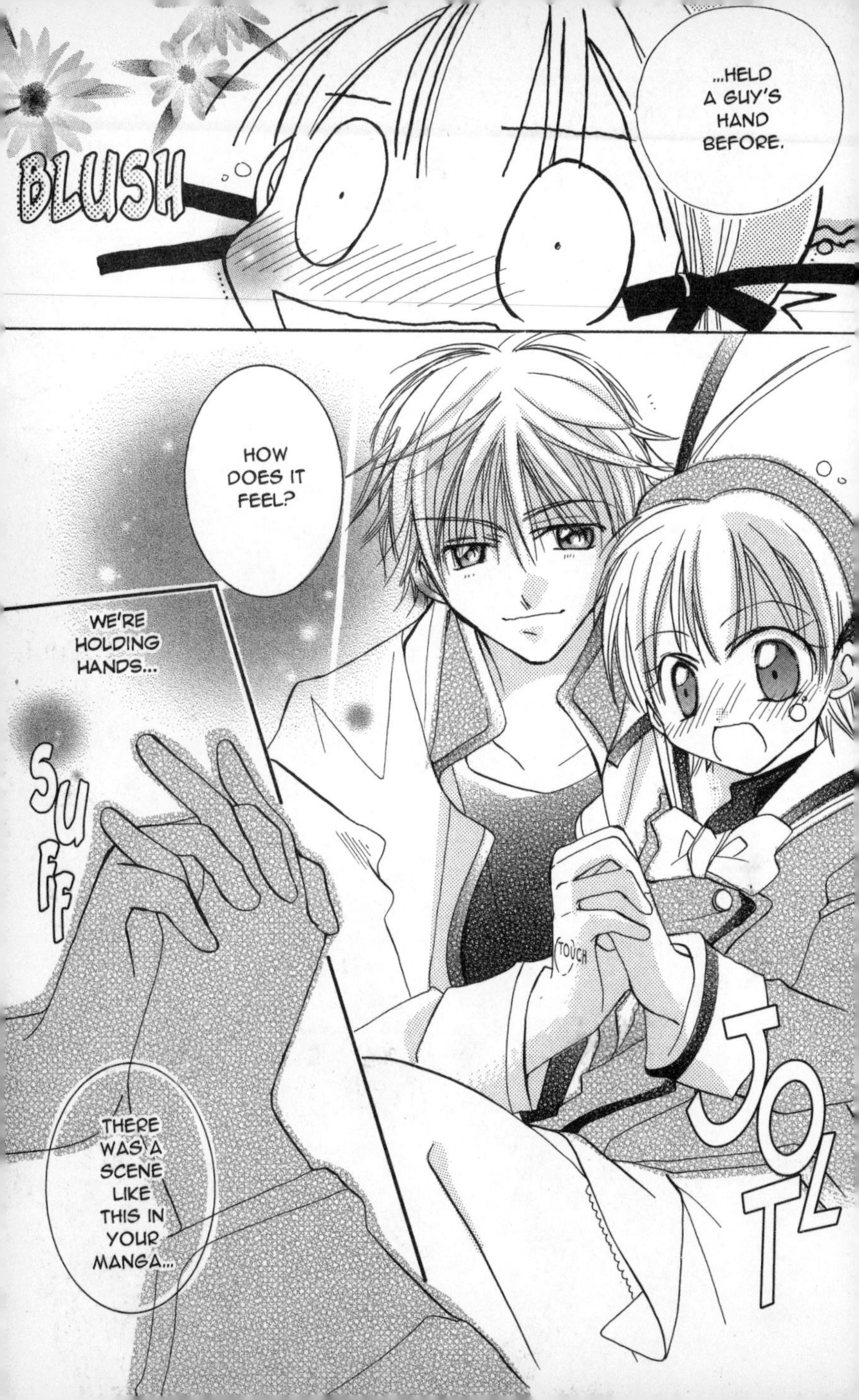
...HELD A GUY'S HAND BEFORE.
BLUSH
JOLT
TOUCH
HOW DOES IT FEEL?
WE'RE HOLDING HANDS...
SUFF
THERE WAS A SCENE LIKE THIS IN YOUR MANGA...

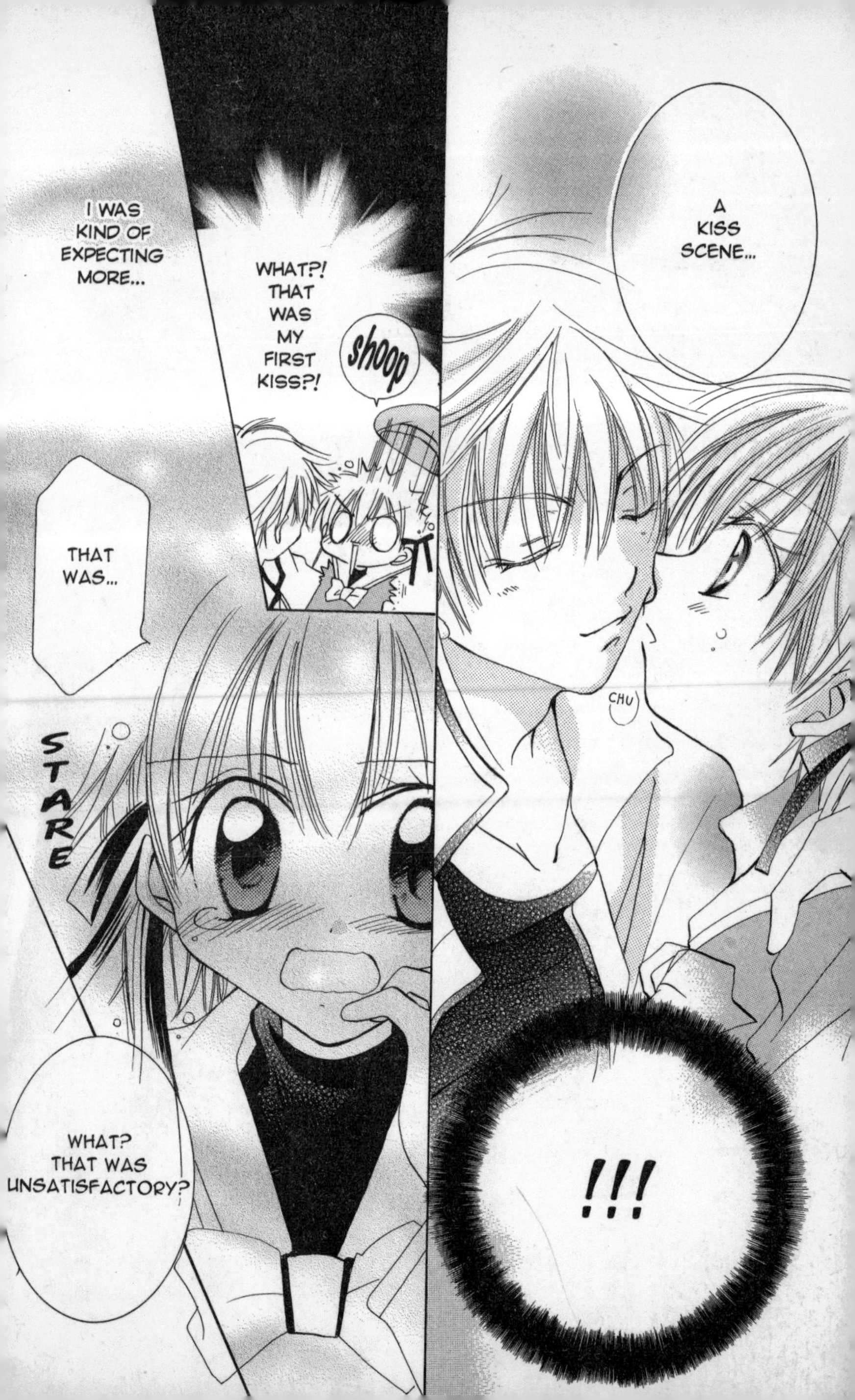
A KISS SCENE...
CHU
!!!
WHAT?! THAT WAS MY FIRST KISS?!
shoop
I WAS KIND OF EXPECTING MORE...
THAT WAS...
STARE
WHAT? THAT WAS UNSATISFACTORY?

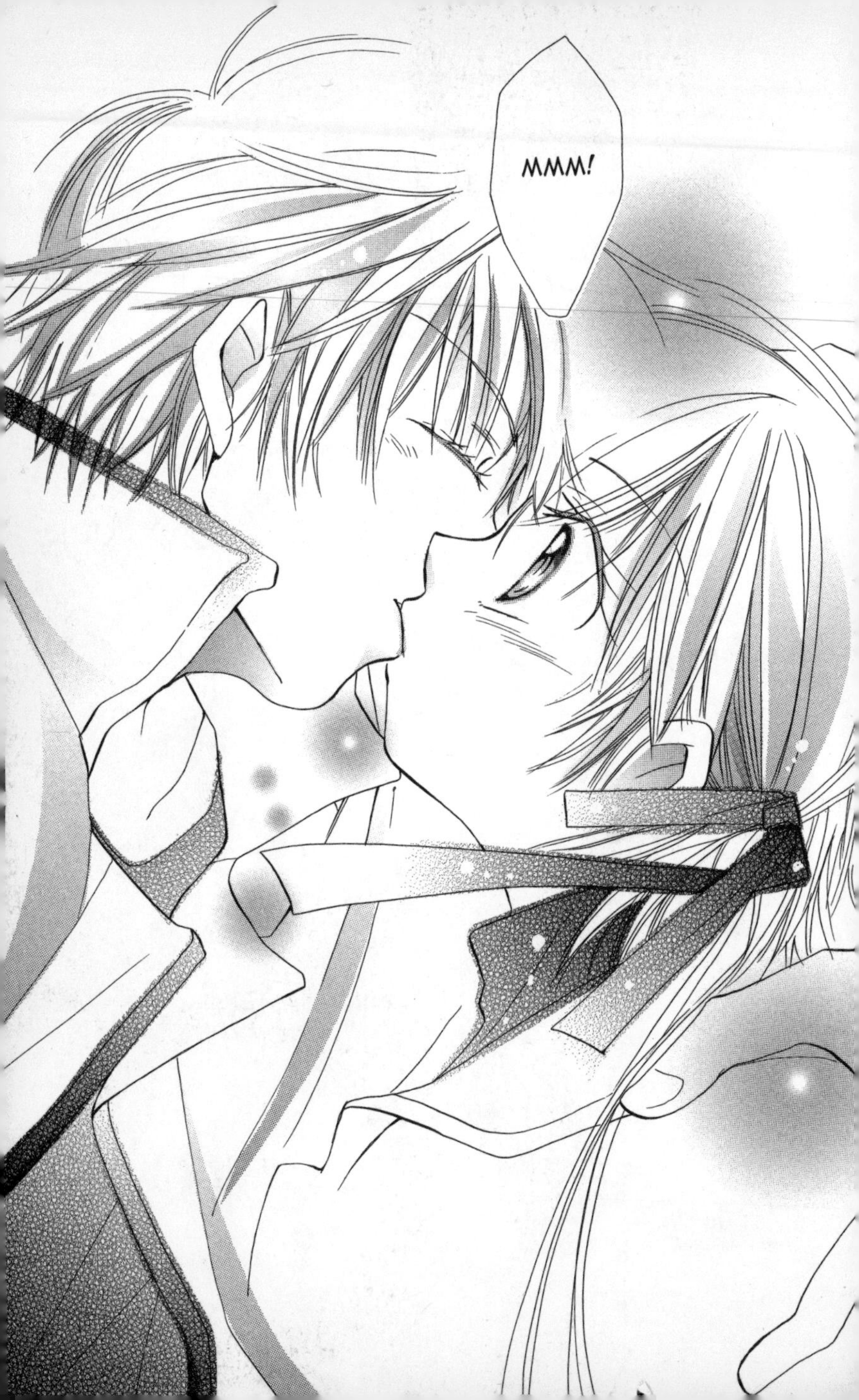
MMM!

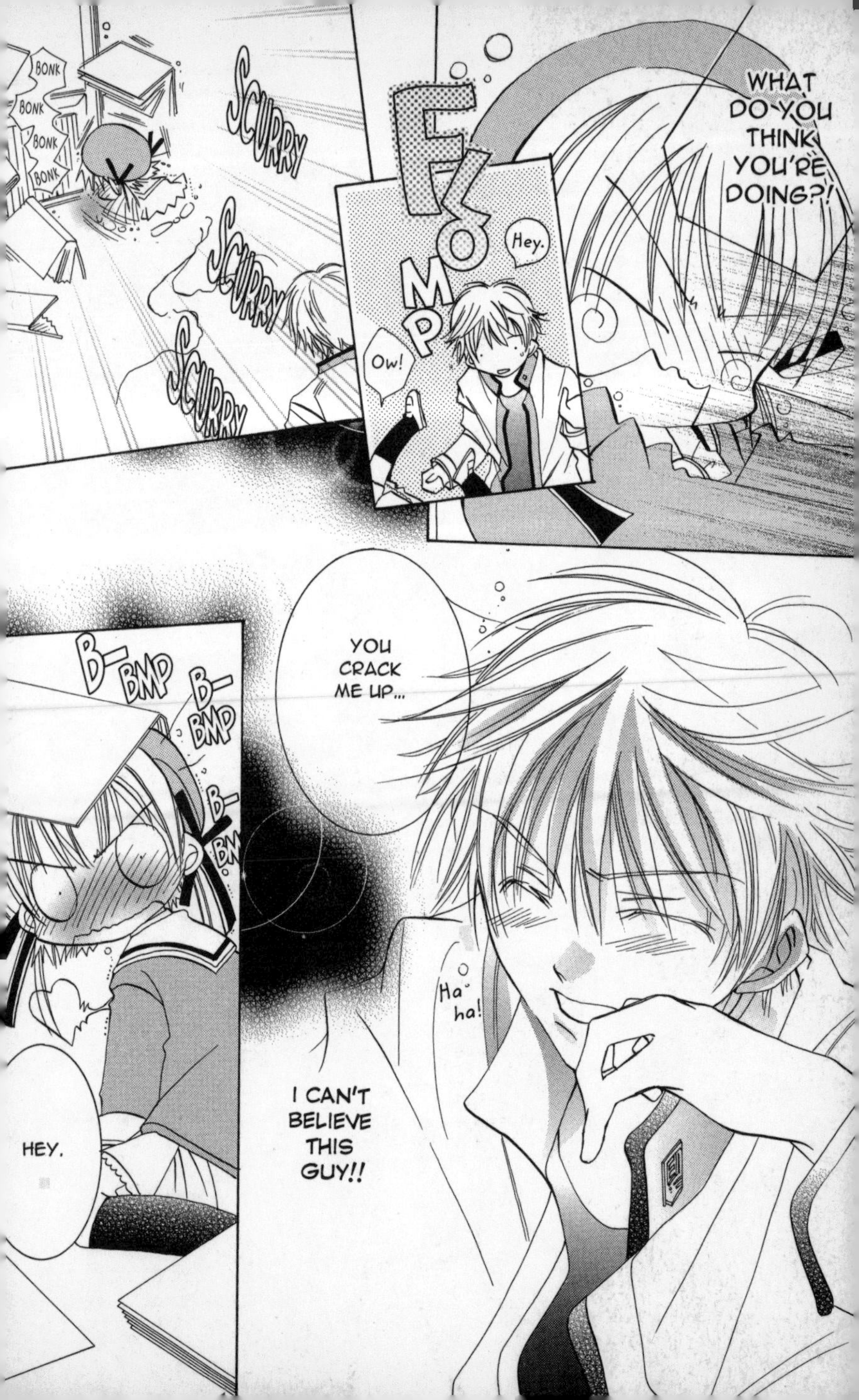
WHAT DO YOU THINK YOU'RE DOING?!
FLOMP
Hey.
Ow!
BONK
BONK
BONK
BONK
SCURRY
SCURRY
SCURRY
YOU CRACK ME UP...
Ha ha!
I CAN'T BELIEVE THIS GUY!!
B-BMP
B-BMP
B-BM
HEY.

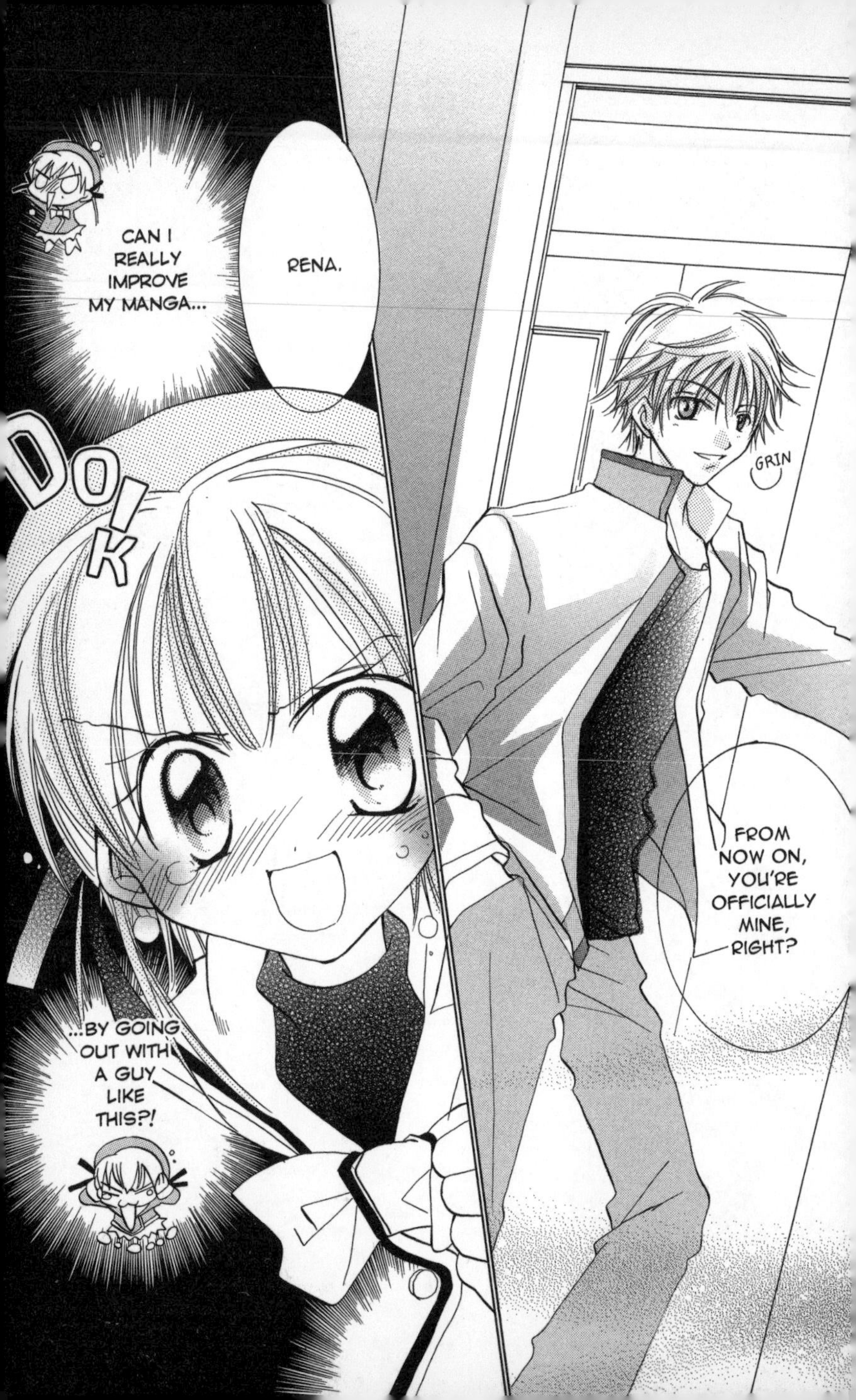

RENA.
GRIN
FROM NOW ON, YOU'RE OFFICIALLY MINE, RIGHT?
CAN I REALLY IMPROVE MY MANGA...
DOIK
...BY GOING OUT WITH A GUY LIKE THIS?!

CHARACTER INTRO

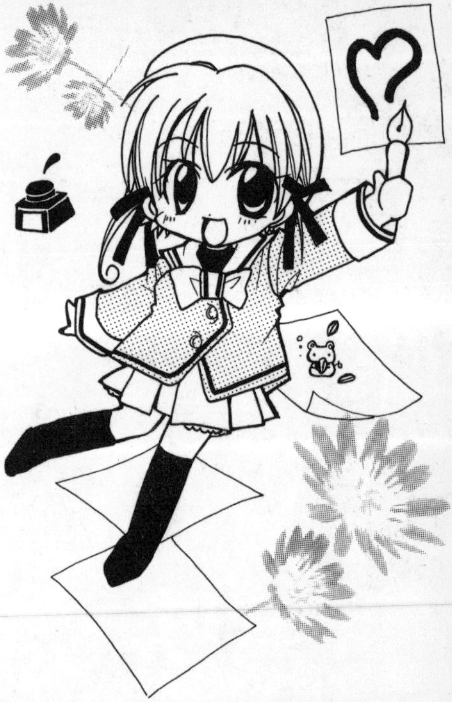

Rena Sakura

The heroine in the one-shot manga I was working on before this series, *Kiss Me♡Psychic Girl*, was quite the character. I had a hard time then creating Rena's character for the first chapter.

We have a lot in common because we share the same professions, but she's in a manga... Even the pandemonium she encounters looks like fun. (laugh)

When I went to go to hang out--that is, went to a meeting--my editor told me I was sacrificing my life to draw this manga. I think it was a compliment... (laugh) But it's really true. There were days I was so busy, I couldn't even eat...

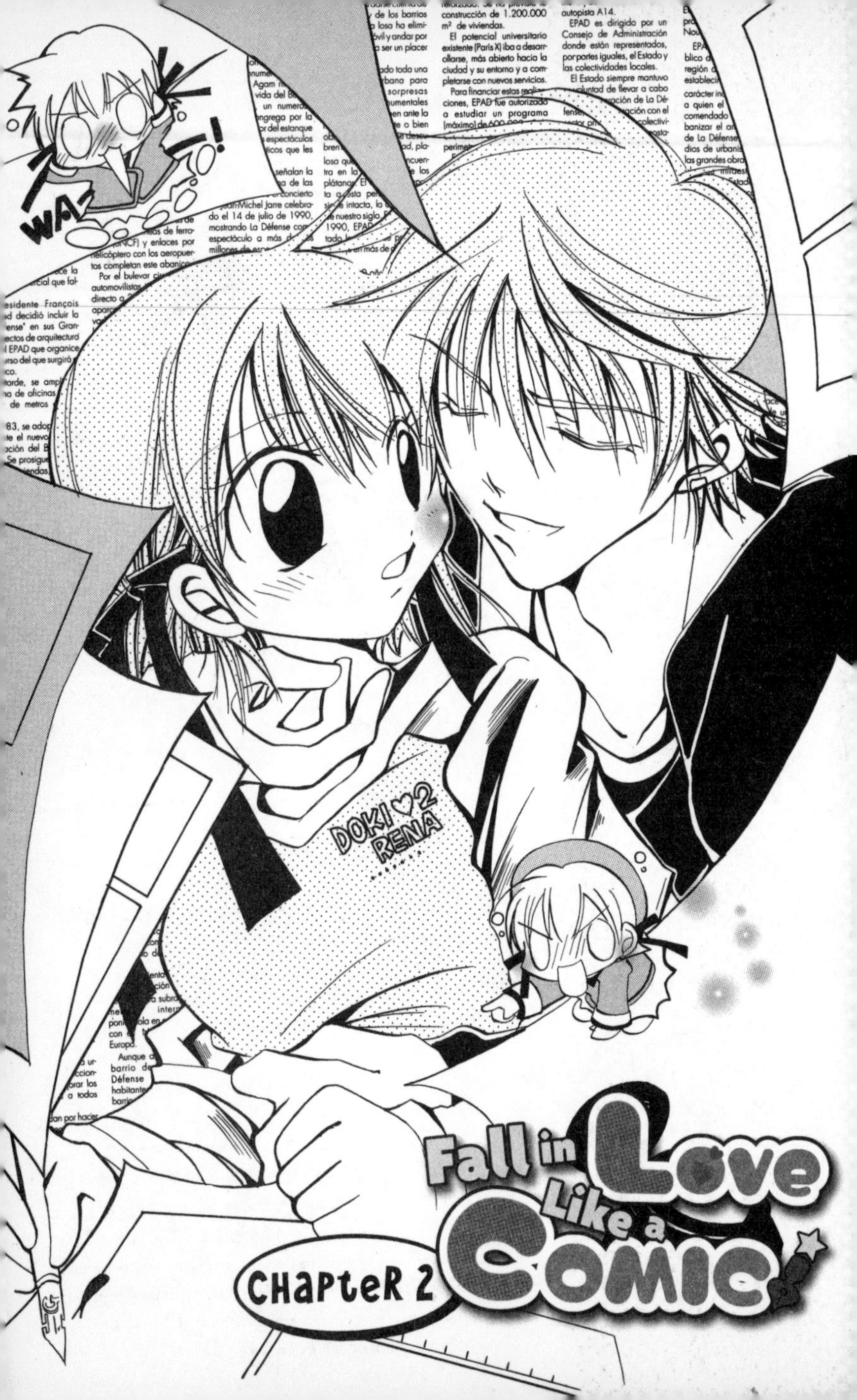
WA—!
DOKI♥2 RENA
Fall in Love Like a Comic
CHAPTER 2

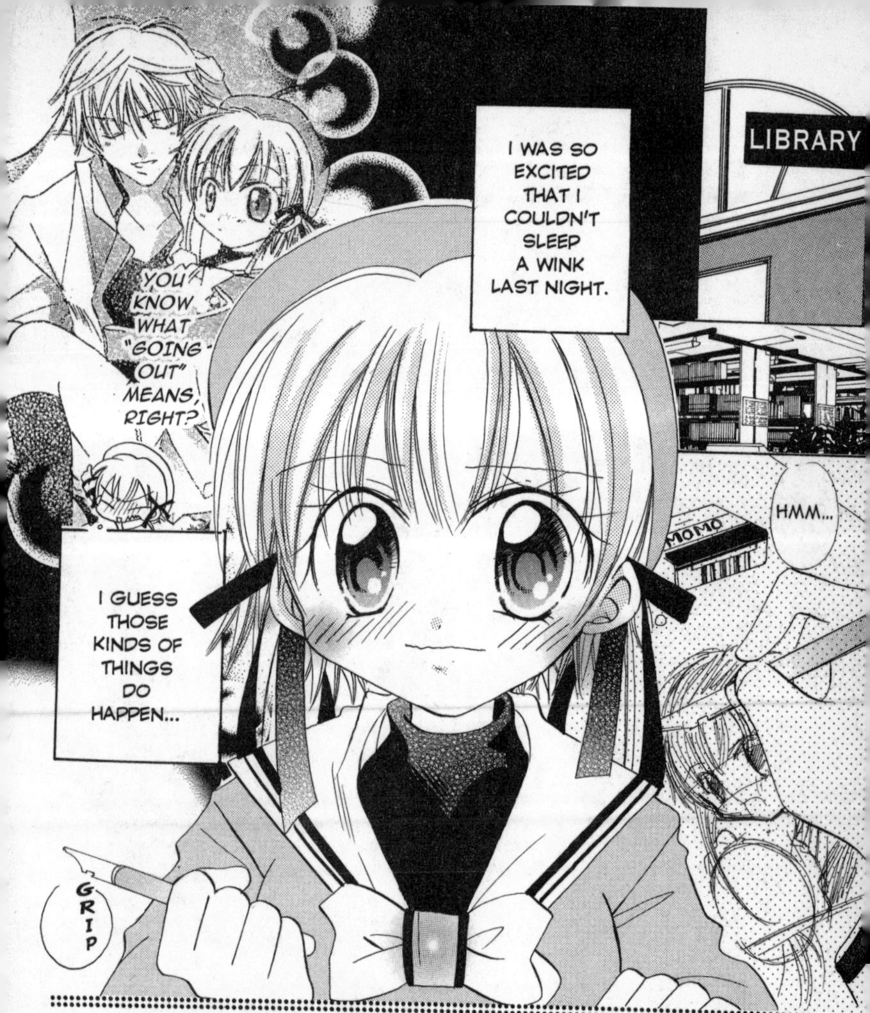
LIBRARY
I WAS SO EXCITED THAT I COULDN'T SLEEP A WINK LAST NIGHT.
YOU KNOW WHAT "GOING OUT" MEANS, RIGHT?
HMM...
MOMO
I GUESS THOSE KINDS OF THINGS DO HAPPEN...
GRIP

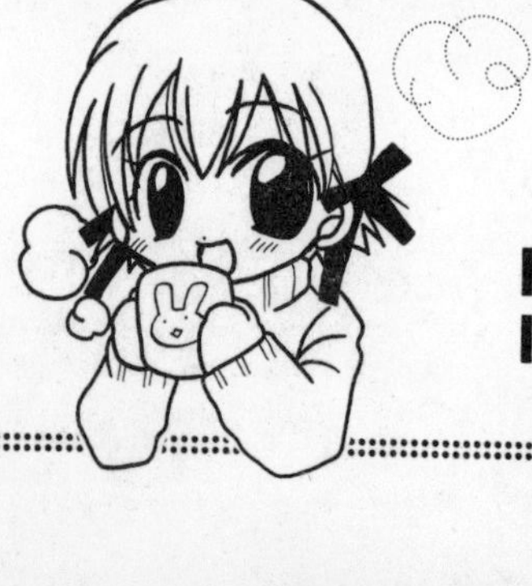

FALL IN LOVE LIKE A COMIC!

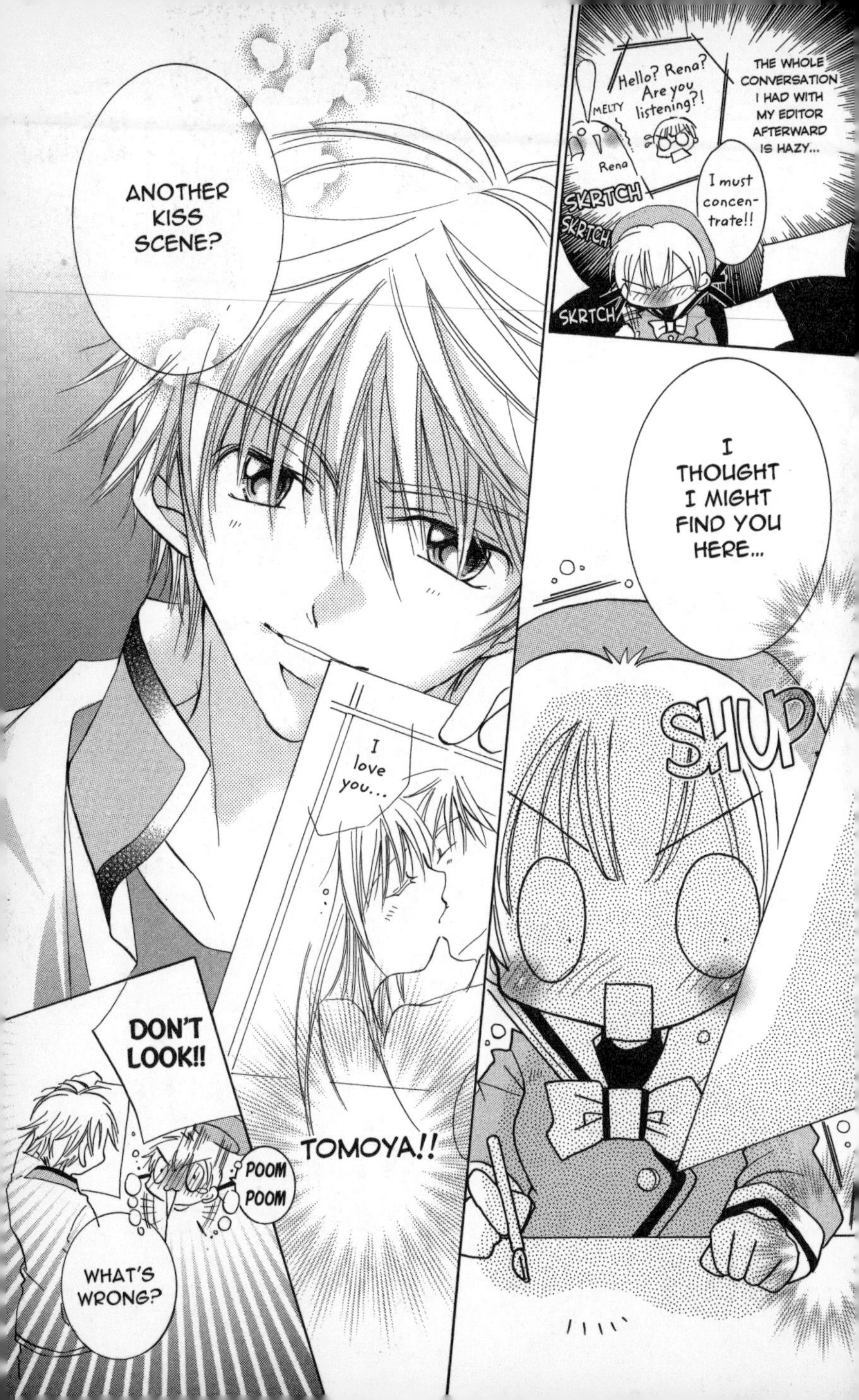
THE WHOLE CONVERSATION I HAD WITH MY EDITOR AFTERWARD IS HAZY...
Hello? Rena? Are you listening?!
MELTY
Rena
I must concen-trate!!
SKRTCH
SKRTCH
SKRTCH
I THOUGHT I MIGHT FIND YOU HERE...
SHUP
ANOTHER KISS SCENE?
I love you...
DON'T LOOK!!
TOMOYA!!
POOM POOM
WHAT'S WRONG?

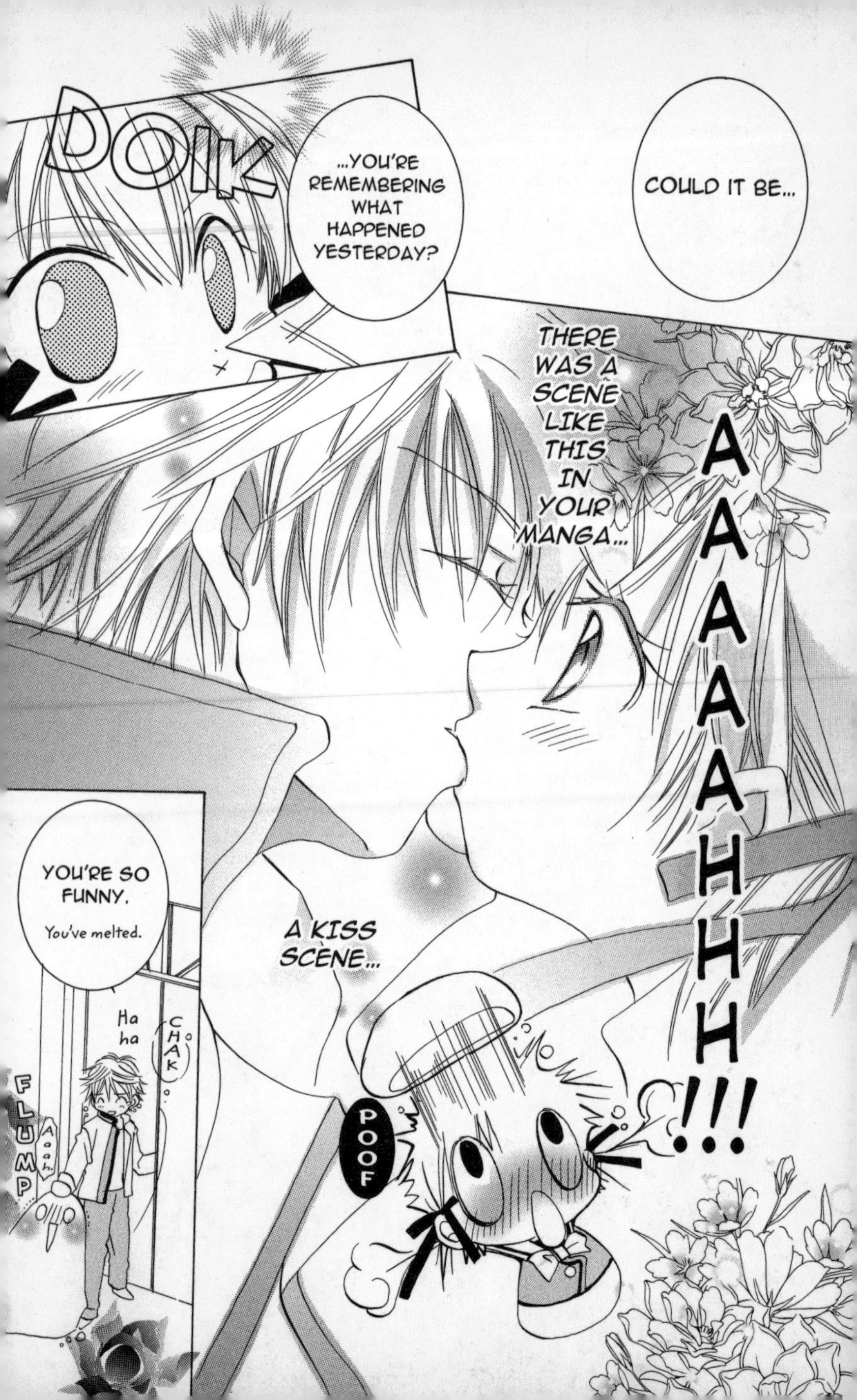
COULD IT BE...
...YOU'RE REMEMBERING WHAT HAPPENED YESTERDAY?
DOIK
THERE WAS A SCENE LIKE THIS IN YOUR MANGA...
AAAAAHH!!!
A KISS SCENE...
POOF
YOU'RE SO FUNNY.
You've melted.
Ha ha
CHAK
FLUMP...
Aaah.

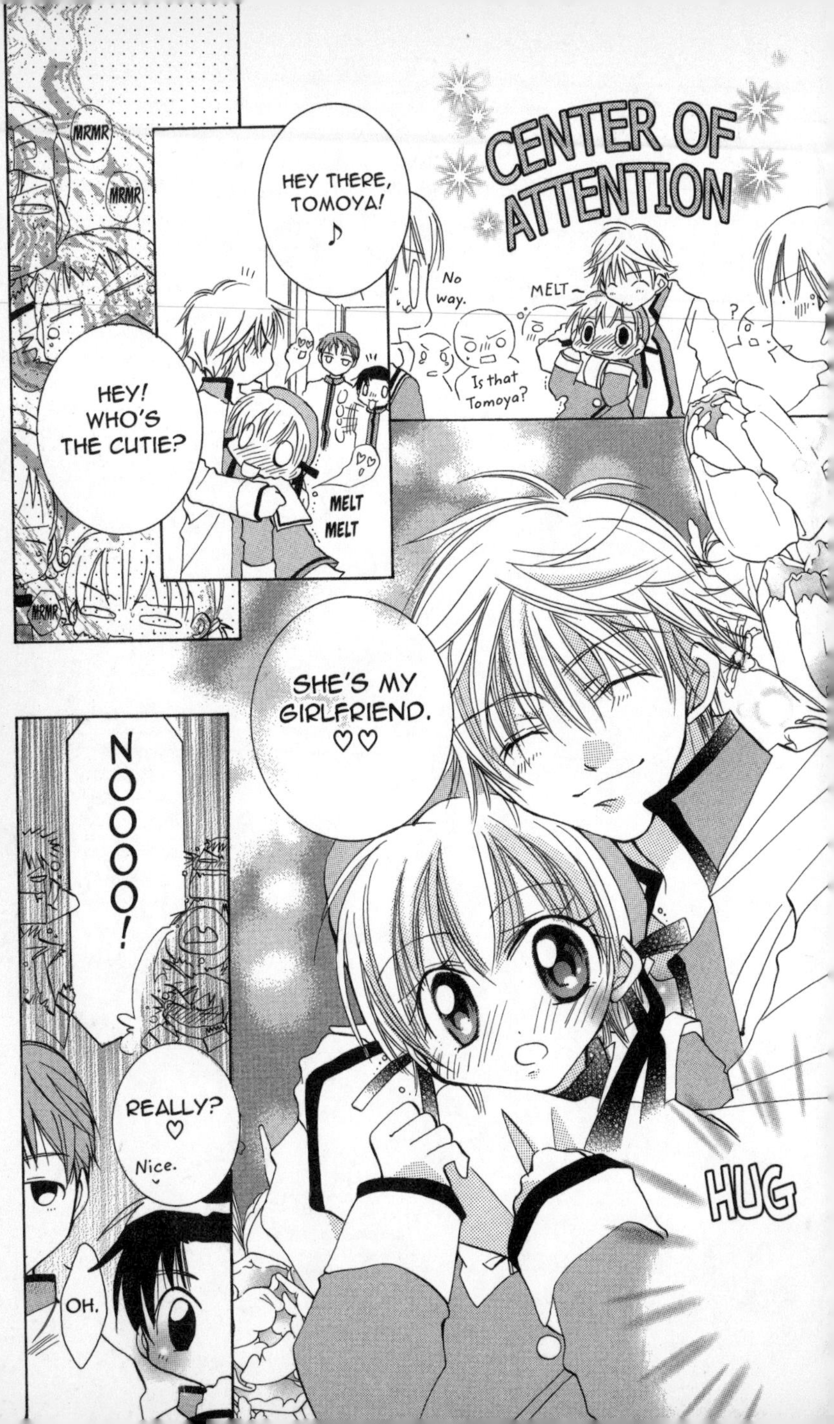
CENTER OF ATTENTION
MELT~
No way.
Is that Tomoya?
?
HEY THERE, TOMOYA! ♪
HEY! WHO'S THE CUTIE?
MELT MELT
MRMR
MRMR
MRMR
SHE'S MY GIRLFRIEND. ♡♡
HUG
NOOOOO!
REALLY? ♡
Nice.
OH.

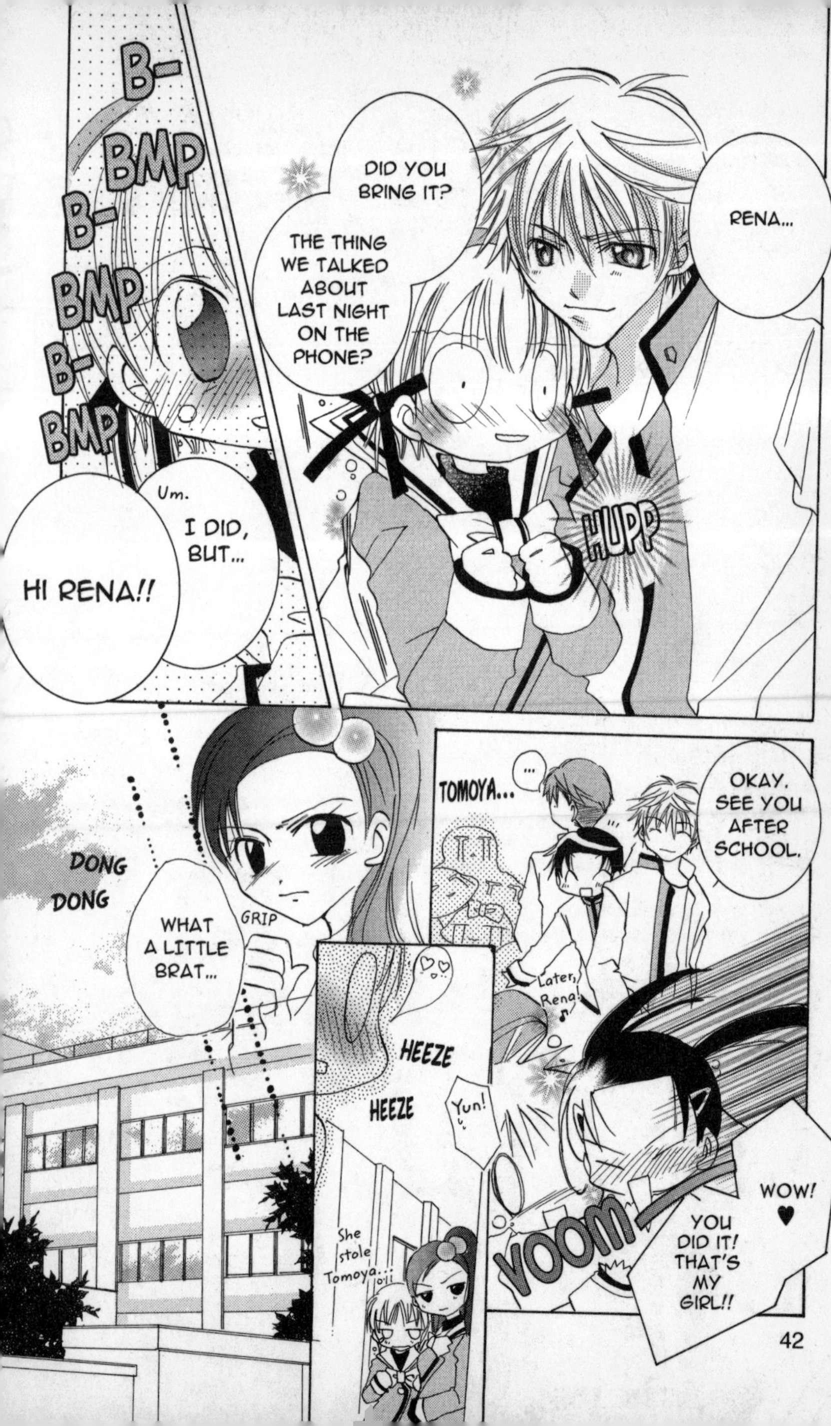
RENA...
DID YOU BRING IT?
THE THING WE TALKED ABOUT LAST NIGHT ON THE PHONE?
HUPP
B-BMP B-BMP B-BMP
Um.
I DID, BUT...
HI RENA!!
OKAY. SEE YOU AFTER SCHOOL.
TOMOYA...
...
Later, Rena! ♪
WOW! ♥
YOU DID IT! THAT'S MY GIRL!!
VOOM
HEEZE
HEEZE
Yun!
She stole Tomoya...
DONG
DONG
WHAT A LITTLE BRAT...
GRIP

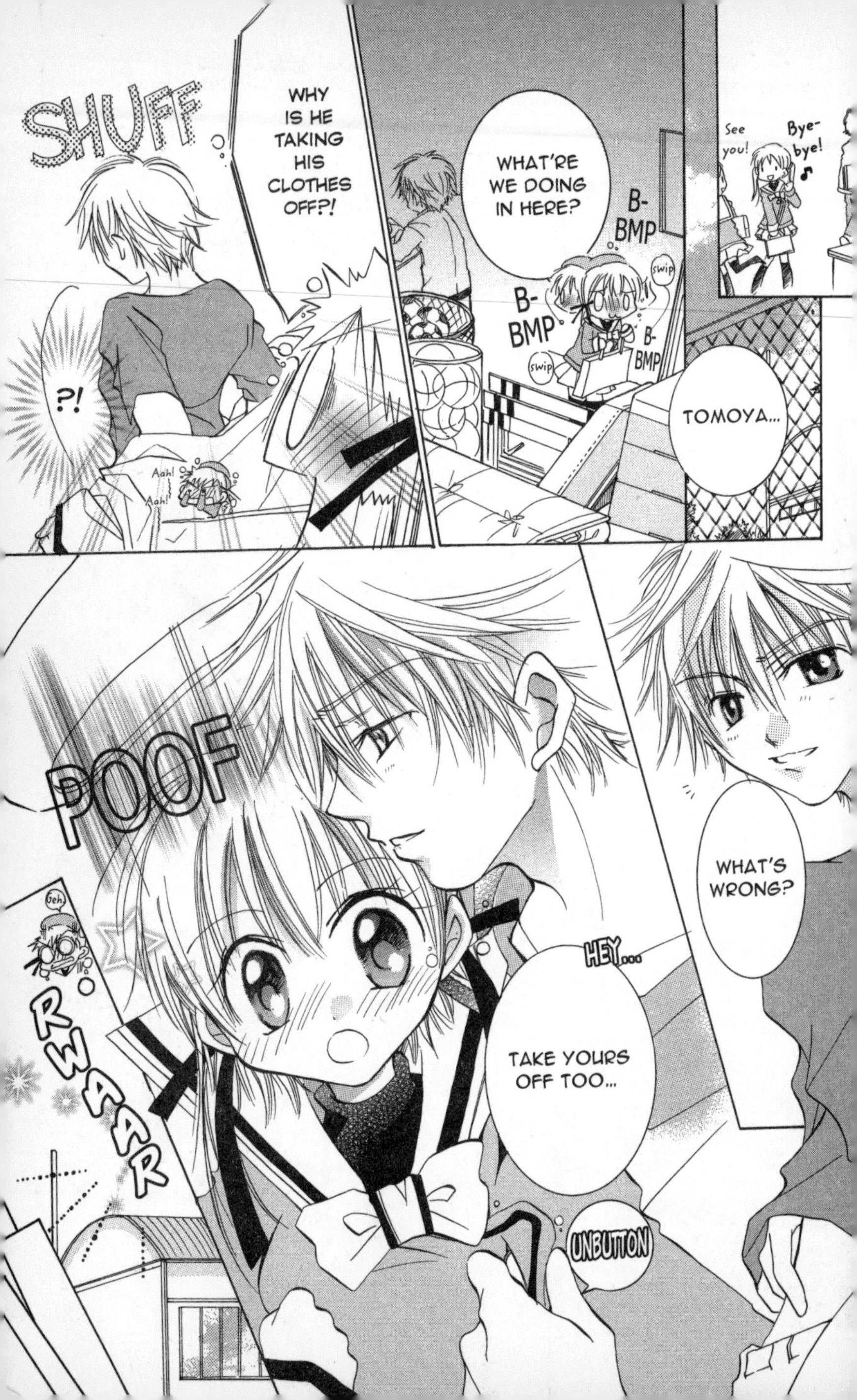
See you!
Bye-bye!
TOMOYA...
WHAT'RE WE DOING IN HERE?
B-BMP
swip
B-BMP
swip
B-BMP
SHUFF
WHY IS HE TAKING HIS CLOTHES OFF?!
?!
Aah!
Aah!
WHAT'S WRONG?
HEY...
TAKE YOURS OFF TOO...
UNBUTTON
POOF
Geh
RWAAAR

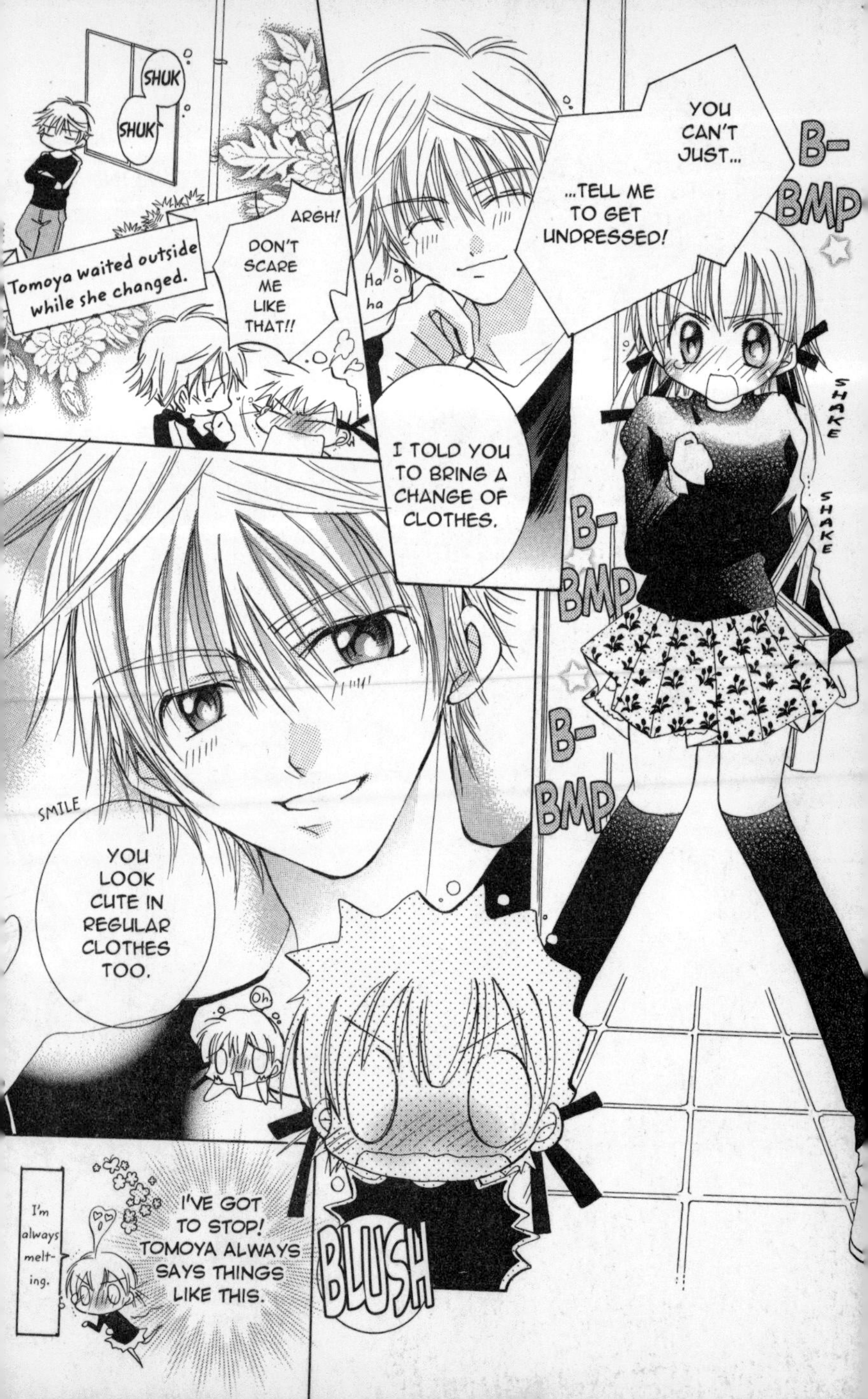
YOU CAN'T JUST...
...TELL ME TO GET UNDRESSED!
B-BMP
SHAKE
SHAKE
B-BMP
B-BMP
Ha ha
I TOLD YOU TO BRING A CHANGE OF CLOTHES.
SHUK
SHUK
ARGH!
DON'T SCARE ME LIKE THAT!!
Tomoya waited outside while she changed.
SMILE
YOU LOOK CUTE IN REGULAR CLOTHES TOO.
Oh
BLUSH
I'VE GOT TO STOP! TOMOYA ALWAYS SAYS THINGS LIKE THIS.
I'm always melt-ing.

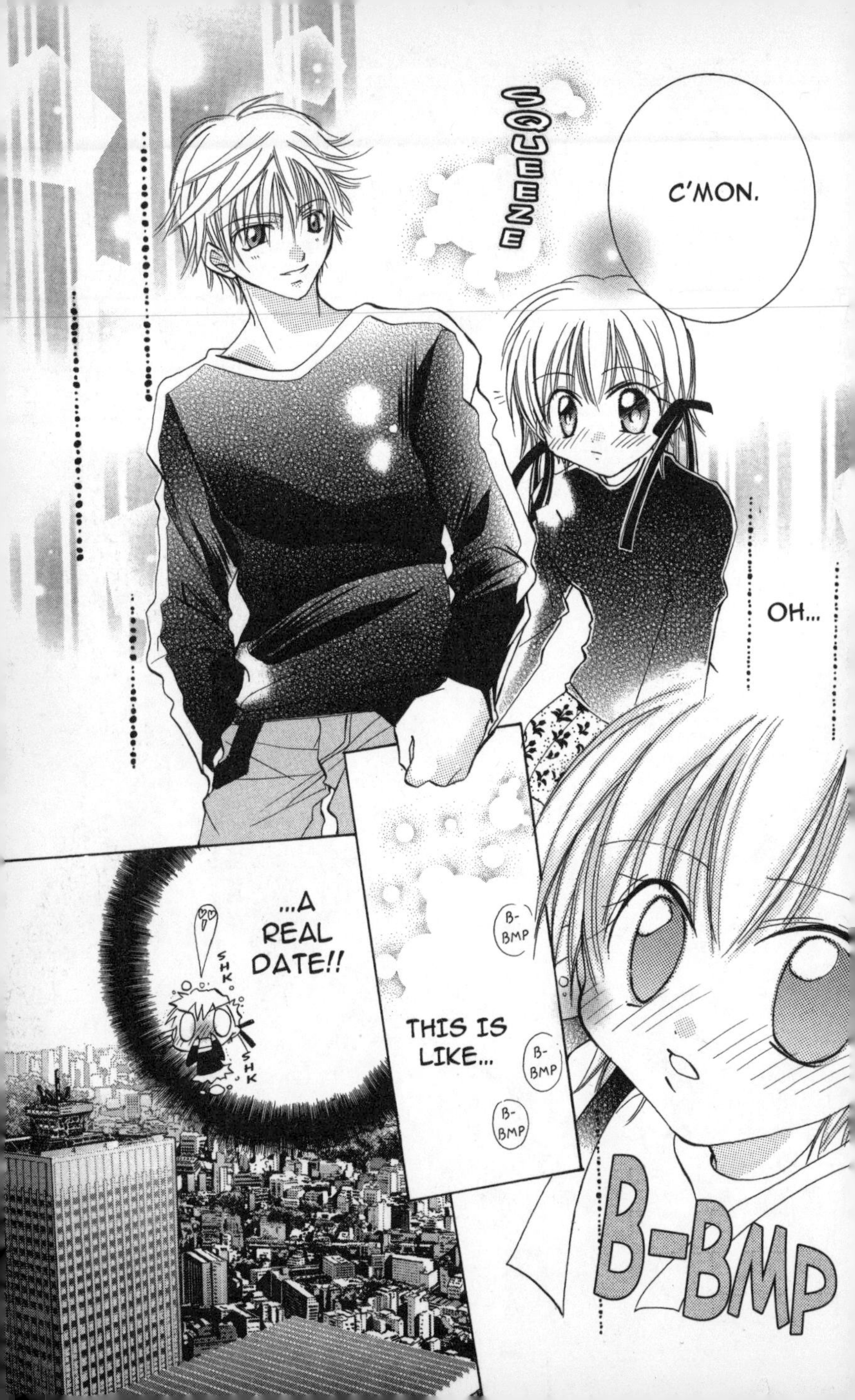
SQUEEZE
C'MON.
OH...
THIS IS LIKE...
B-BMP
B-BMP
B-BMP
...A REAL DATE!!
SHK
SHK
B-BMP

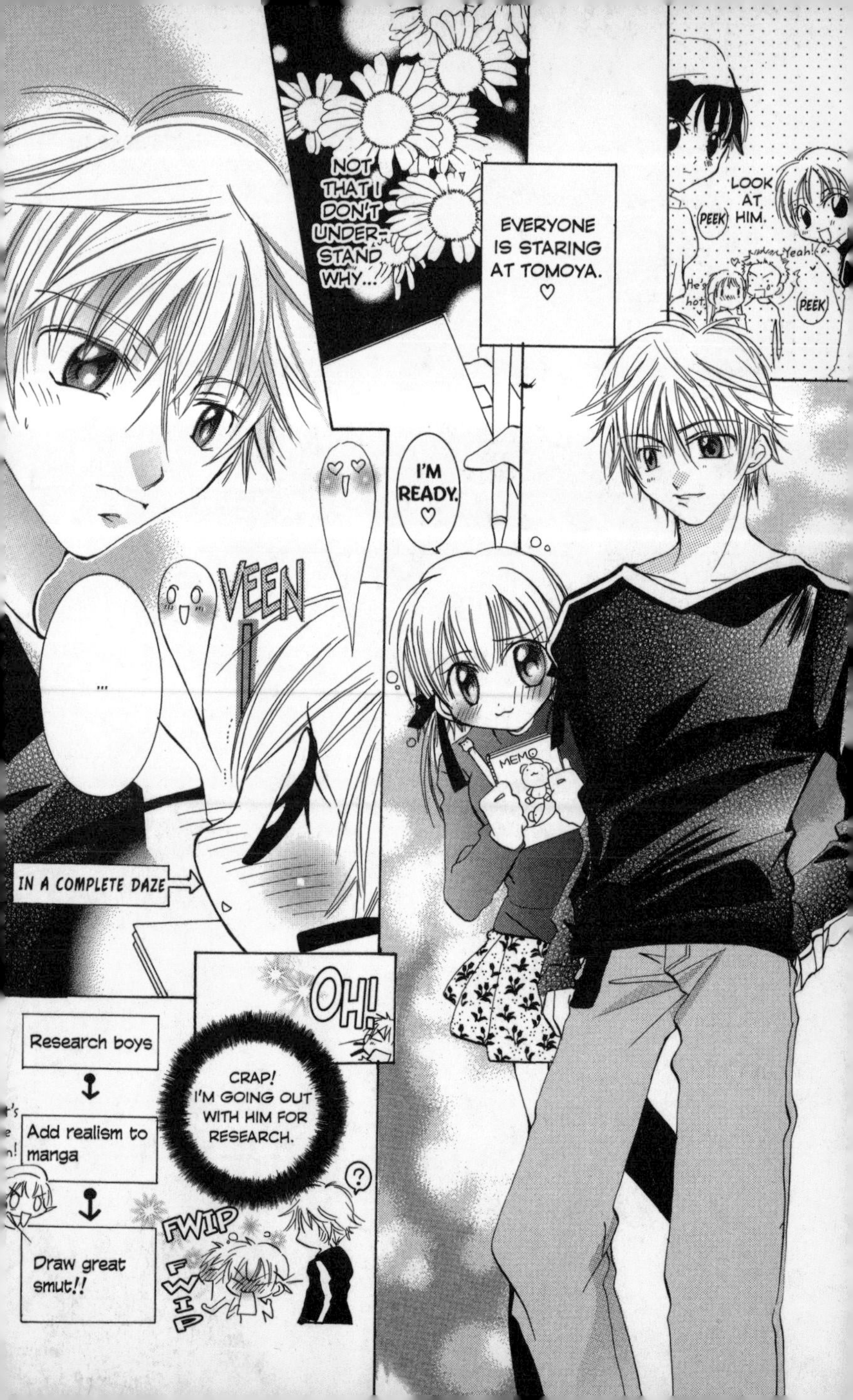
LOOK AT HIM.
PEEK
Yeah!
He's hot.
PEEK
EVERYONE IS STARING AT TOMOYA. ♡
NOT THAT I DON'T UNDER-STAND WHY...
I'M READY. ♡
...
VEEN
IN A COMPLETE DAZE
OH!
CRAP! I'M GOING OUT WITH HIM FOR RESEARCH.
Research boys
Add realism to manga
Draw great smut!!
?
FWIP
FWIP

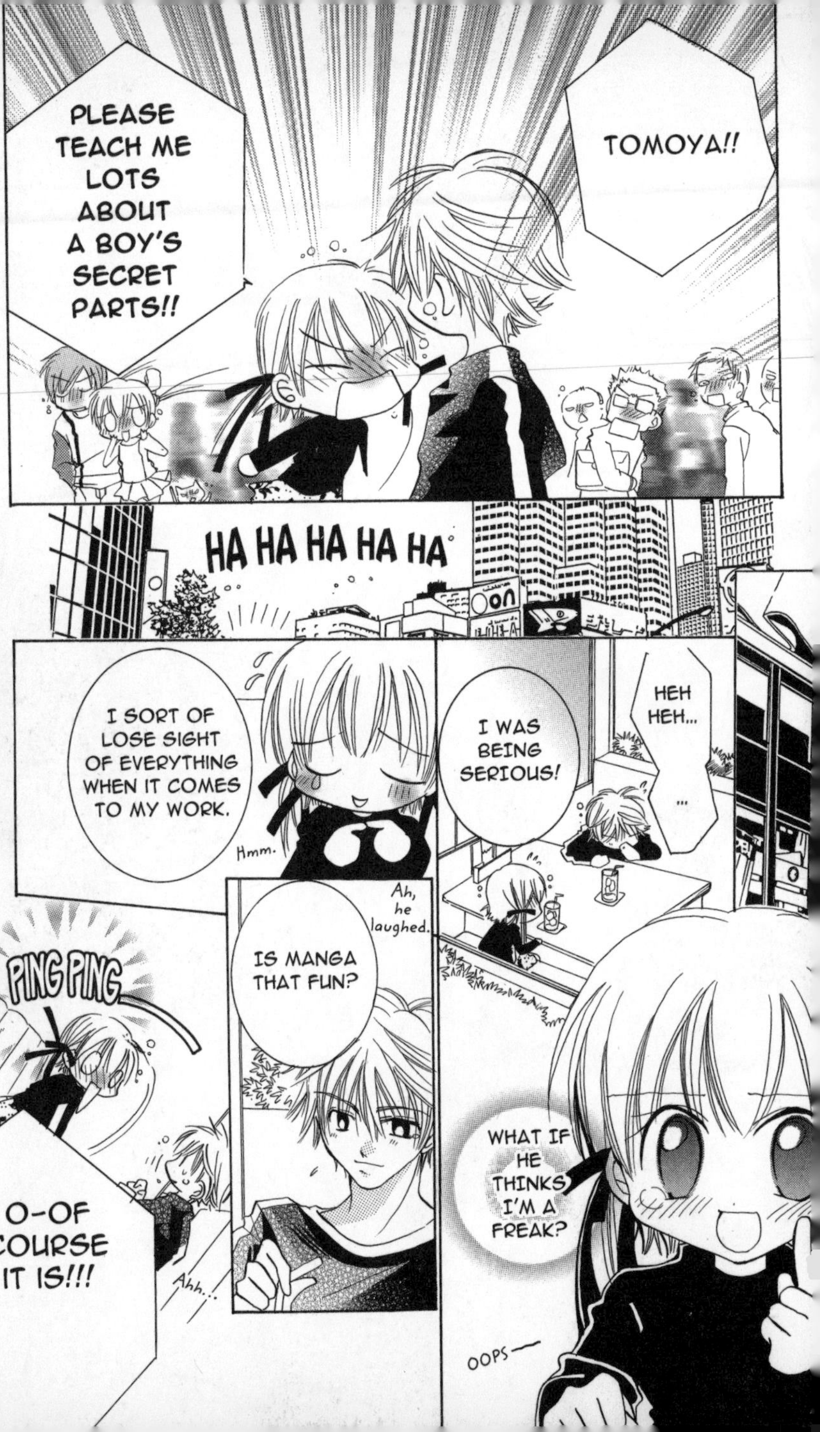
TOMOYA!!
PLEASE TEACH ME LOTS ABOUT A BOY'S SECRET PARTS!!
HA HA HA HA HA
HEH HEH...
I WAS BEING SERIOUS!
...
I SORT OF LOSE SIGHT OF EVERYTHING WHEN IT COMES TO MY WORK.
Hmm.
WHAT IF HE THINKS I'M A FREAK?
OOPS—
Ah, he laughed.
IS MANGA THAT FUN?
PING PING
O-OF COURSE IT IS!!!
Ahh...

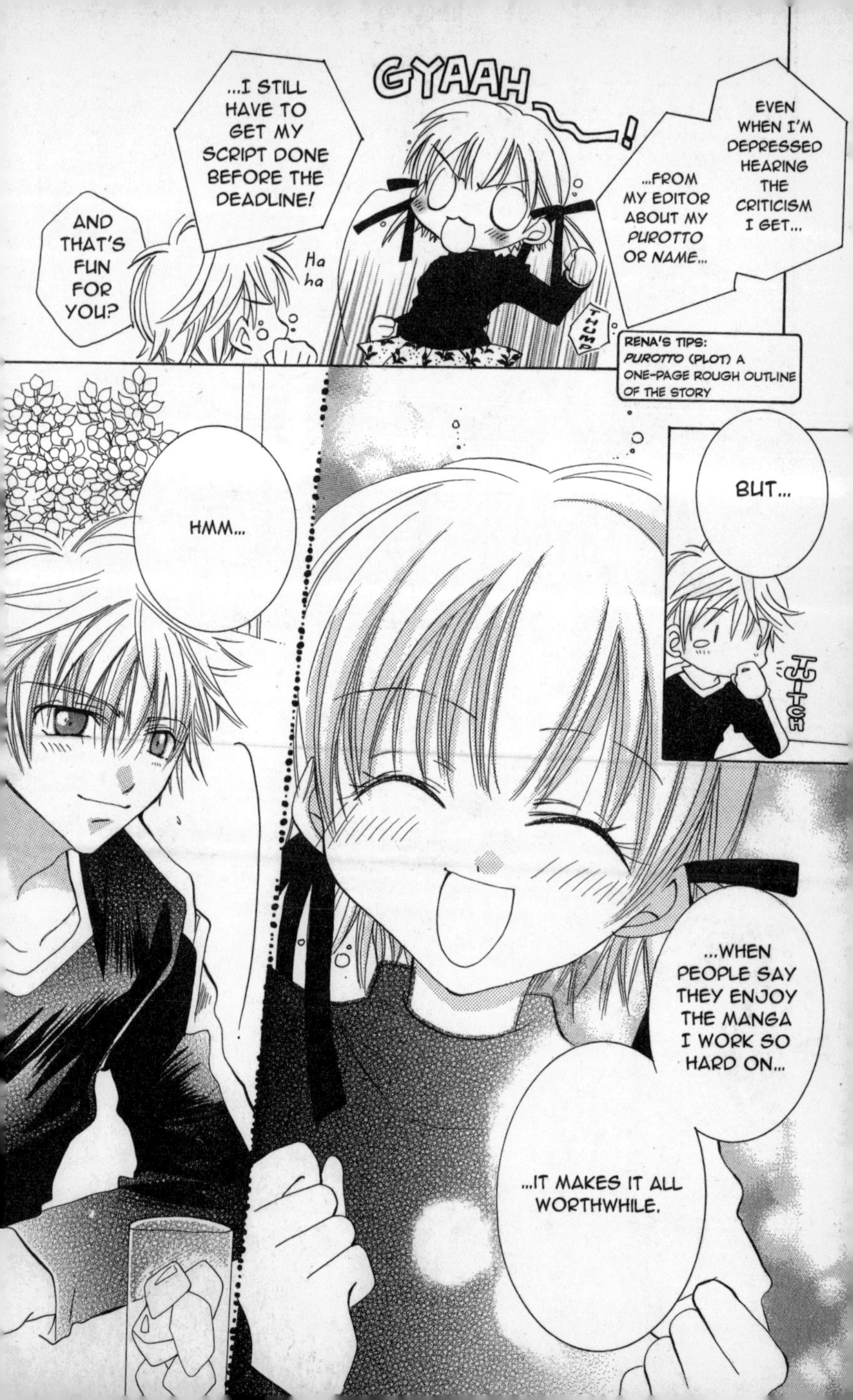
EVEN WHEN I'M DEPRESSED HEARING THE CRITICISM I GET...
...FROM MY EDITOR ABOUT MY *PUROTTO* OR NAME...
GYAAH~~!
THUMP
...I STILL HAVE TO GET MY SCRIPT DONE BEFORE THE DEADLINE!
Ha ha
AND THAT'S FUN FOR YOU?
RENA'S TIPS: *PUROTTO* (PLOT) A ONE-PAGE ROUGH OUTLINE OF THE STORY
BUT...
TWITCH
...WHEN PEOPLE SAY THEY ENJOY THE MANGA I WORK SO HARD ON...
...IT MAKES IT ALL WORTHWHILE.
HMM...

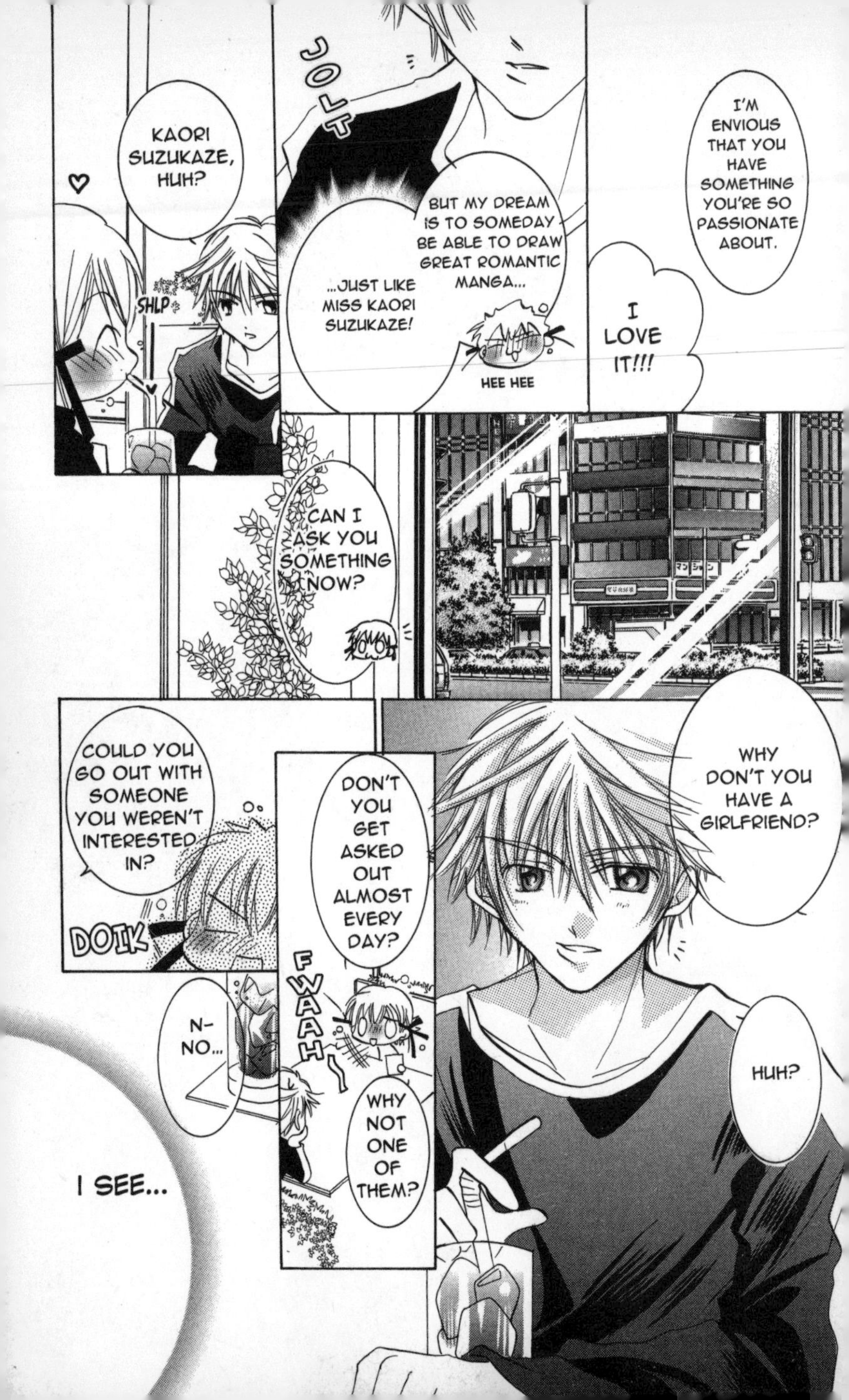
I'M ENVIOUS THAT YOU HAVE SOMETHING YOU'RE SO PASSIONATE ABOUT.
I LOVE IT!!!
JOLT
BUT MY DREAM IS TO SOMEDAY BE ABLE TO DRAW GREAT ROMANTIC MANGA...
...JUST LIKE MISS KAORI SUZUKAZE!
HEE HEE
KAORI SUZUKAZE, HUH?
SHLP
CAN I ASK YOU SOMETHING NOW?
WHY DON'T YOU HAVE A GIRLFRIEND?
HUH?
DON'T YOU GET ASKED OUT ALMOST EVERY DAY?
FWAAAH
WHY NOT ONE OF THEM?
COULD YOU GO OUT WITH SOMEONE YOU WEREN'T INTERESTED IN?
DOIK
N-NO...
I SEE...

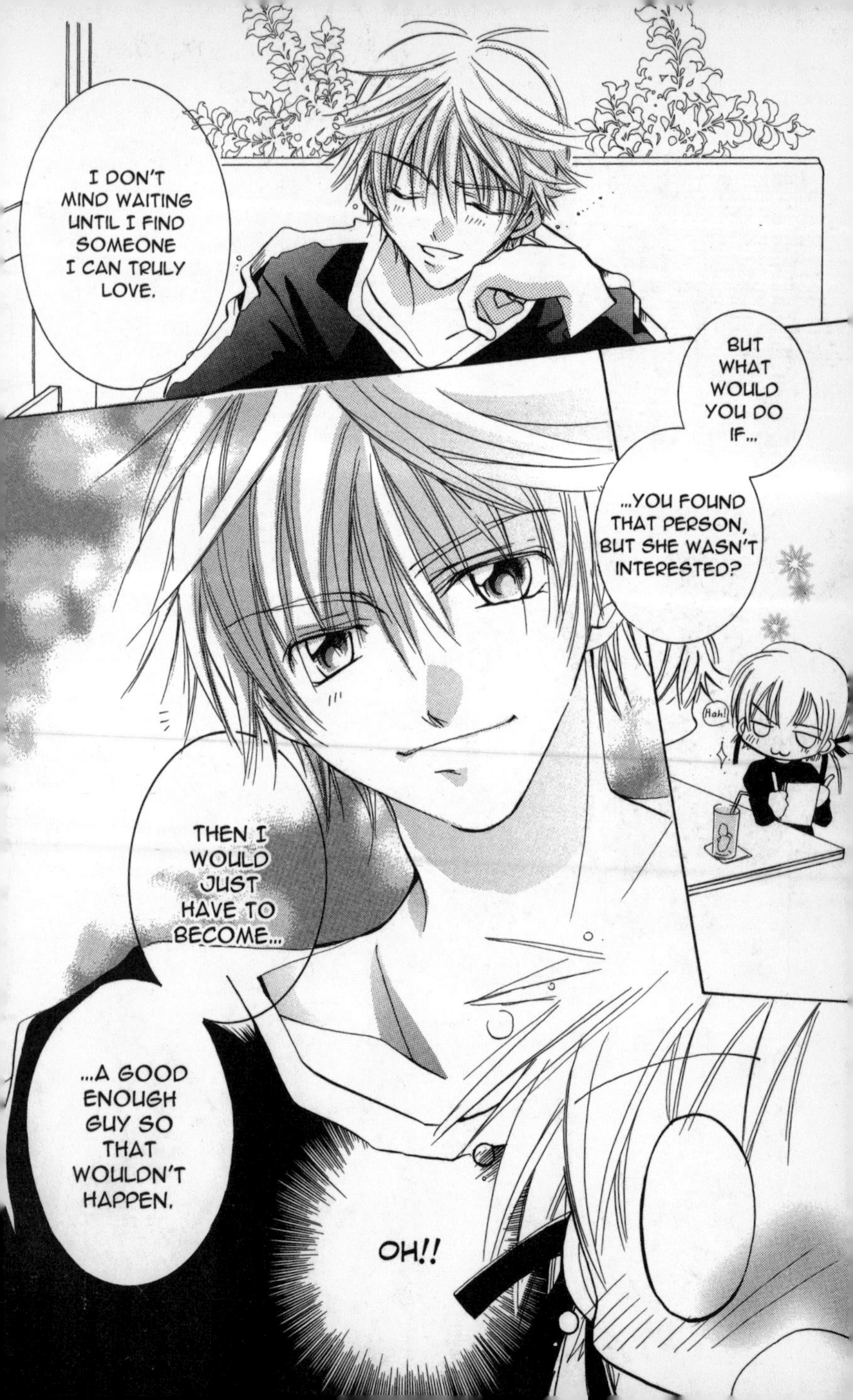
I DON'T MIND WAITING UNTIL I FIND SOMEONE I CAN TRULY LOVE.
BUT WHAT WOULD YOU DO IF...
...YOU FOUND THAT PERSON, BUT SHE WASN'T INTERESTED?
Hah!
THEN I WOULD JUST HAVE TO BECOME...
...A GOOD ENOUGH GUY SO THAT WOULDN'T HAPPEN.
OH!!

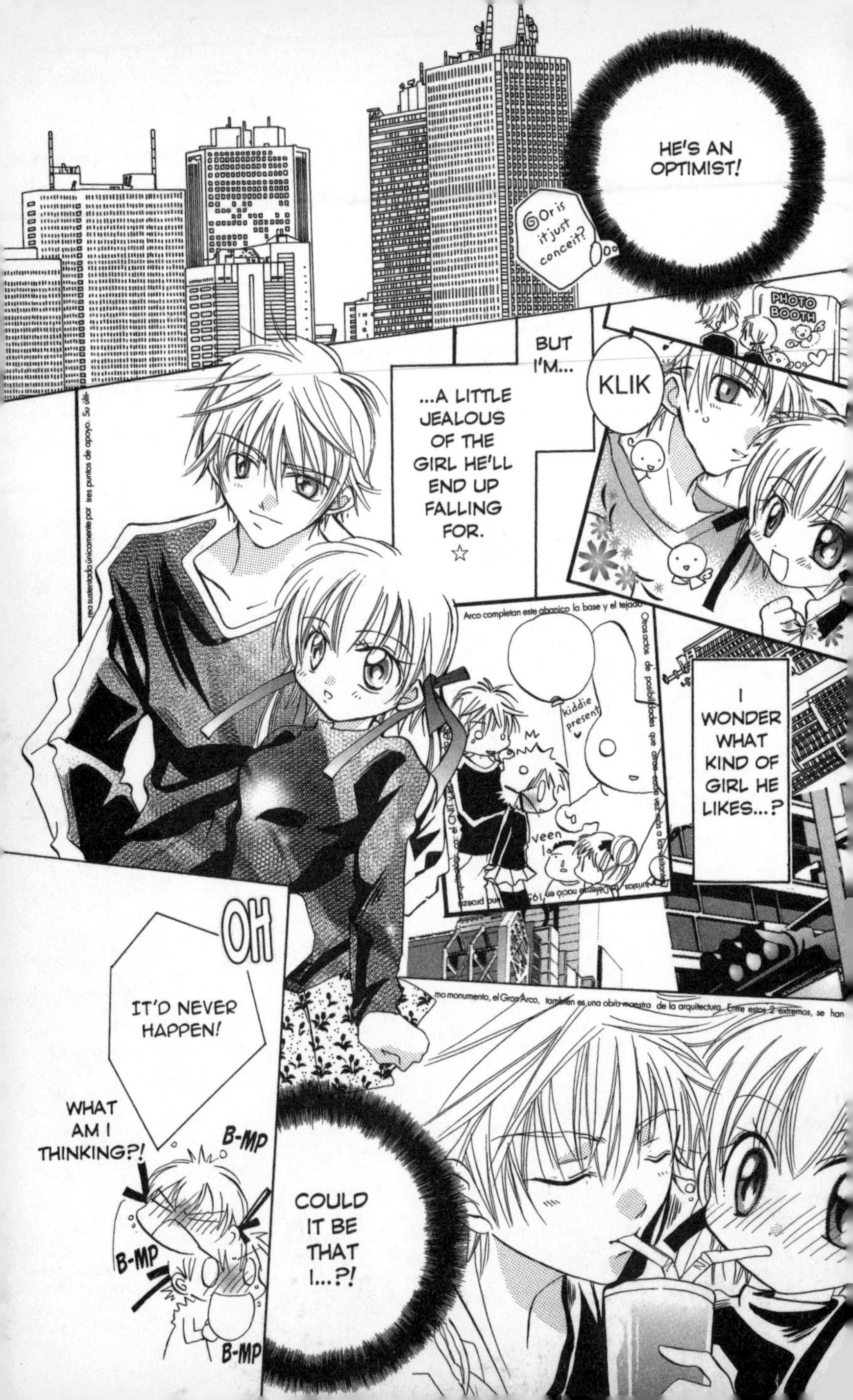
HE'S AN OPTIMIST!
Or is it just conceit?
PHOTO BOOTH
KLIK
BUT I'M...
...A LITTLE JEALOUS OF THE GIRL HE'LL END UP FALLING FOR. ☆
Arco completan este abanico la base y el tejado
kiddie present
I WONDER WHAT KIND OF GIRL HE LIKES...?
mo monumento, el Gran Arco, también es una obra maestra de la arquitectura. Entre estos 2 extremos, se han
COULD IT BE THAT I...?!
OH
IT'D NEVER HAPPEN!
WHAT AM I THINKING?!
B-MP
B-MP
B-MP

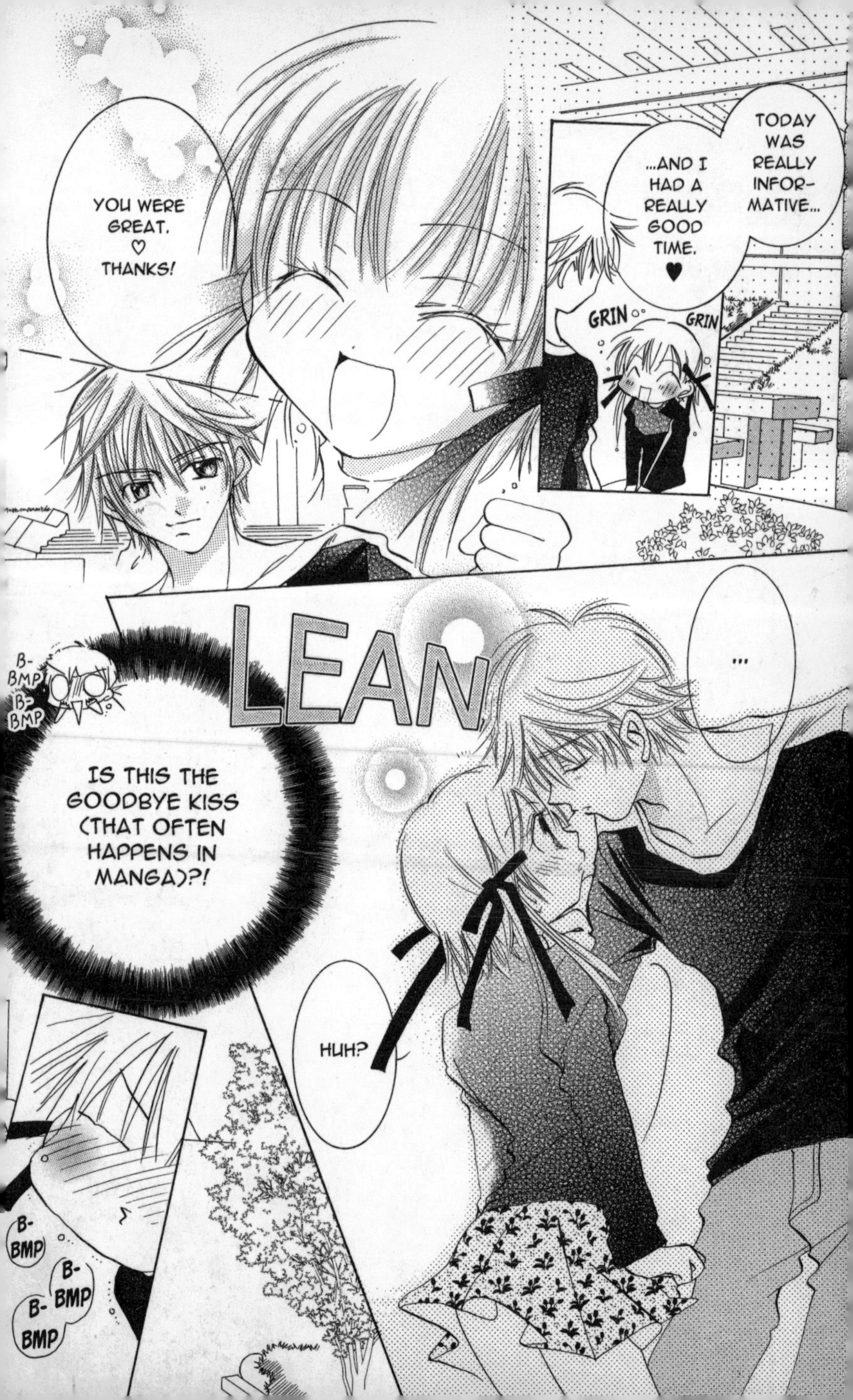
TODAY WAS REALLY INFORMATIVE...
...AND I HAD A REALLY GOOD TIME. ♥
GRIN
GRIN
YOU WERE GREAT. ♡ THANKS!
...
LEAN
B-BMP B-BMP
IS THIS THE GOODBYE KISS (THAT OFTEN HAPPENS IN MANGA)?!
HUH?
B-BMP
B-BMP
B-BMP

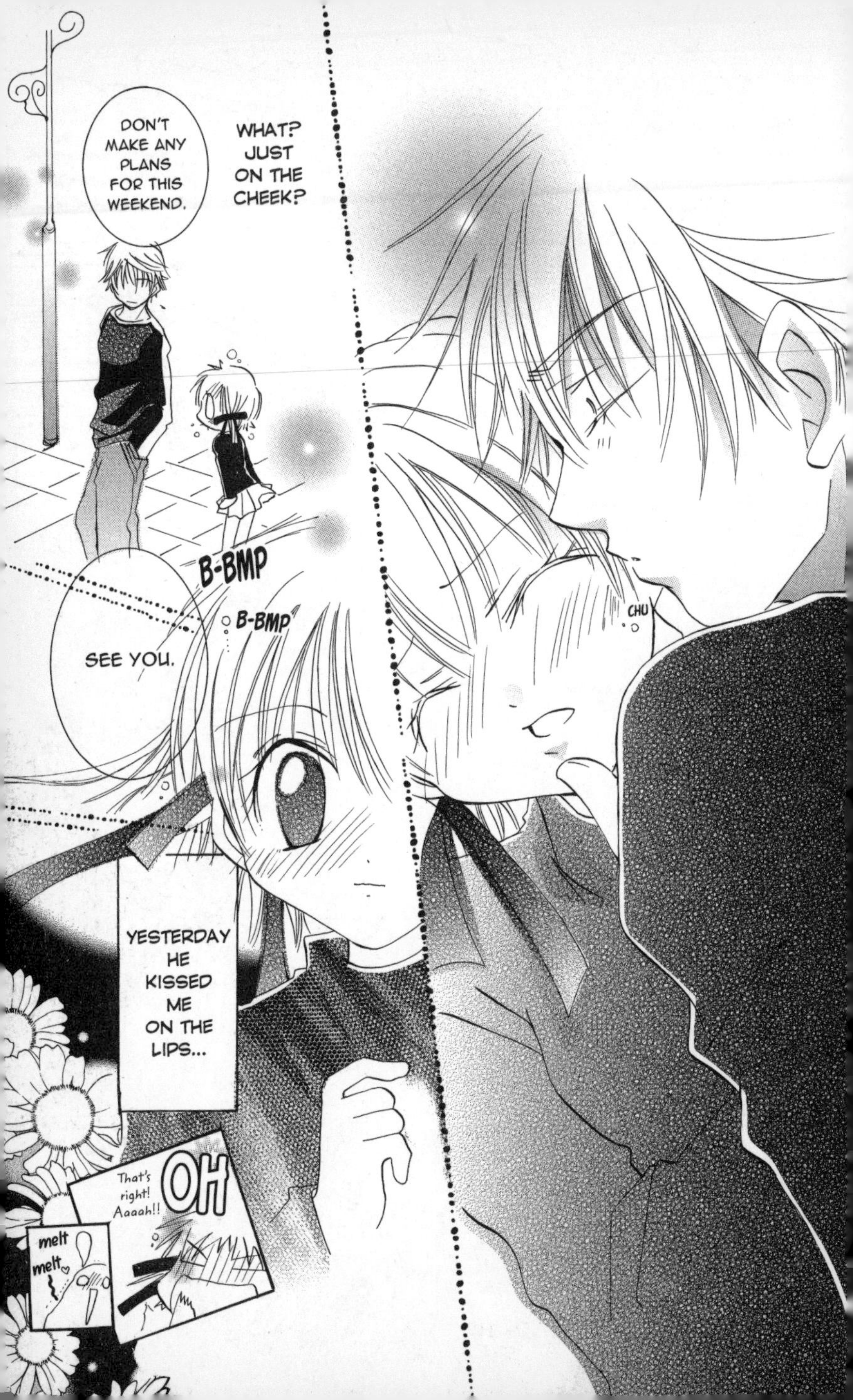
CHU
WHAT? JUST ON THE CHEEK?
DON'T MAKE ANY PLANS FOR THIS WEEKEND.
B-BMP
B-BMP
SEE YOU.
YESTERDAY HE KISSED ME ON THE LIPS...
OH
That's right! Aaaah!!
melt melt

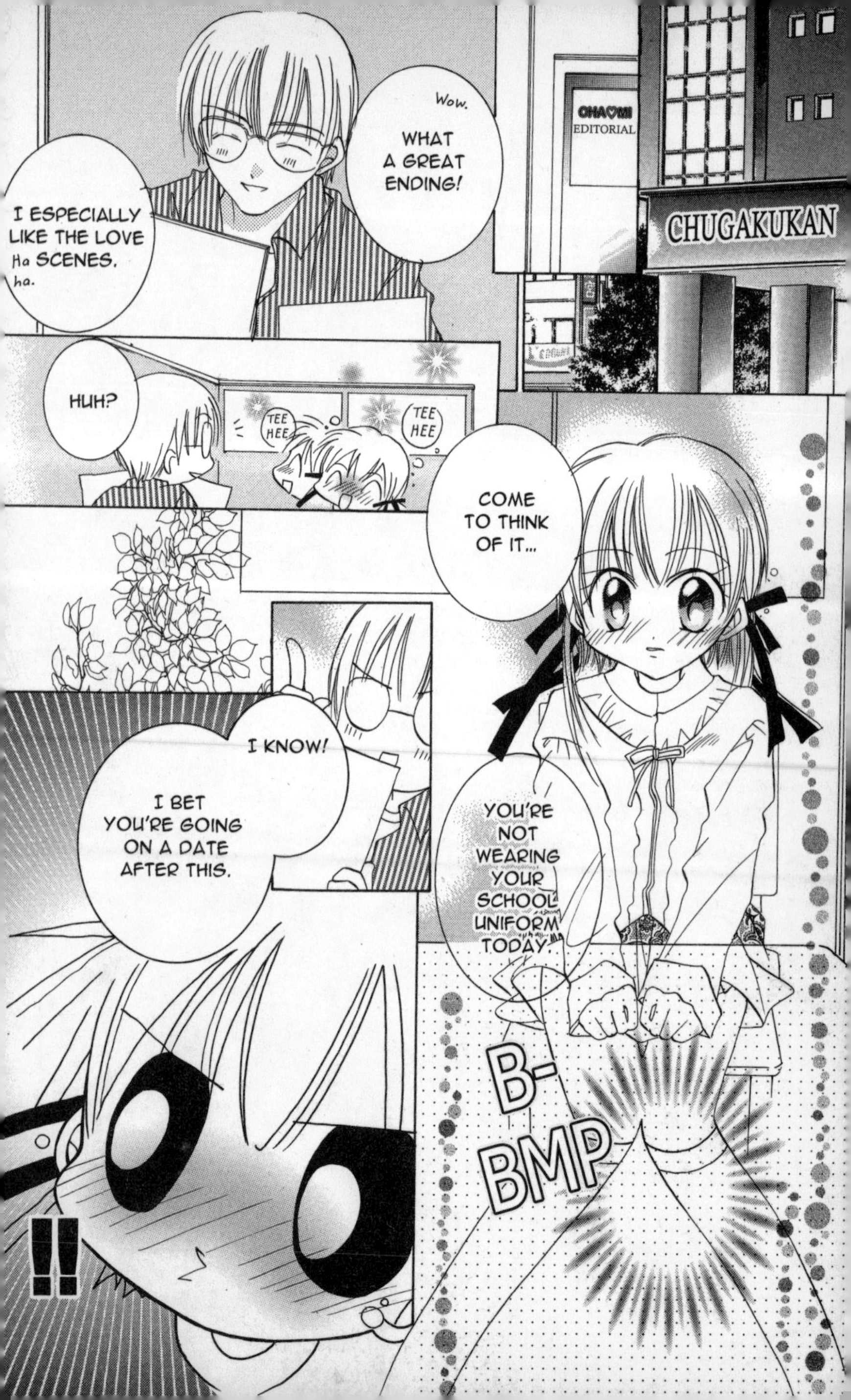
OHA♥MI EDITORIAL
CHUGAKUKAN
Wow.
WHAT A GREAT ENDING!
I ESPECIALLY LIKE THE LOVE SCENES. Ha ha.
HUH?
TEE HEE
TEE HEE
COME TO THINK OF IT...
YOU'RE NOT WEARING YOUR SCHOOL UNIFORM TODAY.
B-BMP
I KNOW!
I BET YOU'RE GOING ON A DATE AFTER THIS.
!!

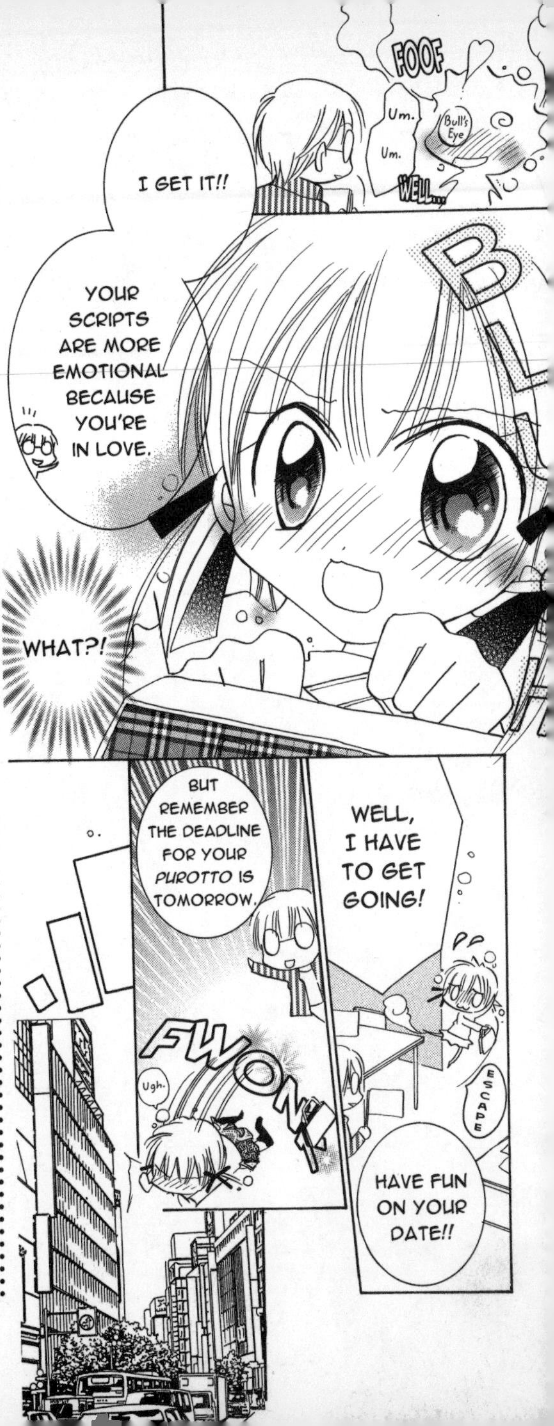
FOOF
Um.
Um.
Bull's Eye
WELL...
I GET IT!!
YOUR SCRIPTS ARE MORE EMOTIONAL BECAUSE YOU'RE IN LOVE.
WHAT?!
WELL, I HAVE TO GET GOING!
BUT REMEMBER THE DEADLINE FOR YOUR *PUROTTO* IS TOMORROW.
ESCAPE
FWON!
Ugh.
HAVE FUN ON YOUR DATE!!

After this manga came out, I was surprised at how many people told me they wanted to become a mangaka.

I'm not sure if this would be of any help to those elementary and middle school kids, but I'd like to introduce some of the tools I use.

Manuscript paper: I use the IC script paper in the B4 size.

Pen nibs: I use the G-pen, the round-nib pen by NIKKO, and also three school pens.

G pen: For sidebars (profiles, etc.)

Round nib pen: I use it for facial features (eyes, nose, mouth), wrinkles on clothes, and other fine parts like hair.

School pen: I use it for hair when the character has an up-do or to outline black hair.

(continues)

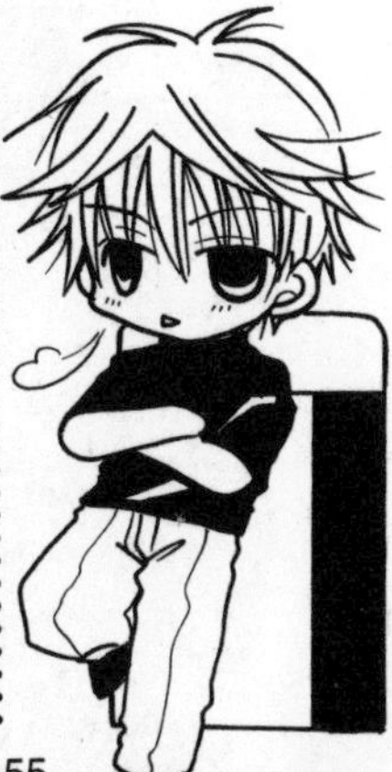

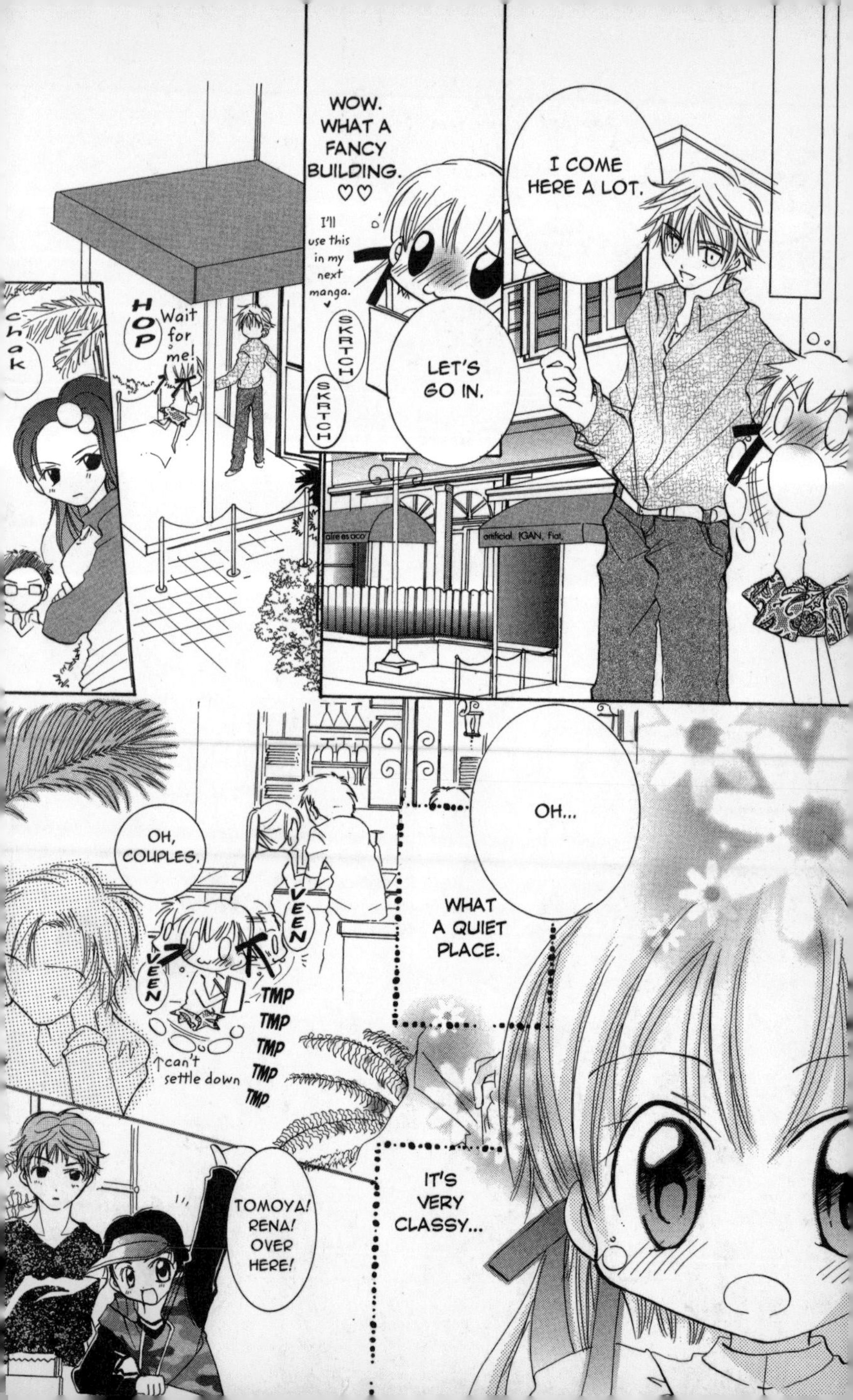
I COME HERE A LOT.
LET'S GO IN.
WOW. WHAT A FANCY BUILDING. ♡♡
I'll use this in my next manga. ♥
SKRTCH
SKRTCH
HOP
Wait for me!
Chak
OH...
WHAT A QUIET PLACE.
IT'S VERY CLASSY...
OH, COUPLES.
VEEN
VEEN
TMP TMP TMP TMP TMP
↑can't settle down
TOMOYA! RENA! OVER HERE!

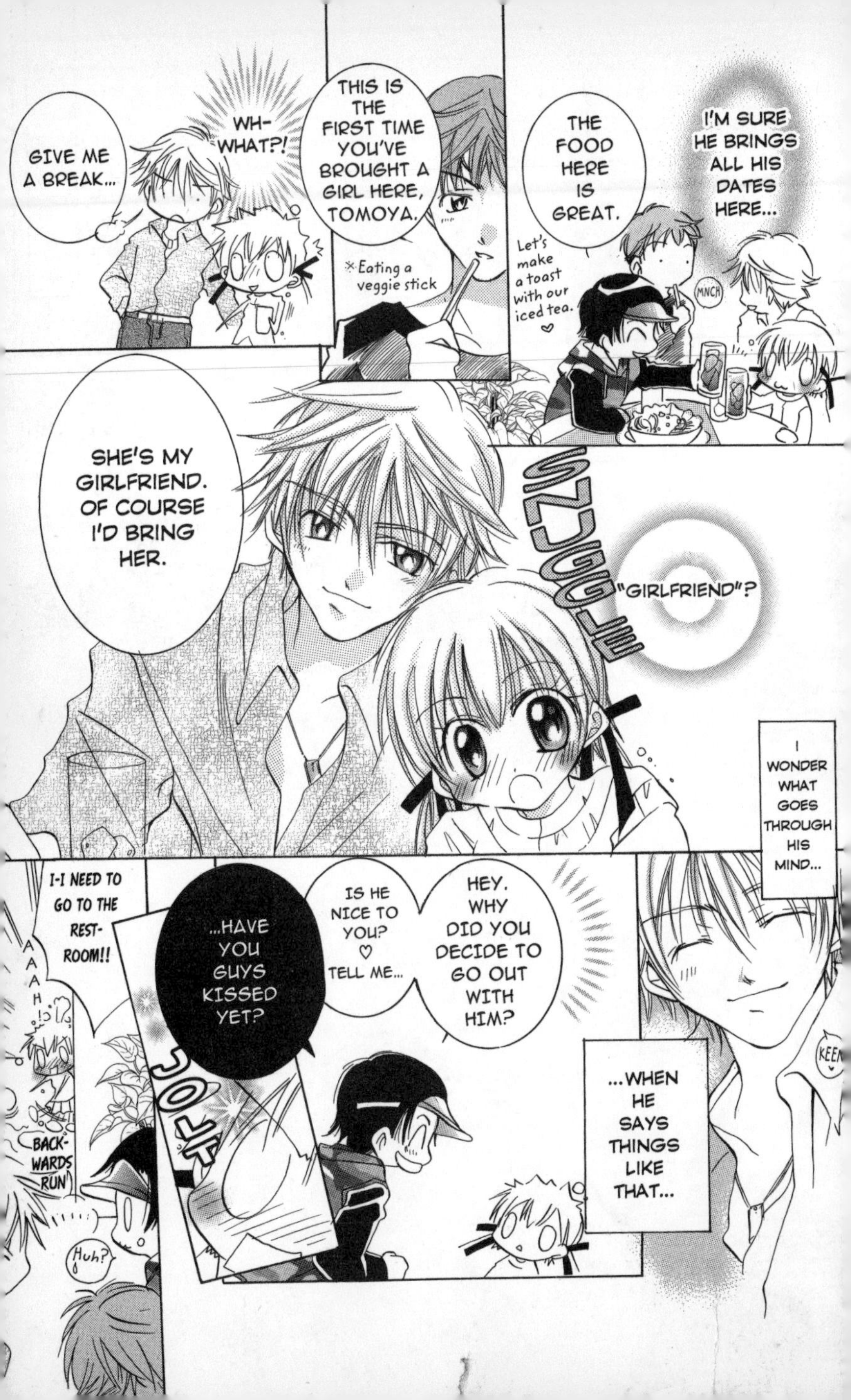
I'M SURE HE BRINGS ALL HIS DATES HERE...
THE FOOD HERE IS GREAT.
Let's make a toast with our iced tea. ♡
MNCH
THIS IS THE FIRST TIME YOU'VE BROUGHT A GIRL HERE, TOMOYA.
※Eating a veggie stick
WH-WHAT?!
GIVE ME A BREAK...
SHE'S MY GIRLFRIEND. OF COURSE I'D BRING HER.
SNUGGLE
"GIRLFRIEND"?
I WONDER WHAT GOES THROUGH HIS MIND...
...WHEN HE SAYS THINGS LIKE THAT...
KEEN
HEY. WHY DID YOU DECIDE TO GO OUT WITH HIM?
IS HE NICE TO YOU? ♡ TELL ME...
...HAVE YOU GUYS KISSED YET?
JOLT
I-I NEED TO GO TO THE REST-ROOM!!
AAAH
BACK-WARDS RUN
Huh?

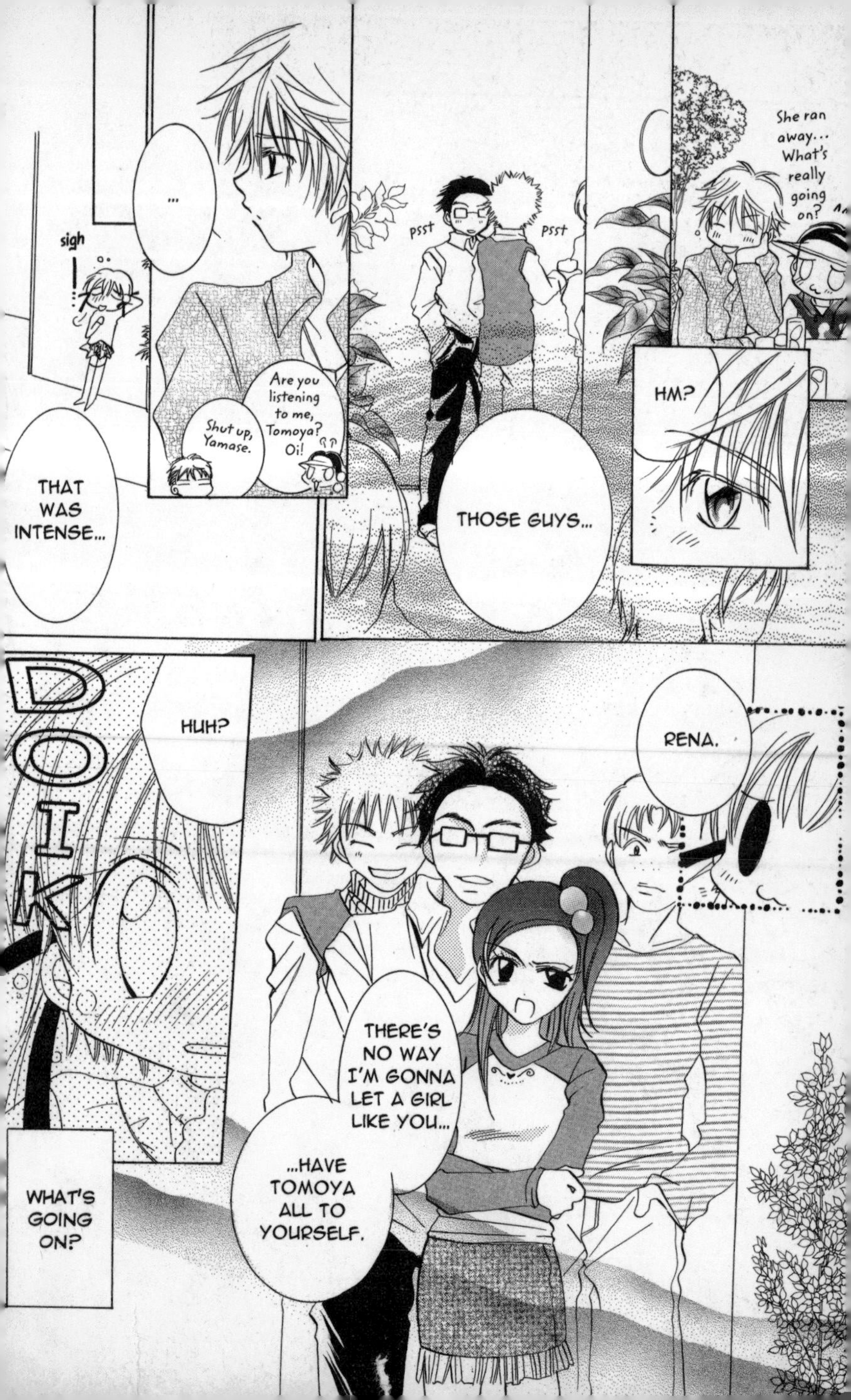
She ran away... What's really going on?
HM?
psst
psst
THOSE GUYS...
...
Are you listening to me, Tomoya? Oi!
Shut up, Yamase.
sigh
THAT WAS INTENSE...
RENA.
THERE'S NO WAY I'M GONNA LET A GIRL LIKE YOU...
...HAVE TOMOYA ALL TO YOURSELF.
HUH?
DOIK
WHAT'S GOING ON?

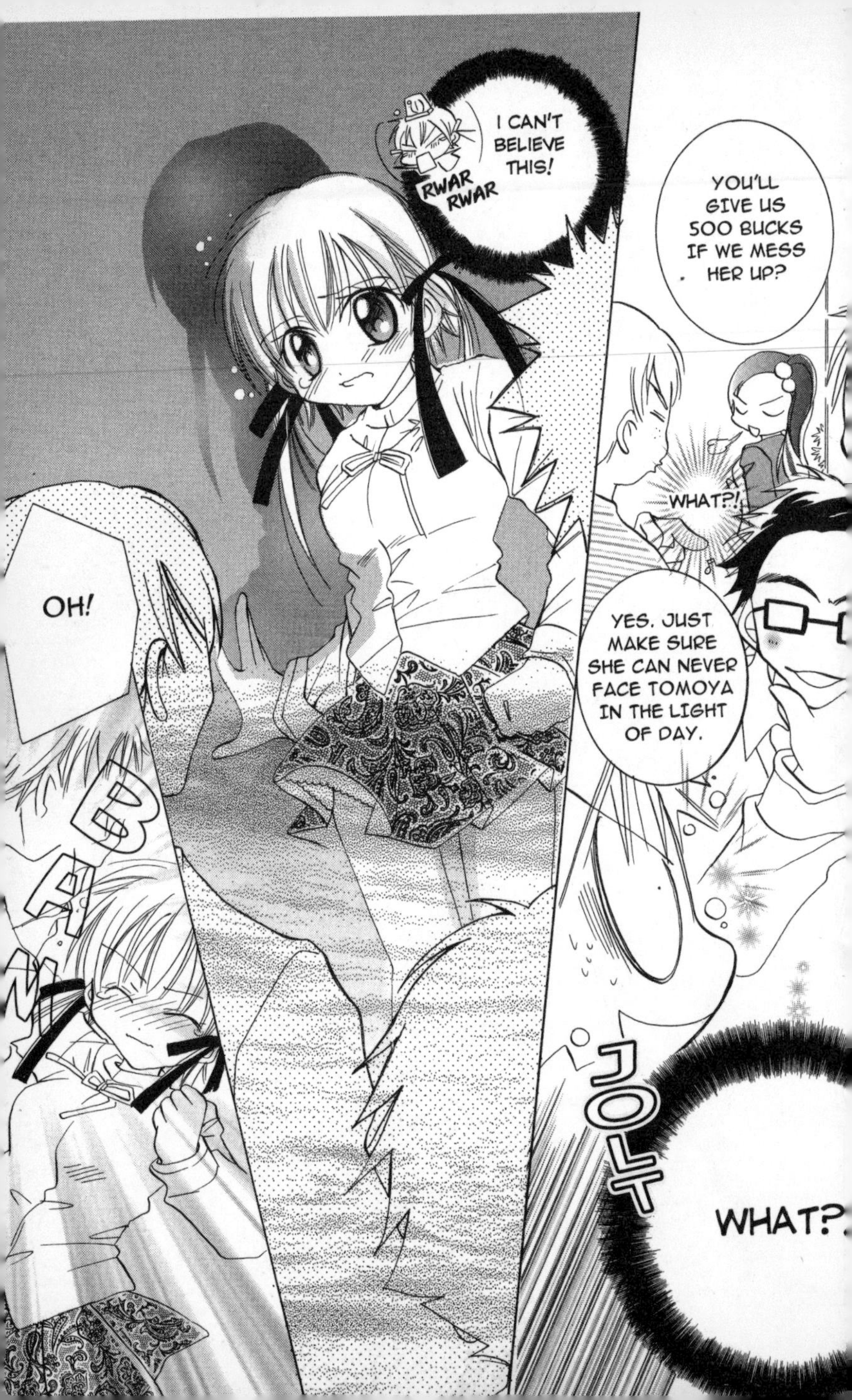
YOU'LL GIVE US 500 BUCKS IF WE MESS HER UP?
WHAT?!
YES. JUST MAKE SURE SHE CAN NEVER FACE TOMOYA IN THE LIGHT OF DAY.
JOLT
WHAT?
I CAN'T BELIEVE THIS!
RWAR RWAR
OH!
BAM

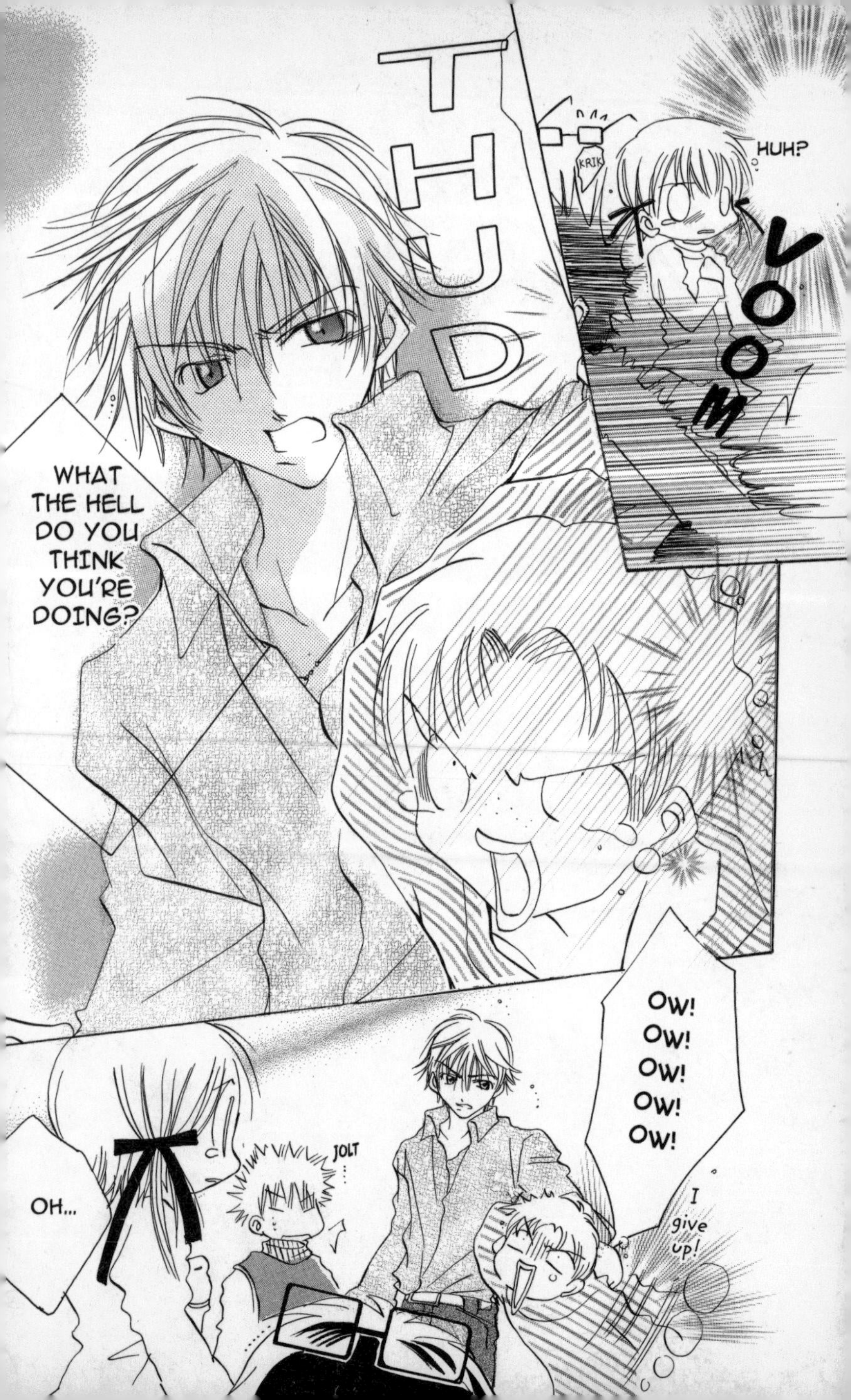
KRIK
HUH?
VOOM
THUD
WHAT THE HELL DO YOU THINK YOU'RE DOING?
OW! OW! OW! OW! OW!
I give up!
JOLT
OH...

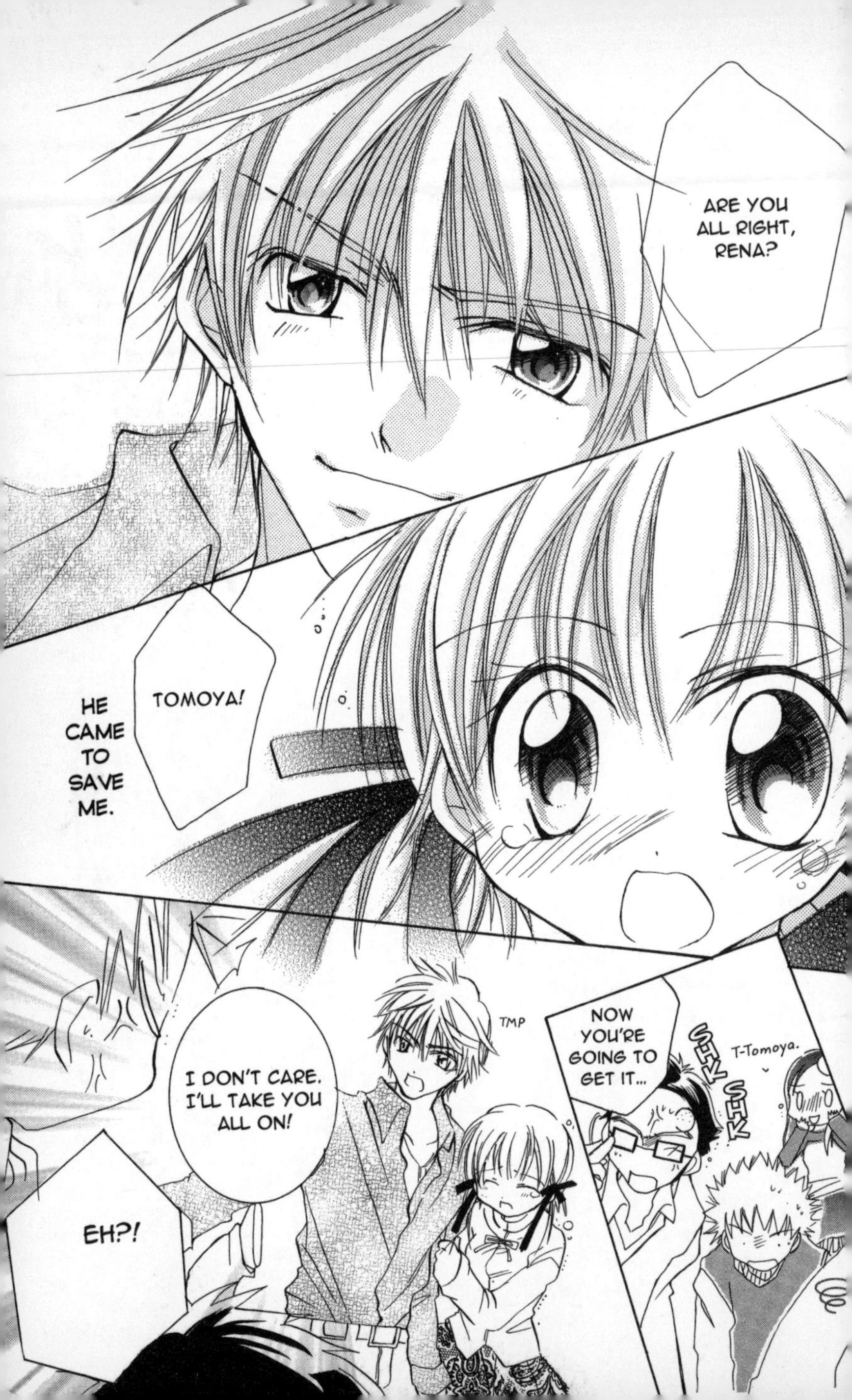
ARE YOU ALL RIGHT, RENA?
TOMOYA!
HE CAME TO SAVE ME.
T-Tomoya.
SHK SHK
NOW YOU'RE GOING TO GET IT...
TMP
I DON'T CARE. I'LL TAKE YOU ALL ON!
EH?!

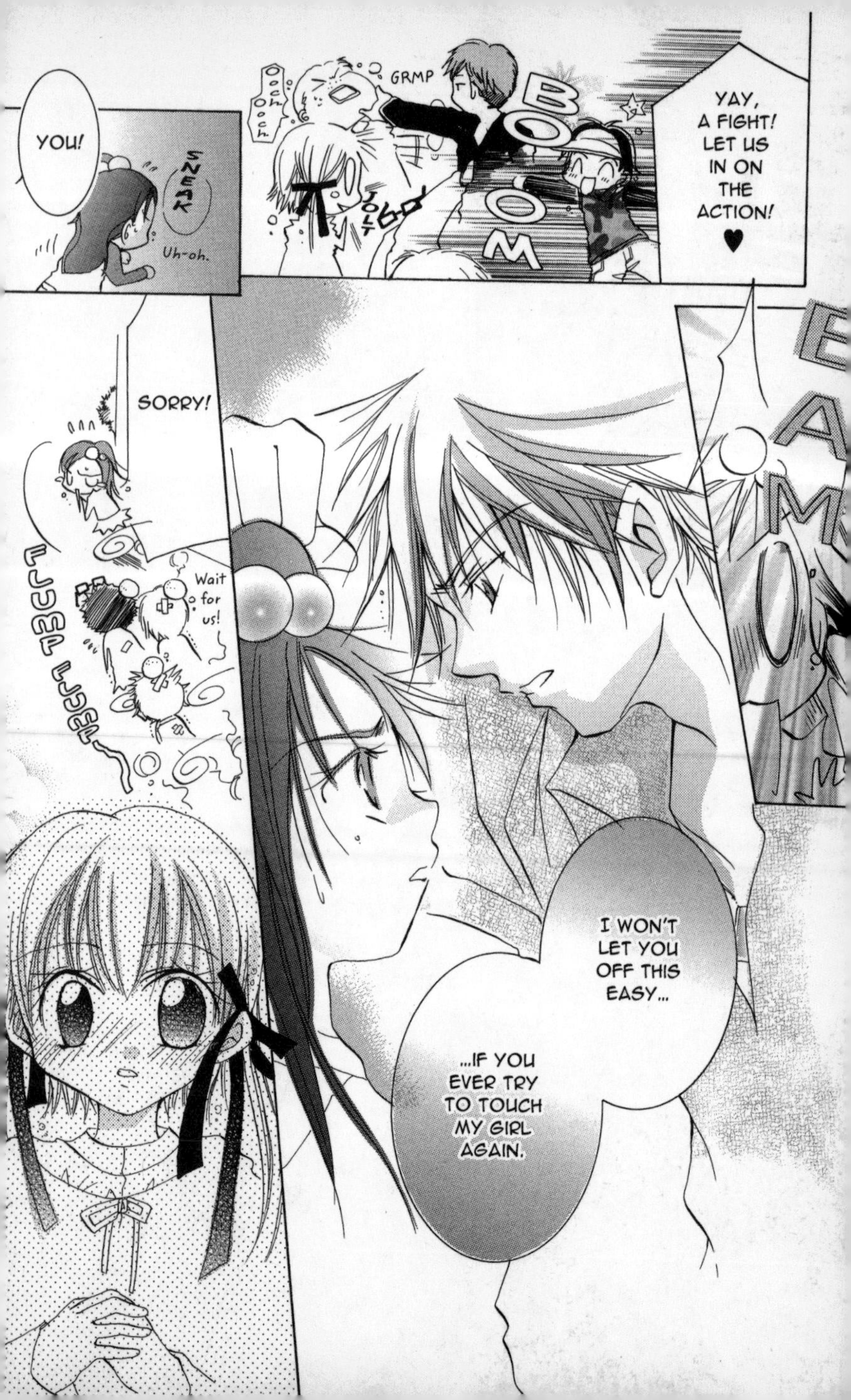
YAY, A FIGHT! LET US IN ON THE ACTION! ♥
BOOM
GRMP
Ooch ooch
JOLT
YOU!
SNEAK
Uh-oh.
BAM
I WON'T LET YOU OFF THIS EASY...
...IF YOU EVER TRY TO TOUCH MY GIRL AGAIN.
SORRY!
FLUMP FLUMP
Wait for us!

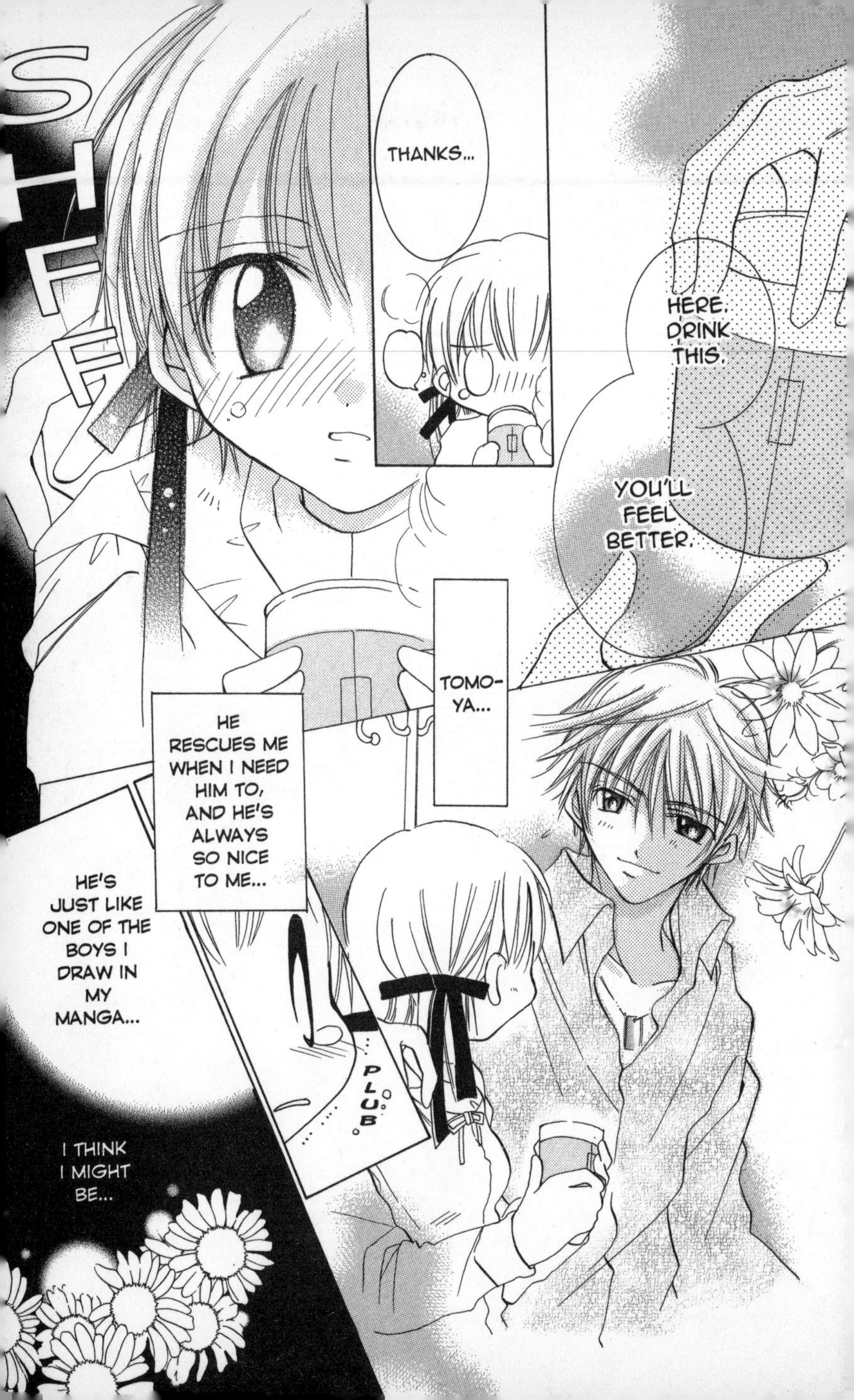
HERE. DRINK THIS.
YOU'LL FEEL BETTER.
THANKS...
SHFF
TOMO-YA...
HE RESCUES ME WHEN I NEED HIM TO, AND HE'S ALWAYS SO NICE TO ME...
HE'S JUST LIKE ONE OF THE BOYS I DRAW IN MY MANGA...
PLUB
I THINK I MIGHT BE...

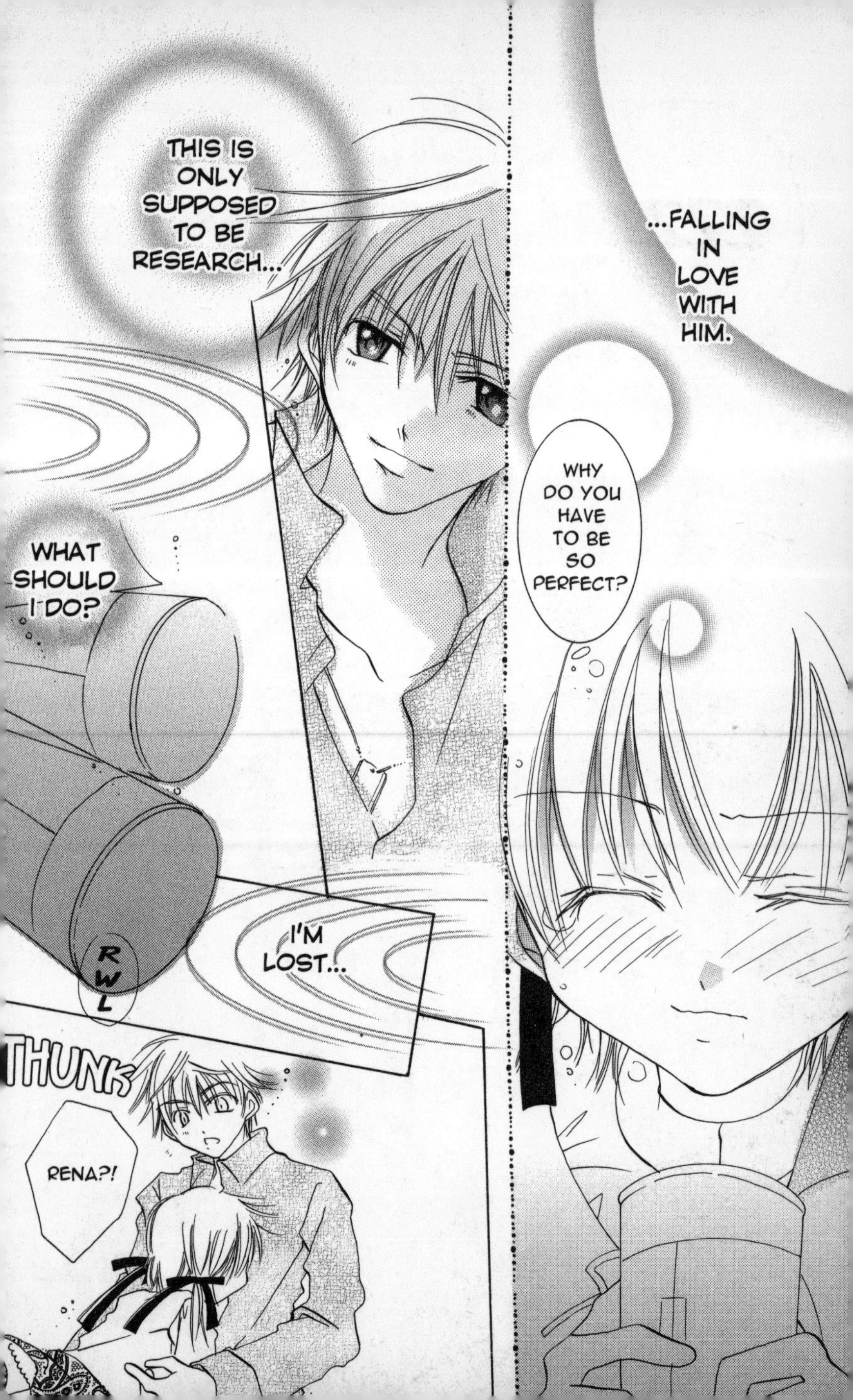
...FALLING IN LOVE WITH HIM.
WHY DO YOU HAVE TO BE SO PERFECT?
THIS IS ONLY SUPPOSED TO BE RESEARCH...
WHAT SHOULD I DO?
I'M LOST...
RWL
THUNK
RENA?!

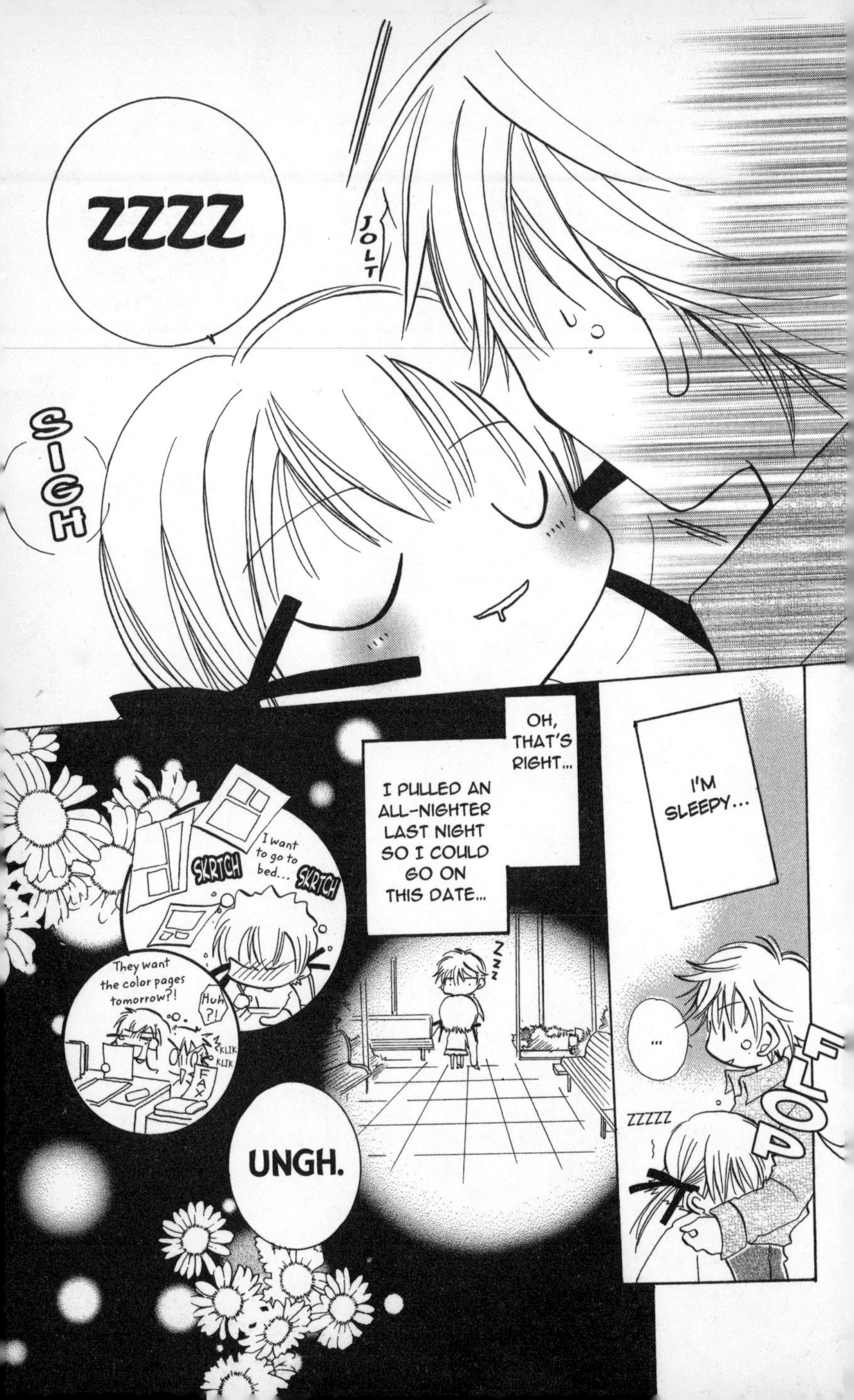
JOLT
ZZZZ
SIGH
I'M SLEEPY...
...
FLOP
ZZZZZ
OH, THAT'S RIGHT...
I PULLED AN ALL-NIGHTER LAST NIGHT SO I COULD GO ON THIS DATE...
ZZZ
I want to go to bed...
SKRTCH
SKRTCH
They want the color pages tomorrow?!
Huh?!
KLIK KLIK
FAX
UNGH.

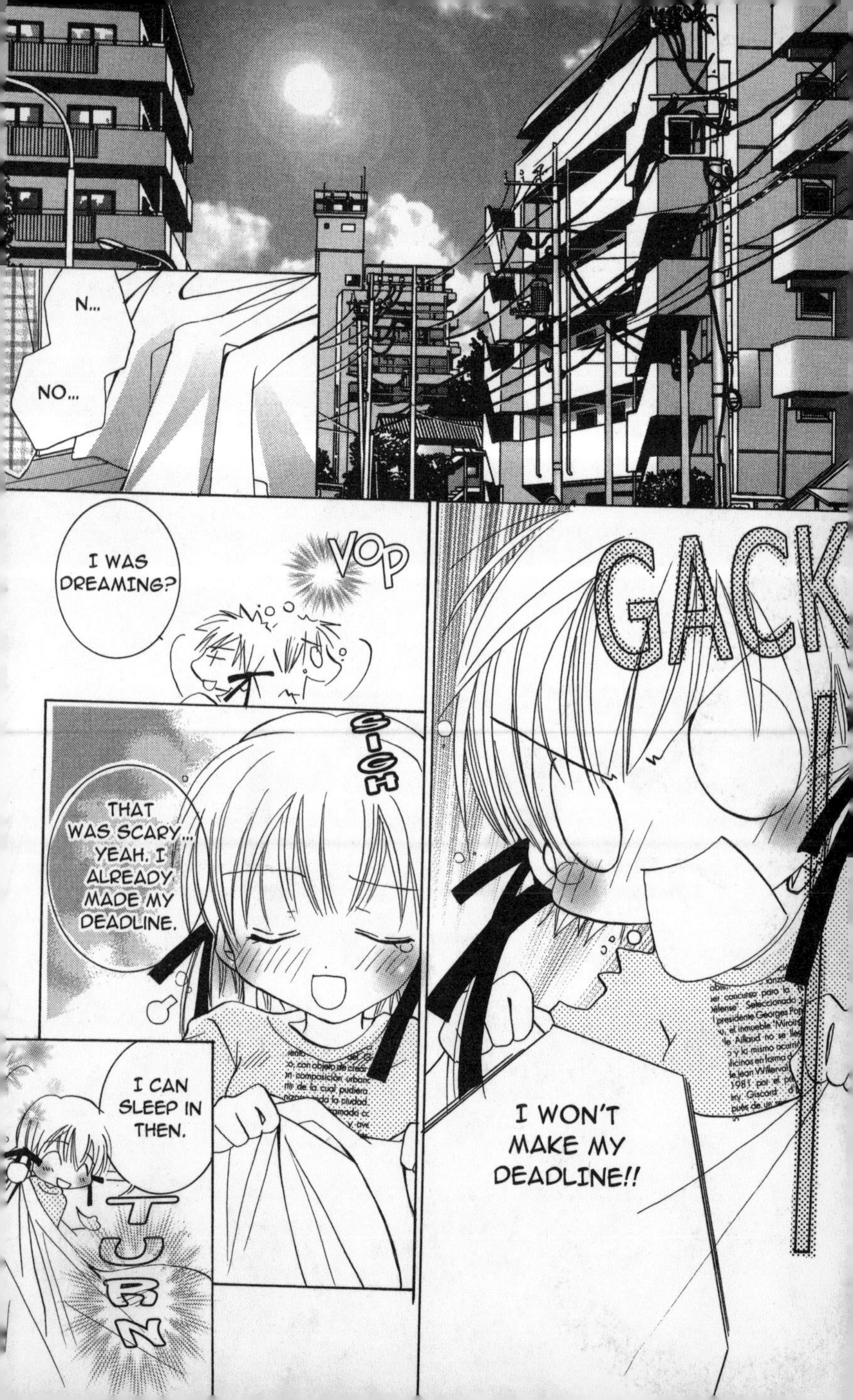
N...
NO...
I WAS DREAMING?
VOP
SIGH
THAT WAS SCARY... YEAH. I ALREADY MADE MY DEADLINE.
I CAN SLEEP IN THEN.
TURN
GACK
I WON'T MAKE MY DEADLINE!!

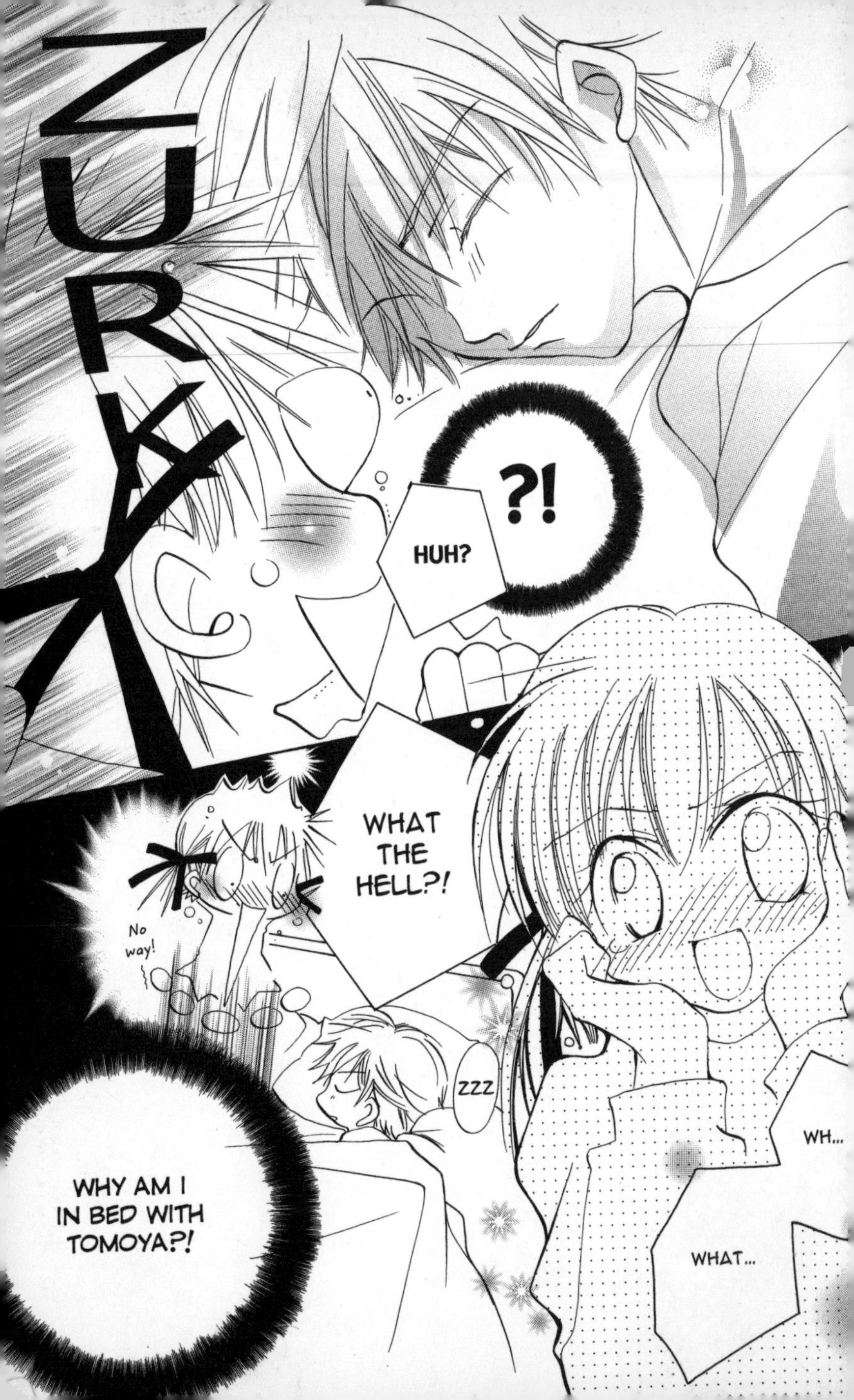
?!
HUH?
ZURK
WH...
WHAT...
WHAT THE HELL?!
ZZZ
No way!
WHY AM I IN BED WITH TOMOYA?!

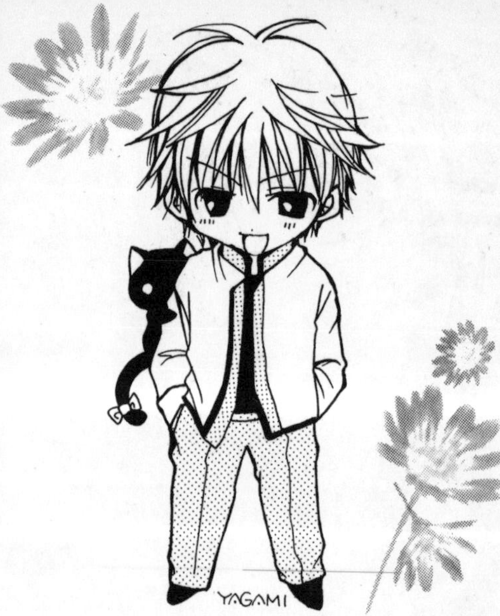
YAGAMI

CHARACTER INTRO

Tomoya Okita

He's the product of a lot of work. I'm happy that so many girls like him! I really enjoyed reading the fan mail--some *Ciao*-girls referred to the couple as "Rena and Prince Tomoya." (laugh) Some people wrote to tell me they wished there were a boy like Tomoya in their class.

But... I think it would only wreak havoc... ◊

I had a hard time with his personality at the *shitae* stage. But by the time I started the *name*, I was having a lot of fun. ◊

A behind-the-scenes story: I actually thought about putting Tomoya in a band. (laugh) But that idea didn't last long...

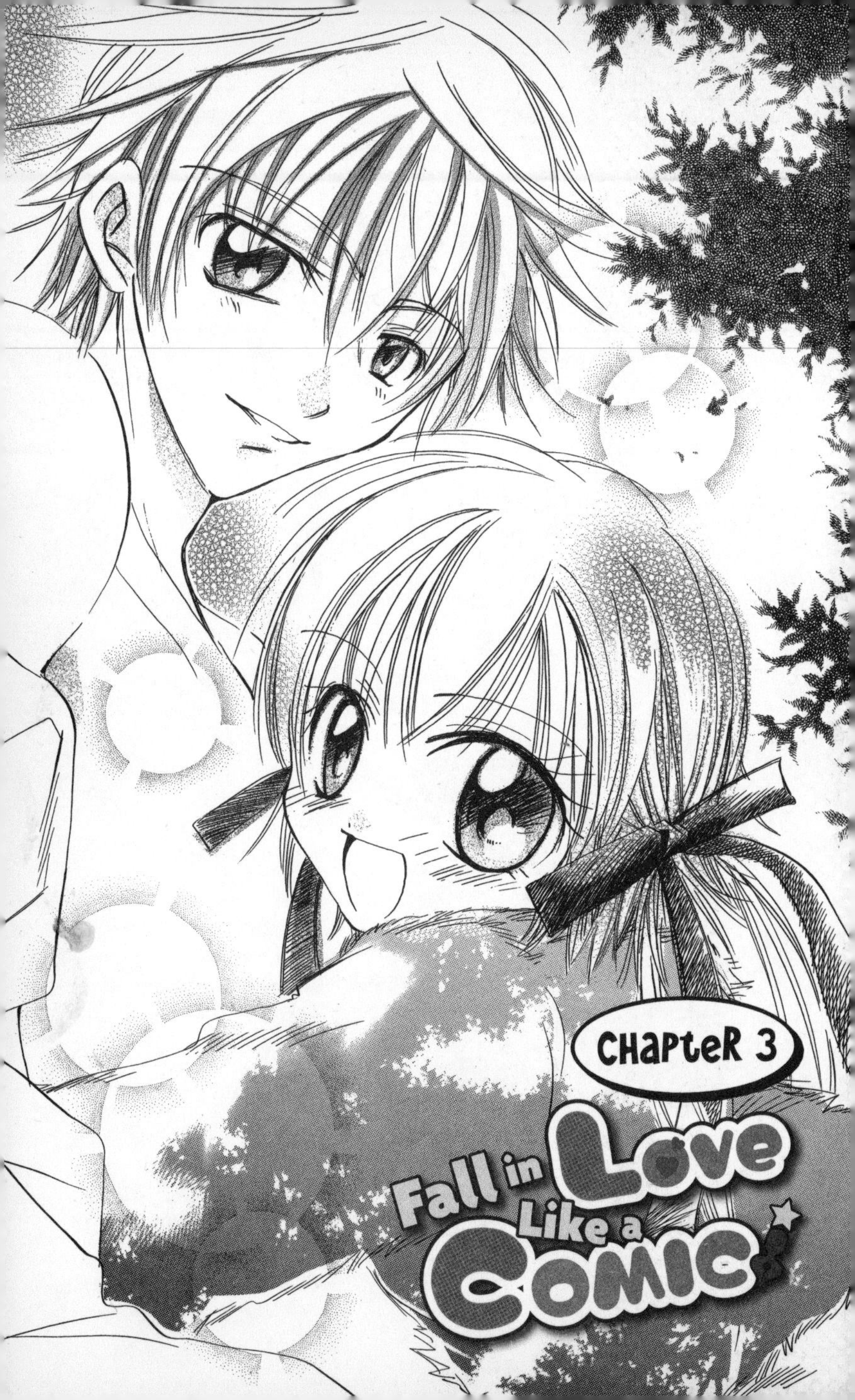
CHAPTER 3
Fall in Love Like a Comic!

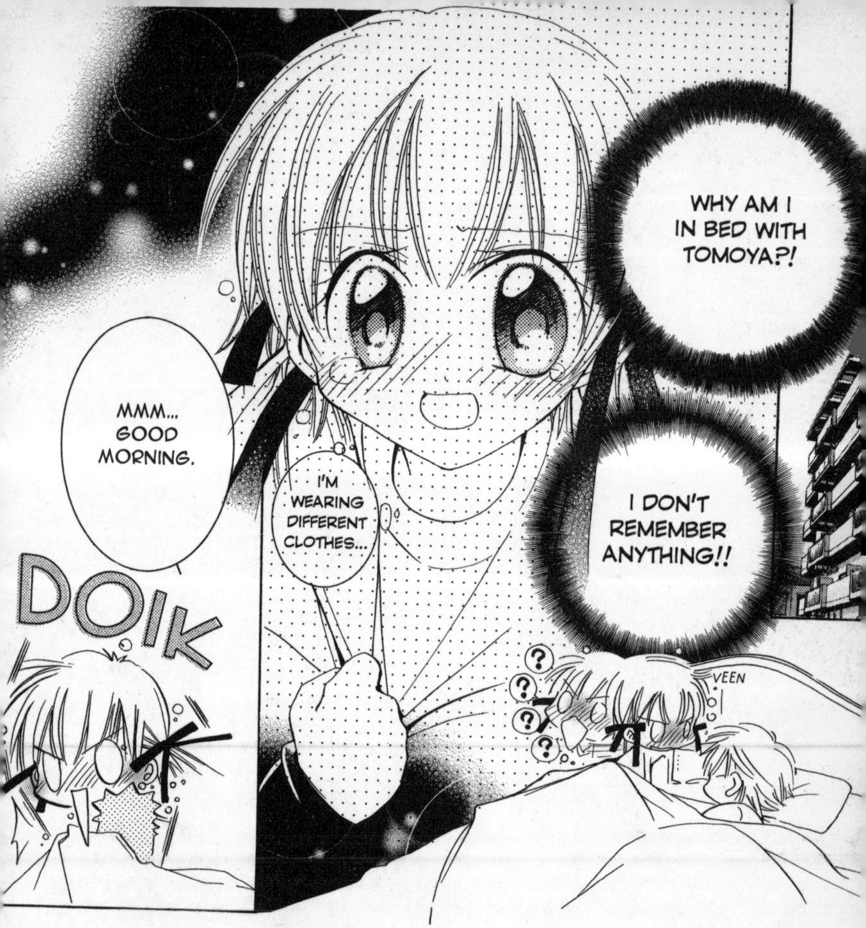
WHY AM I IN BED WITH TOMOYA?!
I DON'T REMEMBER ANYTHING!!
I'M WEARING DIFFERENT CLOTHES...
VEEN
MMM... GOOD MORNING.
DOIK

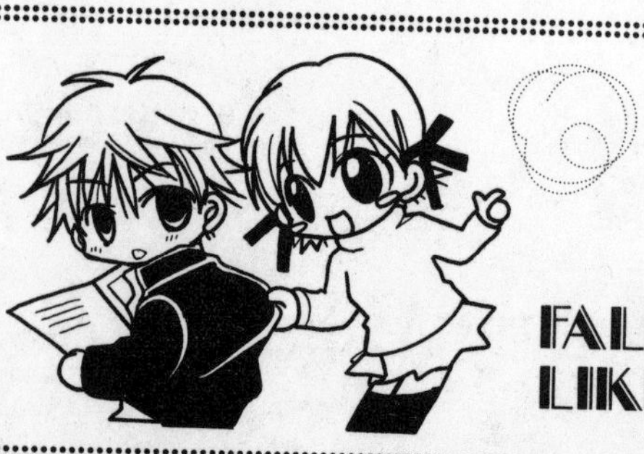

FALL IN LOVE LIKE A COMIC!

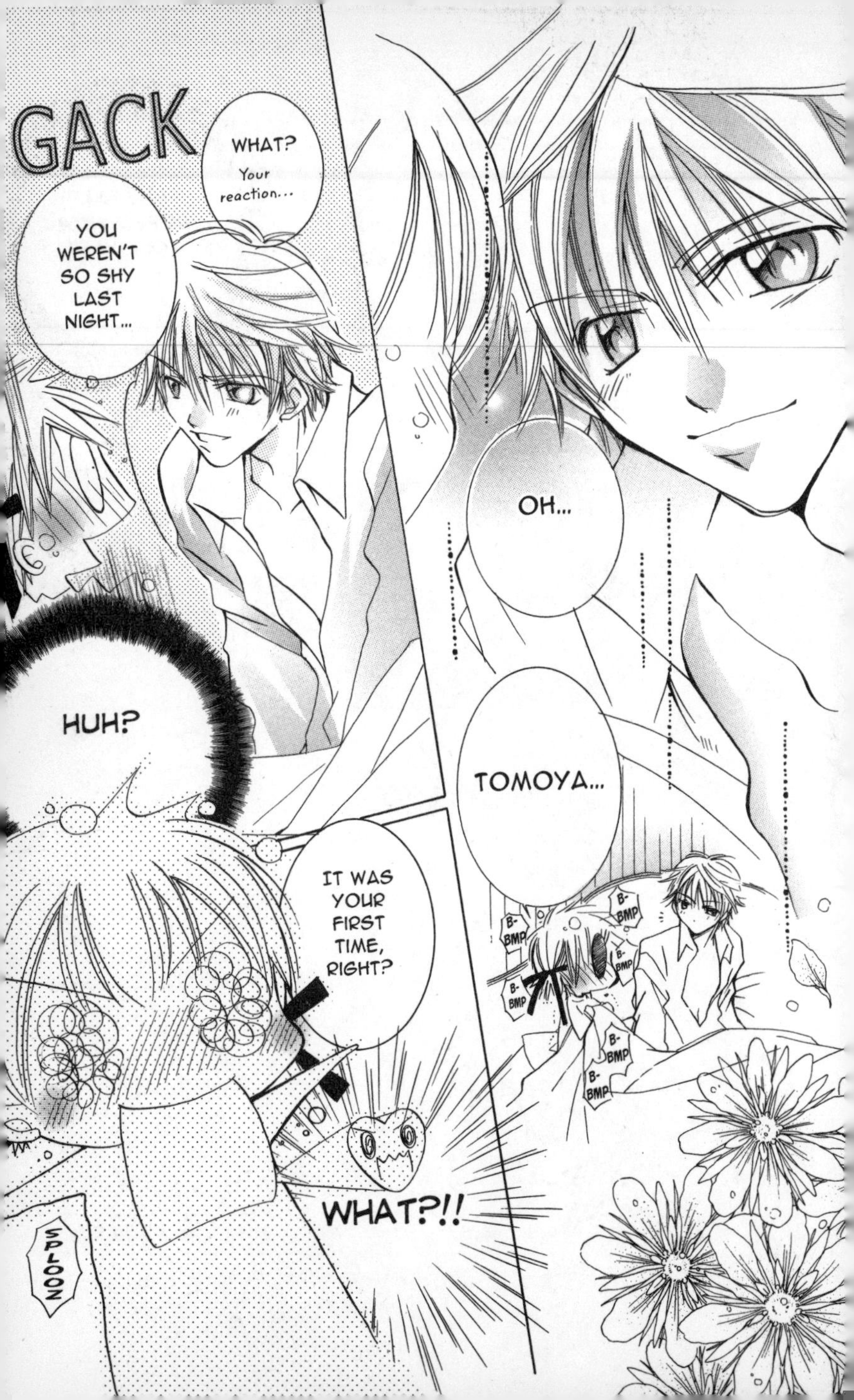
OH...
TOMOYA...
B-BMP
B-BMP
B-BMP
B-BMP
B-BMP
B-BMP
WHAT? Your reaction...
GACK
YOU WEREN'T SO SHY LAST NIGHT...
HUH?
IT WAS YOUR FIRST TIME, RIGHT?
WHAT?!!
SPLOOZ

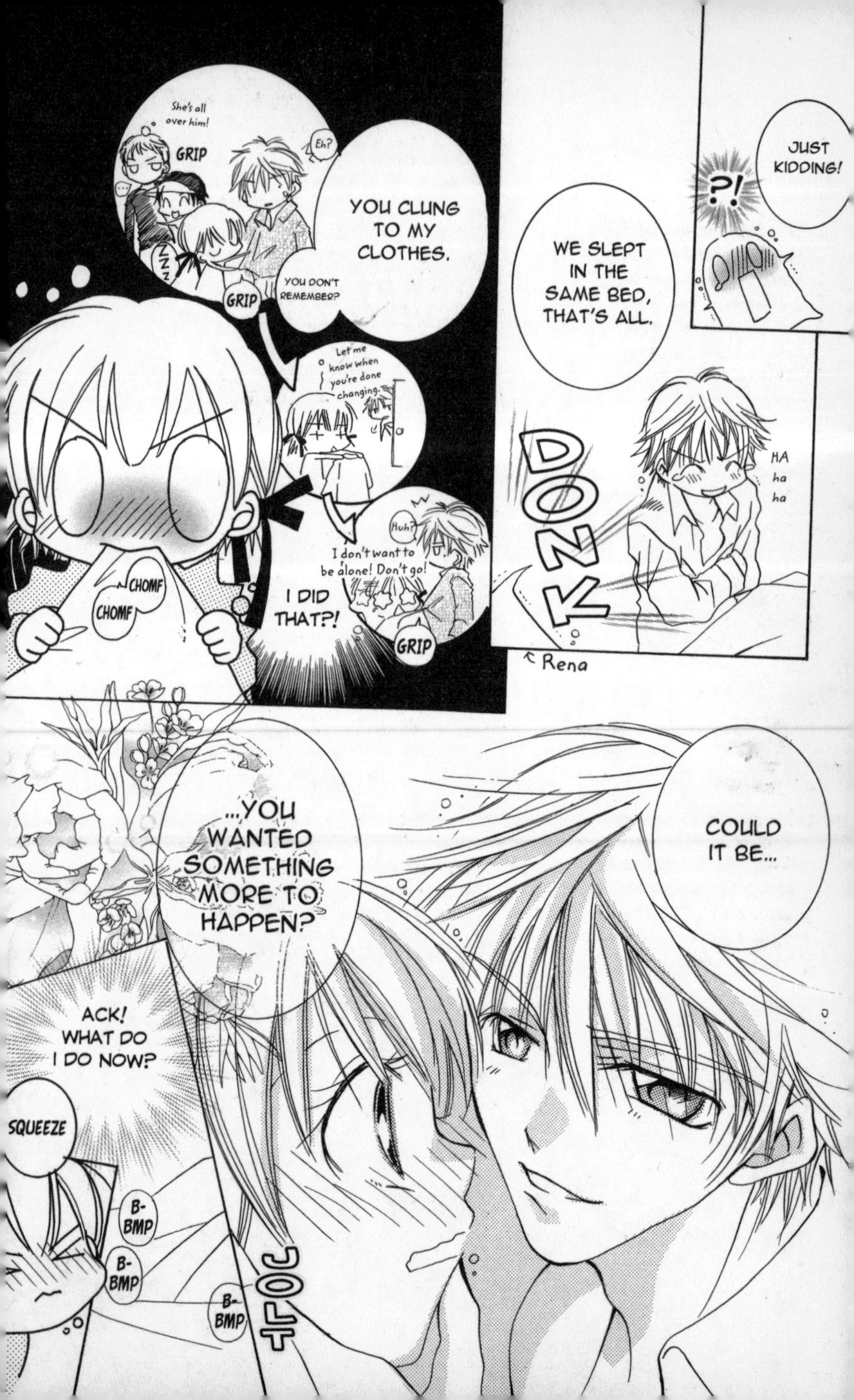
WE SLEPT IN THE SAME BED, THAT'S ALL.
?!
JUST KIDDING!
DONK
HA ha ha
← Rena
YOU CLUNG TO MY CLOTHES.
Eh?
She's all over him!
GRIP
YOU DON'T REMEMBER?
GRIP
Let me know when you're done changing.
Huh?
I don't want to be alone! Don't go!
GRIP
I DID THAT?!
CHOMF
CHOMF
COULD IT BE...
...YOU WANTED SOMETHING MORE TO HAPPEN?
ACK! WHAT DO I DO NOW?
SQUEEZE
B-BMP
B-BMP
B-BMP
JOLT

Ink: I use drawing ink for the most part. For coloring I used oil-based markers and pigment ink. The "shine" on hair is done using a brush pen (2 or 3 different types).

Screentones: You can get some for less than a couple dollars. I'm not really a stickler for brand names as long as I like the pattern.

Other art supplies...
30/45 cm ruler, curve templates, templates, correction ink, tape, light box, knives, etc.

I use anything that comes in handy.

Color art supplies:
I use my PC to color and I mainly use PhotoShop. I would like to learn more about Painter when I have some time. I usually use Copics colored paper for Ciao promotions.

But, the rule of thumb is to use whatever works for you!

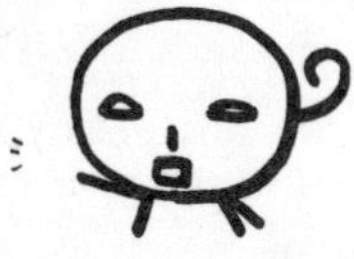

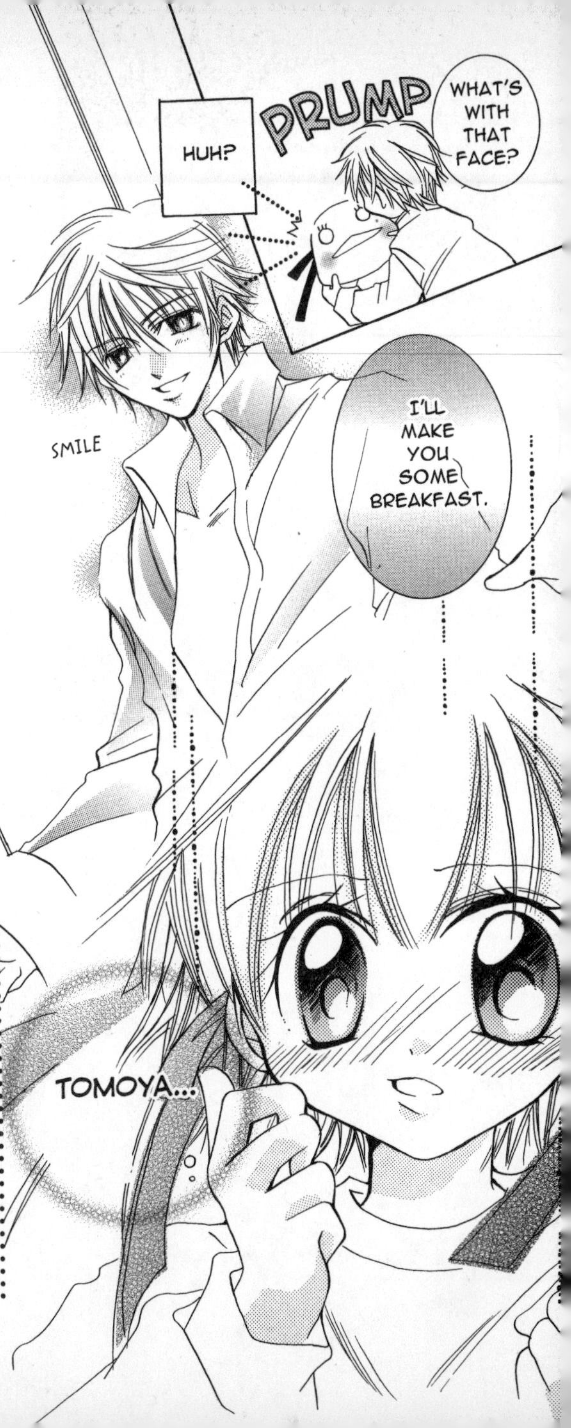
WHAT'S WITH THAT FACE?
PRUMP
HUH?
I'LL MAKE YOU SOME BREAKFAST.
SMILE
TOMOYA...

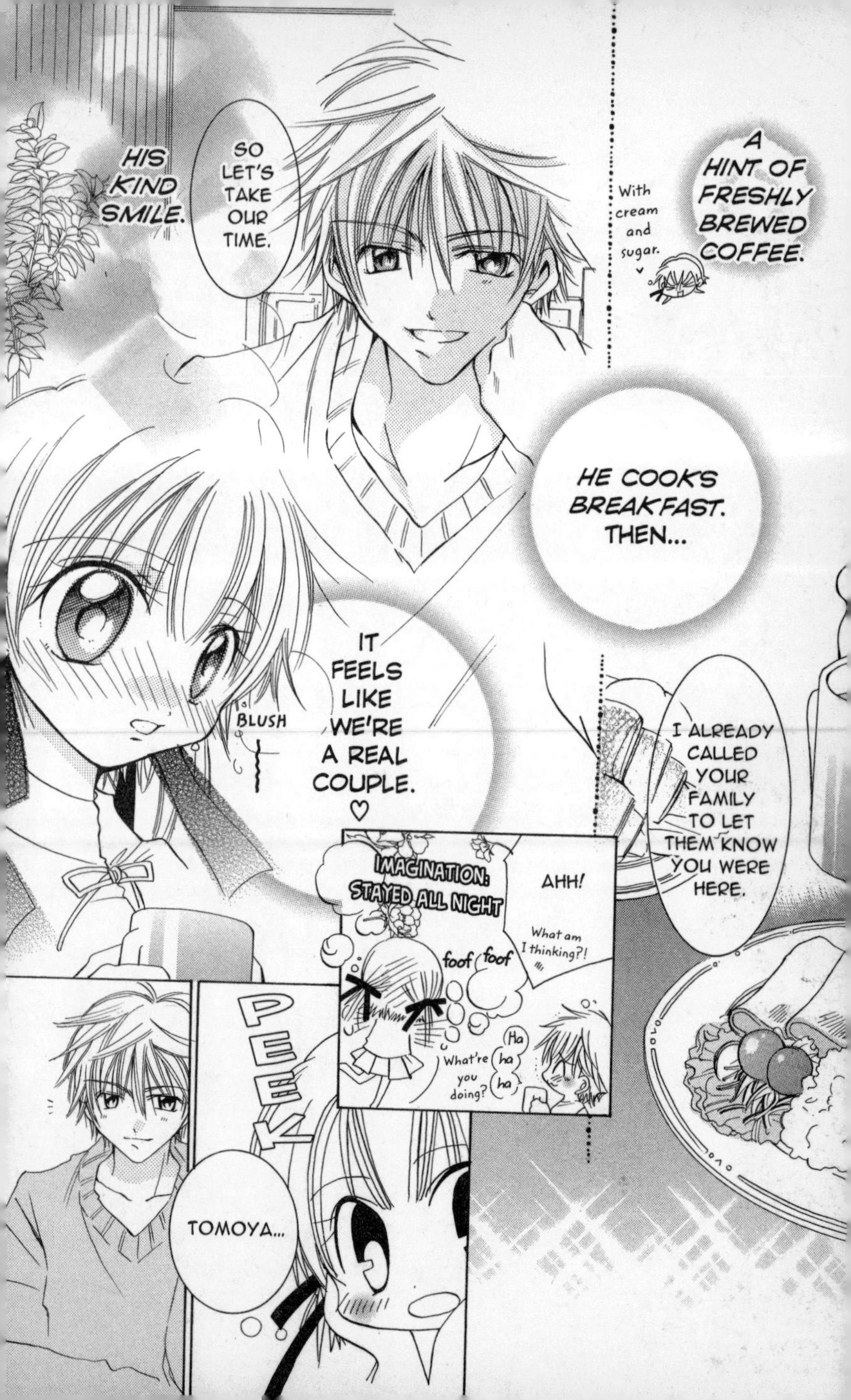
A HINT OF FRESHLY BREWED COFFEE.
With cream and sugar.
SO LET'S TAKE OUR TIME.
HIS KIND SMILE.
HE COOKS BREAKFAST. THEN...
IT FEELS LIKE WE'RE A REAL COUPLE. ♡
BLUSH
I ALREADY CALLED YOUR FAMILY TO LET THEM KNOW YOU WERE HERE.
AHH!
What am I thinking?!
IMAGINATION: STAYED ALL NIGHT
foof foof
Ha ha ha
What're you doing?
PEEK
TOMOYA...

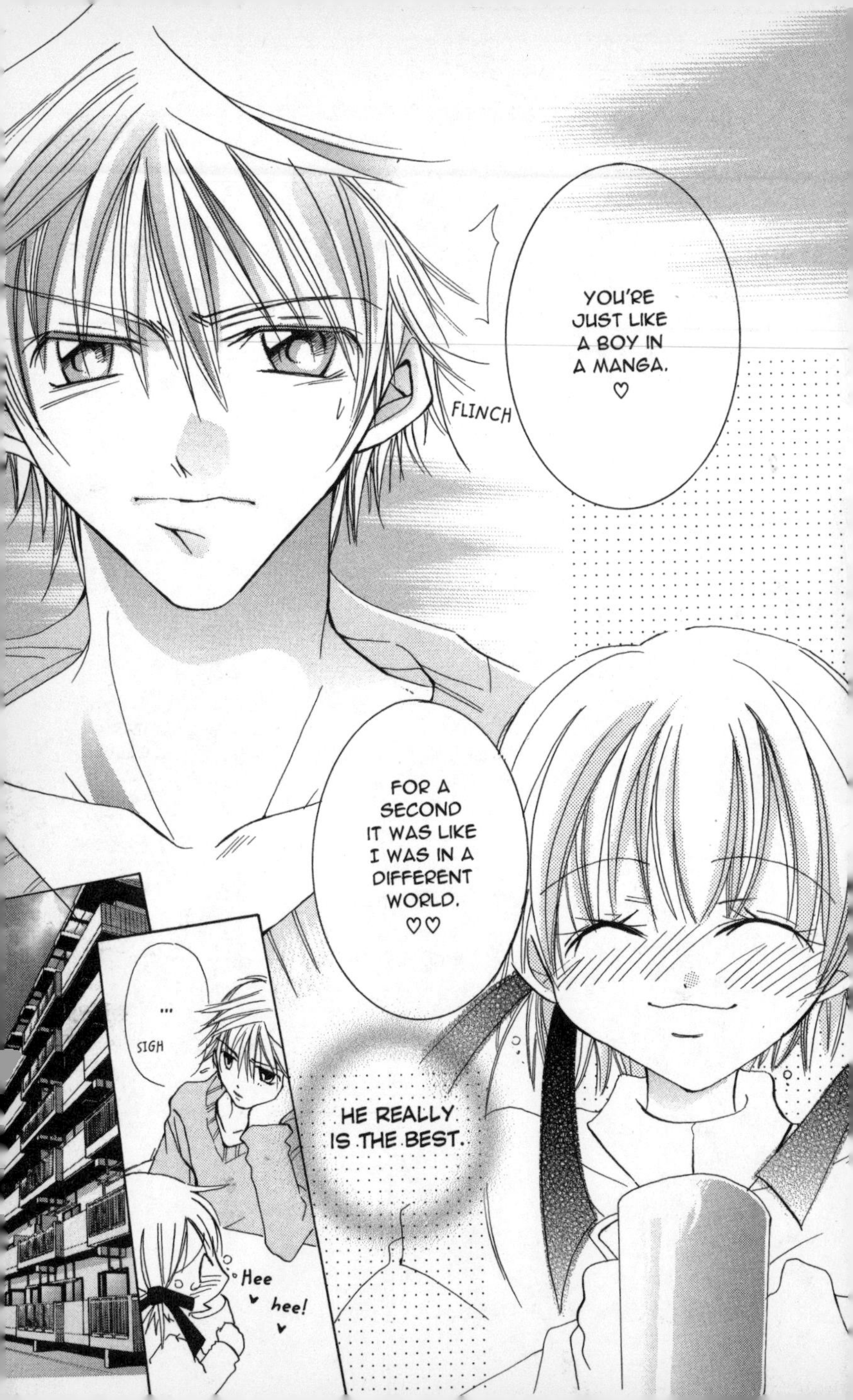
YOU'RE JUST LIKE A BOY IN A MANGA. ♡
FLINCH
FOR A SECOND IT WAS LIKE I WAS IN A DIFFERENT WORLD. ♡♡
HE REALLY IS THE BEST.
...
SIGH
Hee ♥ hee! ♥

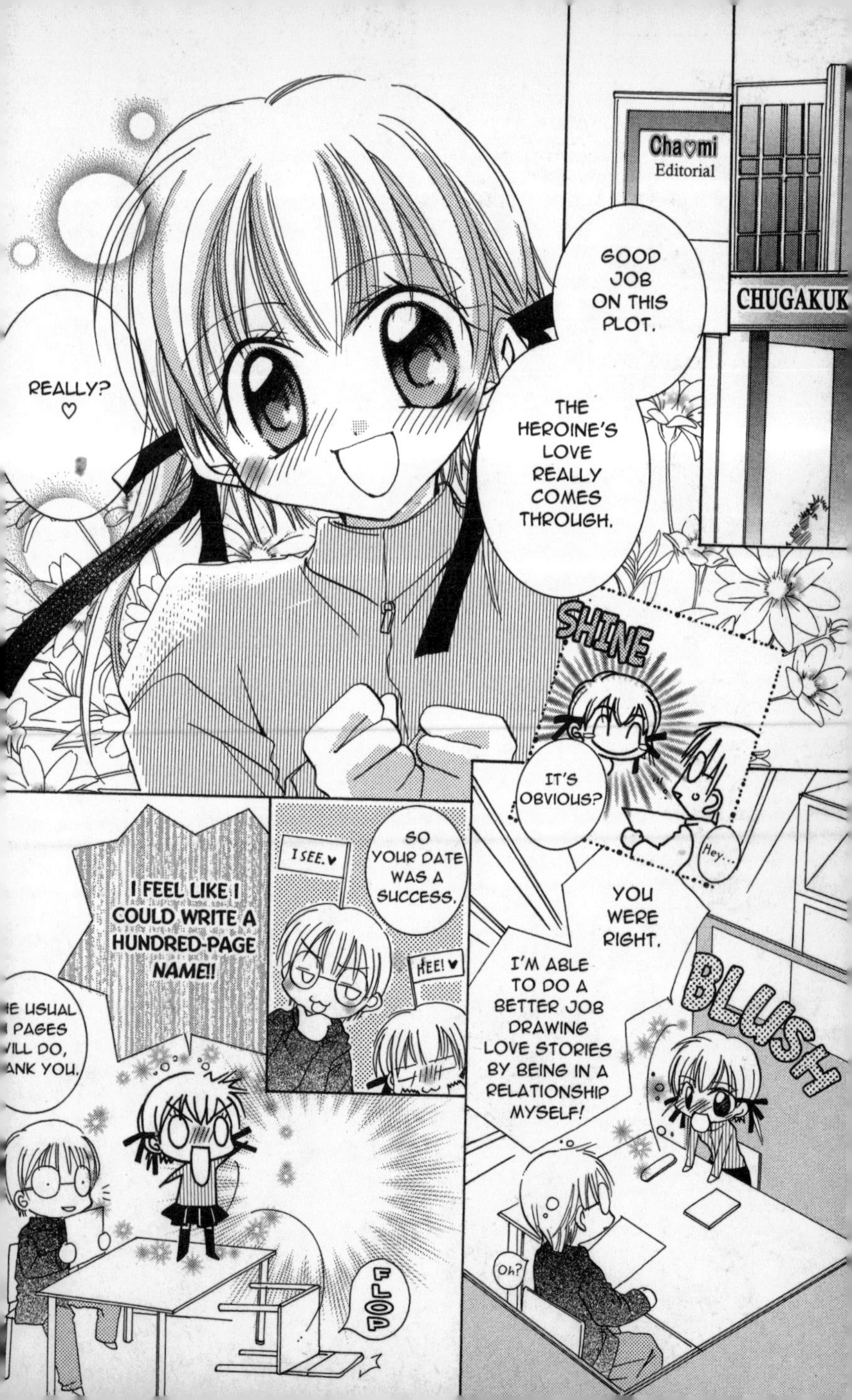
Cha♡mi Editorial
CHUGAKUK
GOOD JOB ON THIS PLOT.
THE HEROINE'S LOVE REALLY COMES THROUGH.
REALLY? ♡
SHINE
IT'S OBVIOUS?
Hey...
YOU WERE RIGHT.
I'M ABLE TO DO A BETTER JOB DRAWING LOVE STORIES BY BEING IN A RELATIONSHIP MYSELF!
BLUSH
Oh?
SO YOUR DATE WAS A SUCCESS.
I SEE.♥
HEE!♥
I FEEL LIKE I COULD WRITE A HUNDRED-PAGE NAME!!
HE USUAL PAGES ILL DO, ANK YOU.
FLOP

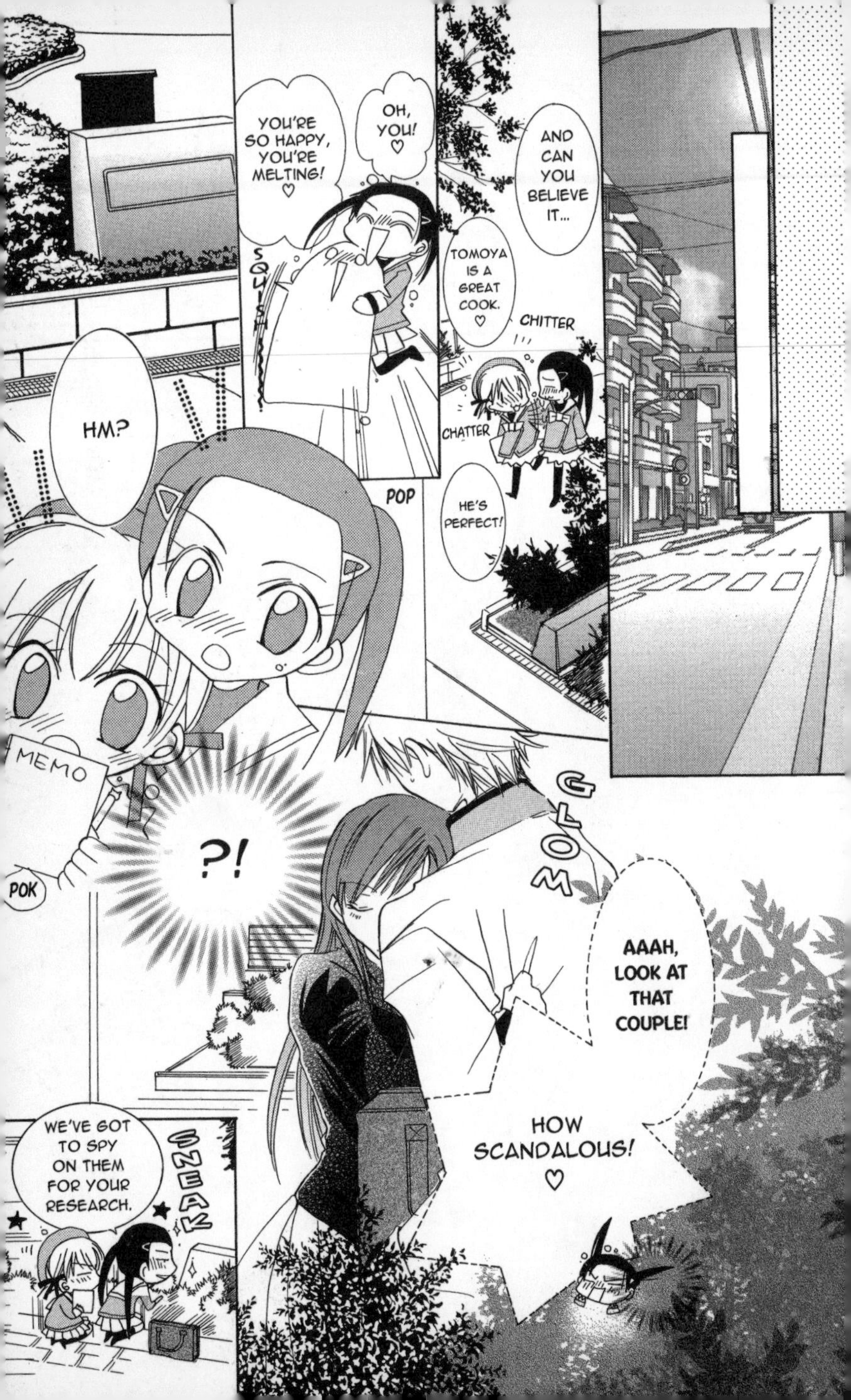
AND CAN YOU BELIEVE IT...
TOMOYA IS A GREAT COOK. ♡
CHITTER
CHATTER
HE'S PERFECT!
OH, YOU! ♡
YOU'RE SO HAPPY, YOU'RE MELTING! ♡
SQUISH
POP
HM?
GLOMP
AAAH, LOOK AT THAT COUPLE!
HOW SCANDALOUS! ♡
?!
MEMO
POK
SNEAK
WE'VE GOT TO SPY ON THEM FOR YOUR RESEARCH.

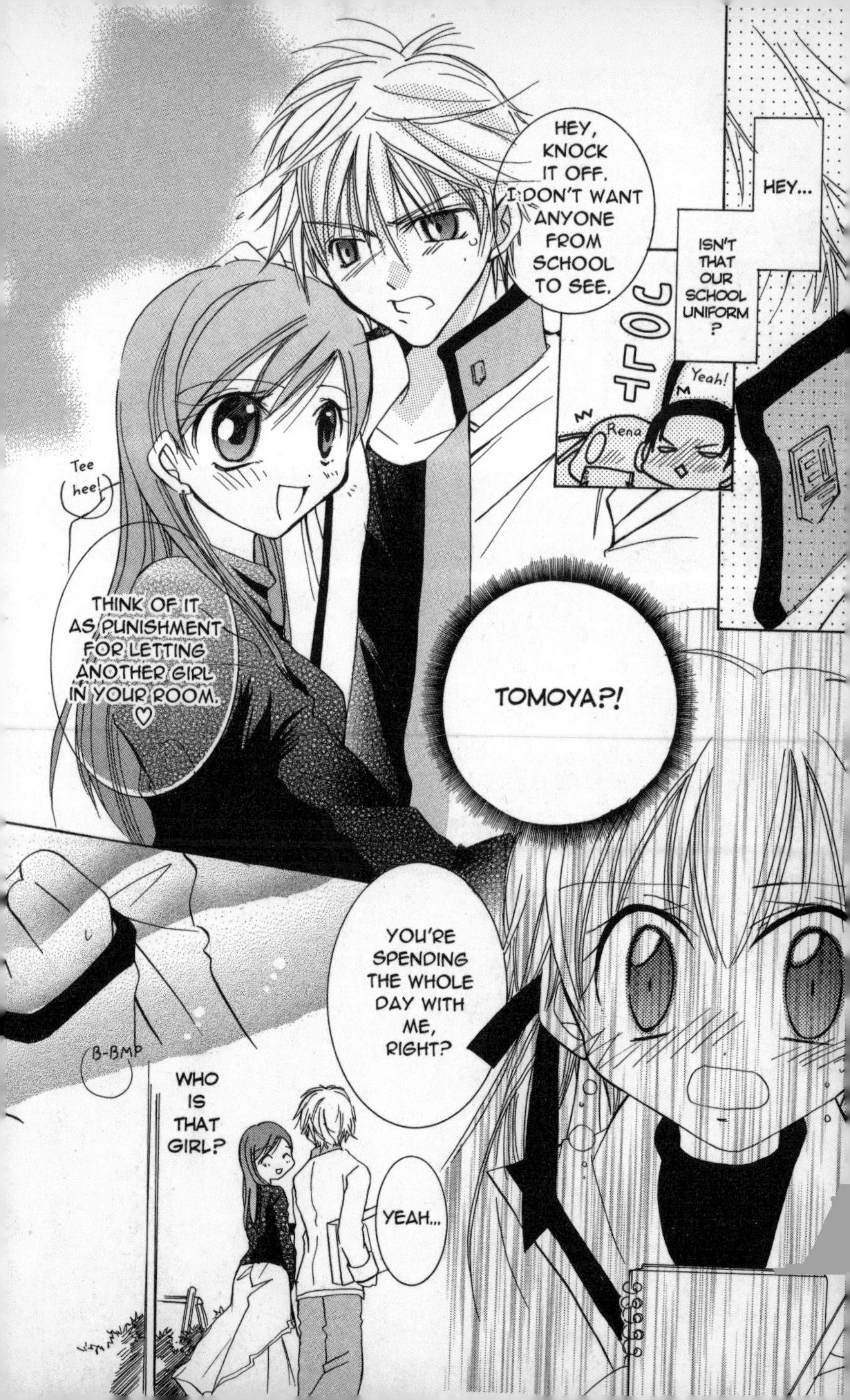
HEY...
ISN'T THAT OUR SCHOOL UNIFORM?
Yeah!
Rena
JOLT
HEY, KNOCK IT OFF. I DON'T WANT ANYONE FROM SCHOOL TO SEE.
Tee hee!
THINK OF IT AS PUNISHMENT FOR LETTING ANOTHER GIRL IN YOUR ROOM. ♡
TOMOYA?!
YOU'RE SPENDING THE WHOLE DAY WITH ME, RIGHT?
YEAH...
WHO IS THAT GIRL?
B-BMP

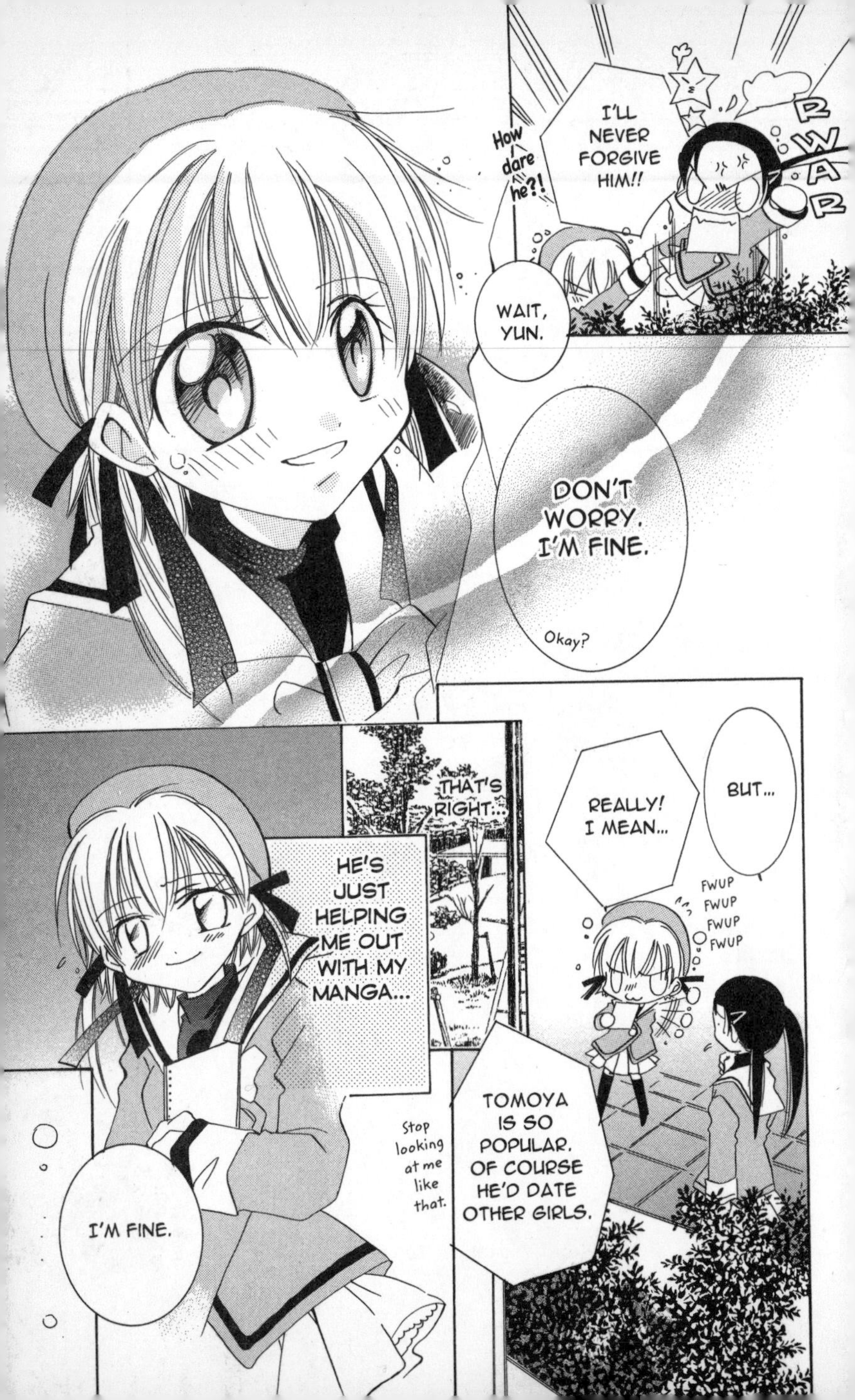
I'LL NEVER FORGIVE HIM!!
How dare he?!
RWAR
WAIT, YUN.
DON'T WORRY. I'M FINE.
Okay?
BUT...
REALLY! I MEAN...
FWUP FWUP FWUP FWUP
TOMOYA IS SO POPULAR. OF COURSE HE'D DATE OTHER GIRLS.
Stop looking at me like that.
THAT'S RIGHT...
HE'S JUST HELPING ME OUT WITH MY MANGA...
I'M FINE.

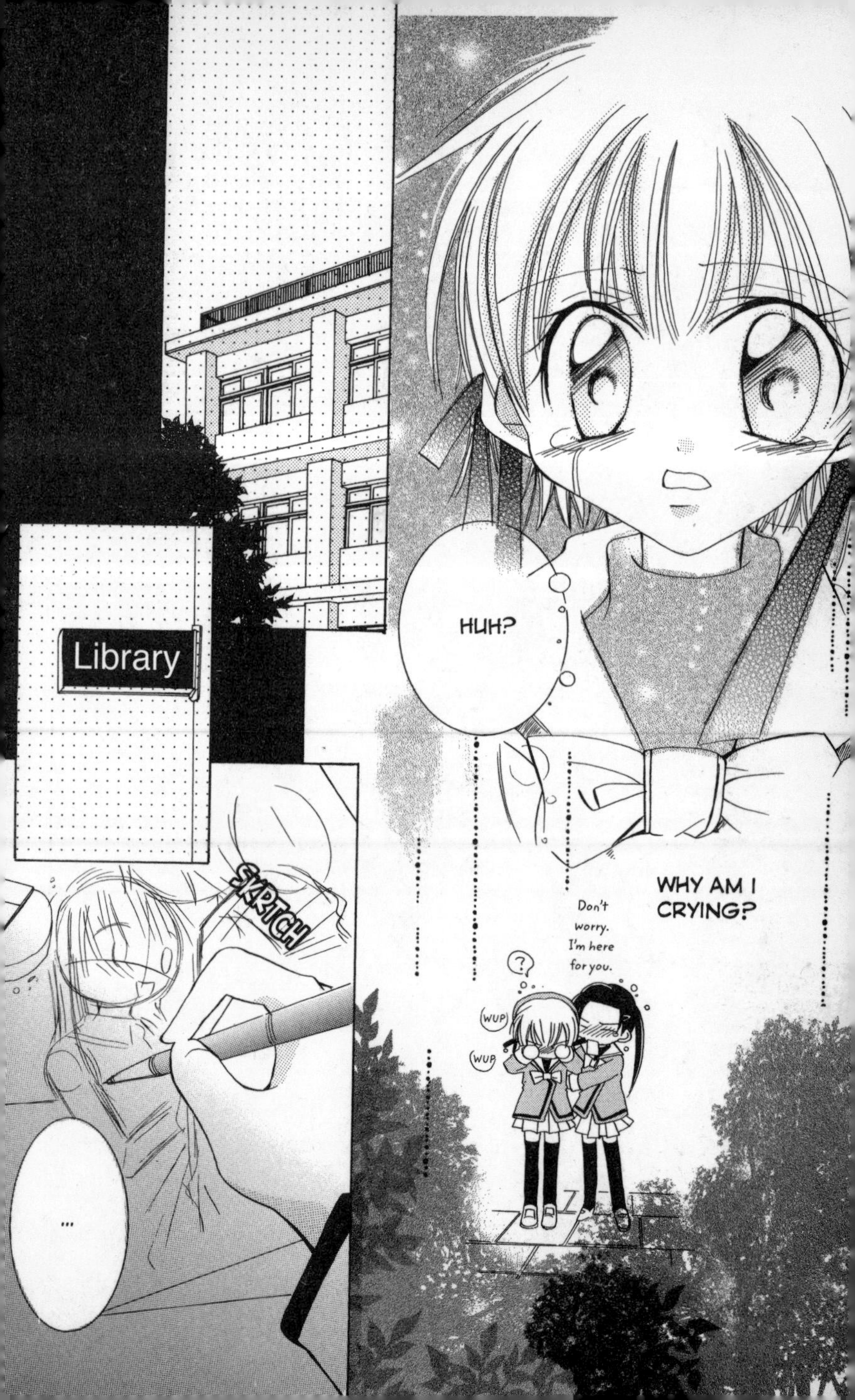
HUH?
WHY AM I CRYING?
Don't worry. I'm here for you.
?
WUP
WUP
Library
SKRTCH
...

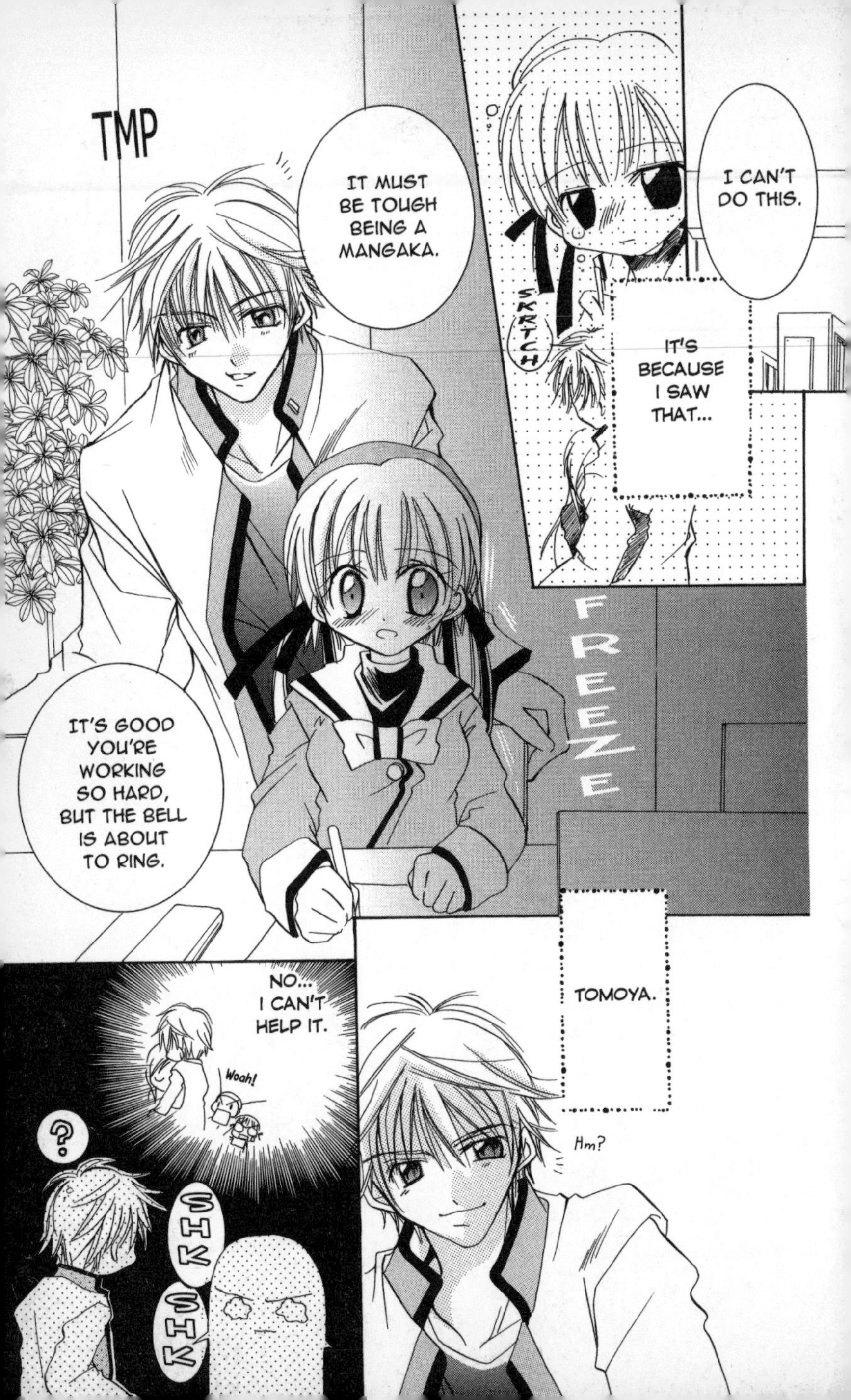
I CAN'T DO THIS.
SKRTCH
IT'S BECAUSE I SAW THAT...
TMP
IT MUST BE TOUGH BEING A MANGAKA.
FREEZE
IT'S GOOD YOU'RE WORKING SO HARD, BUT THE BELL IS ABOUT TO RING.
TOMOYA.
Hm?
NO... I CAN'T HELP IT.
Woah!
?
SHK
SHK

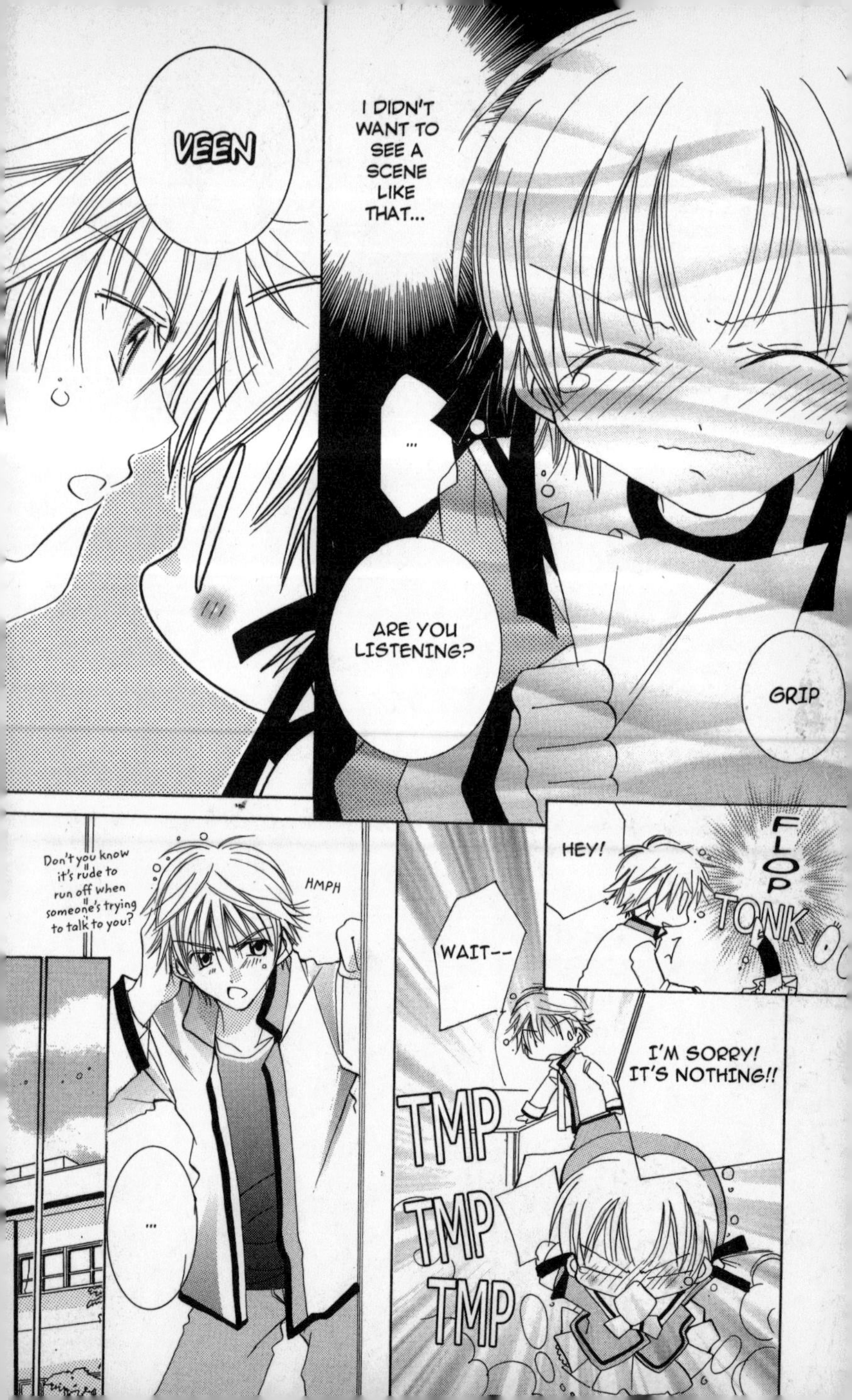
I DIDN'T WANT TO SEE A SCENE LIKE THAT...
...
ARE YOU LISTENING?
GRIP
VEEN
HEY!
FLOP
TONK
WAIT--
I'M SORRY! IT'S NOTHING!!
TMP
TMP
TMP
Don't you know it's rude to run off when someone's trying to talk to you?
HMPH
...

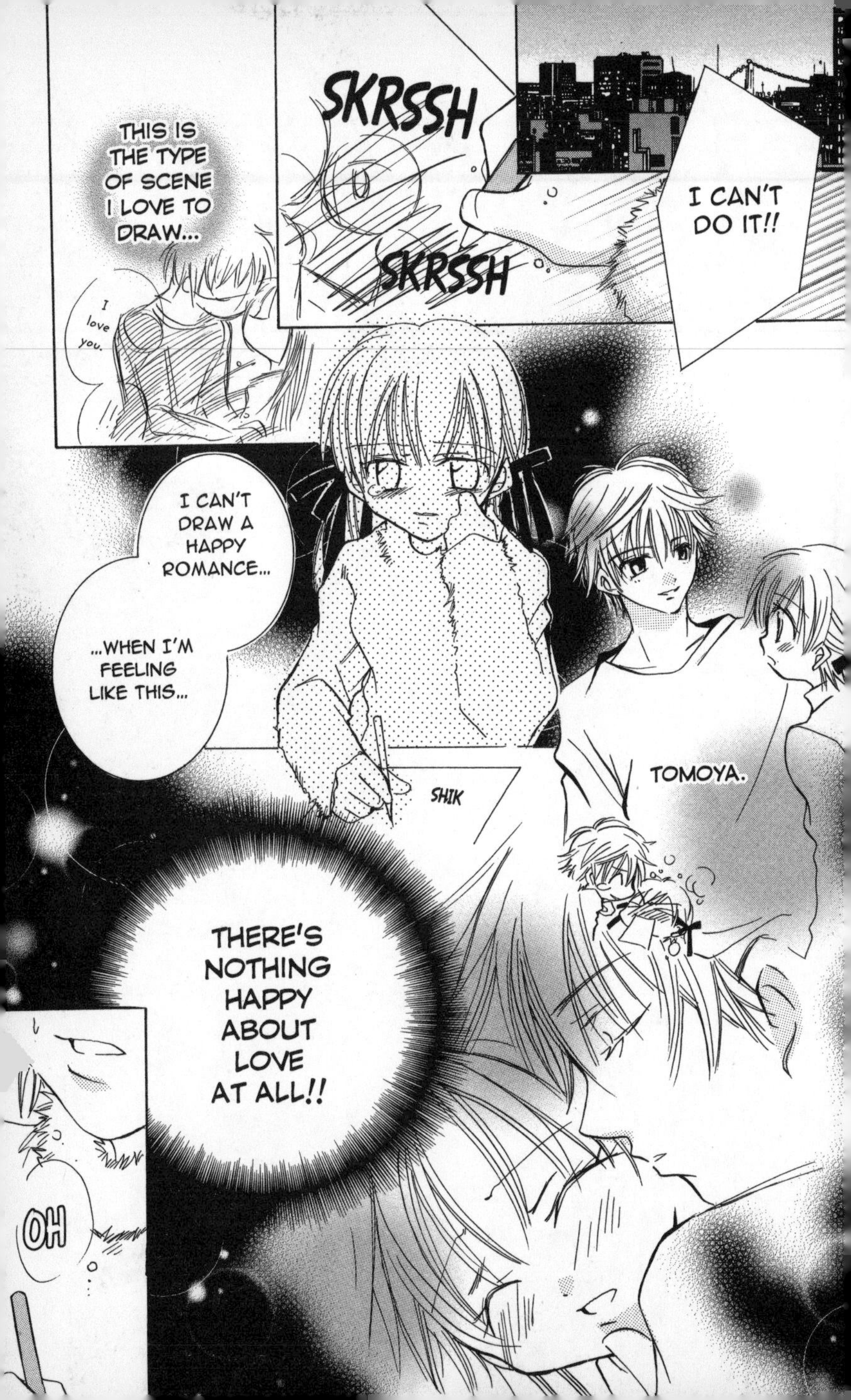
I CAN'T DO IT!!
SKRSSH
SKRSSH
THIS IS THE TYPE OF SCENE I LOVE TO DRAW...
I love you.
TOMOYA.
I CAN'T DRAW A HAPPY ROMANCE...
...WHEN I'M FEELING LIKE THIS...
SHIK
THERE'S NOTHING HAPPY ABOUT LOVE AT ALL!!
OH
...

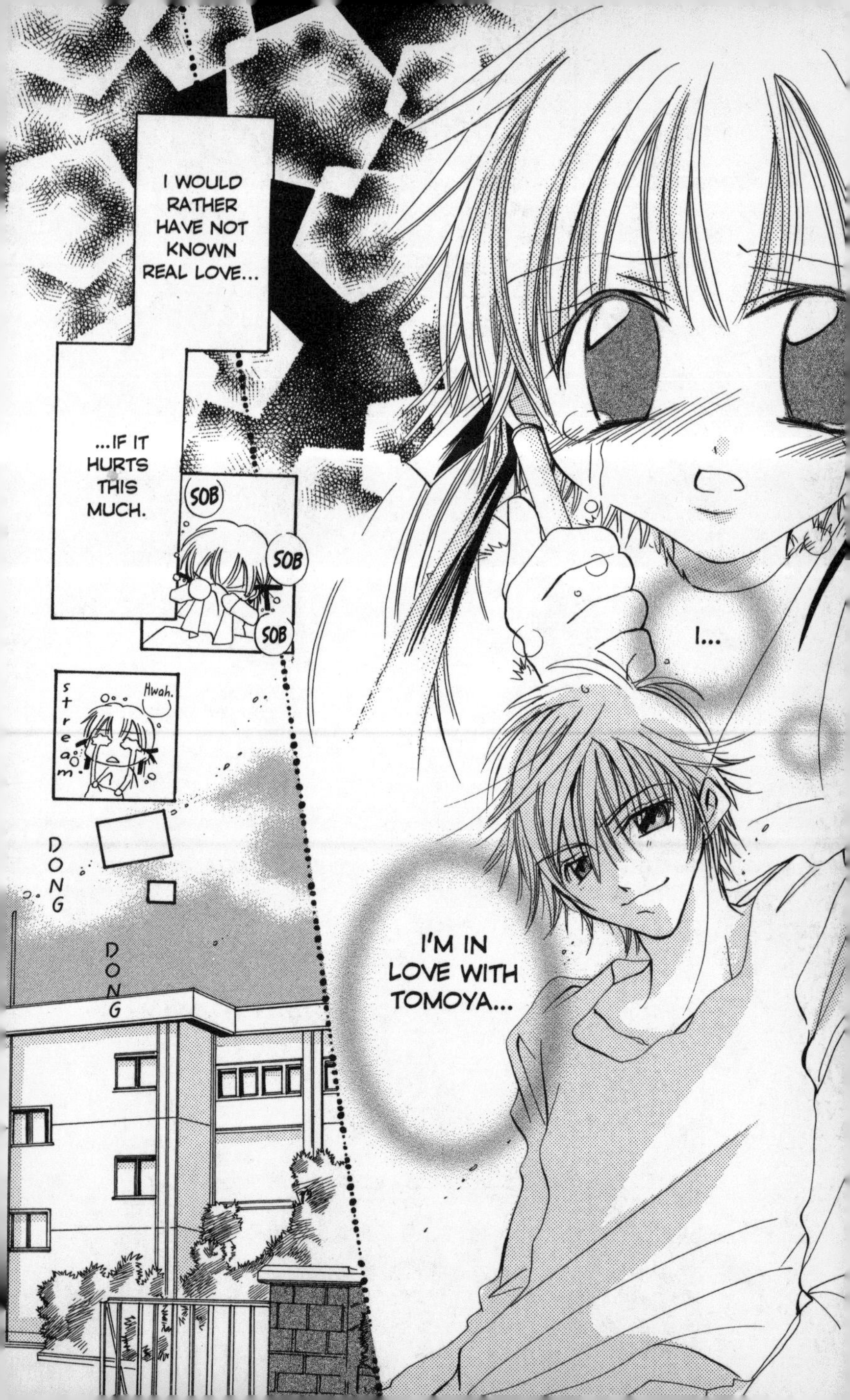
I...
I'M IN LOVE WITH TOMOYA...
I WOULD RATHER HAVE NOT KNOWN REAL LOVE...
...IF IT HURTS THIS MUCH.
SOB
SOB
SOB
Hwah.
stream
DONG
DONG

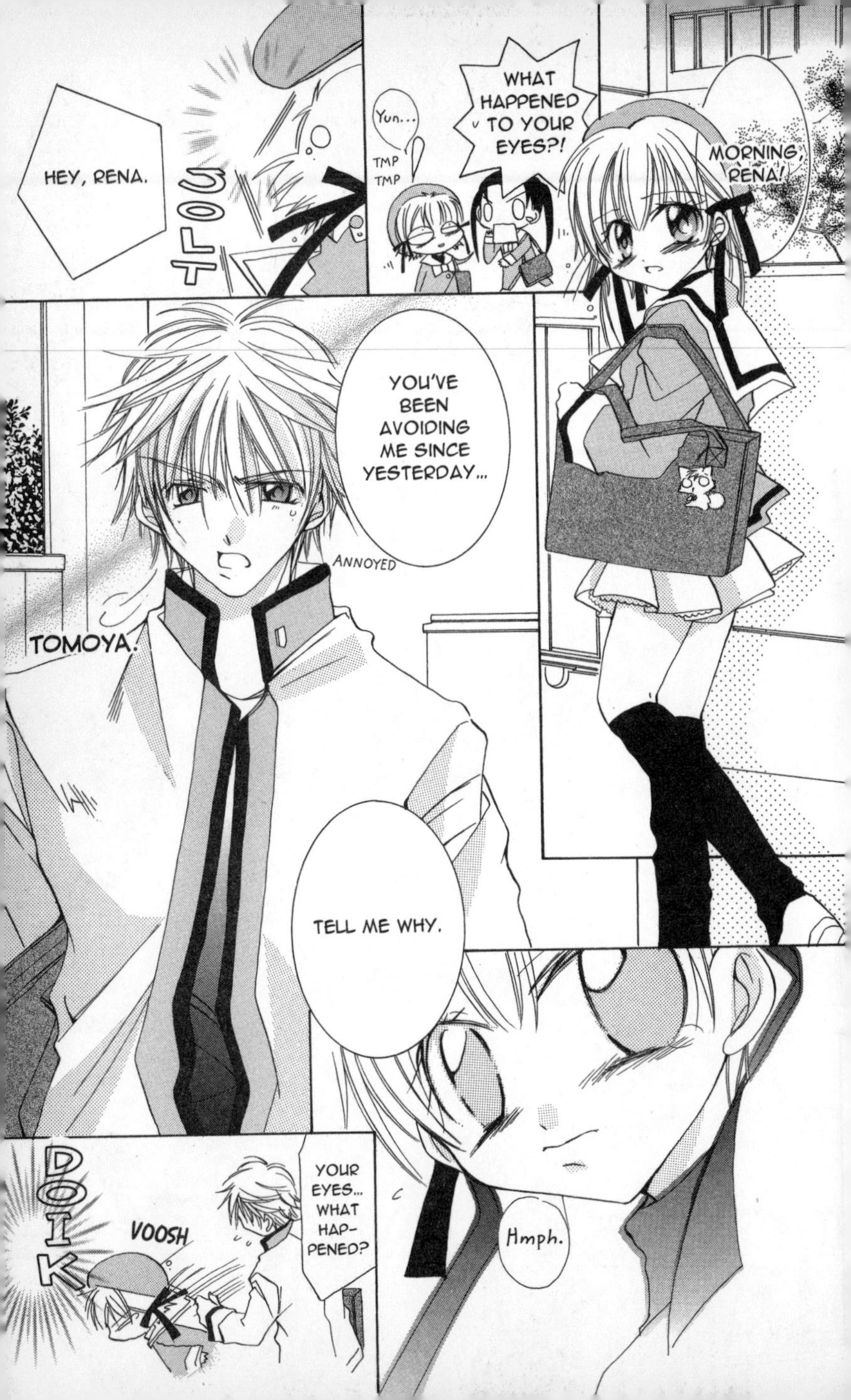
MORNING, RENA!
WHAT HAPPENED TO YOUR EYES?!
Yun...
TMP TMP
HEY, RENA.
JOLT
YOU'VE BEEN AVOIDING ME SINCE YESTERDAY...
ANNOYED
TOMOYA.
TELL ME WHY.
Hmph.
YOUR EYES... WHAT HAP-PENED?
DOIK
VOOSH

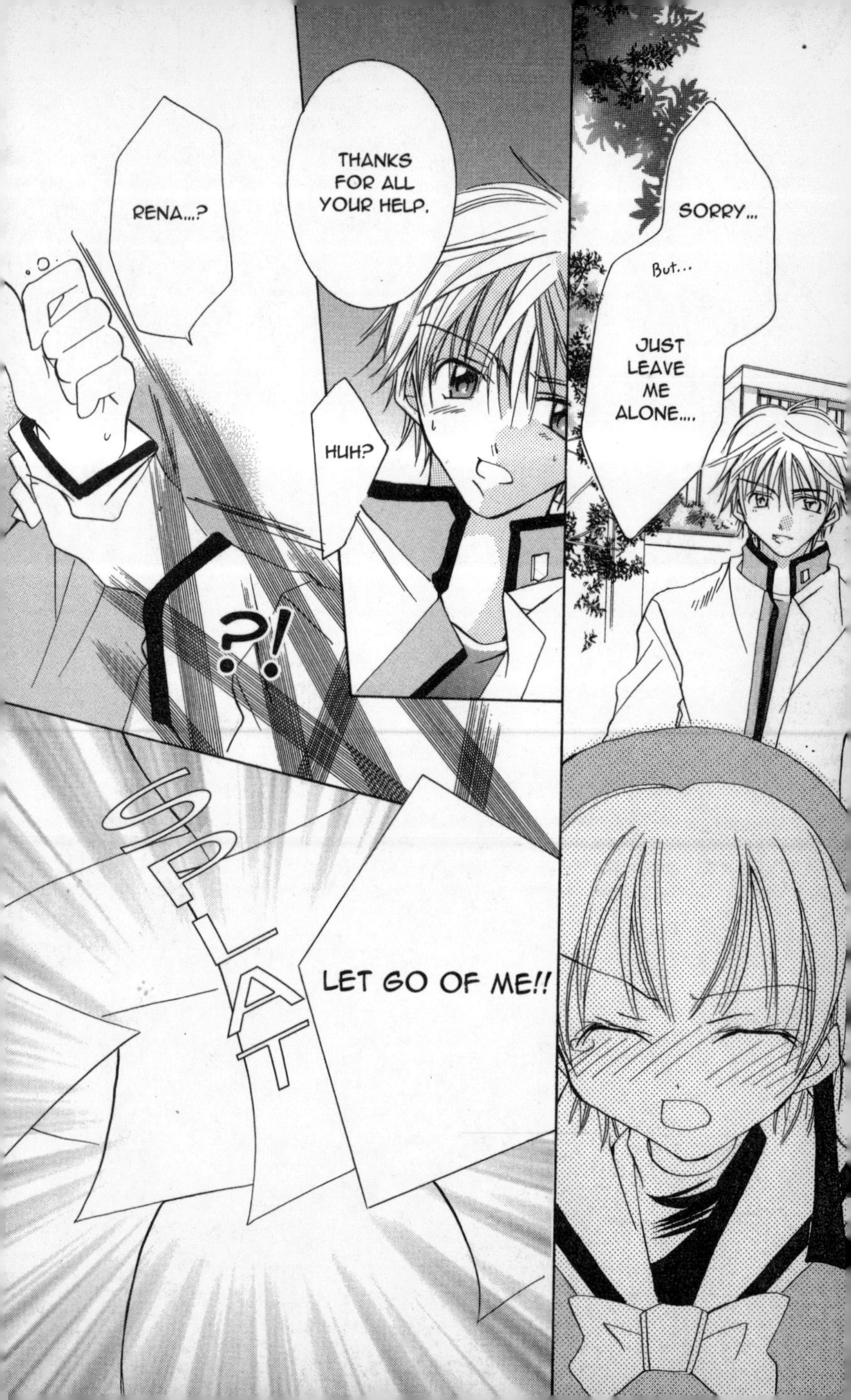
SORRY...
But...
JUST LEAVE ME ALONE....
THANKS FOR ALL YOUR HELP.
HUH?
RENA...?
?!
LET GO OF ME!!
SPLAT

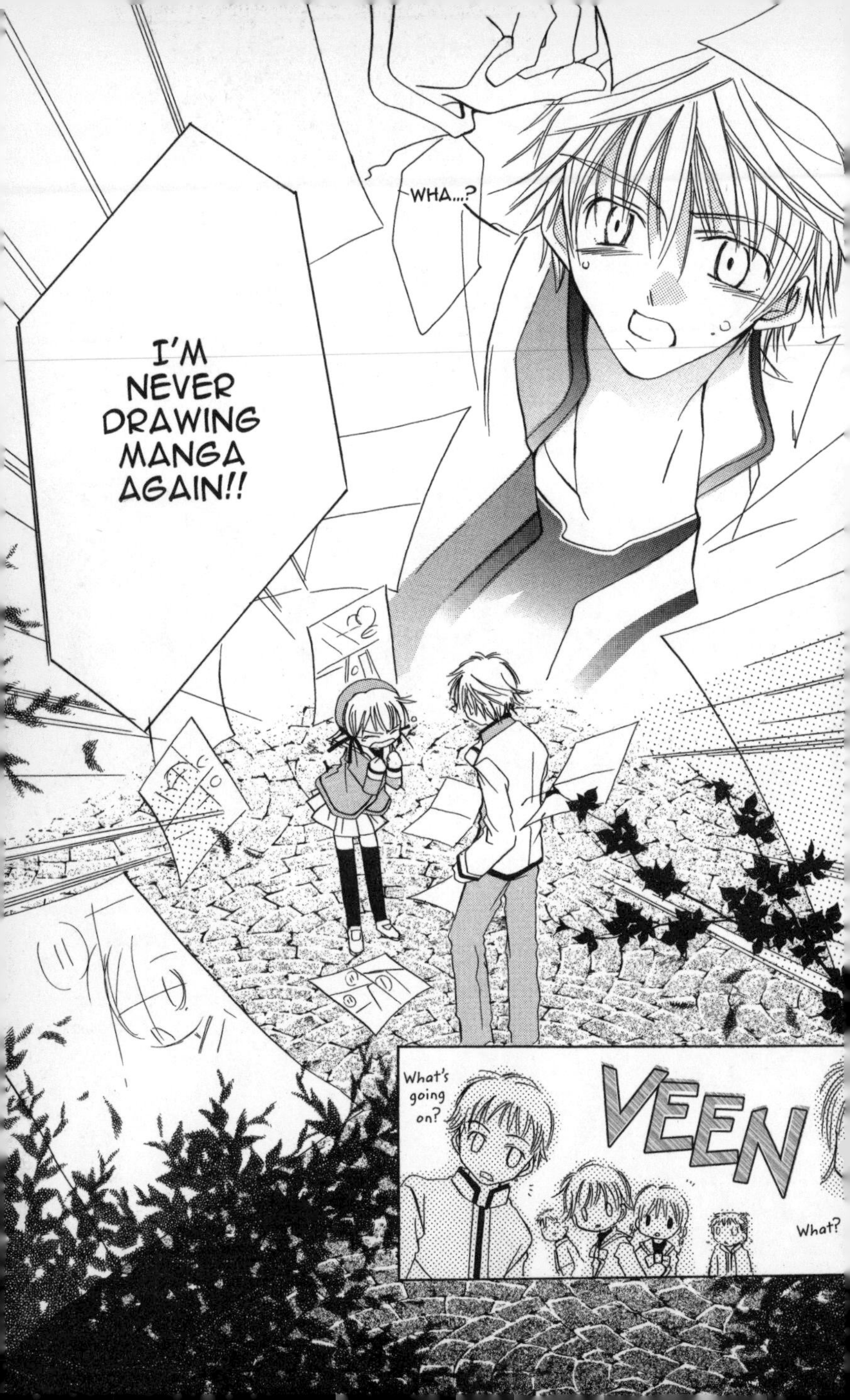

I'M NEVER DRAWING MANGA AGAIN!!
WHA...?
What?
VEEN
What's going on?

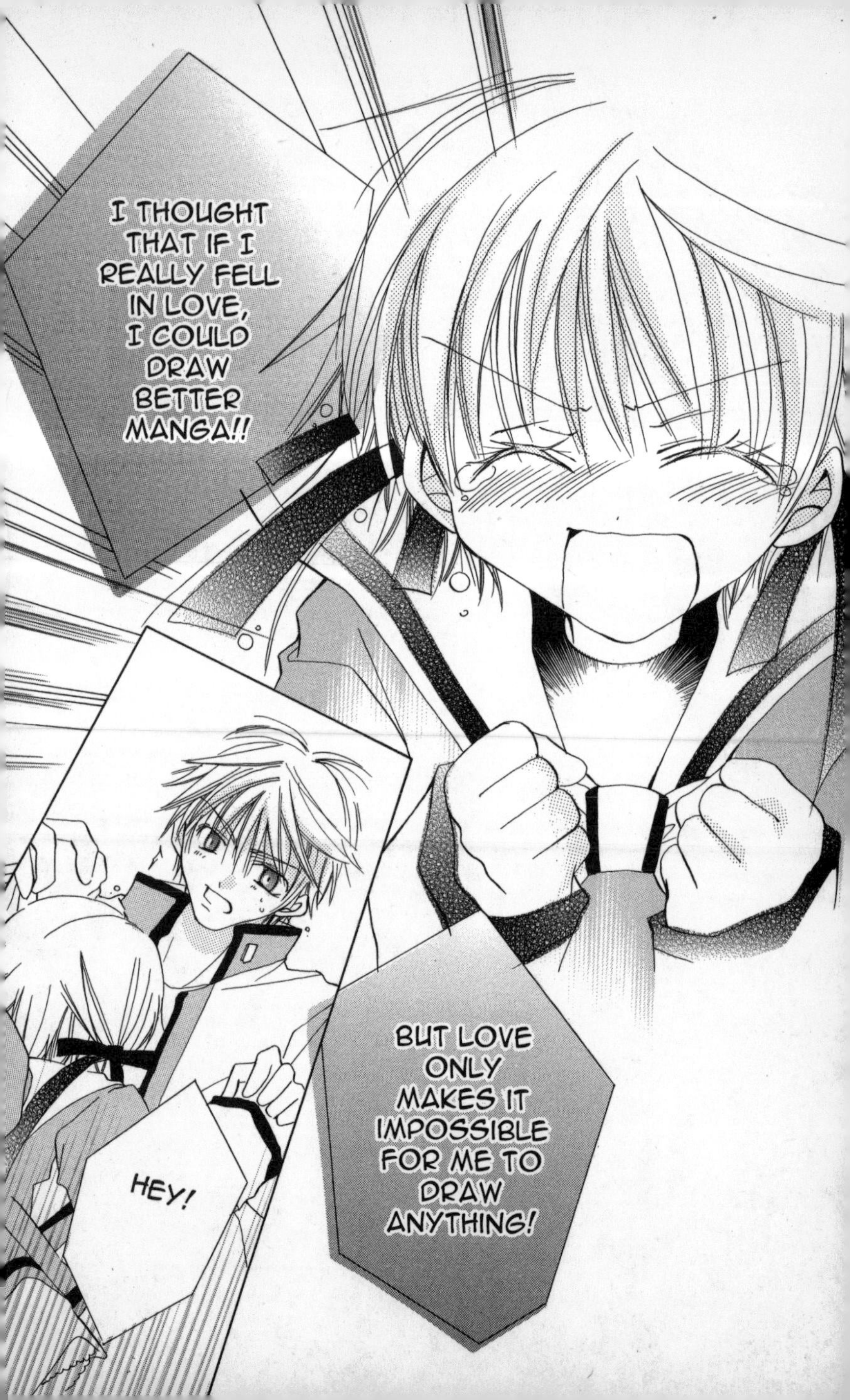
I THOUGHT THAT IF I REALLY FELL IN LOVE, I COULD DRAW BETTER MANGA!!
BUT LOVE ONLY MAKES IT IMPOSSIBLE FOR ME TO DRAW ANYTHING!
HEY!

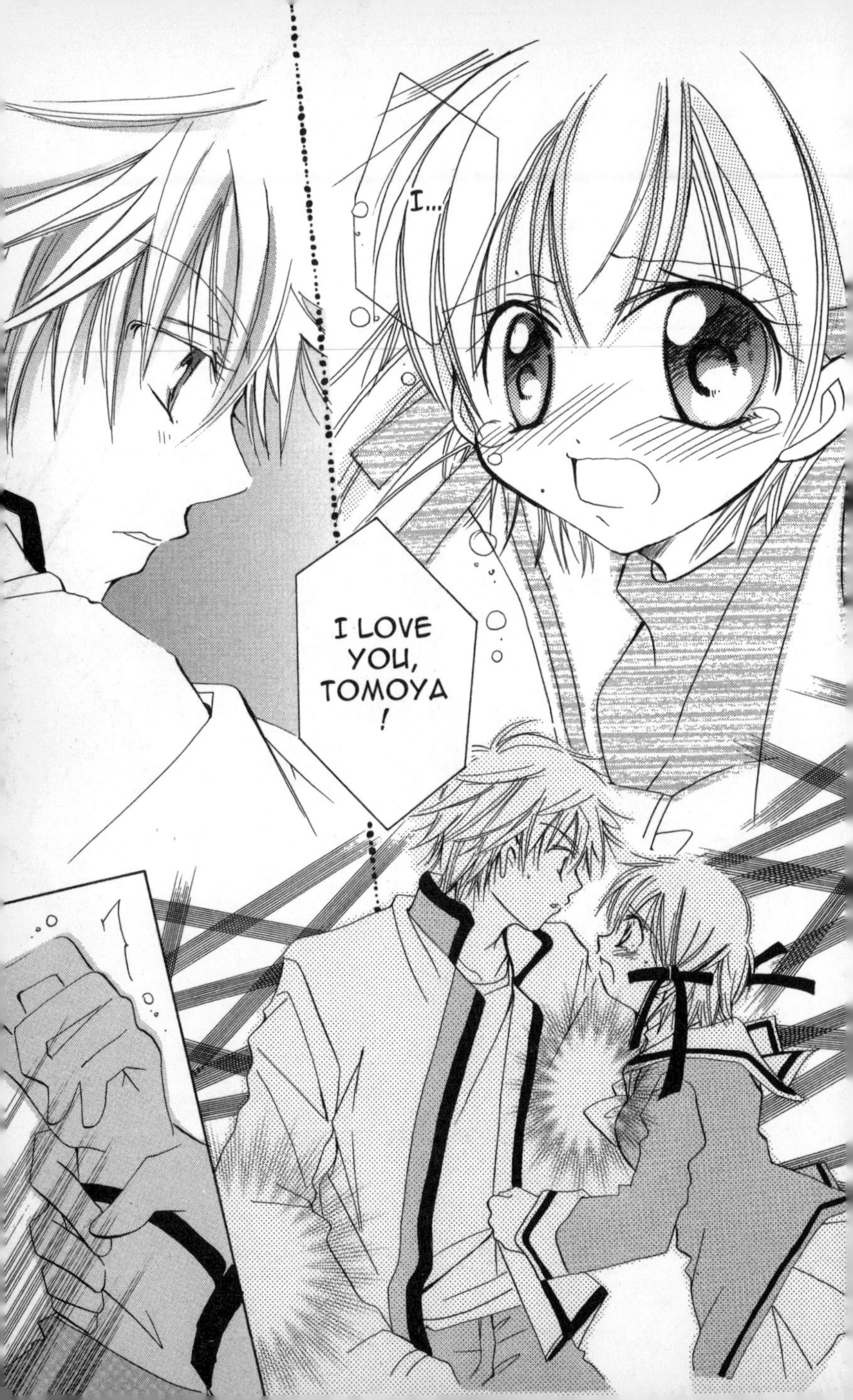
I...
I LOVE YOU, TOMOYA!

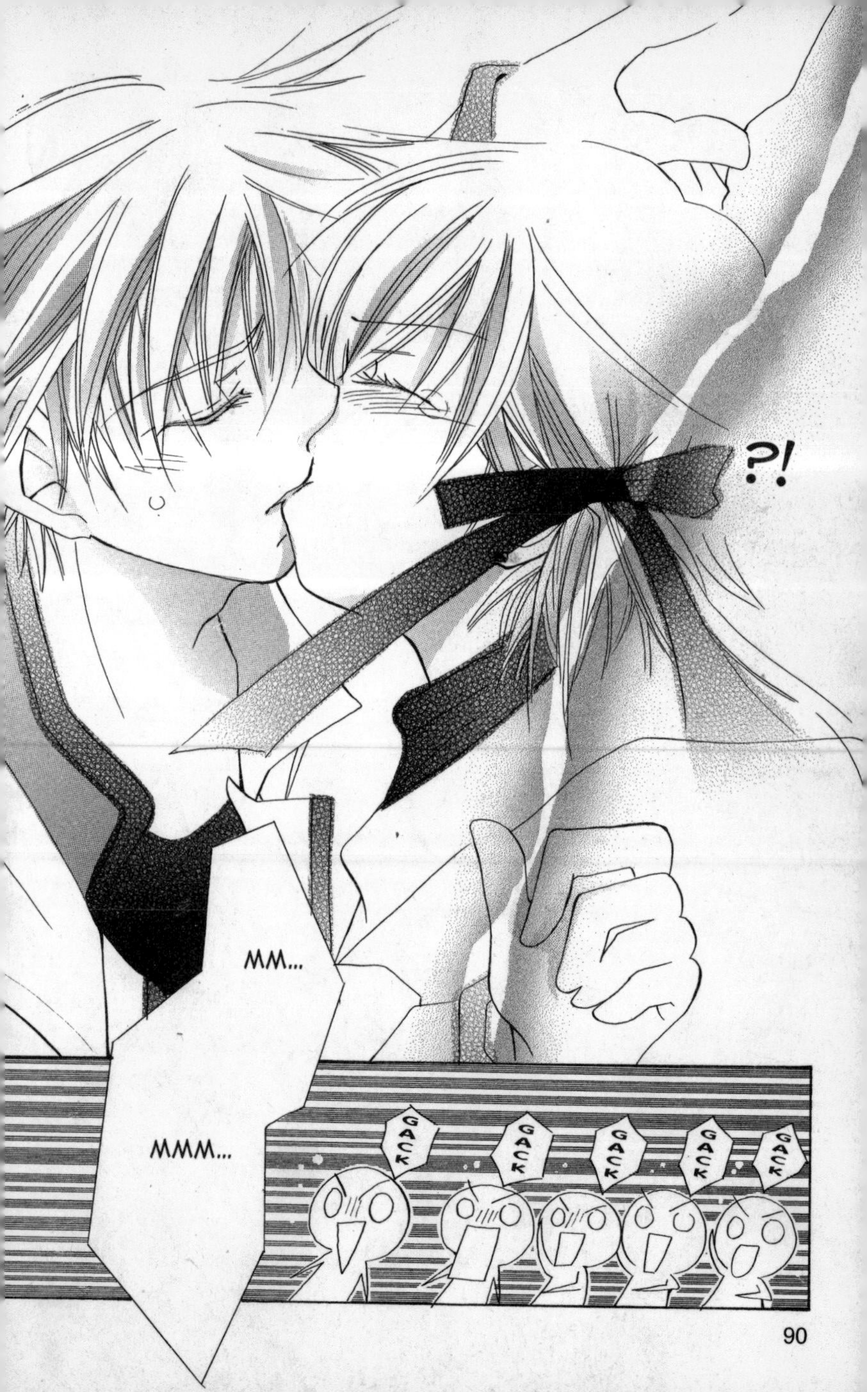
?!
MM...
MMM...
GACK
GACK
GACK
GACK
GACK

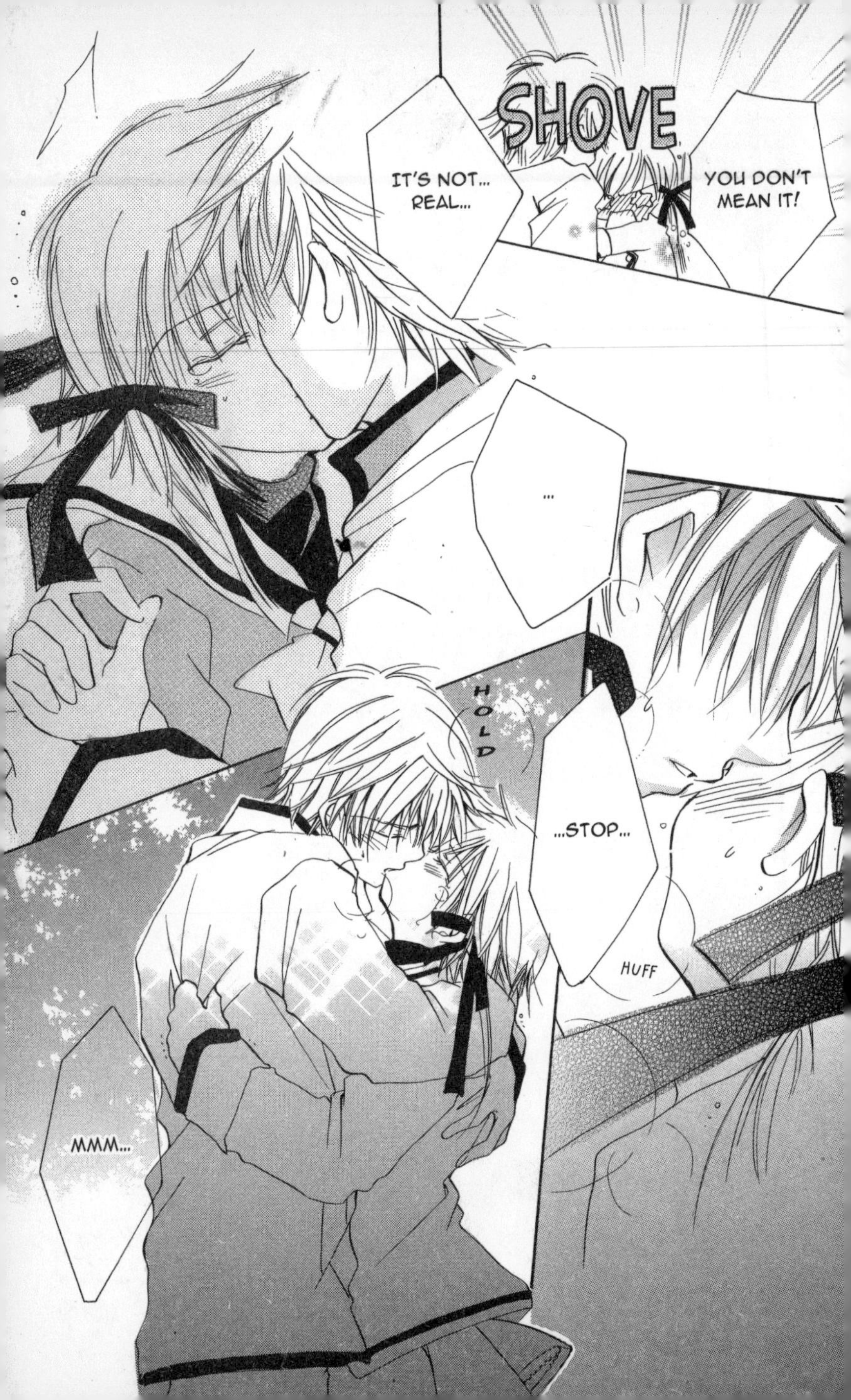
YOU DON'T MEAN IT!
SHOVE
IT'S NOT... REAL...
...
...STOP...
HUFF
HOLD
MMM...

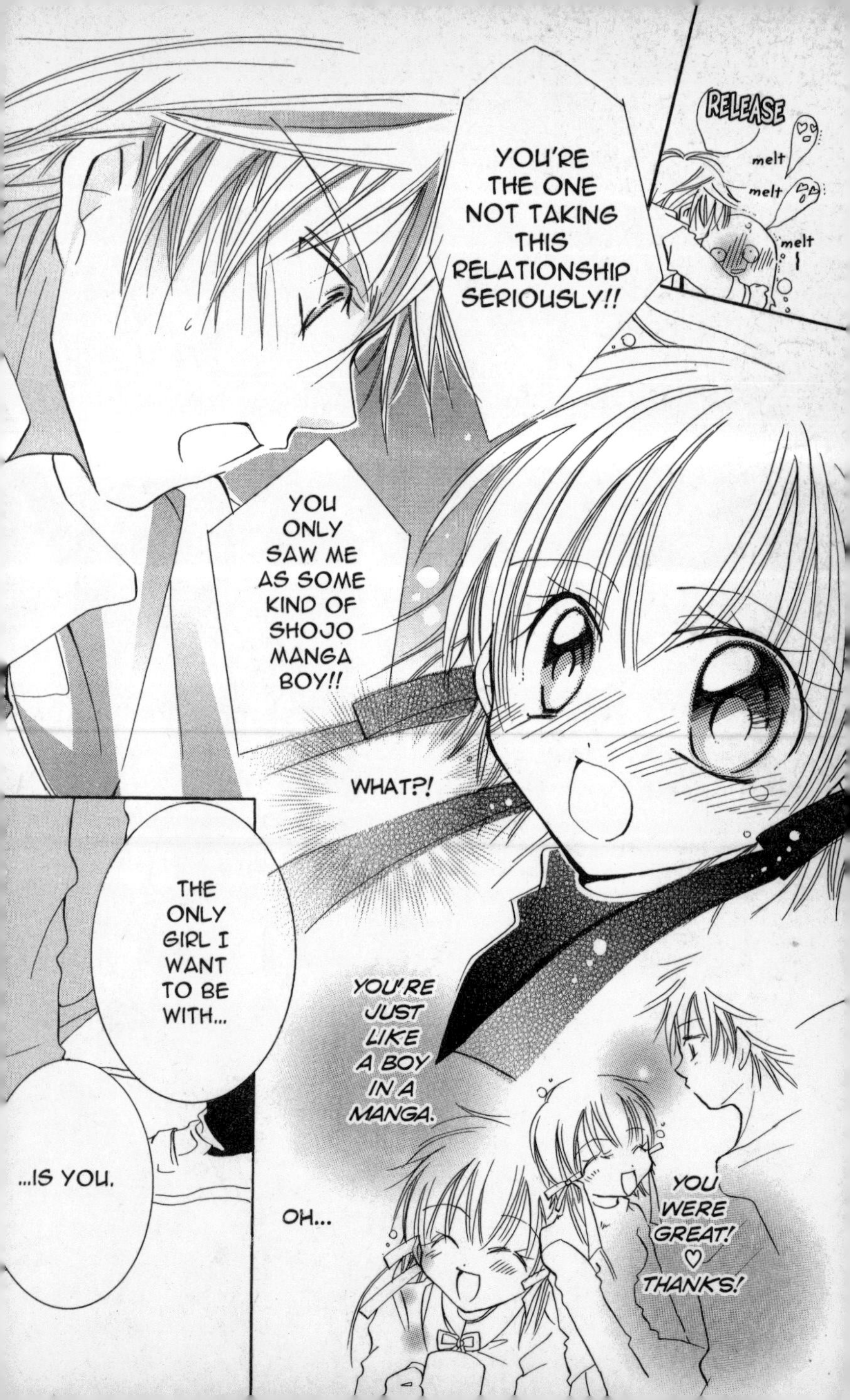
RELEASE
melt
melt
melt
YOU'RE THE ONE NOT TAKING THIS RELATIONSHIP SERIOUSLY!!
YOU ONLY SAW ME AS SOME KIND OF SHOJO MANGA BOY!!
WHAT?!
YOU'RE JUST LIKE A BOY IN A MANGA.
YOU WERE GREAT! ♡
THANKS!
OH...
THE ONLY GIRL I WANT TO BE WITH...
...IS YOU.

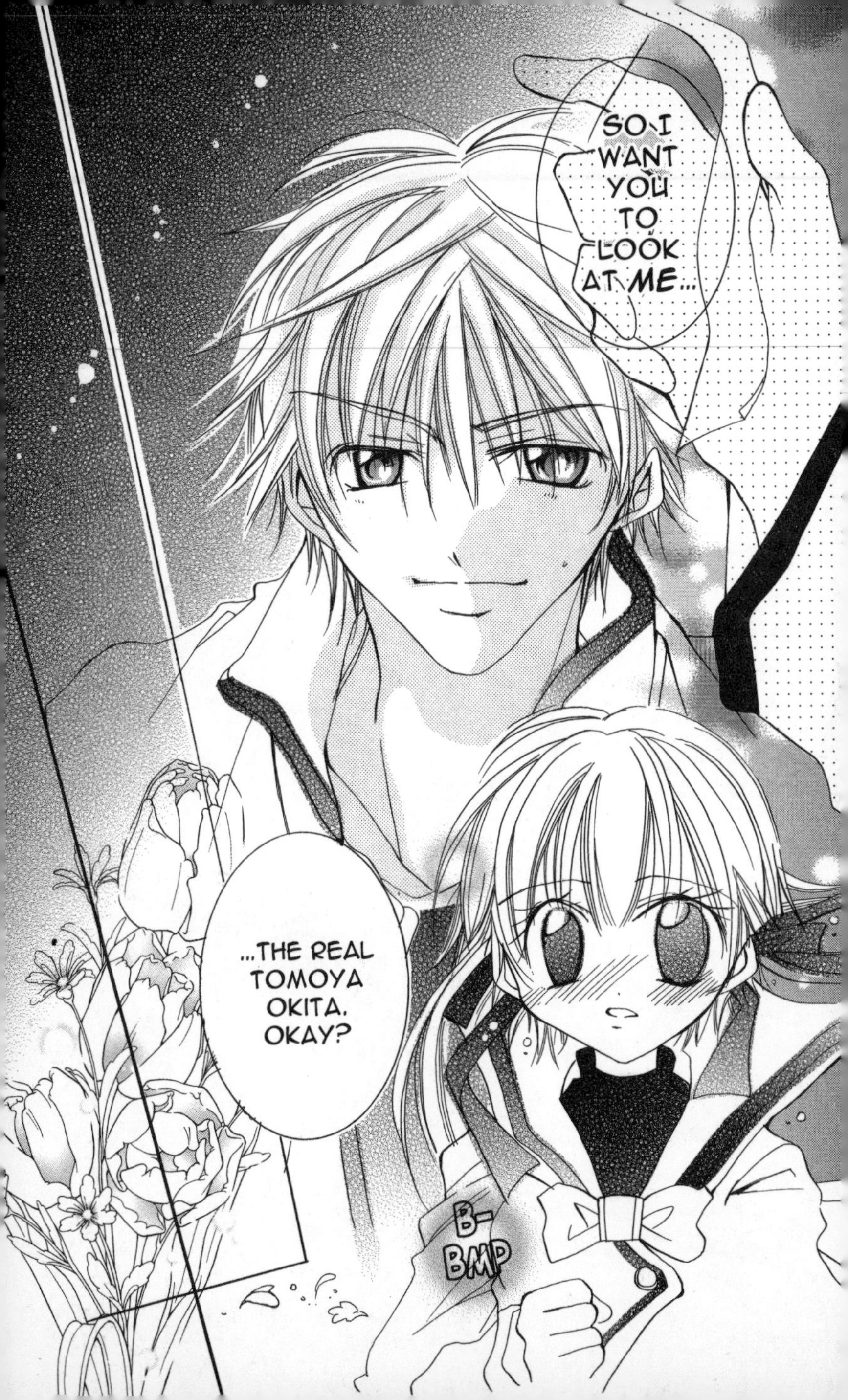
SO I WANT YOU TO LOOK AT ME...
...THE REAL TOMOYA OKITA. OKAY?
B-BMP

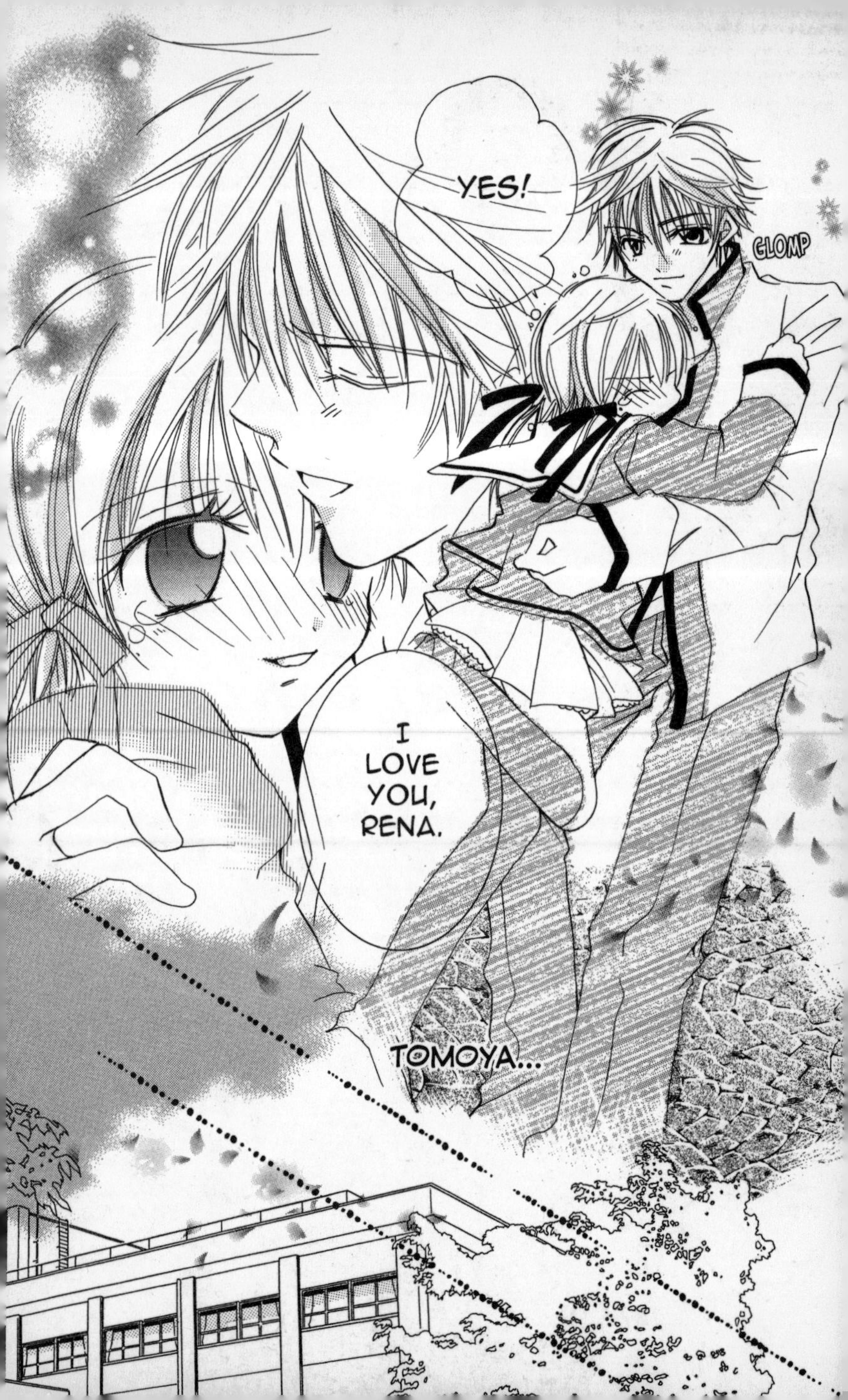
GLOMP
YES!
I LOVE YOU, RENA.
TOMOYA...

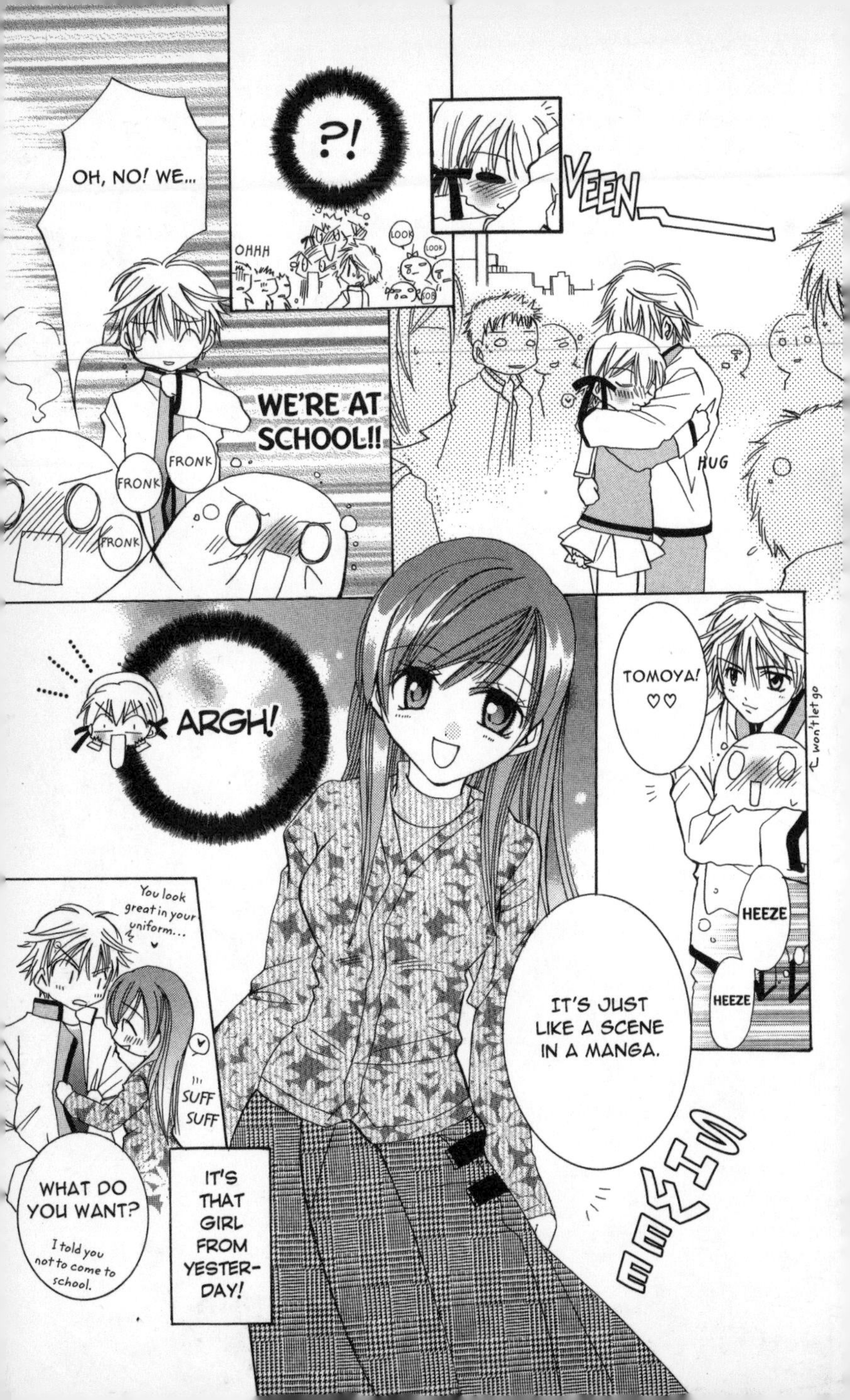
VEEN
HUG
?!
OHHH
LOOK
LOOK
SOB
OH, NO! WE...
WE'RE AT SCHOOL!!
FRONK
FRONK
FRONK
TOMOYA! ♡♡
won't let go
HEEZE
HEEZE
IT'S JUST LIKE A SCENE IN A MANGA.
ARGH!
IT'S THAT GIRL FROM YESTERDAY!
You look great in your uniform...
SUFF SUFF
WHAT DO YOU WANT?
I told you not to come to school.

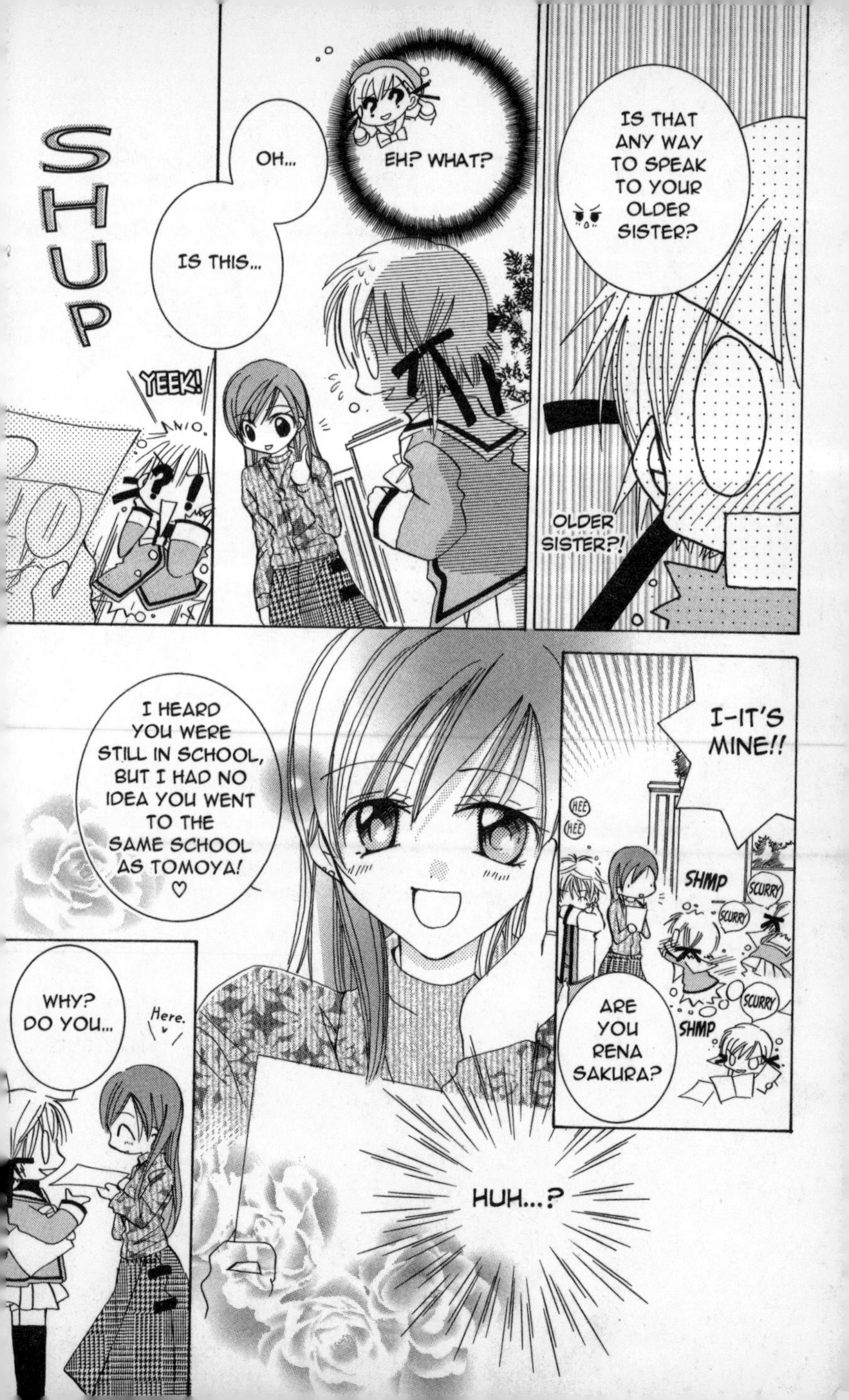
IS THAT ANY WAY TO SPEAK TO YOUR OLDER SISTER?
OLDER SISTER?!
EH? WHAT?
OH...
IS THIS...
SHUP
YEEK!
I-IT'S MINE!!
HEE
HEE
SHMP
SCURRY
SCURRY
SCURRY
SHMP
ARE YOU RENA SAKURA?
I HEARD YOU WERE STILL IN SCHOOL, BUT I HAD NO IDEA YOU WENT TO THE SAME SCHOOL AS TOMOYA! ♡
HUH...?
WHY? DO YOU...
Here.

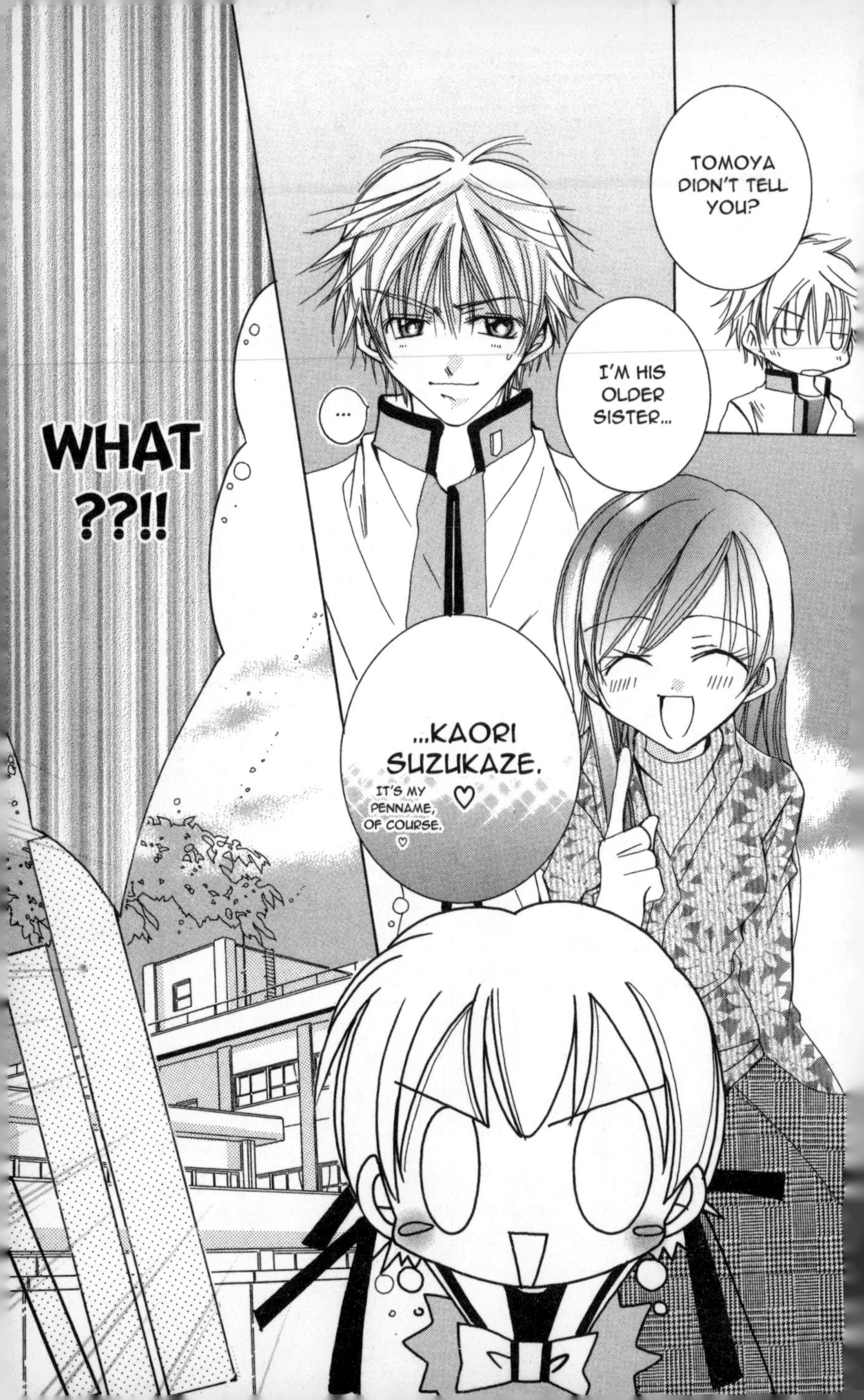
TOMOYA DIDN'T TELL YOU?
I'M HIS OLDER SISTER...
...
...KAORI SUZUKAZE. ♡
IT'S MY PENNAME, OF COURSE. ♡
WHAT ??!!

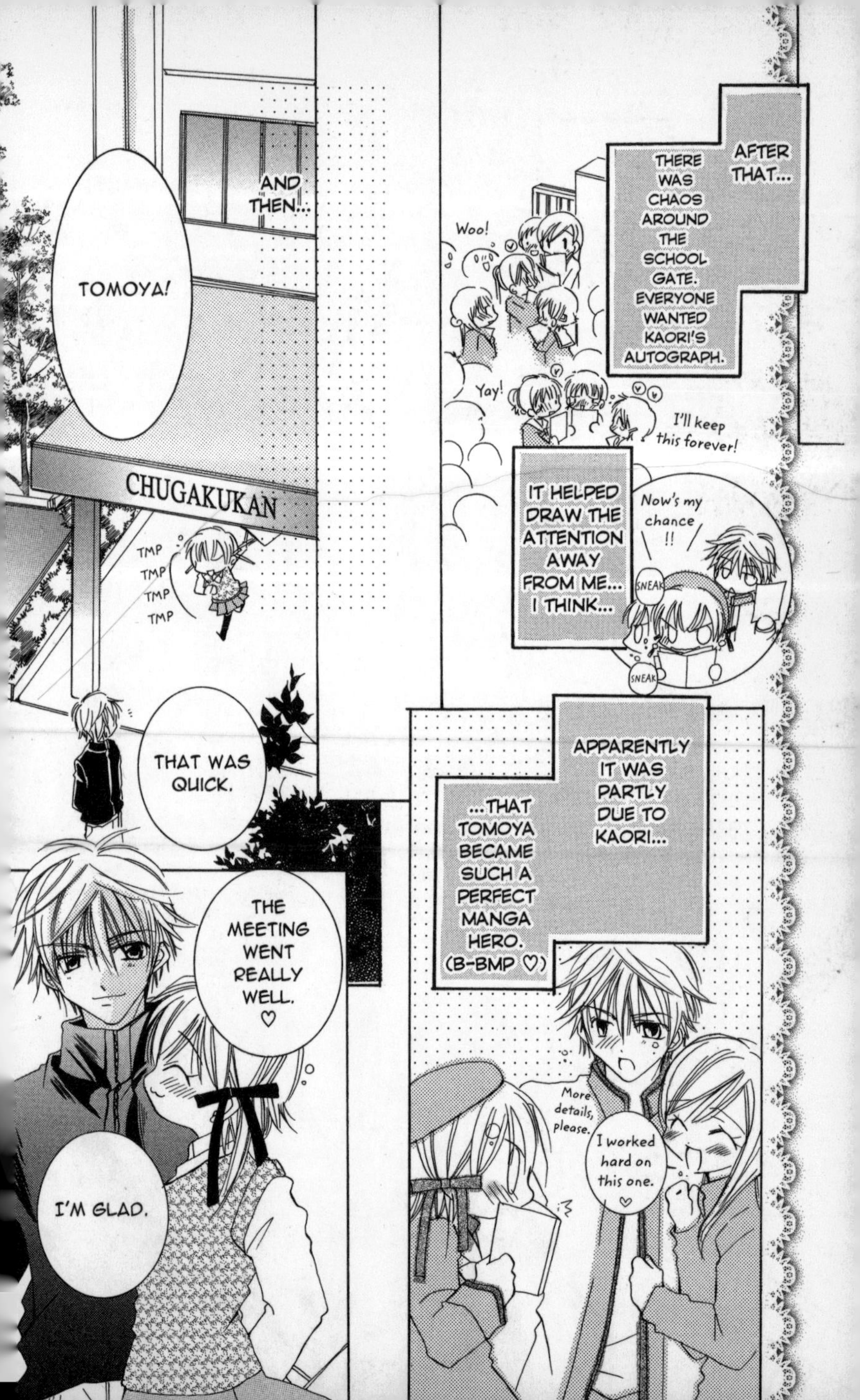
AFTER THAT...
THERE WAS CHAOS AROUND THE SCHOOL GATE. EVERYONE WANTED KAORI'S AUTOGRAPH.
Woo!
Yay!
I'll keep this forever!
IT HELPED DRAW THE ATTENTION AWAY FROM ME... I THINK...
Now's my chance !!
SNEAK
SNEAK
APPARENTLY IT WAS PARTLY DUE TO KAORI...
...THAT TOMOYA BECAME SUCH A PERFECT MANGA HERO. (B-BMP ♡)
More details, please.
I worked hard on this one. ♡
AND THEN...
TOMOYA!
CHUGAKUKAN
TMP
TMP
TMP
TMP
THAT WAS QUICK.
THE MEETING WENT REALLY WELL. ♡
I'M GLAD.

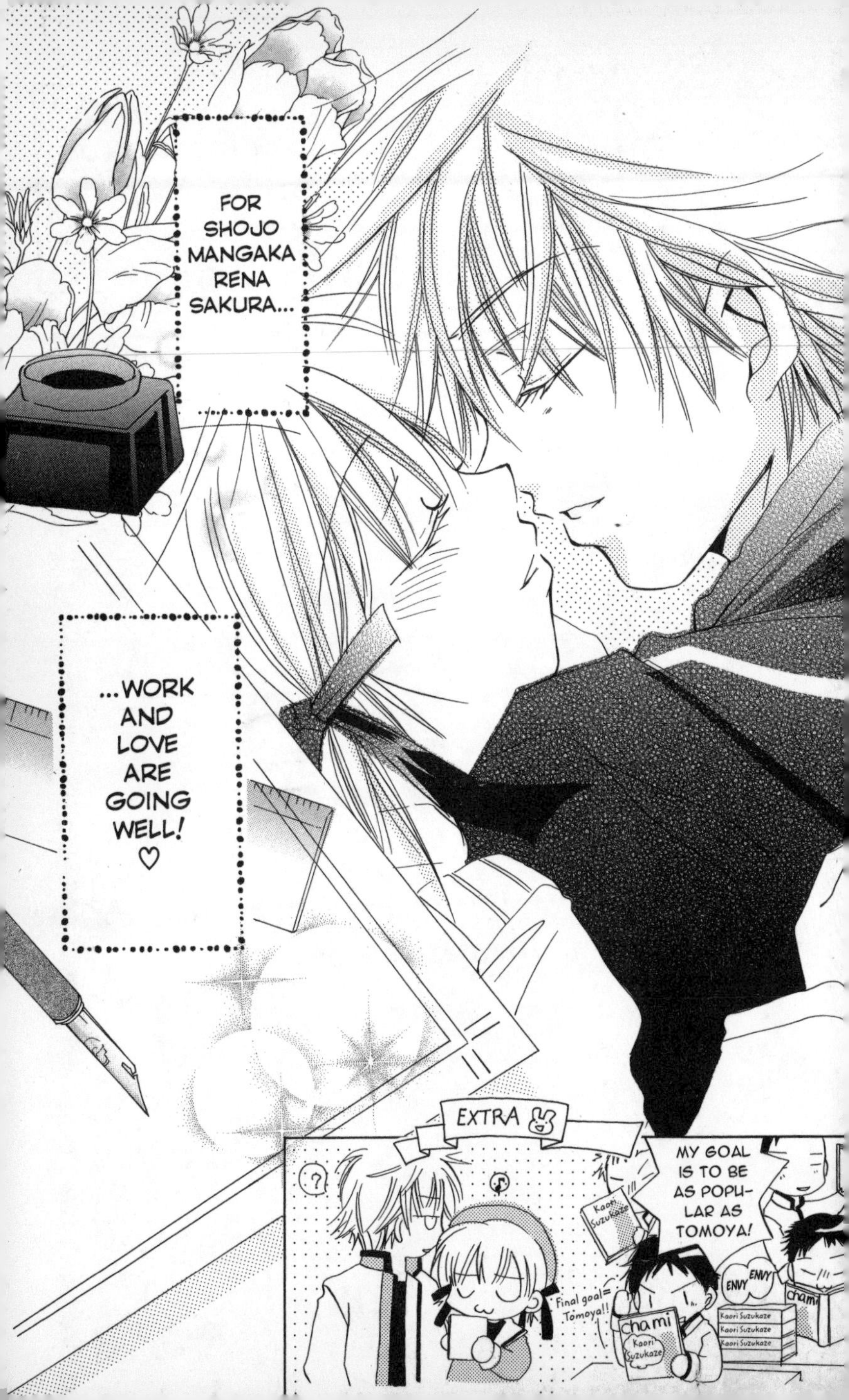
FOR SHOJO MANGAKA RENA SAKURA...
...WORK AND LOVE ARE GOING WELL! ♡
EXTRA
MY GOAL IS TO BE AS POPU-LAR AS TOMOYA!
chami
Kaori Suzukaze
Kaori Suzukaze
Kaori Suzukaze
Kaori Suzukaze
ENVY ENVY
chami
Kaori Suzukaze
Kaori Suzukaze
Final goal= Tomoya!!

CHARACTER INTRO

Yun

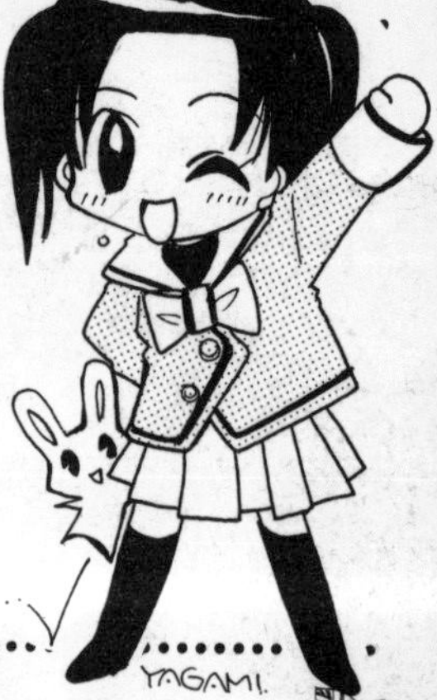
YAGAMI

She is Rena's partner in crime... Some readers really liked her. I got letters saying, "I wish I had a friend like Yun." I'm glad you like her despite her few appearances.

Yamase

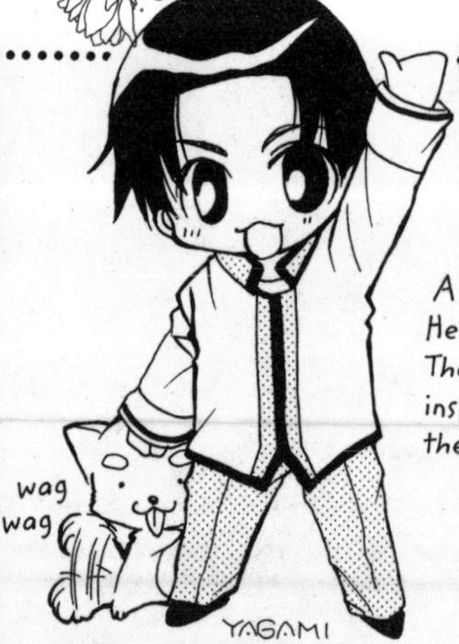
wag
wag
YAGAMI

A voice said that he is "cute like a girl." He is the second most popular boy after Tomoya. There's actually someone who was the source of inspiration for this character... (laugh) Yes, it was the ever-popular comedian from Kansai. v"

Sunahara

He had hardly any lines. I personally wish I had given him a bigger role. I named him after a friend of mine who helps me with my scripts.

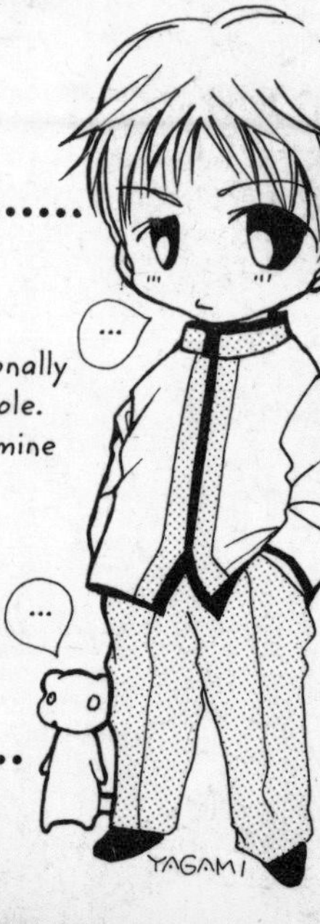
...
...
YAGAMI

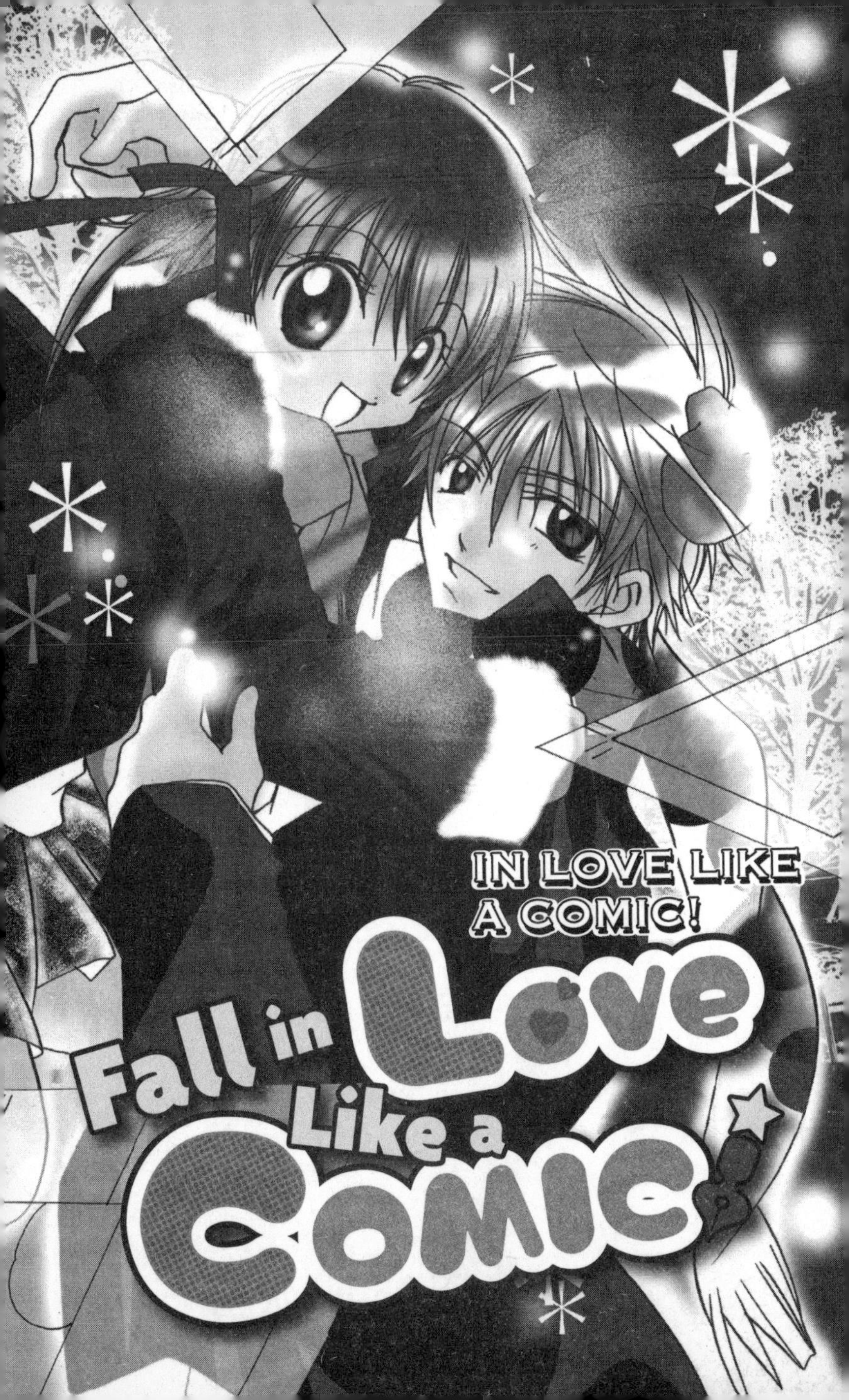
IN LOVE LIKE A COMIC!
Fall in Love Like a Comic!

FALL IN LOVE LIKE A COMIC!

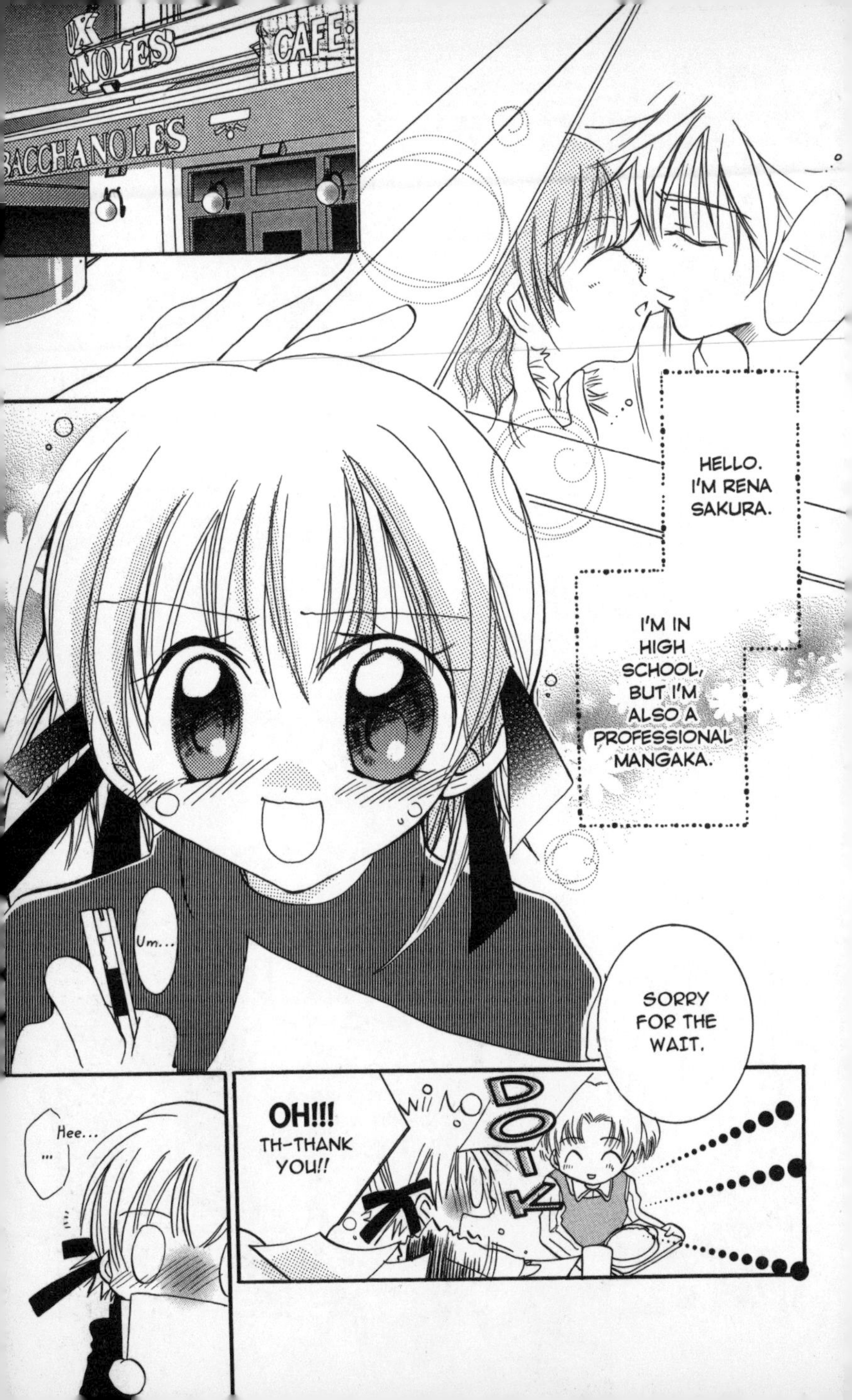
BACCHANOLES
CAFE
HELLO. I'M RENA SAKURA.
I'M IN HIGH SCHOOL, BUT I'M ALSO A PROFESSIONAL MANGAKA.
Um...
SORRY FOR THE WAIT.
DOINK
OH!!!! TH-THANK YOU!!
Hee... ...

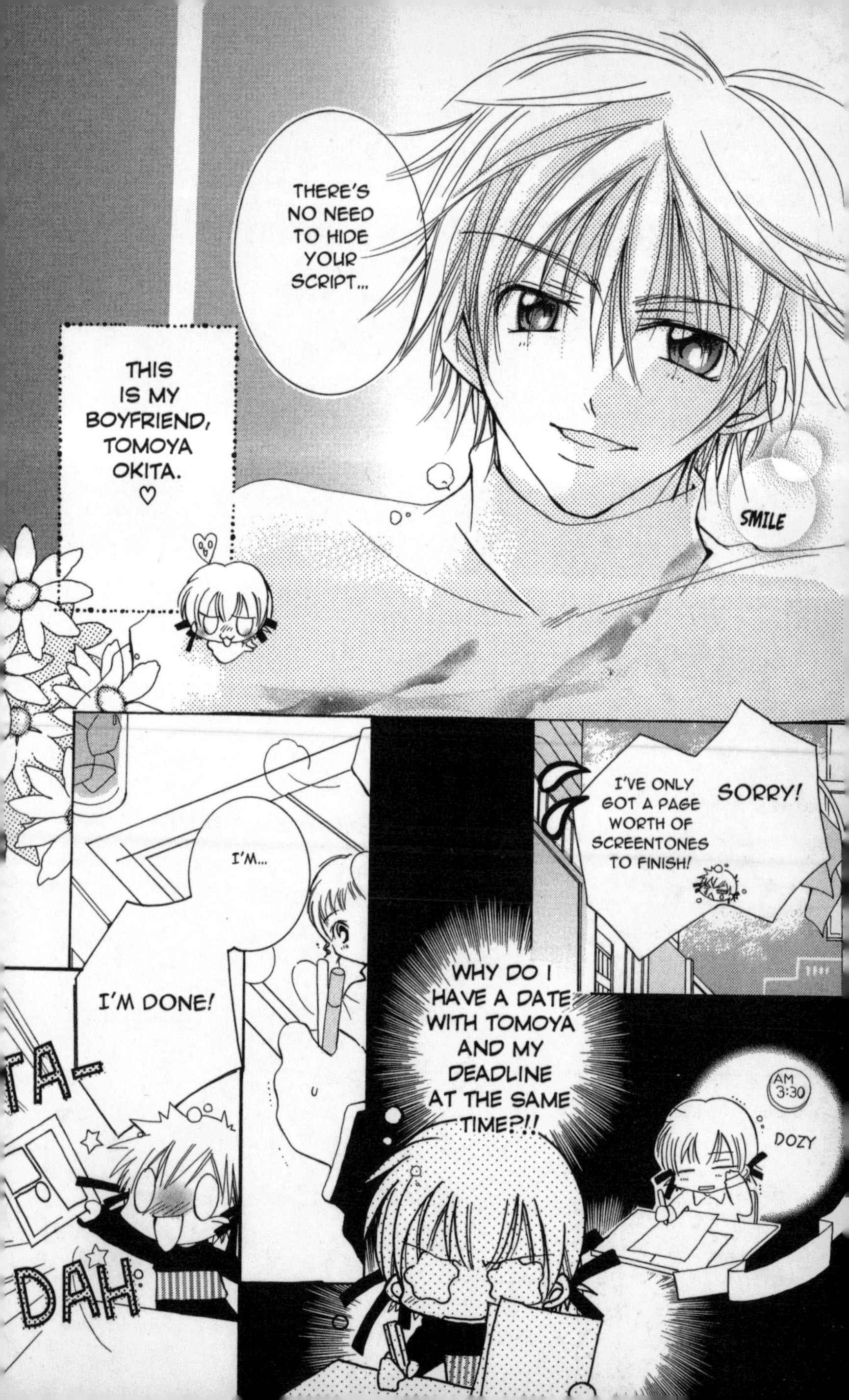
THERE'S NO NEED TO HIDE YOUR SCRIPT...
THIS IS MY BOYFRIEND, TOMOYA OKITA. ♡
SMILE
SORRY!
I'VE ONLY GOT A PAGE WORTH OF SCREENTONES TO FINISH!
AM 3:30
WHY DO I HAVE A DATE WITH TOMOYA AND MY DEADLINE AT THE SAME TIME?!!
DOZY
I'M...
I'M DONE!
TA-DAH

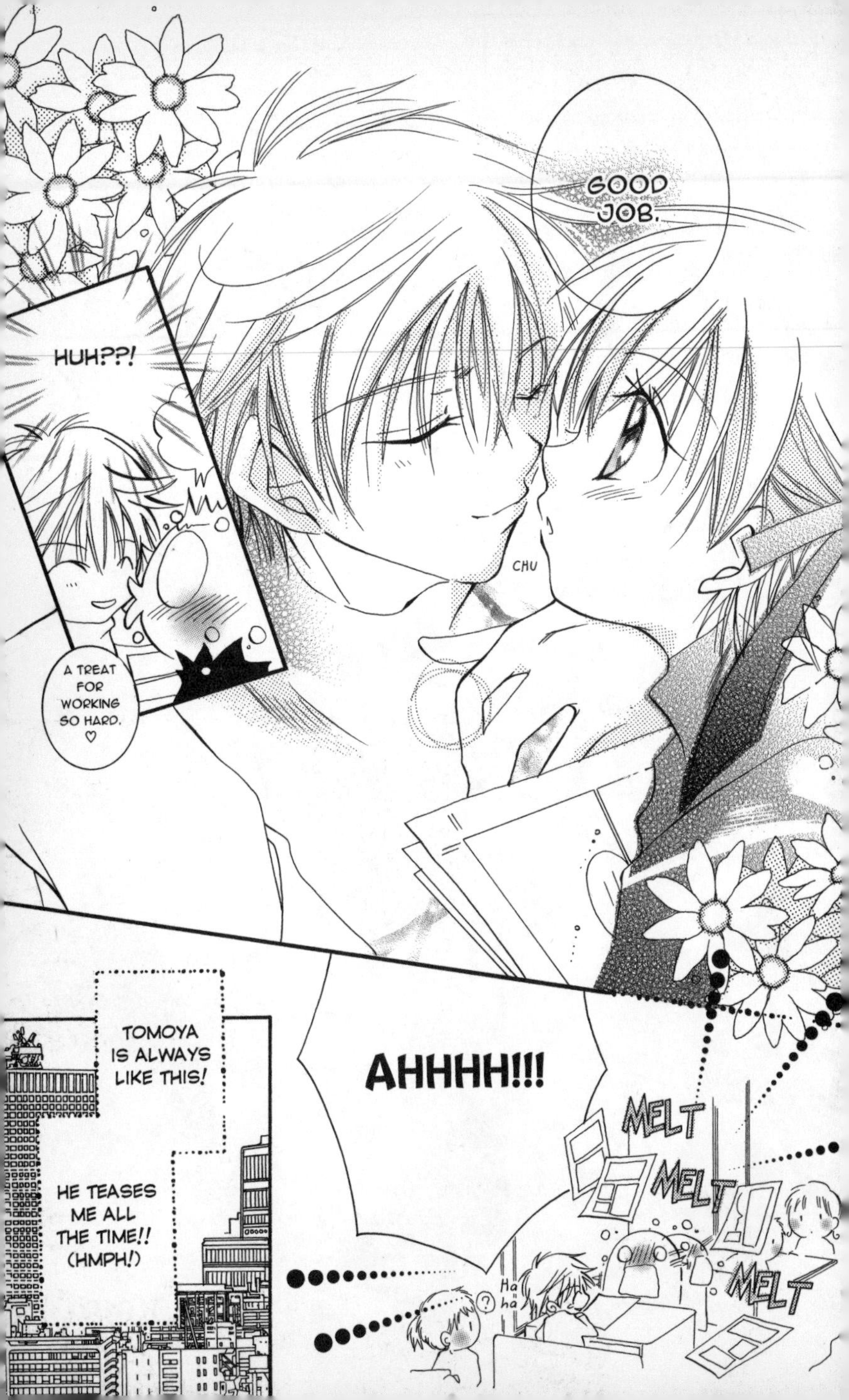
GOOD JOB.
CHU
HUH??!
A TREAT FOR WORKING SO HARD. ♡
AHHHH!!!
MELT
MELT
MELT
Ha ha
TOMOYA IS ALWAYS LIKE THIS!
HE TEASES ME ALL THE TIME!! (HMPH!)

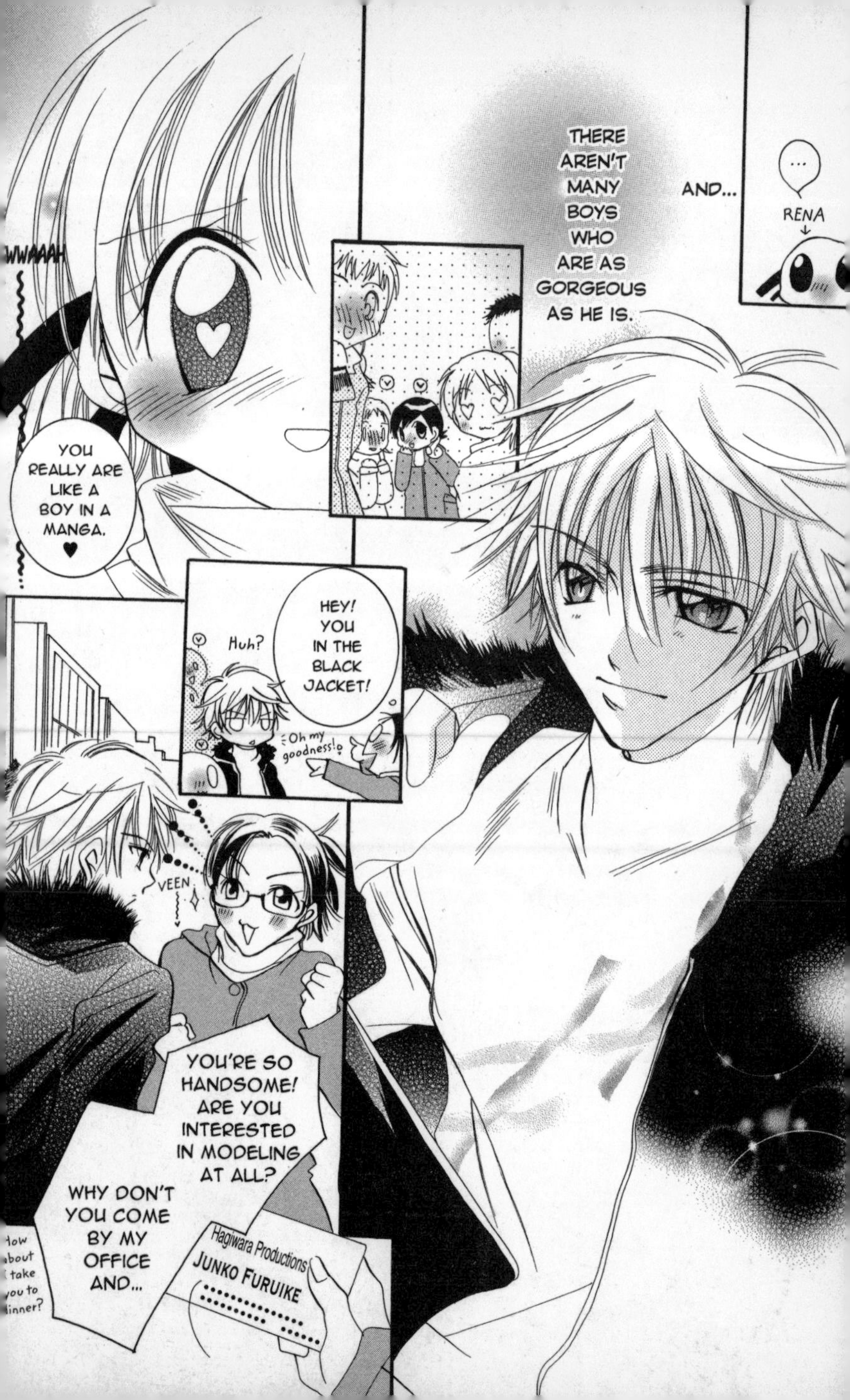
...
RENA
AND...
THERE AREN'T MANY BOYS WHO ARE AS GORGEOUS AS HE IS.
WWAAAH
YOU REALLY ARE LIKE A BOY IN A MANGA. ♥
HEY! YOU IN THE BLACK JACKET!
Huh?
Oh my goodness!
VEEN
YOU'RE SO HANDSOME! ARE YOU INTERESTED IN MODELING AT ALL?
WHY DON'T YOU COME BY MY OFFICE AND...
How about I take you to dinner?
Hagiwara Productions
JUNKO FURUIKE

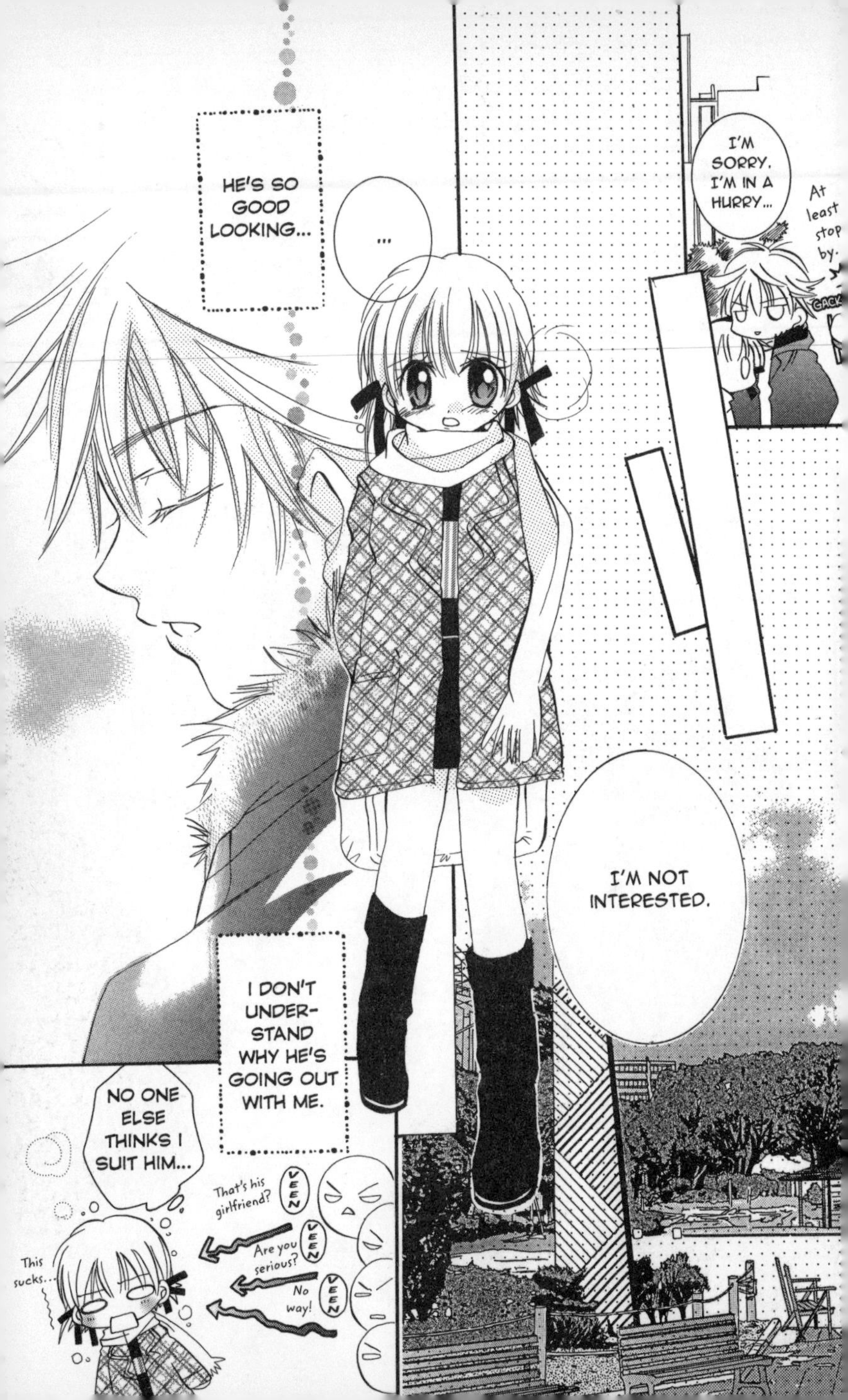
I'M SORRY. I'M IN A HURRY...
At least stop by.
GACK
...
HE'S SO GOOD LOOKING...
I'M NOT INTERESTED.
I DON'T UNDER-STAND WHY HE'S GOING OUT WITH ME.
NO ONE ELSE THINKS I SUIT HIM...
That's his girlfriend?
VEEN
Are you serious?
VEEN
No way!
VEEN
This sucks...

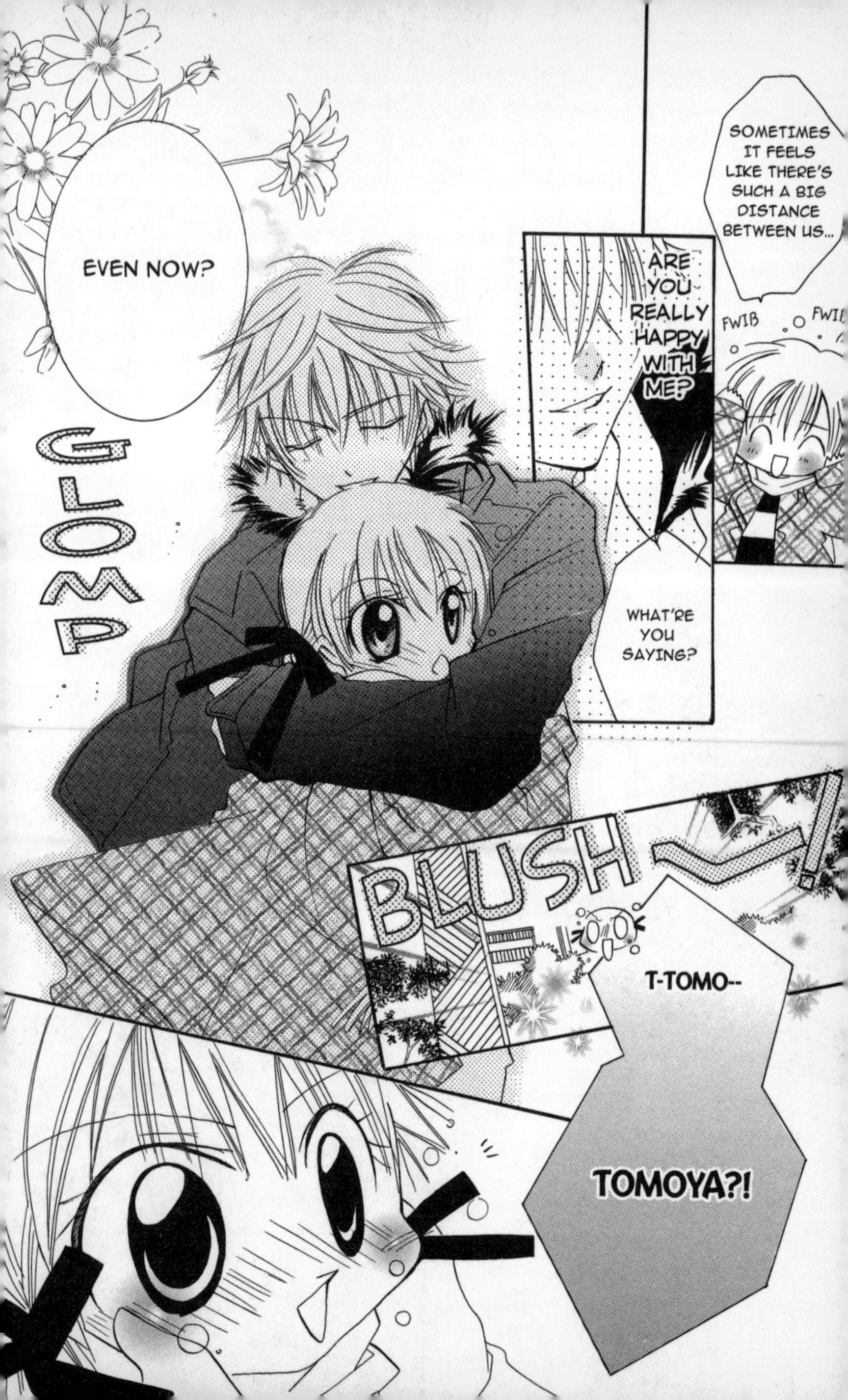
SOMETIMES IT FEELS LIKE THERE'S SUCH A BIG DISTANCE BETWEEN US...
FWIB
FWIB
ARE YOU REALLY HAPPY WITH ME?
WHAT'RE YOU SAYING?
EVEN NOW?
GLOMP
BLUSH~~!
T-TOMO--
TOMOYA?!

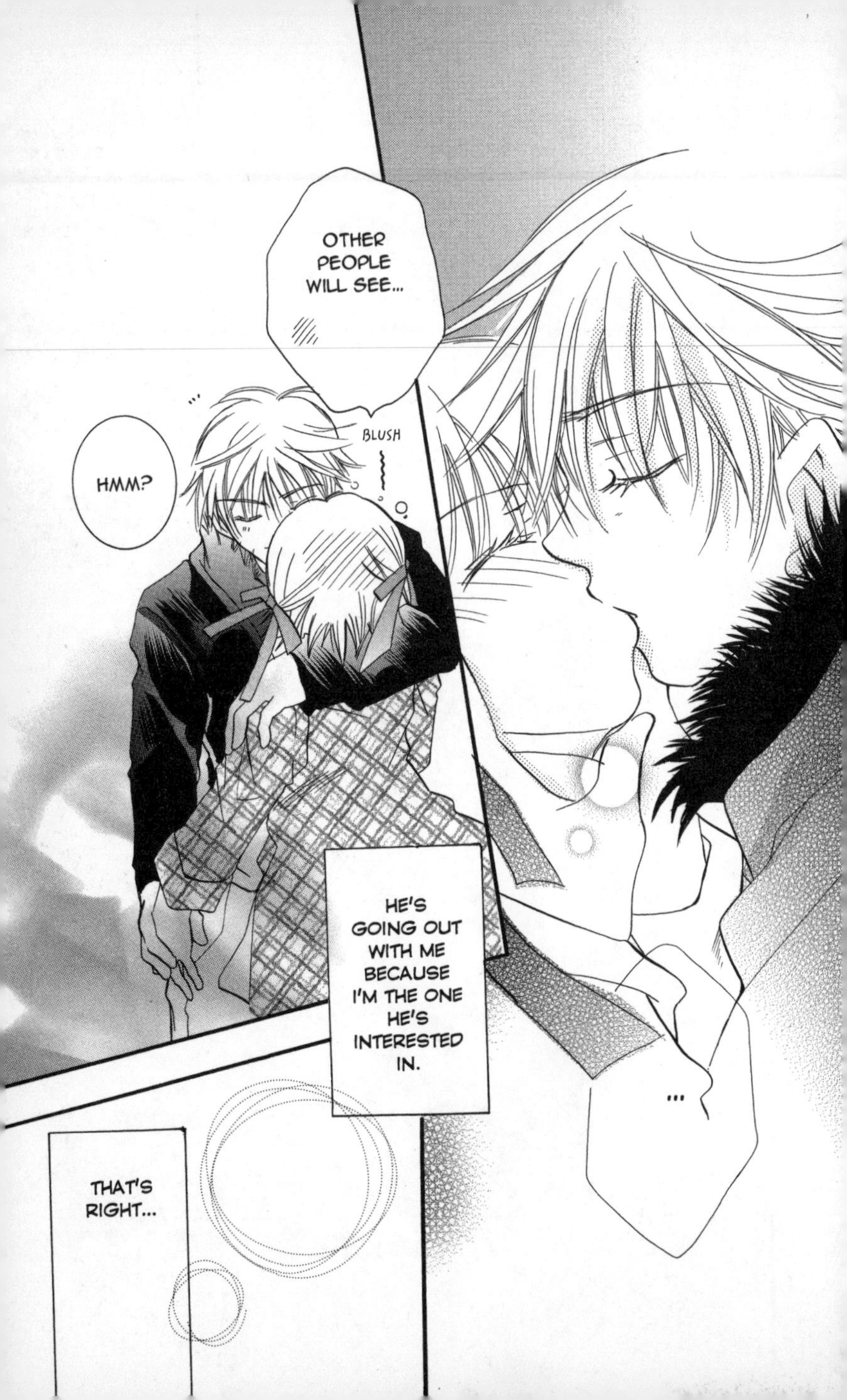

...
HE'S GOING OUT WITH ME BECAUSE I'M THE ONE HE'S INTERESTED IN.
OTHER PEOPLE WILL SEE...
BLUSH
HMM?
...
THAT'S RIGHT...

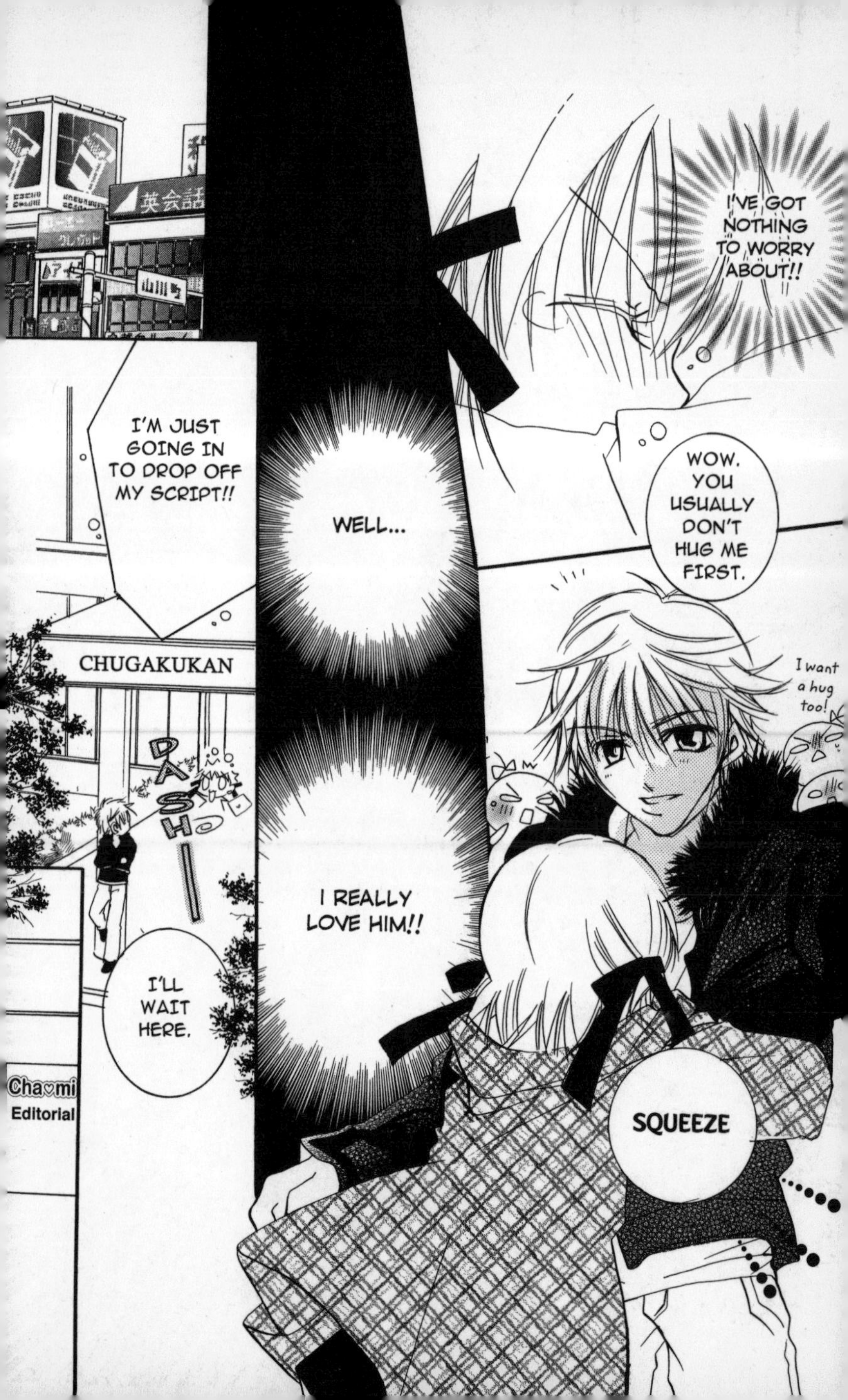
I'VE GOT NOTHING TO WORRY ABOUT!!
英会話
WOW. YOU USUALLY DON'T HUG ME FIRST.
I want a hug too!
SQUEEZE
WELL...
I REALLY LOVE HIM!!
I'M JUST GOING IN TO DROP OFF MY SCRIPT!!
CHUGAKUKAN
DASH
I'LL WAIT HERE.
Cha♡mi Editorial

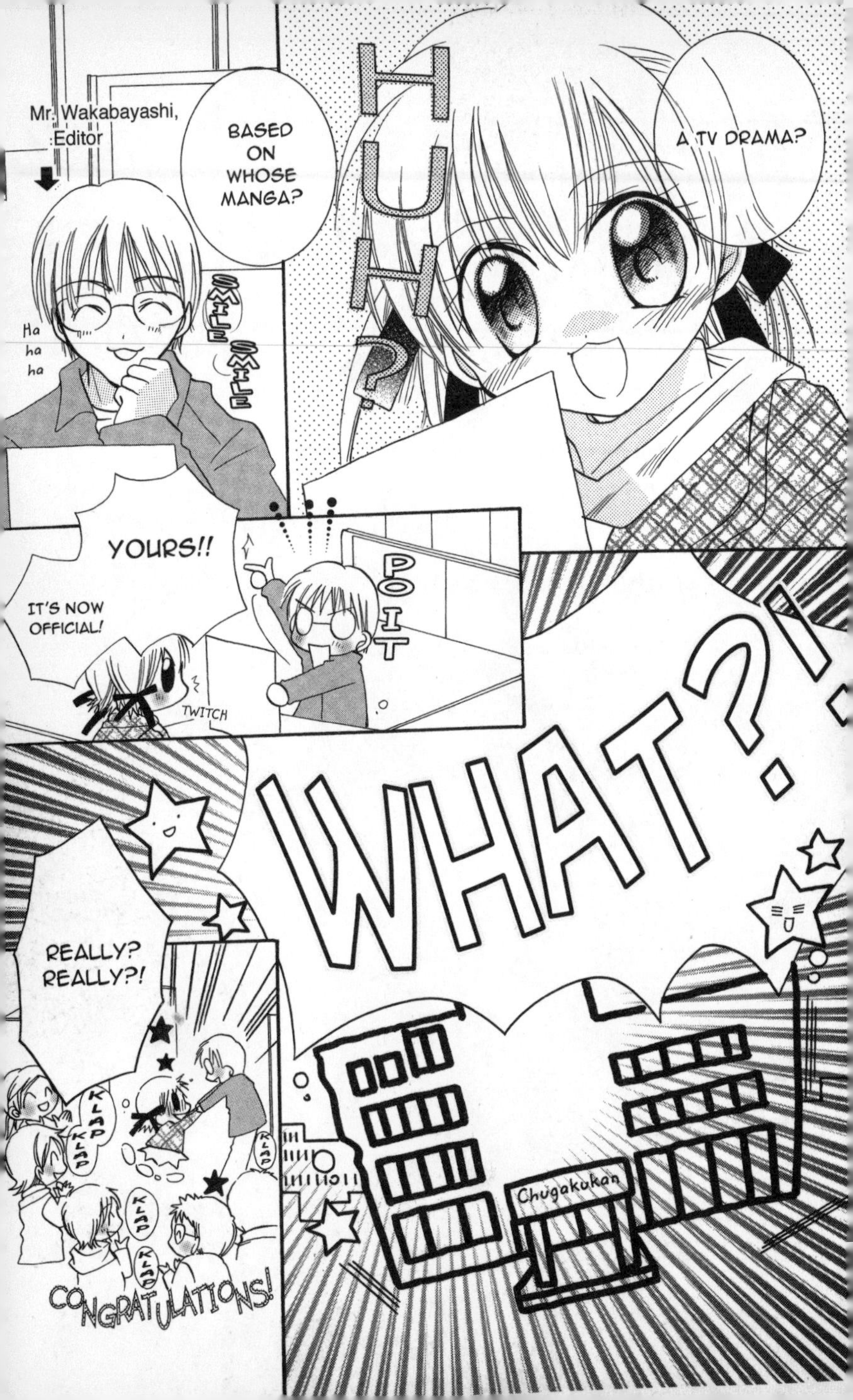
A TV DRAMA?
HUH?
BASED ON WHOSE MANGA?
Mr. Wakabayashi, Editor
SMILE SMILE
Ha ha ha
YOURS!!
IT'S NOW OFFICIAL!
POIT
TWITCH
WHAT?!
Chugakukan
REALLY? REALLY?!
KLAP KLAP KLAP KLAP KLAP KLAP
CONGRATULATIONS!

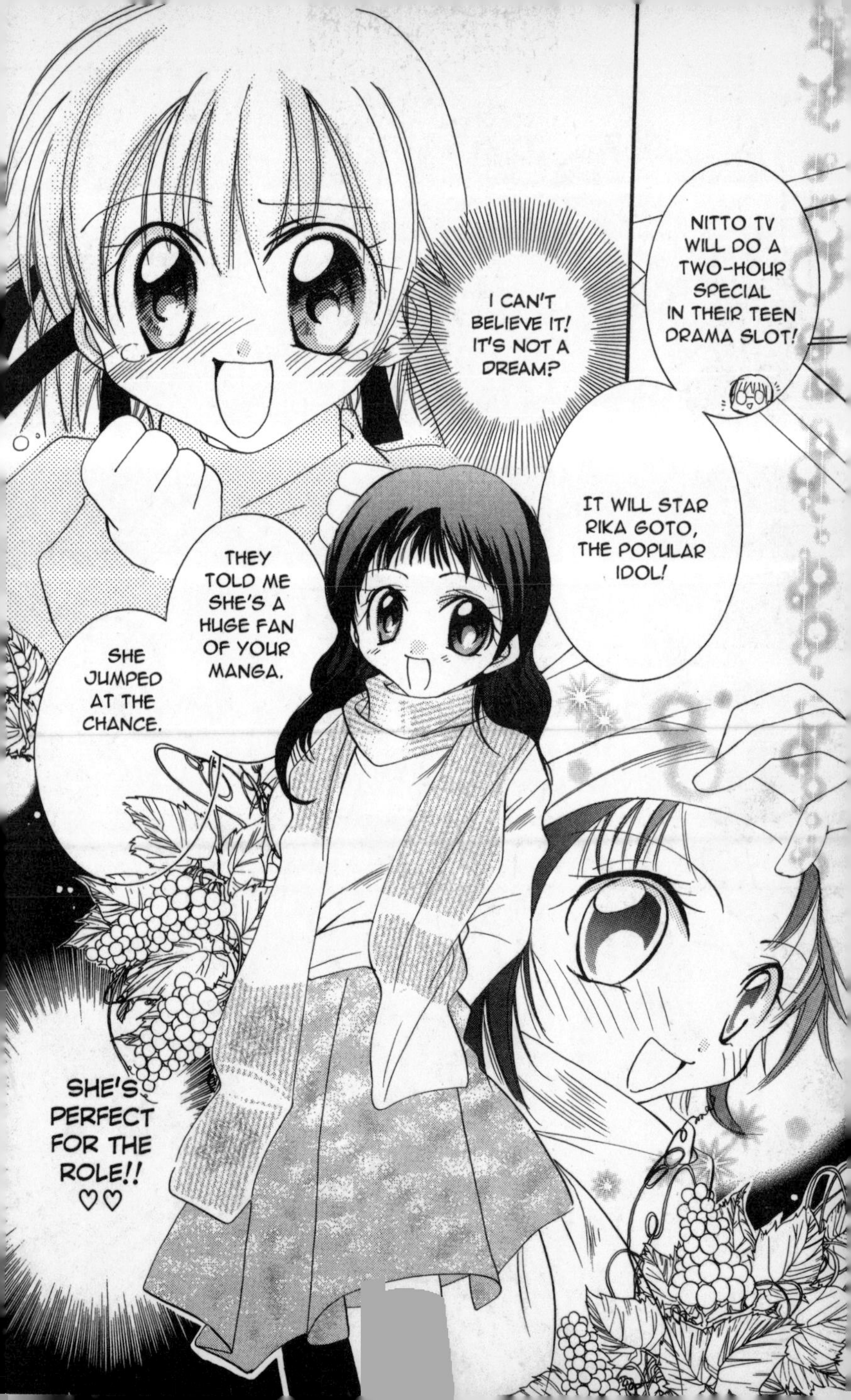
NITTO TV WILL DO A TWO-HOUR SPECIAL IN THEIR TEEN DRAMA SLOT!
IT WILL STAR RIKA GOTO, THE POPULAR IDOL!
I CAN'T BELIEVE IT! IT'S NOT A DREAM?
THEY TOLD ME SHE'S A HUGE FAN OF YOUR MANGA.
SHE JUMPED AT THE CHANCE.
SHE'S PERFECT FOR THE ROLE!! ♡♡

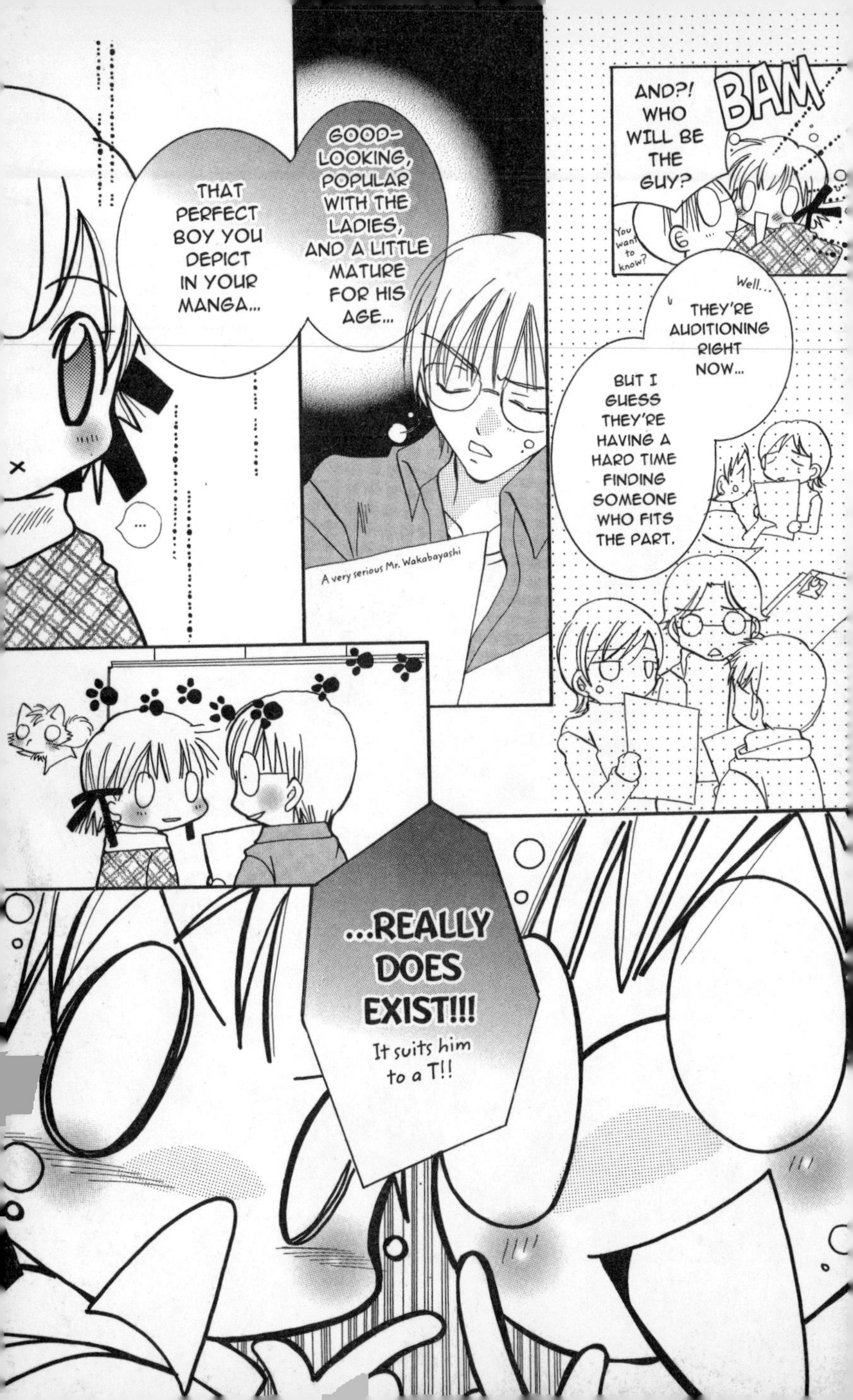
AND?! WHO WILL BE THE GUY?
BAM
You want to know?
Well...
THEY'RE AUDITIONING RIGHT NOW...
BUT I GUESS THEY'RE HAVING A HARD TIME FINDING SOMEONE WHO FITS THE PART.
GOOD-LOOKING, POPULAR WITH THE LADIES, AND A LITTLE MATURE FOR HIS AGE...
A very serious Mr. Wakabayashi
THAT PERFECT BOY YOU DEPICT IN YOUR MANGA...
...
...REALLY DOES EXIST!!!
It suits him to a T!!

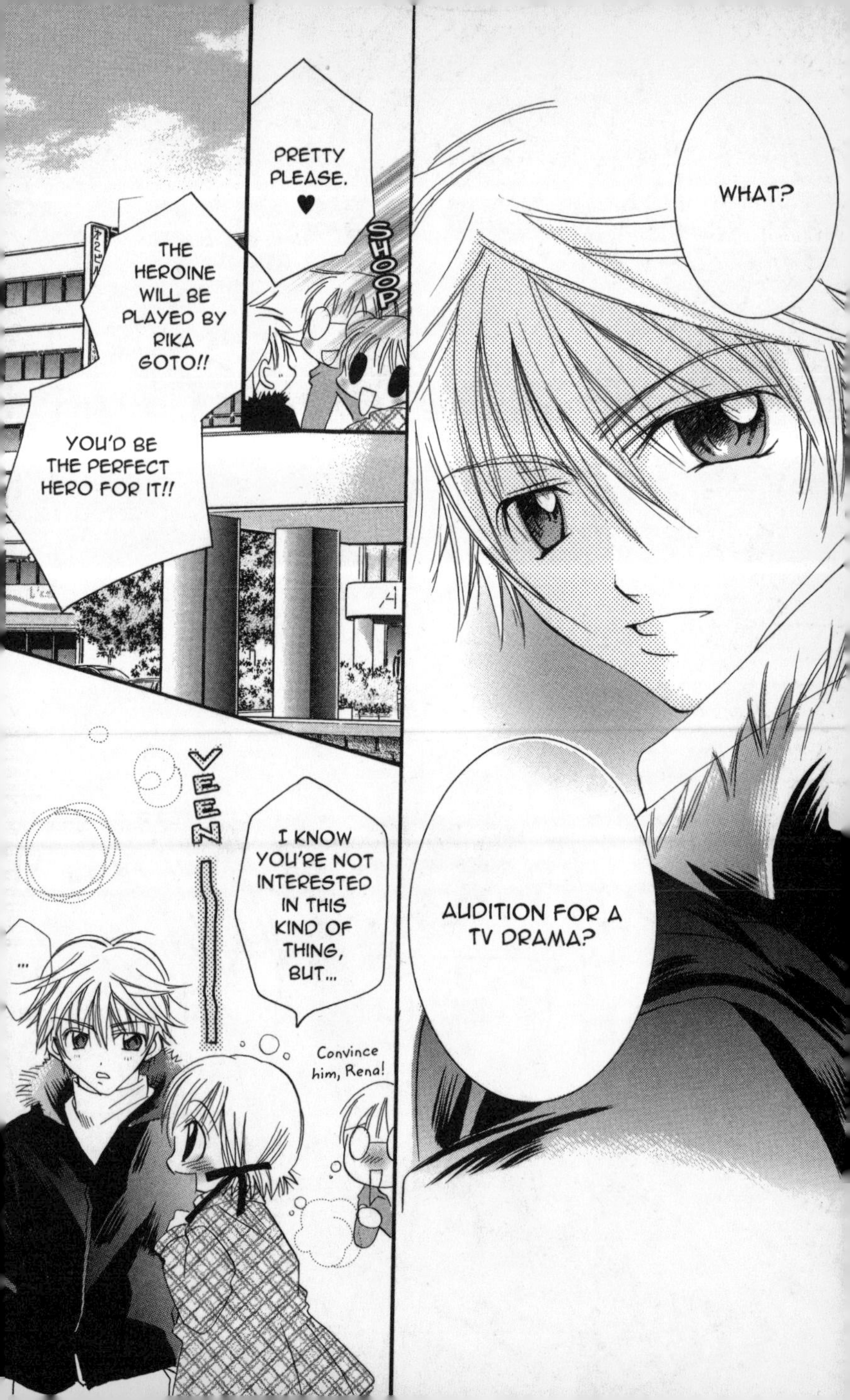
WHAT?
AUDITION FOR A TV DRAMA?
PRETTY PLEASE. ♥
SHOOP
THE HEROINE WILL BE PLAYED BY RIKA GOTO!!
YOU'D BE THE PERFECT HERO FOR IT!!
VEEN
I KNOW YOU'RE NOT INTERESTED IN THIS KIND OF THING, BUT...
Convince him, Rena!
...

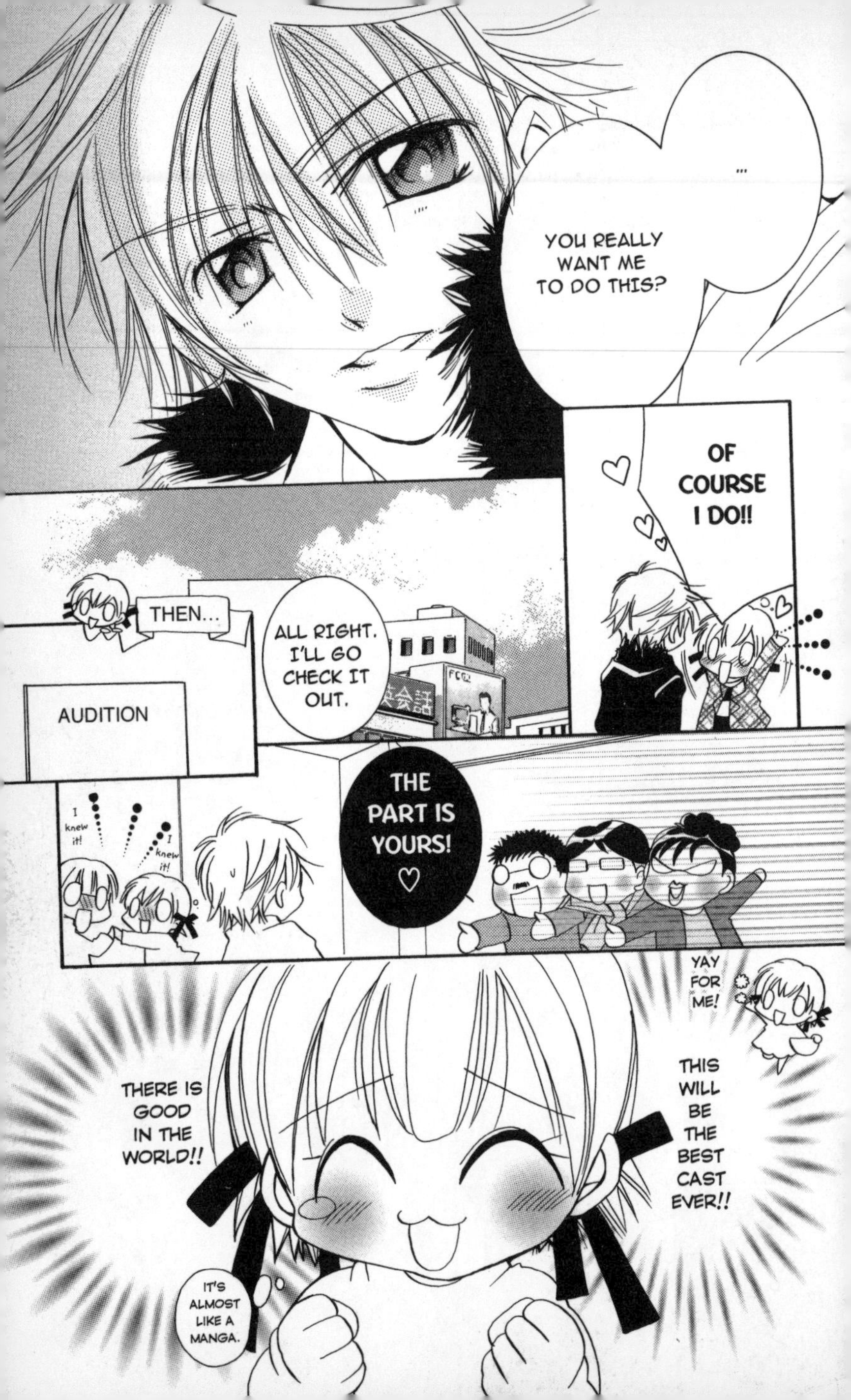
...
YOU REALLY WANT ME TO DO THIS?
OF COURSE I DO!!
ALL RIGHT. I'LL GO CHECK IT OUT.
THEN...
AUDITION
THE PART IS YOURS! ♡
I knew it!
I knew it!
YAY FOR ME!
THIS WILL BE THE BEST CAST EVER!!
THERE IS GOOD IN THE WORLD!!
IT'S ALMOST LIKE A MANGA.

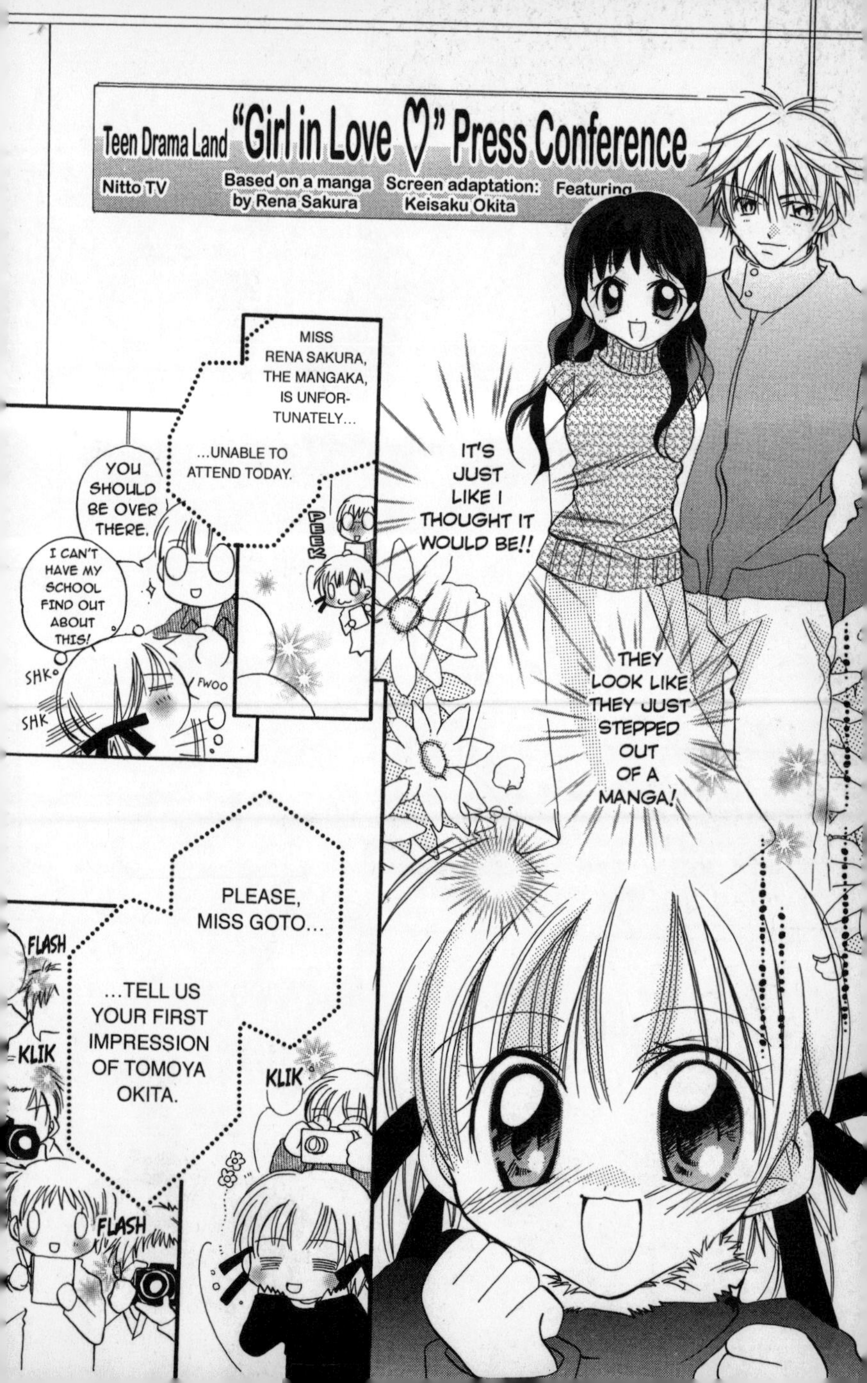
Teen Drama Land "Girl in Love ♡" Press Conference
Nitto TV
Based on a manga by Rena Sakura
Screen adaptation: Keisaku Okita
Featuring
IT'S JUST LIKE I THOUGHT IT WOULD BE!!
THEY LOOK LIKE THEY JUST STEPPED OUT OF A MANGA!
MISS RENA SAKURA, THE MANGAKA, IS UNFORTUNATELY…
…UNABLE TO ATTEND TODAY.
PEEK
YOU SHOULD BE OVER THERE.
I CAN'T HAVE MY SCHOOL FIND OUT ABOUT THIS!
SHK
SHK
FWOO
PLEASE, MISS GOTO…
…TELL US YOUR FIRST IMPRESSION OF TOMOYA OKITA.
FLASH
KLIK
KLIK
FLASH

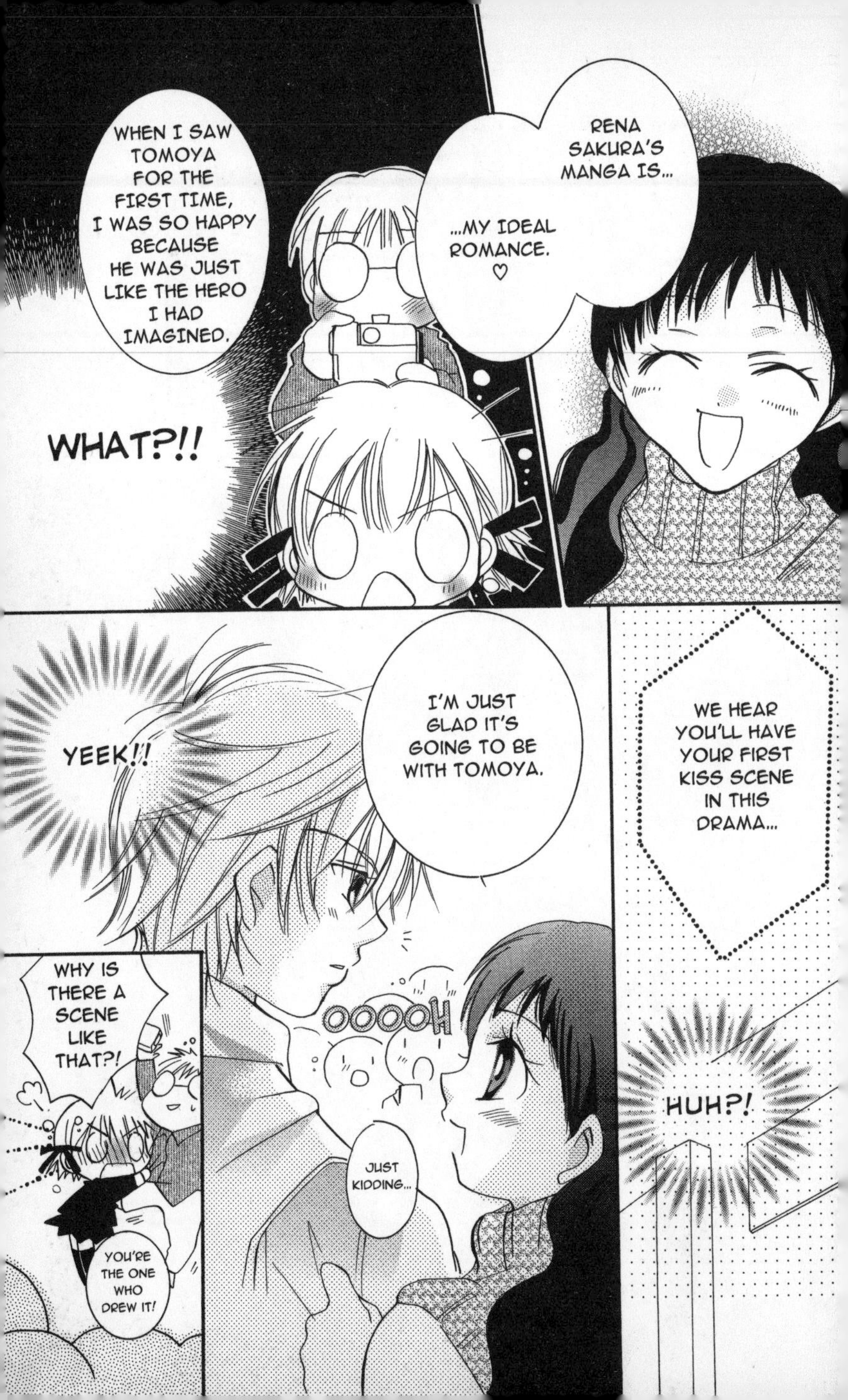
RENA SAKURA'S MANGA IS...
...MY IDEAL ROMANCE. ♡
WHEN I SAW TOMOYA FOR THE FIRST TIME, I WAS SO HAPPY BECAUSE HE WAS JUST LIKE THE HERO I HAD IMAGINED.
WHAT?!!
WE HEAR YOU'LL HAVE YOUR FIRST KISS SCENE IN THIS DRAMA...
HUH?!
I'M JUST GLAD IT'S GOING TO BE WITH TOMOYA.
YEEK!!
OOOOH
JUST KIDDING...
WHY IS THERE A SCENE LIKE THAT?!
YOU'RE THE ONE WHO DREW IT!

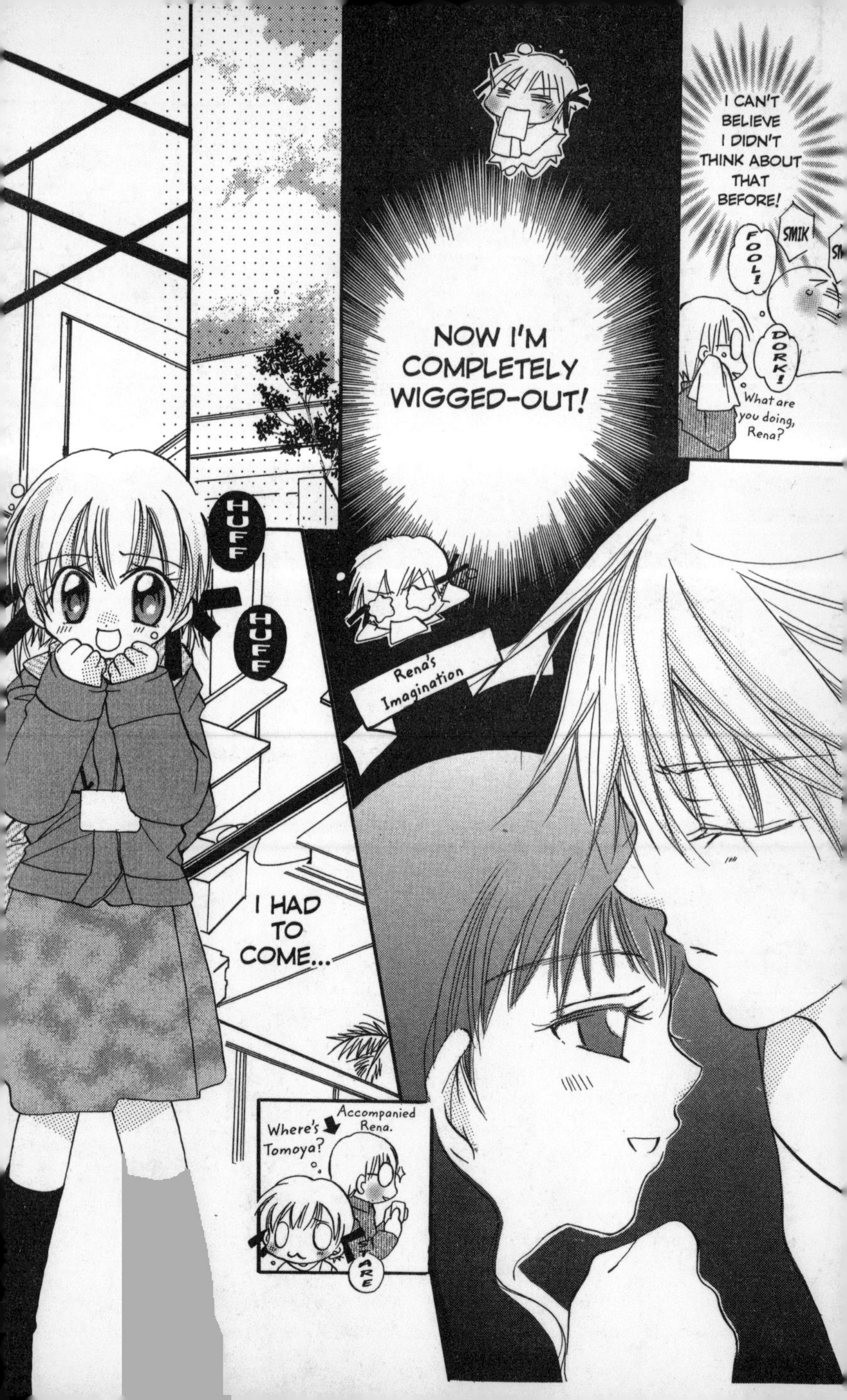
I CAN'T BELIEVE I DIDN'T THINK ABOUT THAT BEFORE!
SMIK
FOOL!
DORK!
What are you doing, Rena?
NOW I'M COMPLETELY WIGGED-OUT!
Rena's Imagination
HUFF
HUFF
I HAD TO COME...
Accompanied Rena.
Where's Tomoya?
STARE

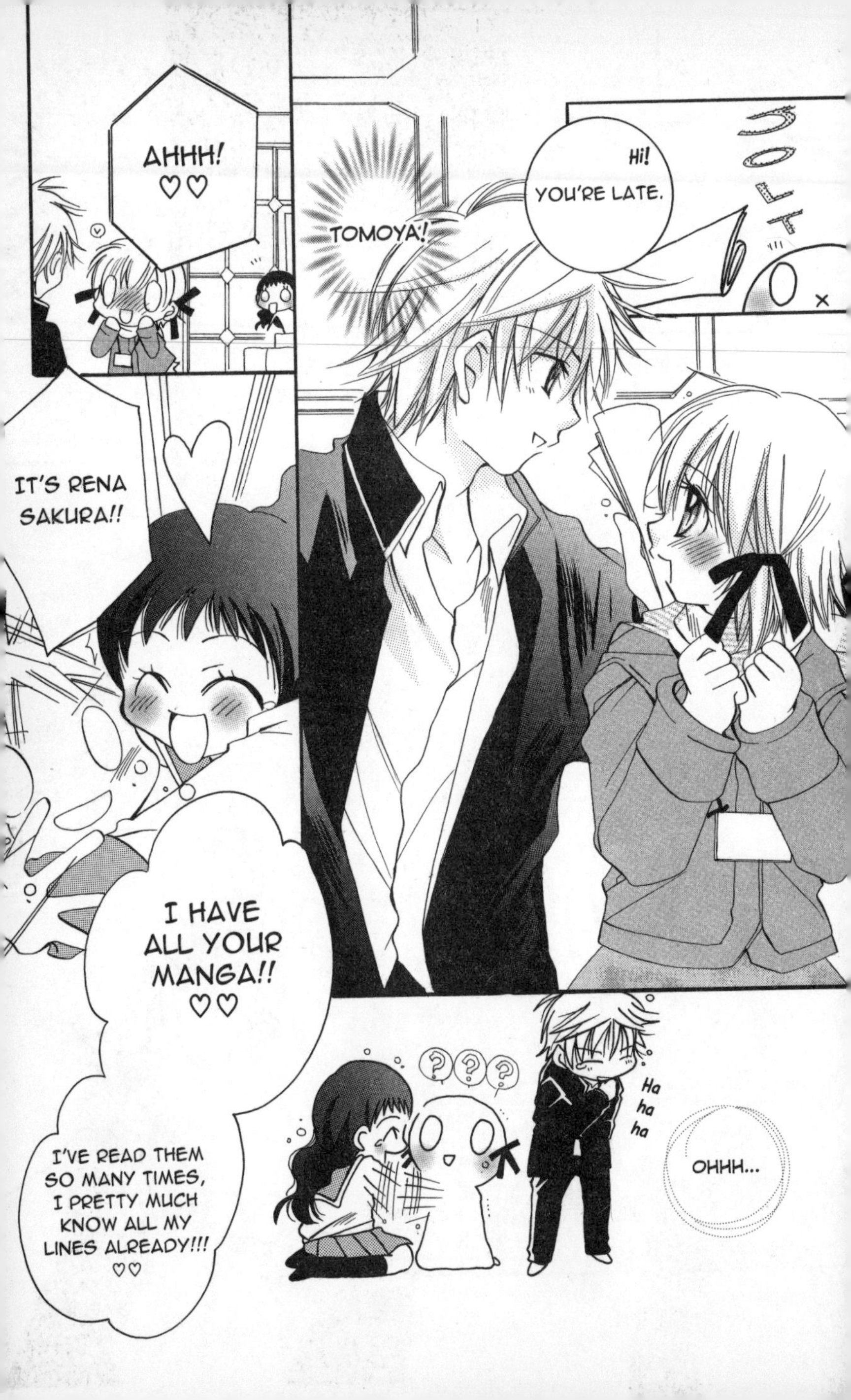
Hi! YOU'RE LATE.
TOMOYA!
AHHH! ♡♡
IT'S RENA SAKURA!!
I HAVE ALL YOUR MANGA!! ♡♡
I'VE READ THEM SO MANY TIMES, I PRETTY MUCH KNOW ALL MY LINES ALREADY!!! ♡♡
OHHH...
Ha ha ha
???

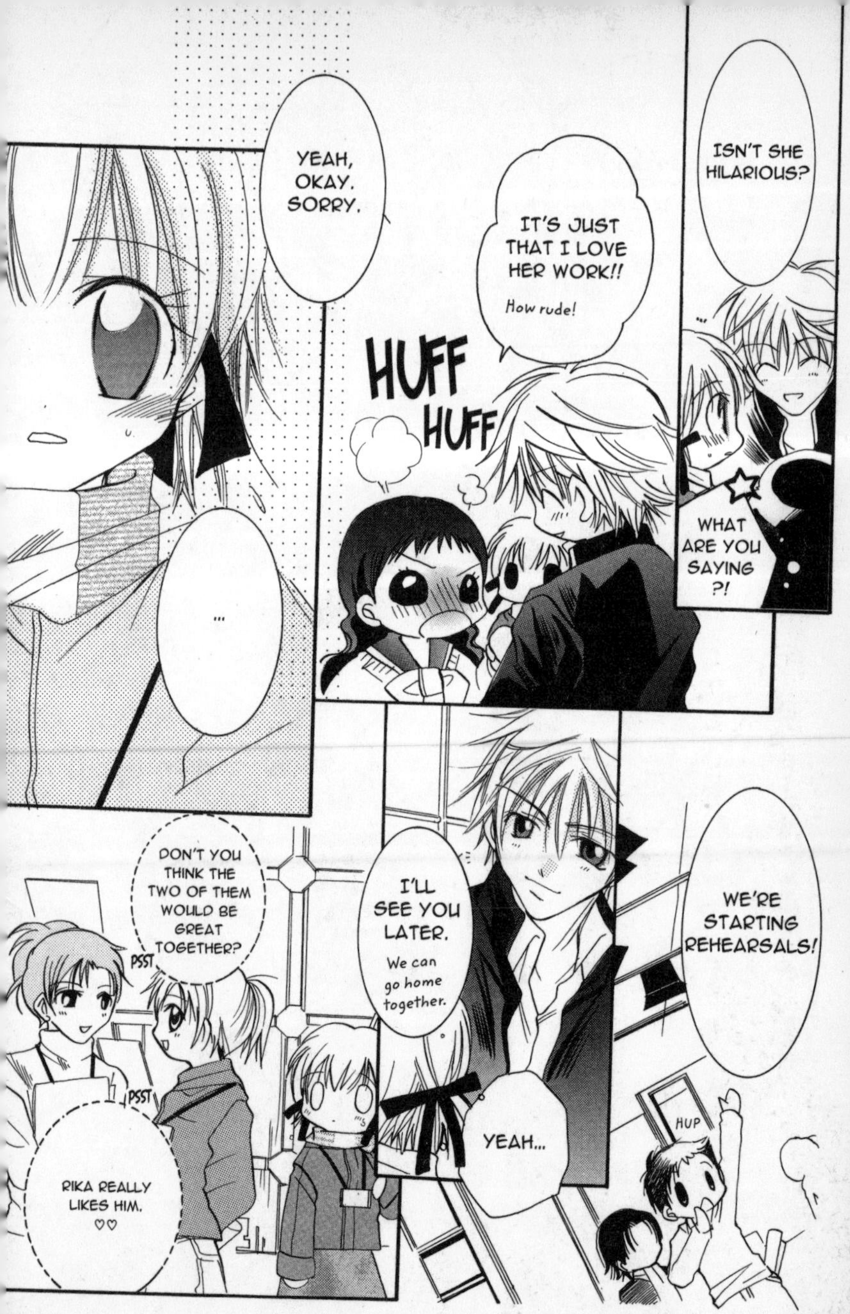

ISN'T SHE HILARIOUS?
...
WHAT ARE YOU SAYING ?!
IT'S JUST THAT I LOVE HER WORK!!
How rude!
HUFF HUFF
YEAH, OKAY. SORRY.
...
WE'RE STARTING REHEARSALS!
HUP
I'LL SEE YOU LATER.
We can go home together.
YEAH...
PSST
DON'T YOU THINK THE TWO OF THEM WOULD BE GREAT TOGETHER?
PSST
RIKA REALLY LIKES HIM. ♡♡

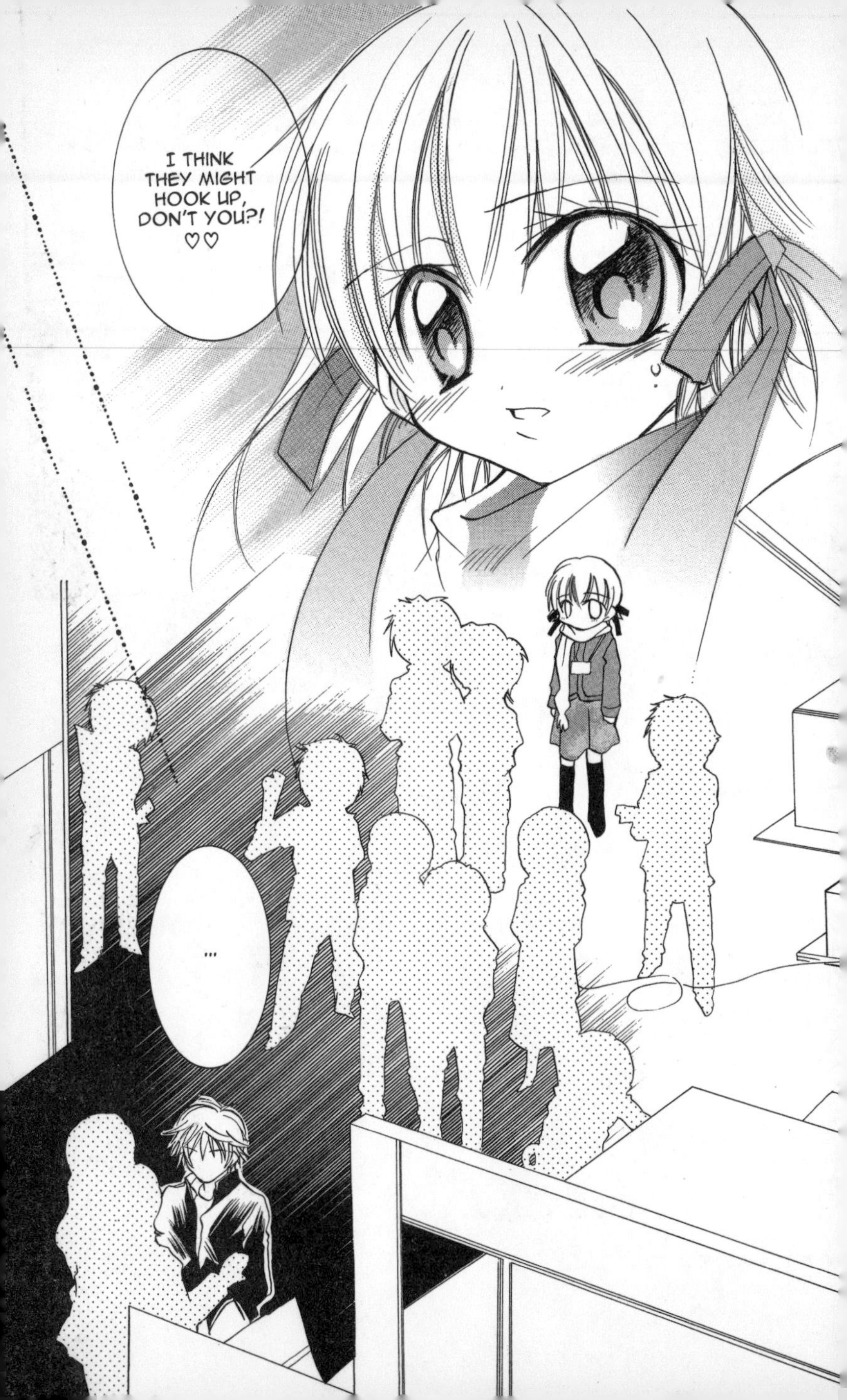
I THINK THEY MIGHT HOOK UP, DON'T YOU?! ♡♡
...

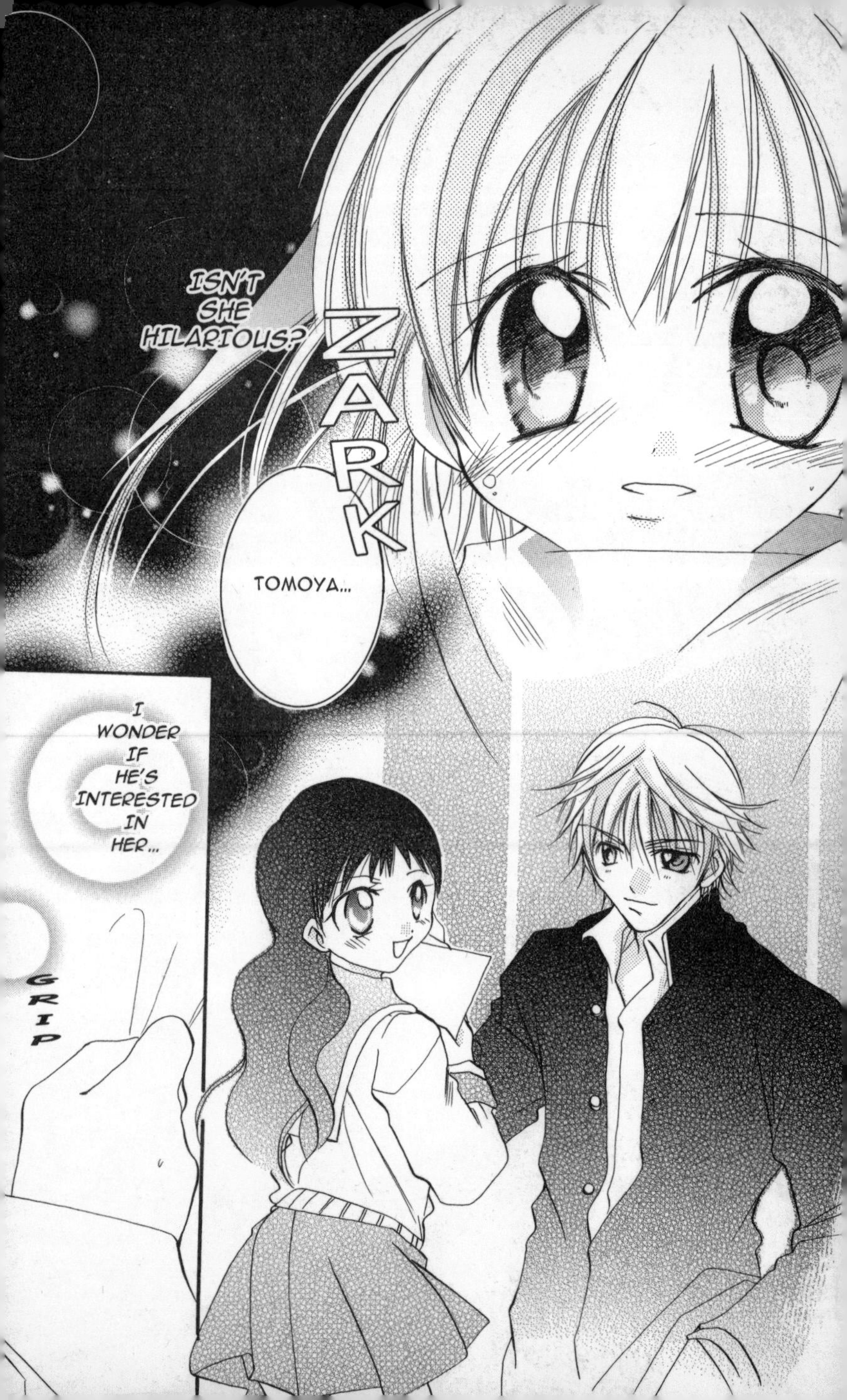
ISN'T SHE HILARIOUS?
ZARK
TOMOYA...
I WONDER IF HE'S INTERESTED IN HER...
GRIP

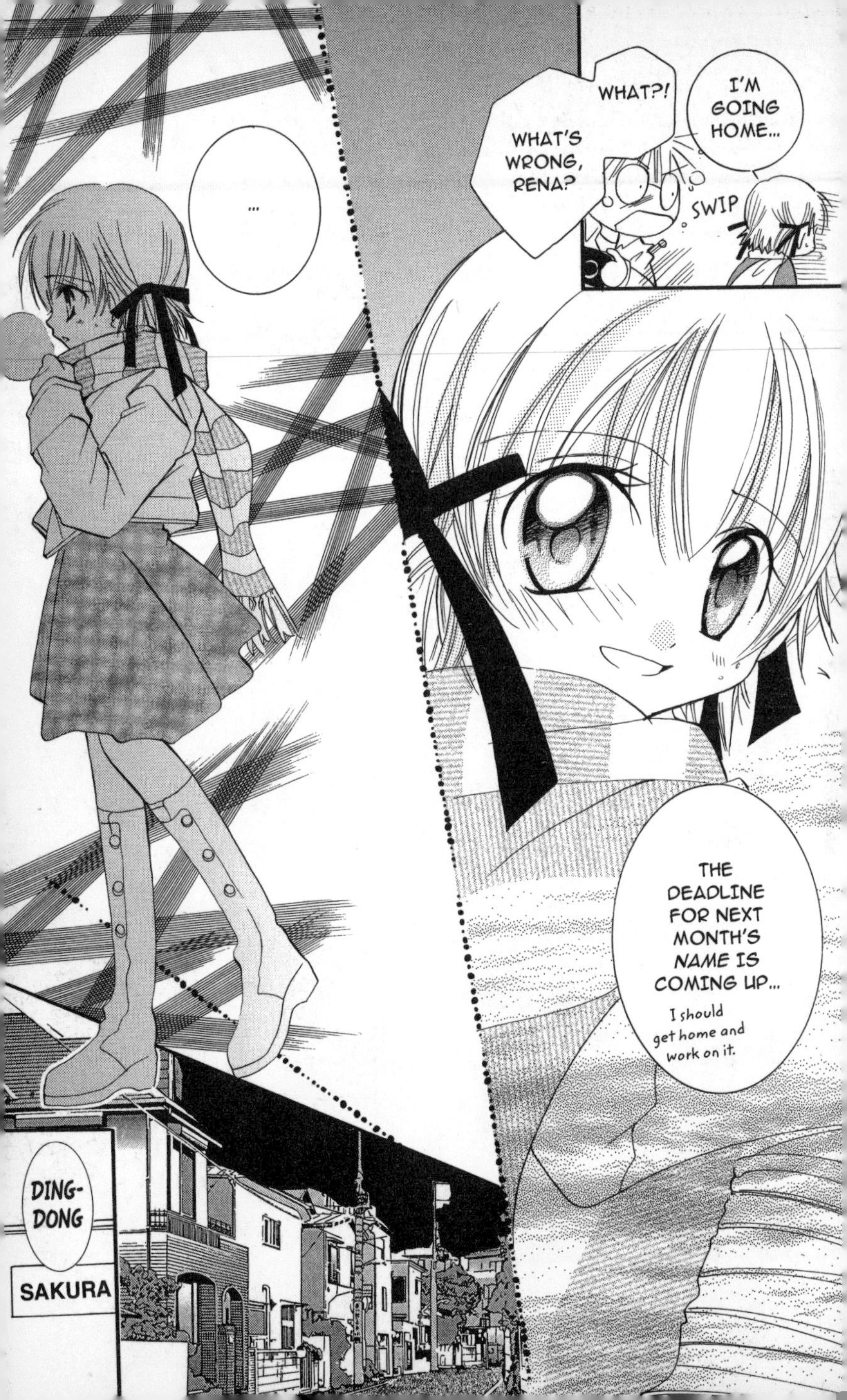
I'M GOING HOME...
WHAT?!
SWIP
WHAT'S WRONG, RENA?
THE DEADLINE FOR NEXT MONTH'S *NAME* IS COMING UP...
I should get home and work on it.
...
DING-DONG
SAKURA

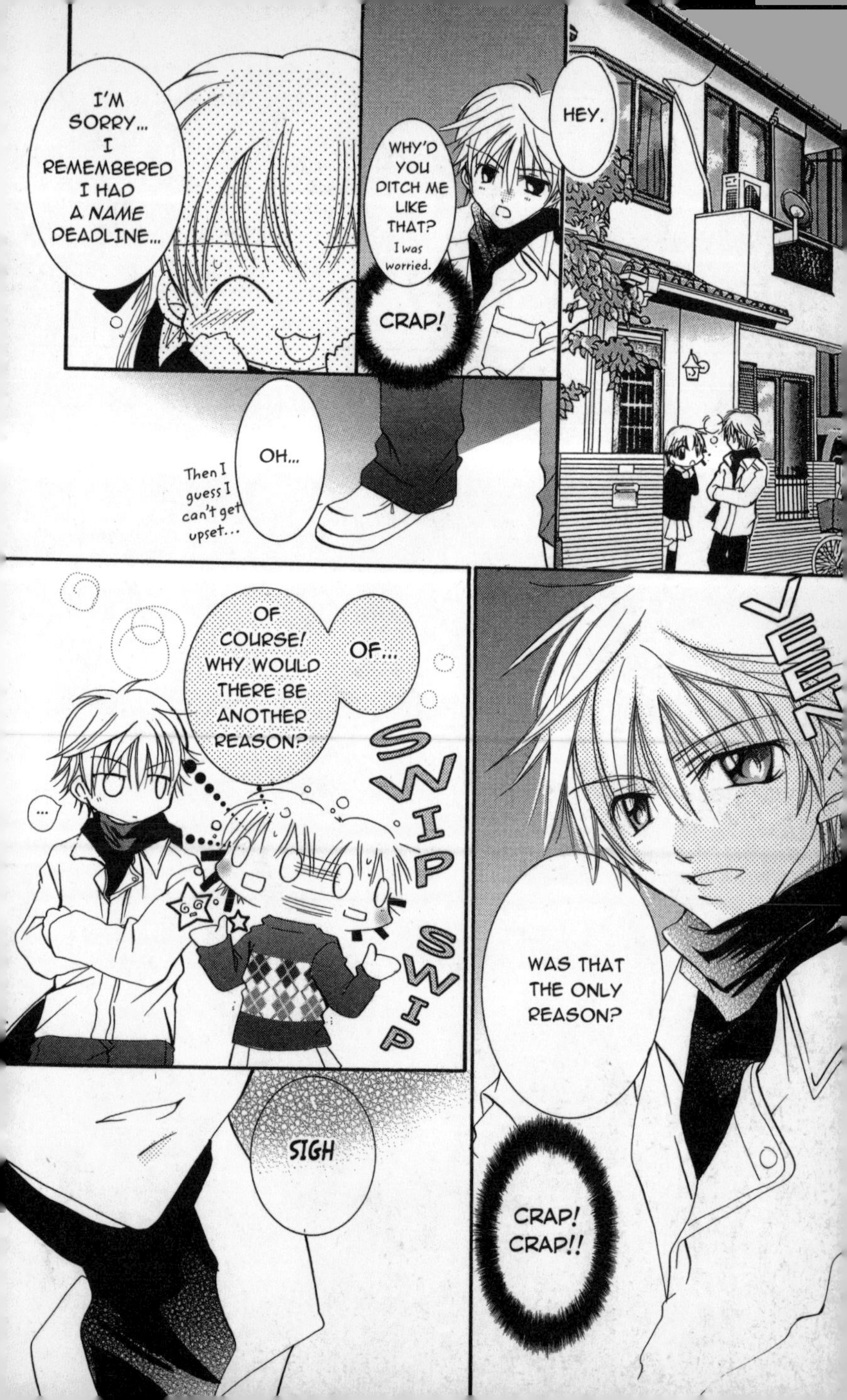
HEY.
WHY'D YOU DITCH ME LIKE THAT? I was worried.
CRAP!
I'M SORRY... I REMEMBERED I HAD A *NAME* DEADLINE...
OH...
Then I guess I can't get upset...
YEEK
WAS THAT THE ONLY REASON?
CRAP! CRAP!!
OF COURSE! WHY WOULD THERE BE ANOTHER REASON?
OF...
SWIP SWIP
...
SIGH

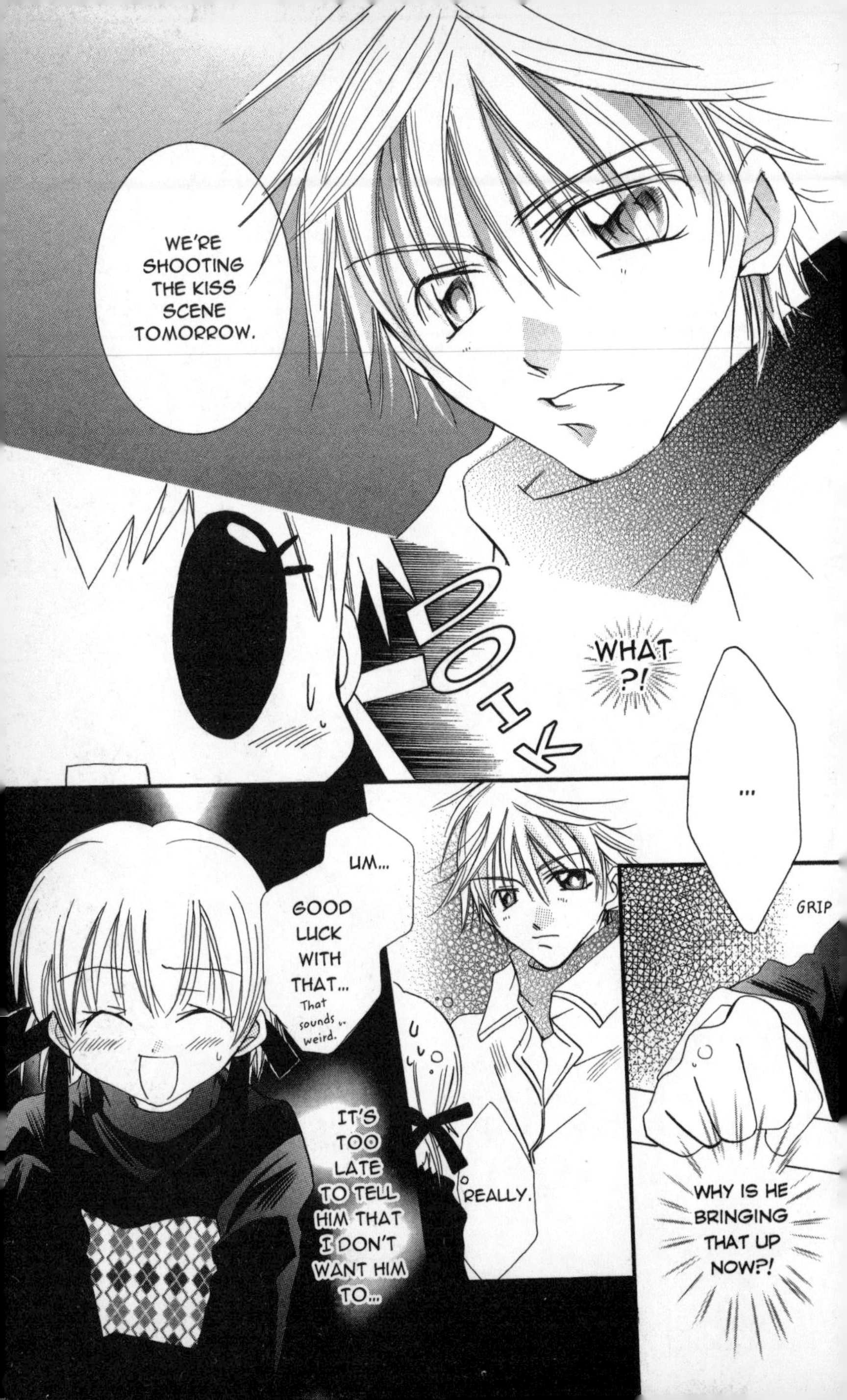
WE'RE SHOOTING THE KISS SCENE TOMORROW.
WHAT?!
DOIK
...
GRIP
WHY IS HE BRINGING THAT UP NOW?!
UM...
GOOD LUCK WITH THAT...
That sounds weird.
REALLY.
IT'S TOO LATE TO TELL HIM THAT I DON'T WANT HIM TO...

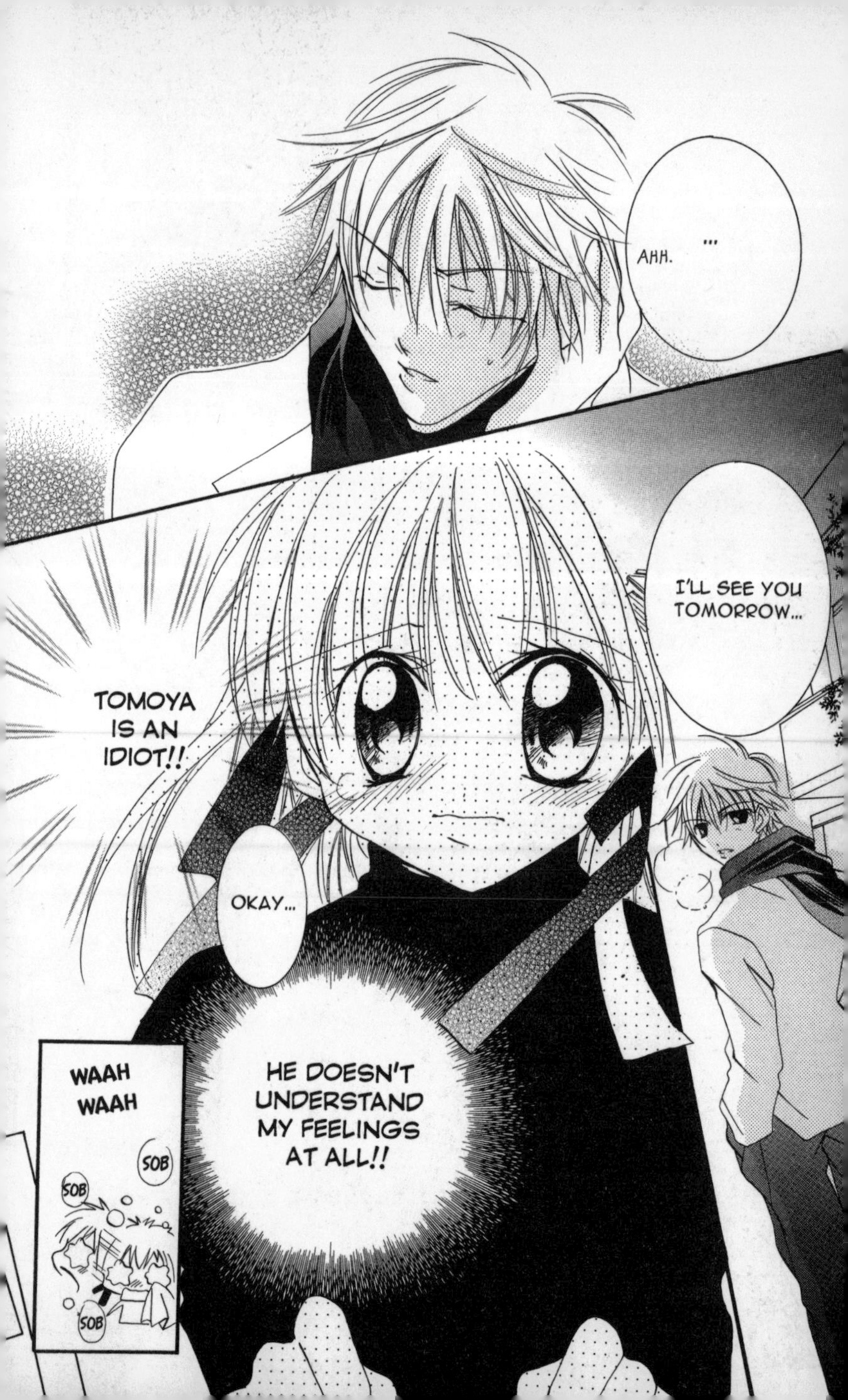
AHH. ...
I'LL SEE YOU TOMORROW...
TOMOYA IS AN IDIOT!!
OKAY...
HE DOESN'T UNDERSTAND MY FEELINGS AT ALL!!
WAAH WAAH
SOB
SOB
SOB

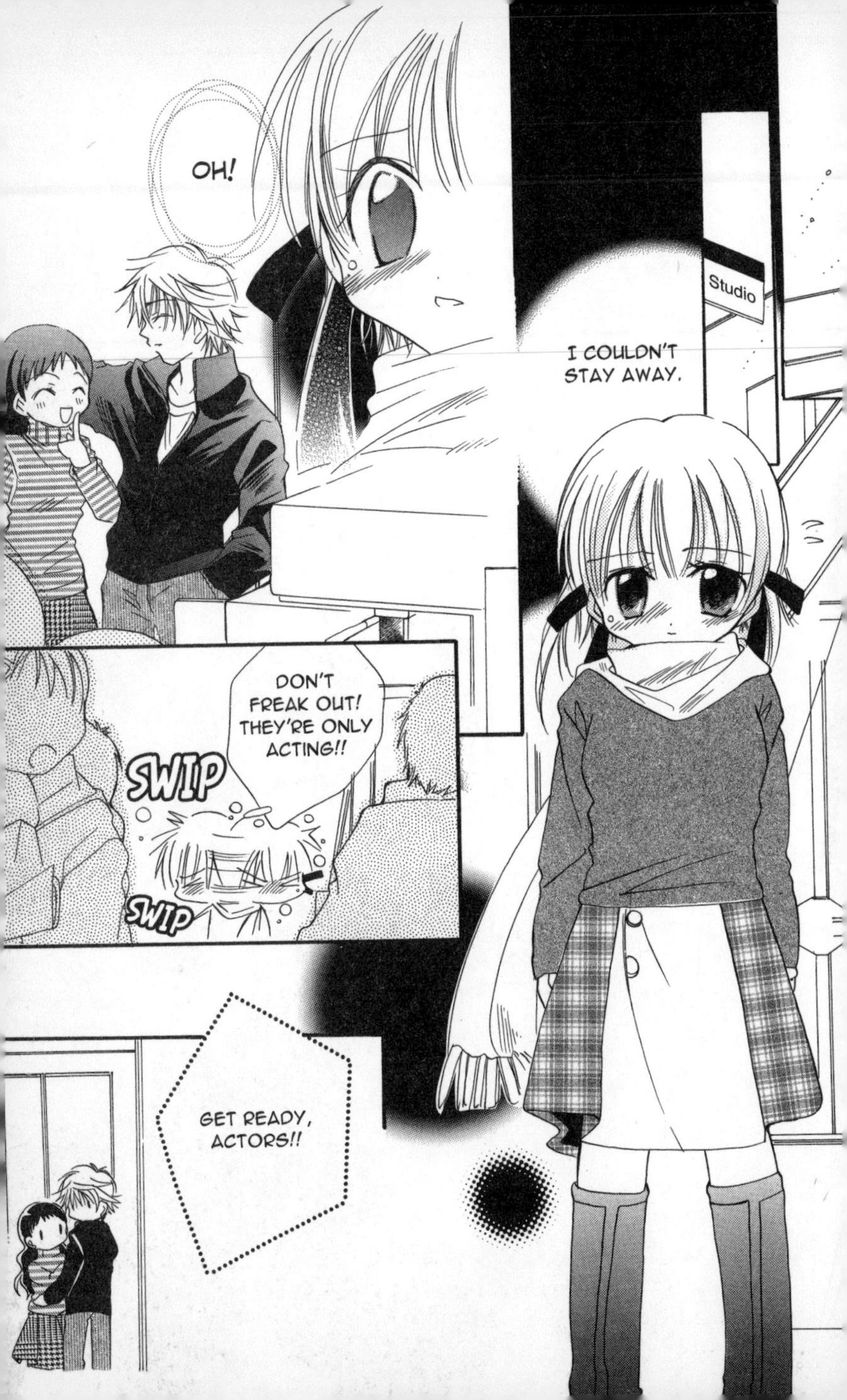
Studio
I COULDN'T STAY AWAY.
OH!
DON'T FREAK OUT! THEY'RE ONLY ACTING!!
SWIP
SWIP
GET READY, ACTORS!!

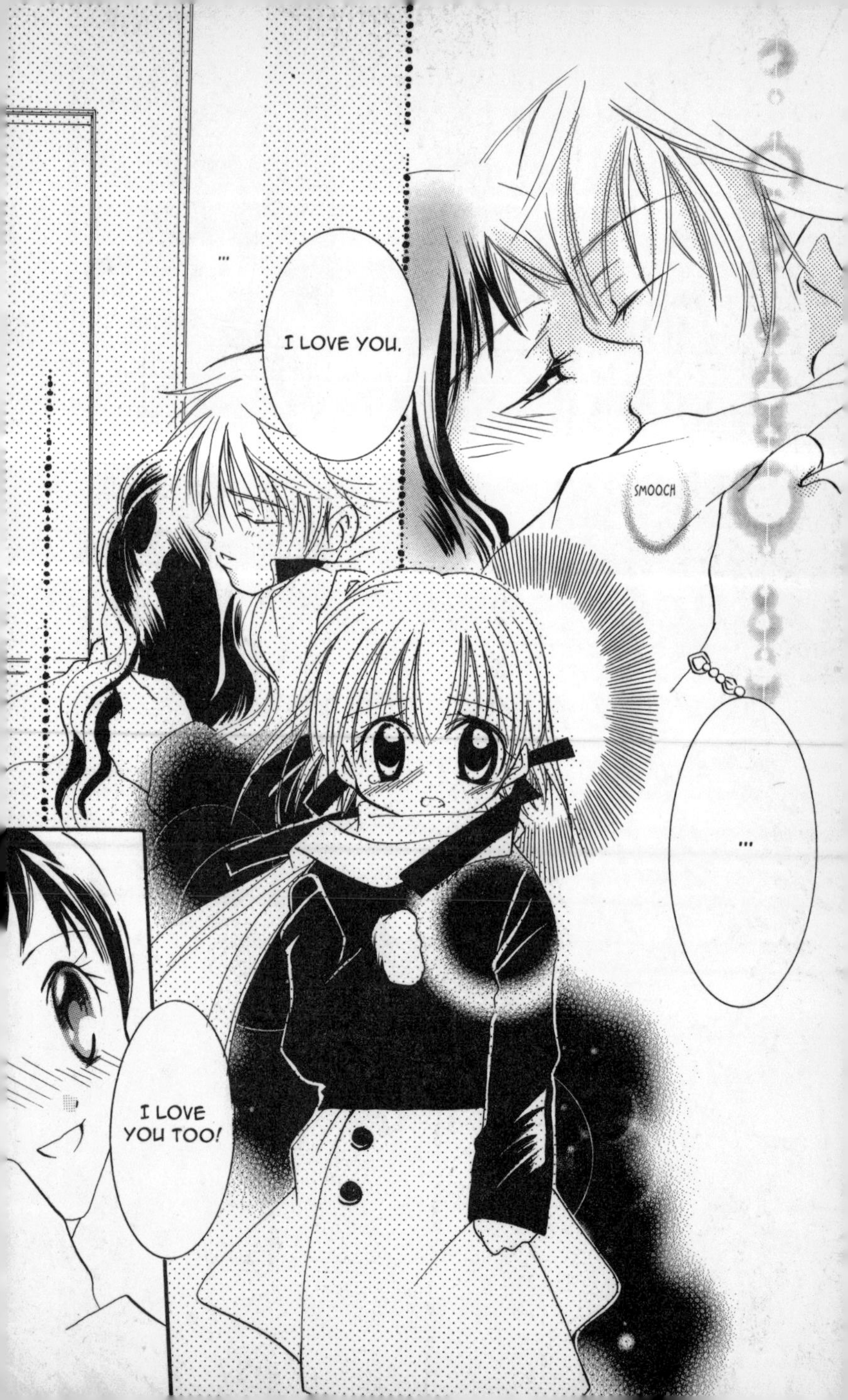
I LOVE YOU.
SMOOCH
...
...
I LOVE YOU TOO!

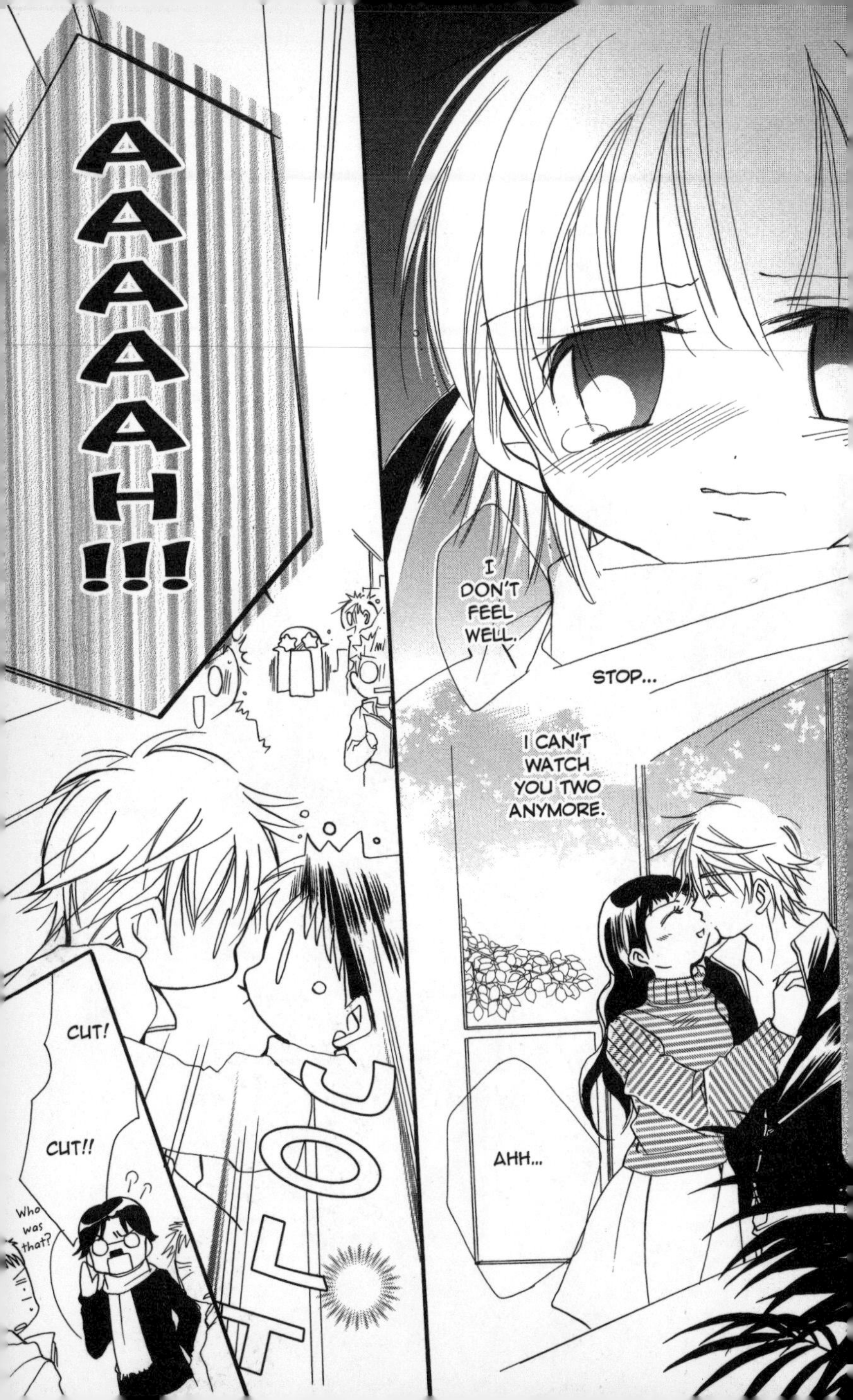
STOP...
I DON'T FEEL WELL.
I CAN'T WATCH YOU TWO ANYMORE.
AHH...
AAAAAH!!!
JOLT
CUT!
CUT!!
Who was that?

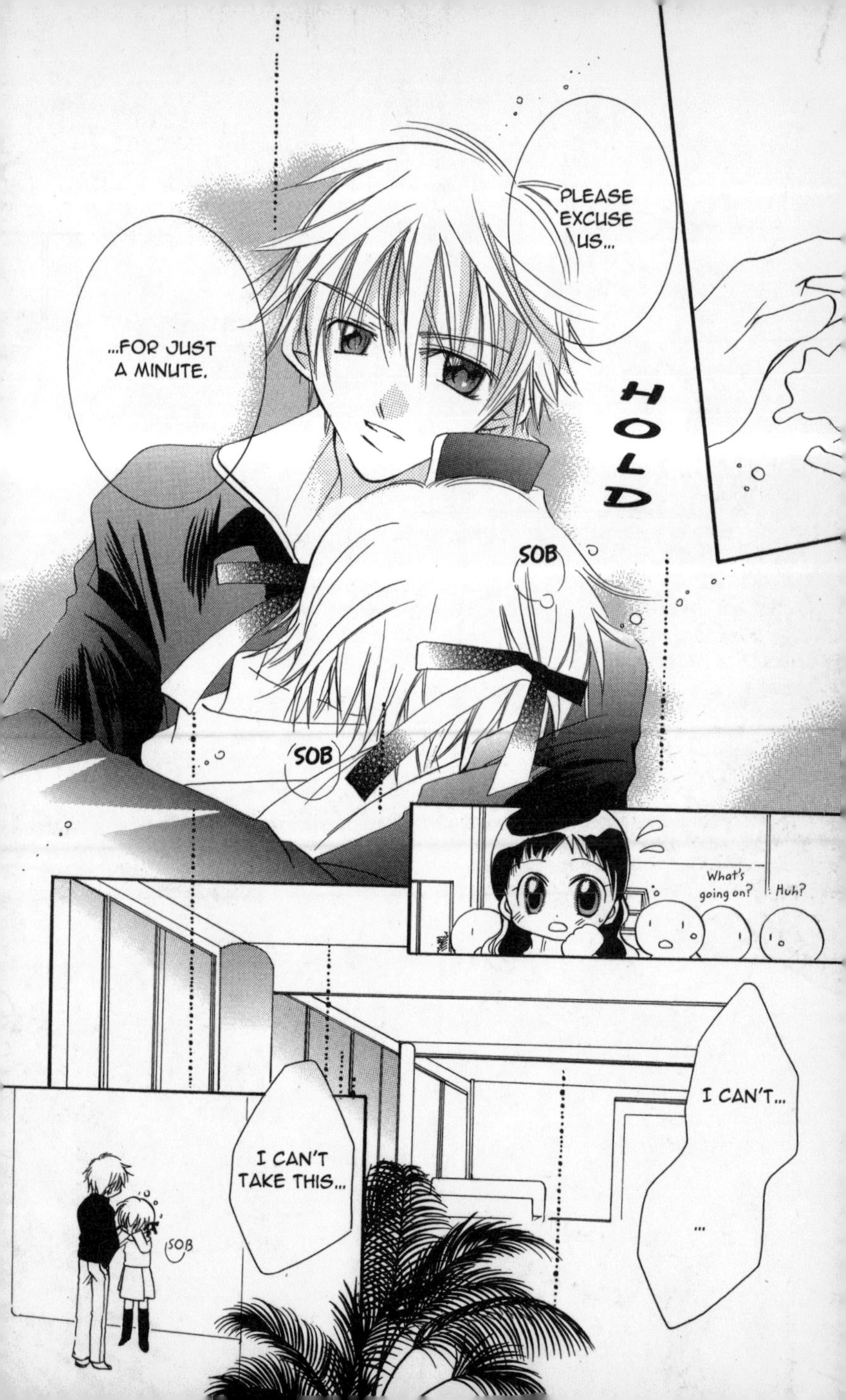
PLEASE EXCUSE US...
HOLD
...FOR JUST A MINUTE.
SOB
SOB
Huh?
What's going on?
I CAN'T...
...
I CAN'T TAKE THIS...
SOB

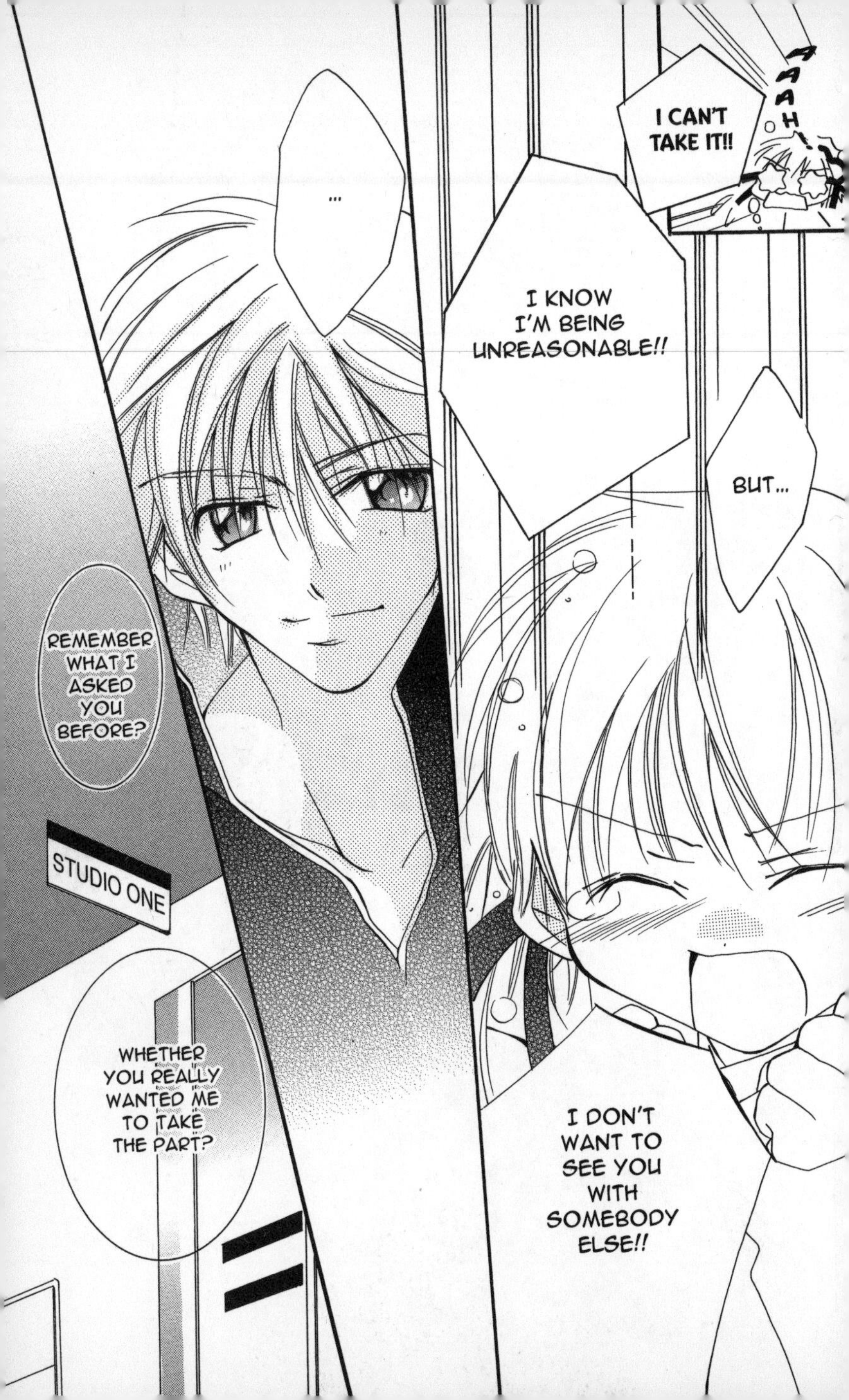

AAAH!!
I CAN'T TAKE IT!!
I KNOW I'M BEING UNREASONABLE!!
BUT...
I DON'T WANT TO SEE YOU WITH SOMEBODY ELSE!!
...
REMEMBER WHAT I ASKED YOU BEFORE?
STUDIO ONE
WHETHER YOU REALLY WANTED ME TO TAKE THE PART?

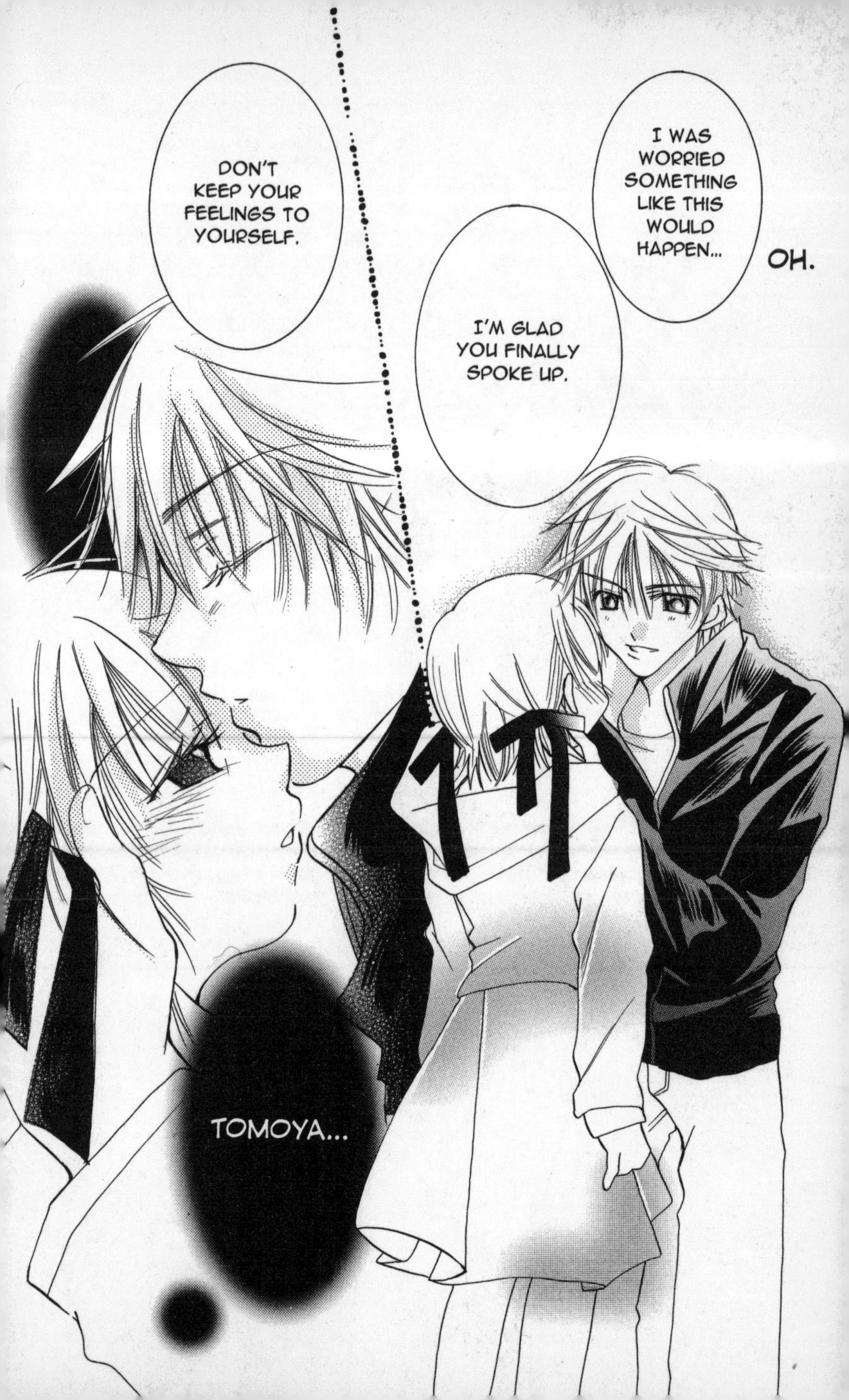
OH.
I WAS WORRIED SOMETHING LIKE THIS WOULD HAPPEN...
I'M GLAD YOU FINALLY SPOKE UP.
DON'T KEEP YOUR FEELINGS TO YOURSELF.
TOMOYA...

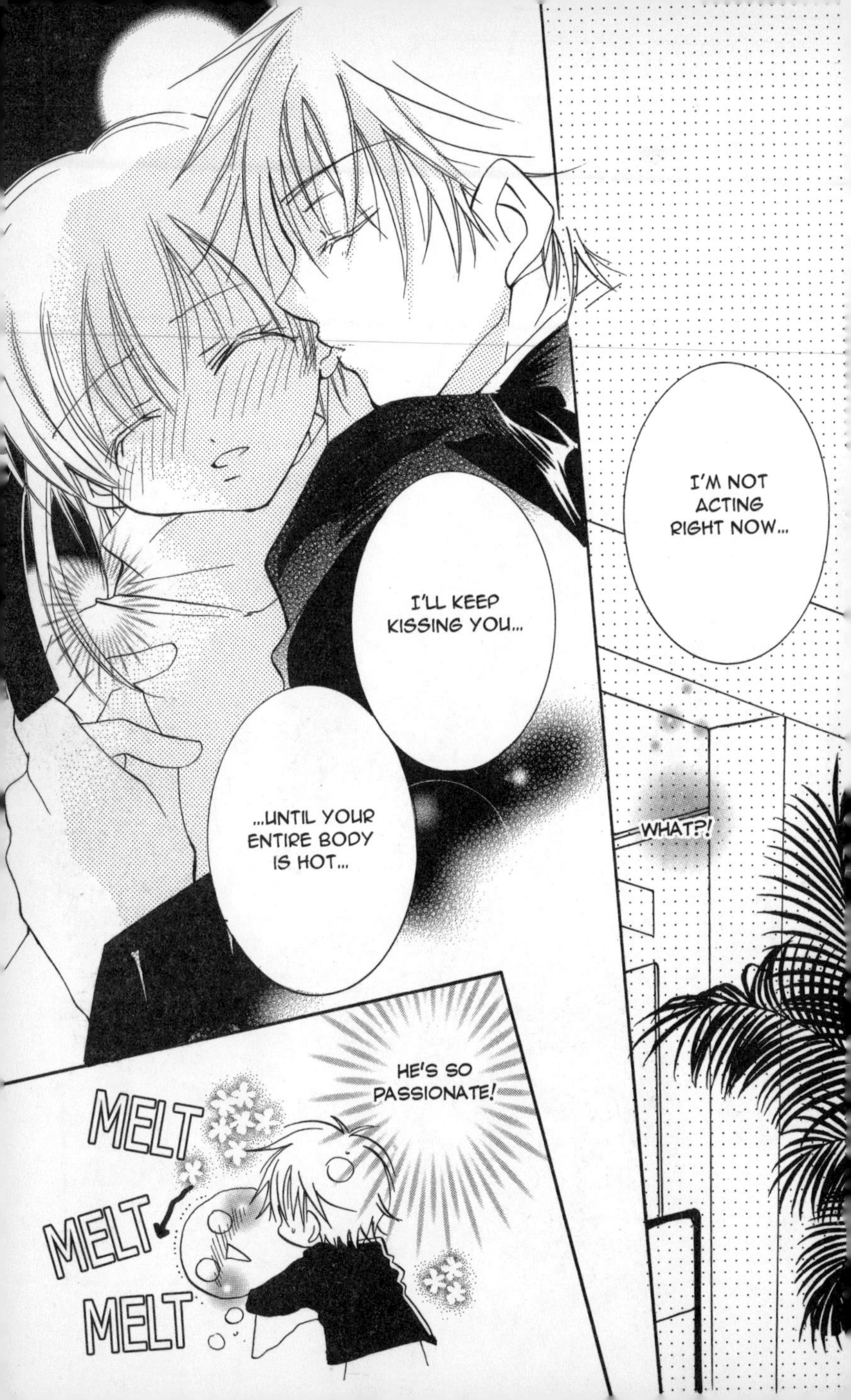
I'M NOT ACTING RIGHT NOW...
WHAT?!
I'LL KEEP KISSING YOU...
...UNTIL YOUR ENTIRE BODY IS HOT...
HE'S SO PASSIONATE!
MELT
MELT
MELT

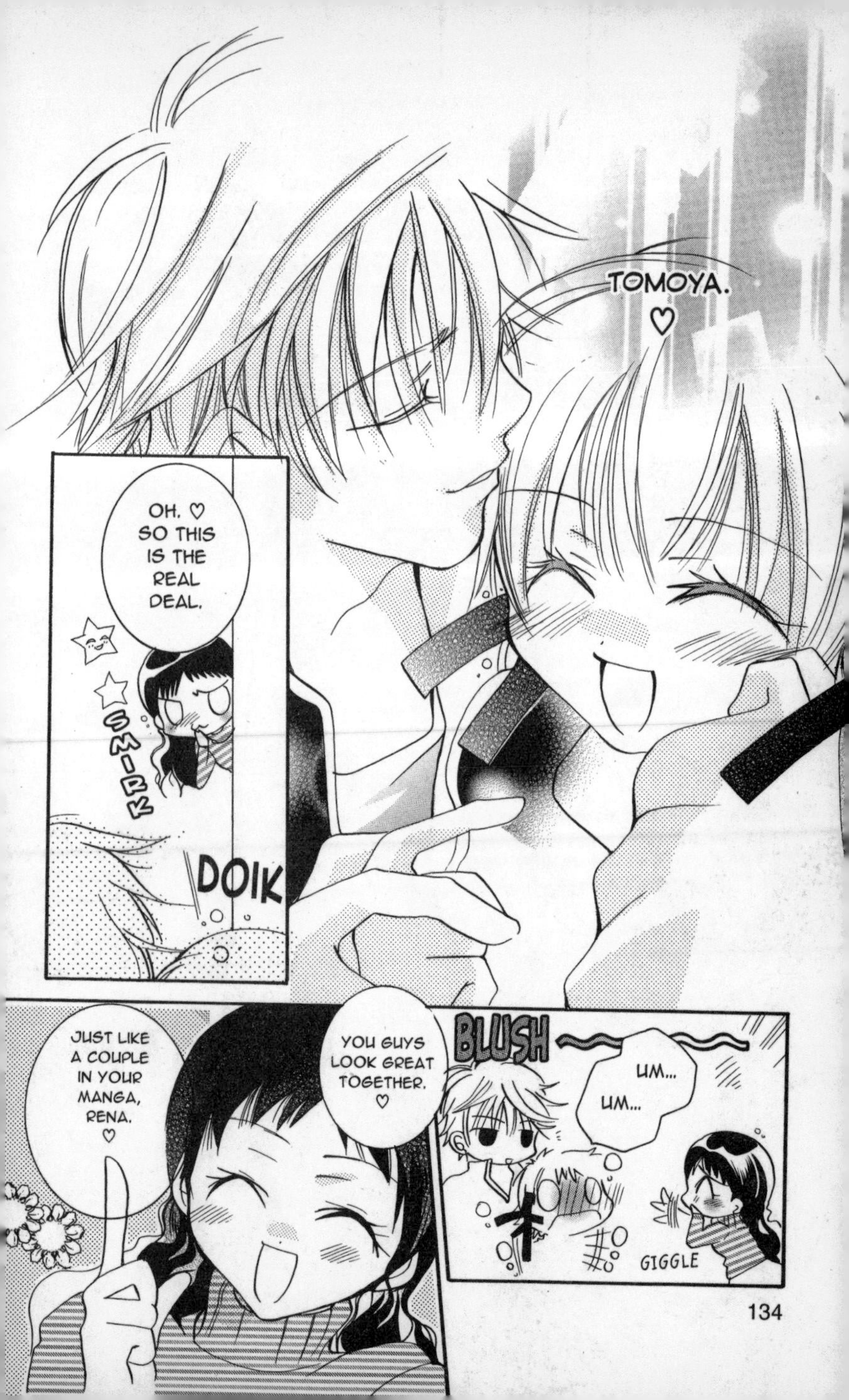
TOMOYA. ♡
OH. ♡ SO THIS IS THE REAL DEAL.
SMIRK
DOIK
BLUSH
UM... UM...
GIGGLE
YOU GUYS LOOK GREAT TOGETHER. ♡
JUST LIKE A COUPLE IN YOUR MANGA, RENA. ♡

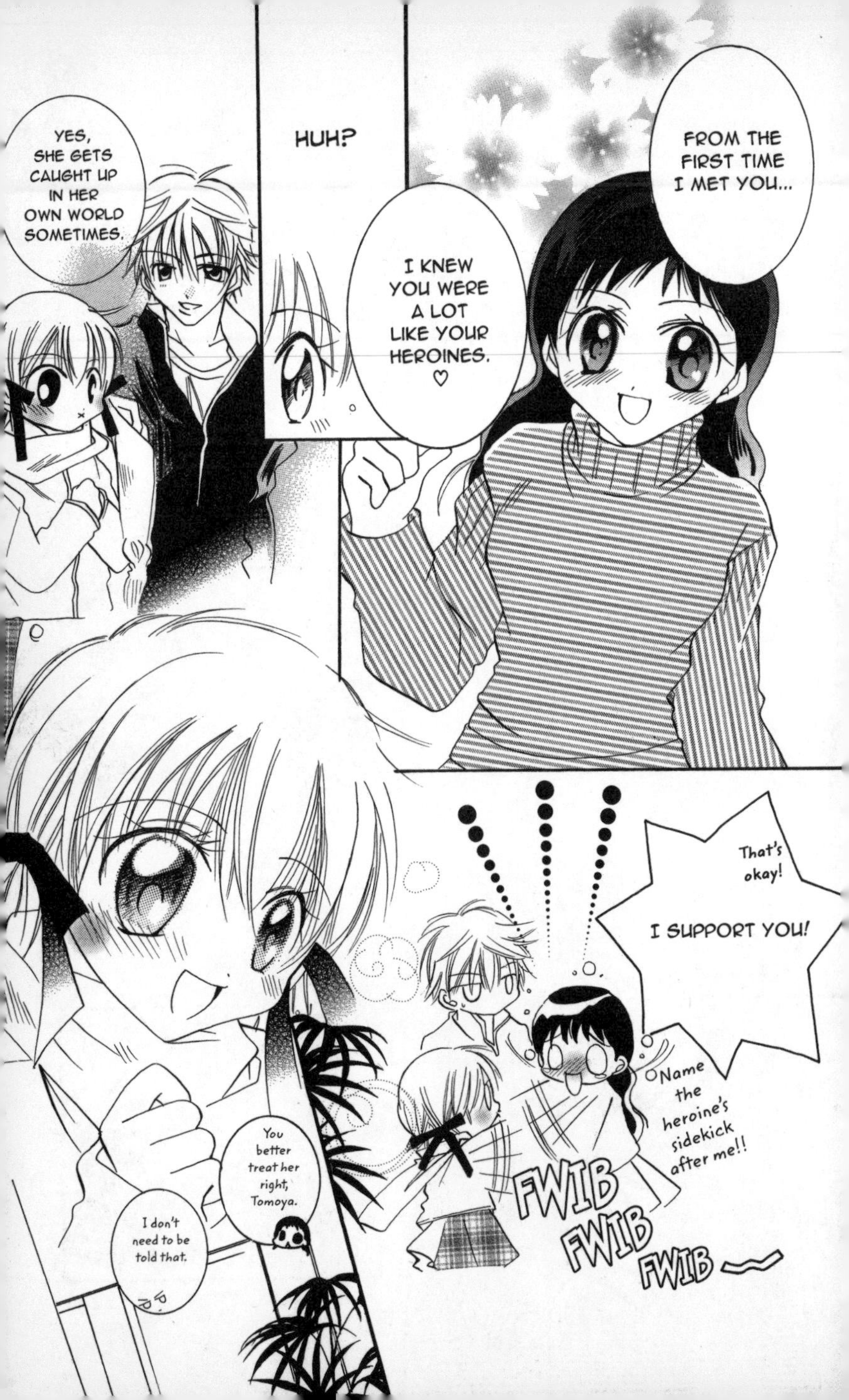
FROM THE FIRST TIME I MET YOU...
I KNEW YOU WERE A LOT LIKE YOUR HEROINES. ♡
HUH?
YES, SHE GETS CAUGHT UP IN HER OWN WORLD SOMETIMES.
That's okay!
I SUPPORT YOU!
Name the heroine's sidekick after me!!
FWIB FWIB FWIB
You better treat her right, Tomoya.
I don't need to be told that.

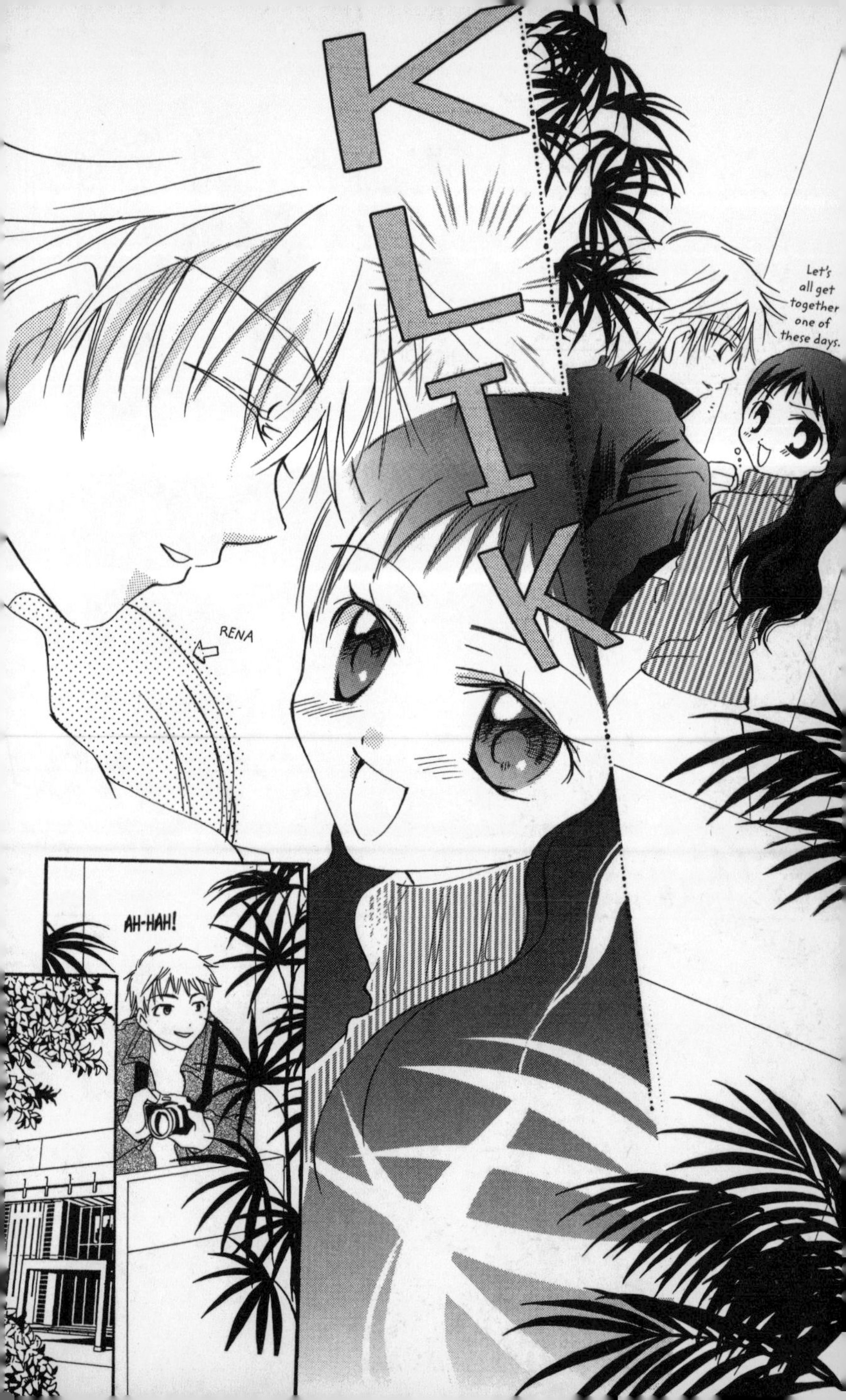
Let's all get together one of these days.
KLIK
RENA
AH-HAH!

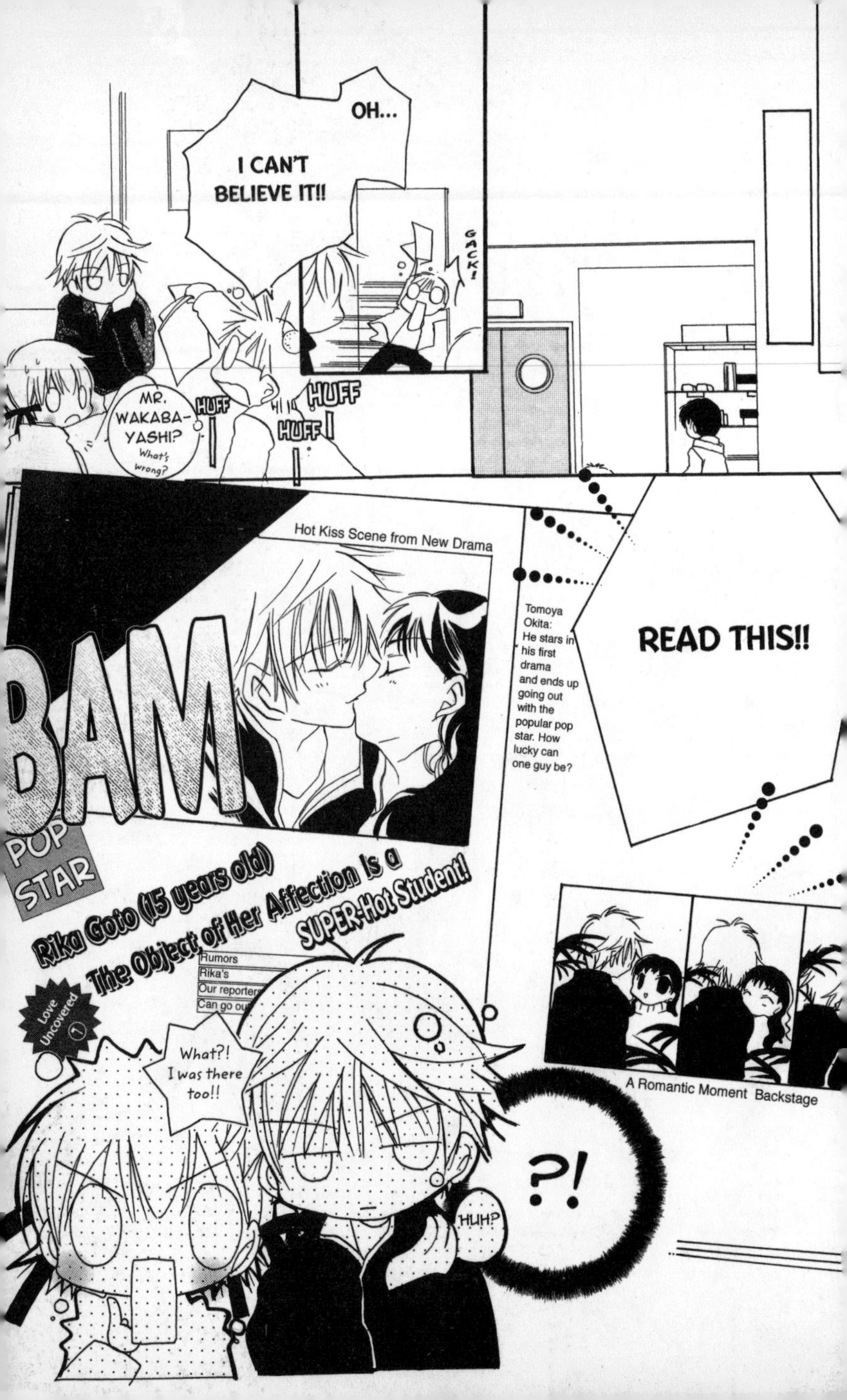
OH...
I CAN'T BELIEVE IT!!
GACK!
HUFF
HUFF
HUFF
MR. WAKABAYASHI? What's wrong?
READ THIS!!
Hot Kiss Scene from New Drama
BAM
Tomoya Okita: He stars in his first drama and ends up going out with the popular pop star. How lucky can one guy be?
A Romantic Moment Backstage
POP STAR
Rika Goto (15 years old)
The Object of Her Affection Is a SUPER-Hot Student!
Love Uncovered 1
Rumors
Rika's
Our reporters
Can go ou
?!
HUH?
What?! I was there too!!

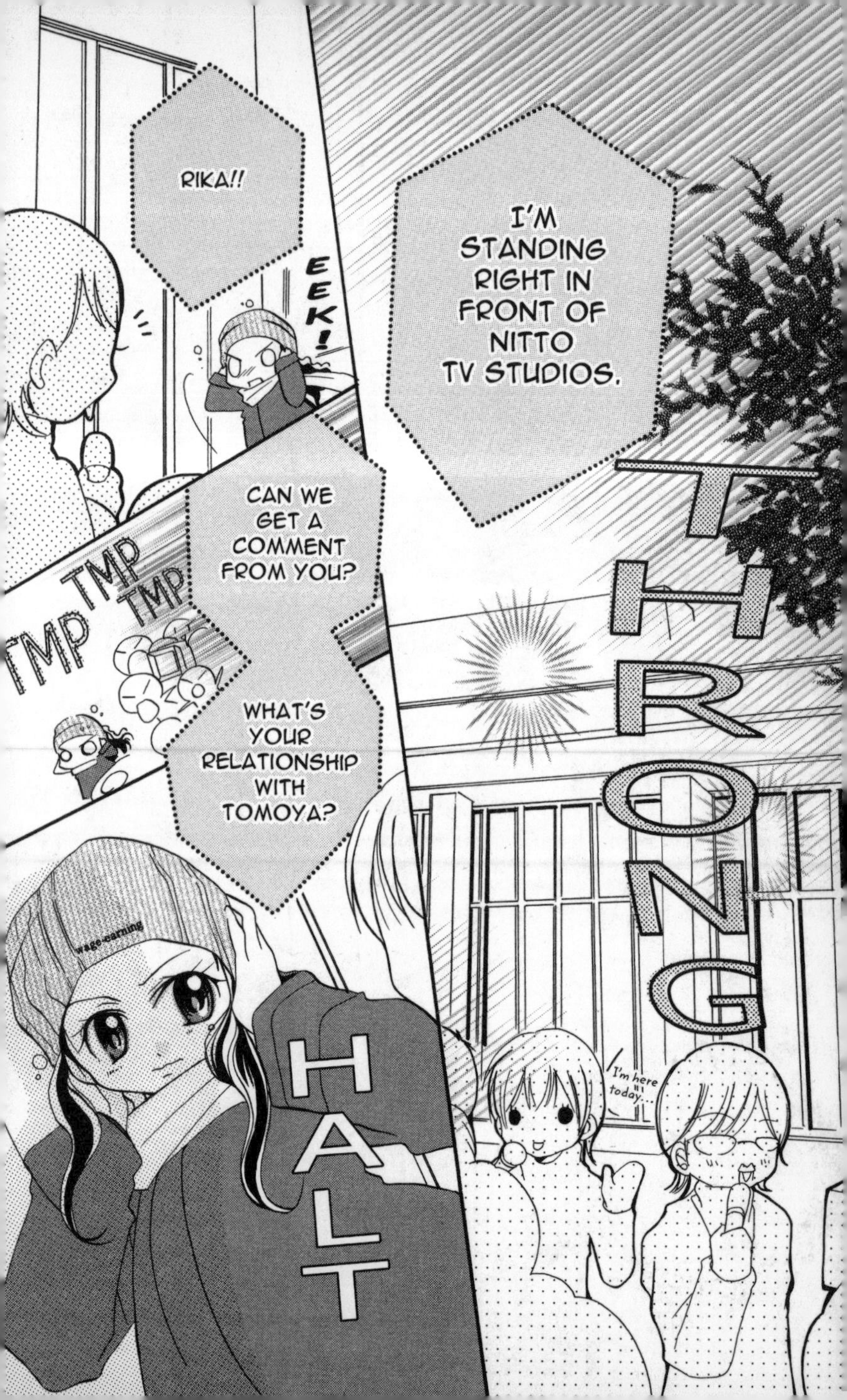
I'M STANDING RIGHT IN FRONT OF NITTO TV STUDIOS.
THRONG
I'm here today...
RIKA!!
EEK!
CAN WE GET A COMMENT FROM YOU?
TMP TMP TMP TMP
WHAT'S YOUR RELATIONSHIP WITH TOMOYA?
wage-earning
HALT

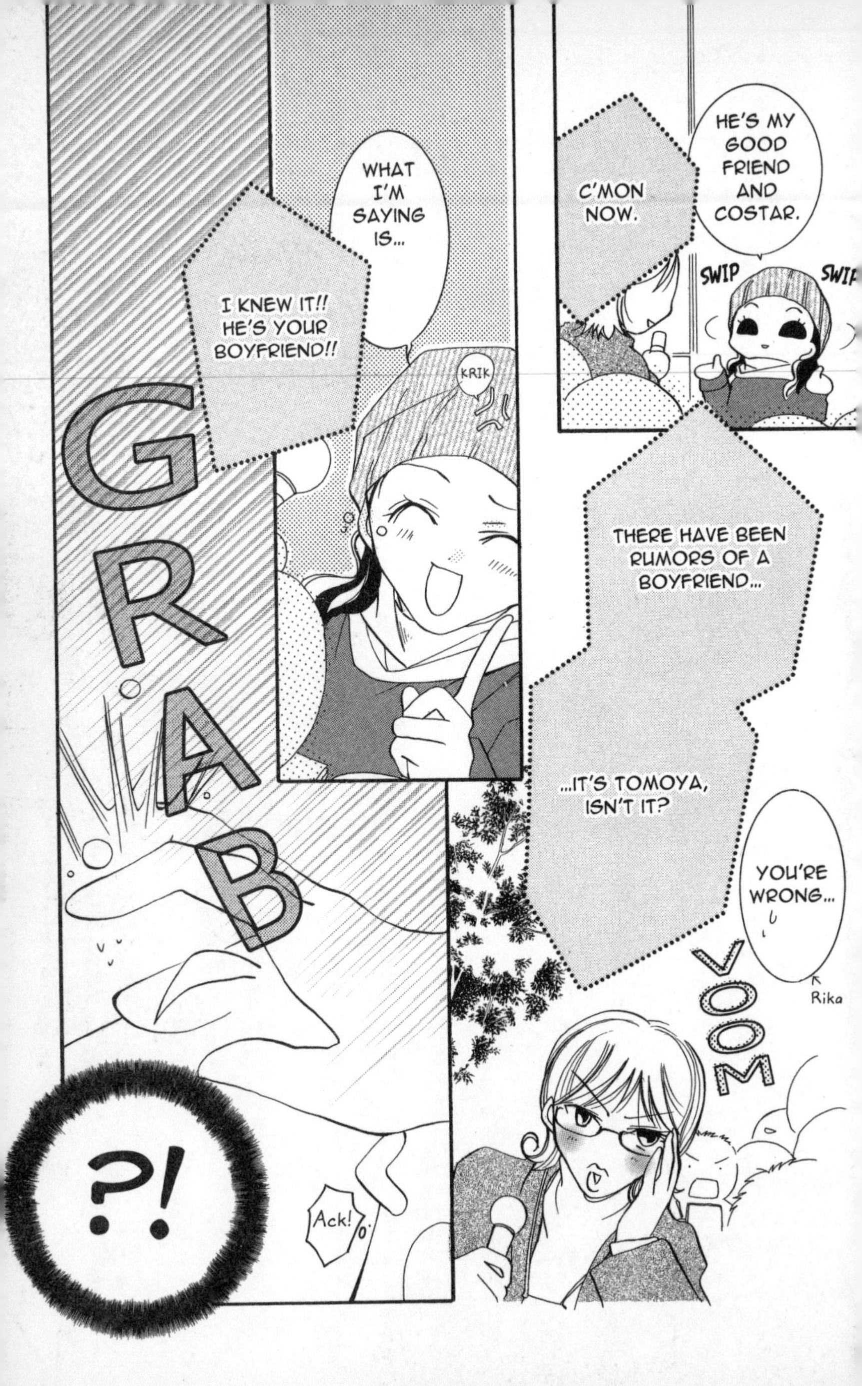
HE'S MY GOOD FRIEND AND COSTAR.
C'MON NOW.
SWIP
SWIP
WHAT I'M SAYING IS...
I KNEW IT!! HE'S YOUR BOYFRIEND!!
KRIK
THERE HAVE BEEN RUMORS OF A BOYFRIEND...
...IT'S TOMOYA, ISN'T IT?
YOU'RE WRONG...
Rika
VOOM
GRAB
Ack!
?!

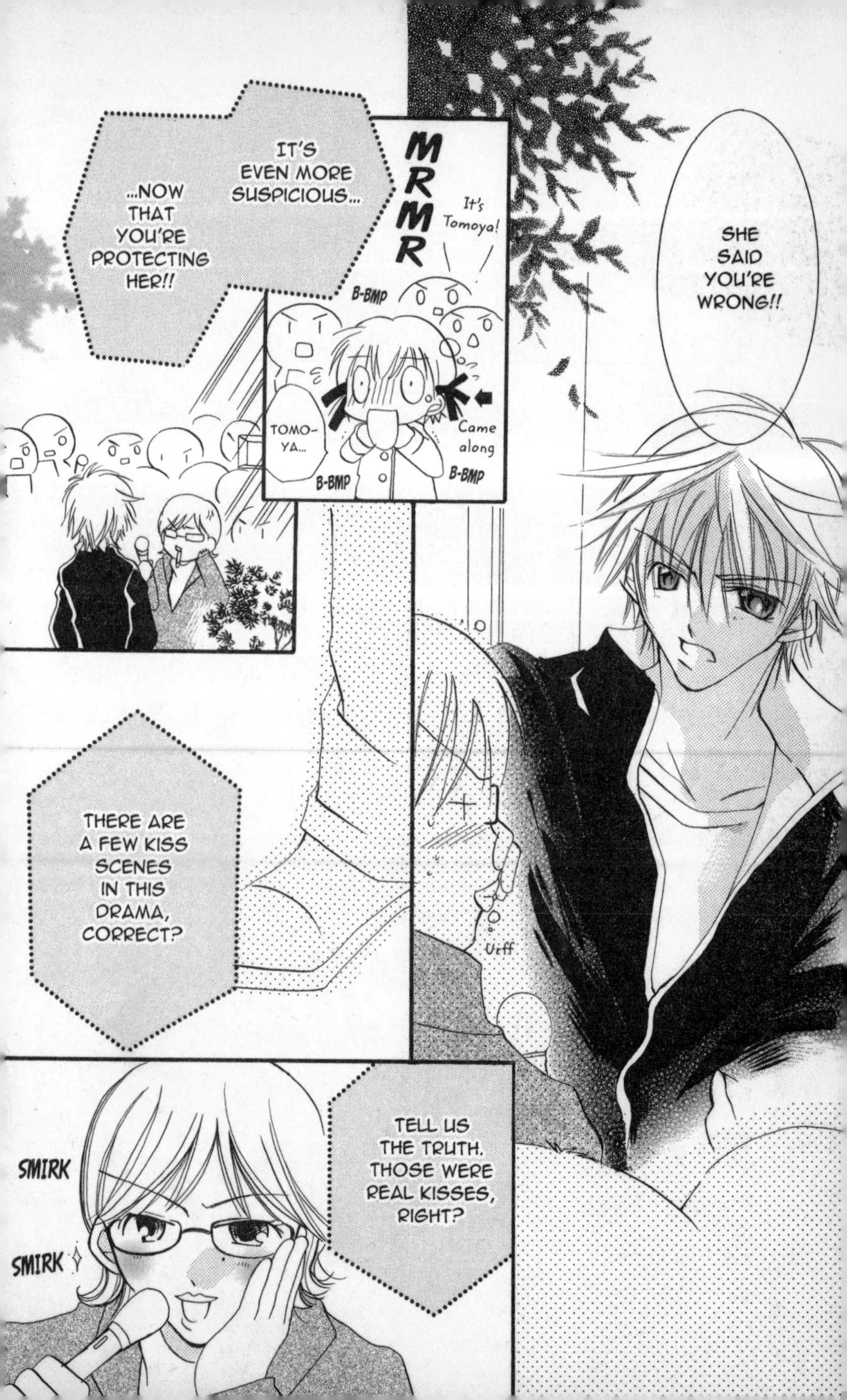
SHE SAID YOU'RE WRONG!!
IT'S EVEN MORE SUSPICIOUS...
...NOW THAT YOU'RE PROTECTING HER!!
MRMR
It's Tomoya!
B-BMP
Came along
TOMO-YA...
B-BMP
B-BMP
THERE ARE A FEW KISS SCENES IN THIS DRAMA, CORRECT?
Urff
TELL US THE TRUTH. THOSE WERE REAL KISSES, RIGHT?
SMIRK
SMIRK

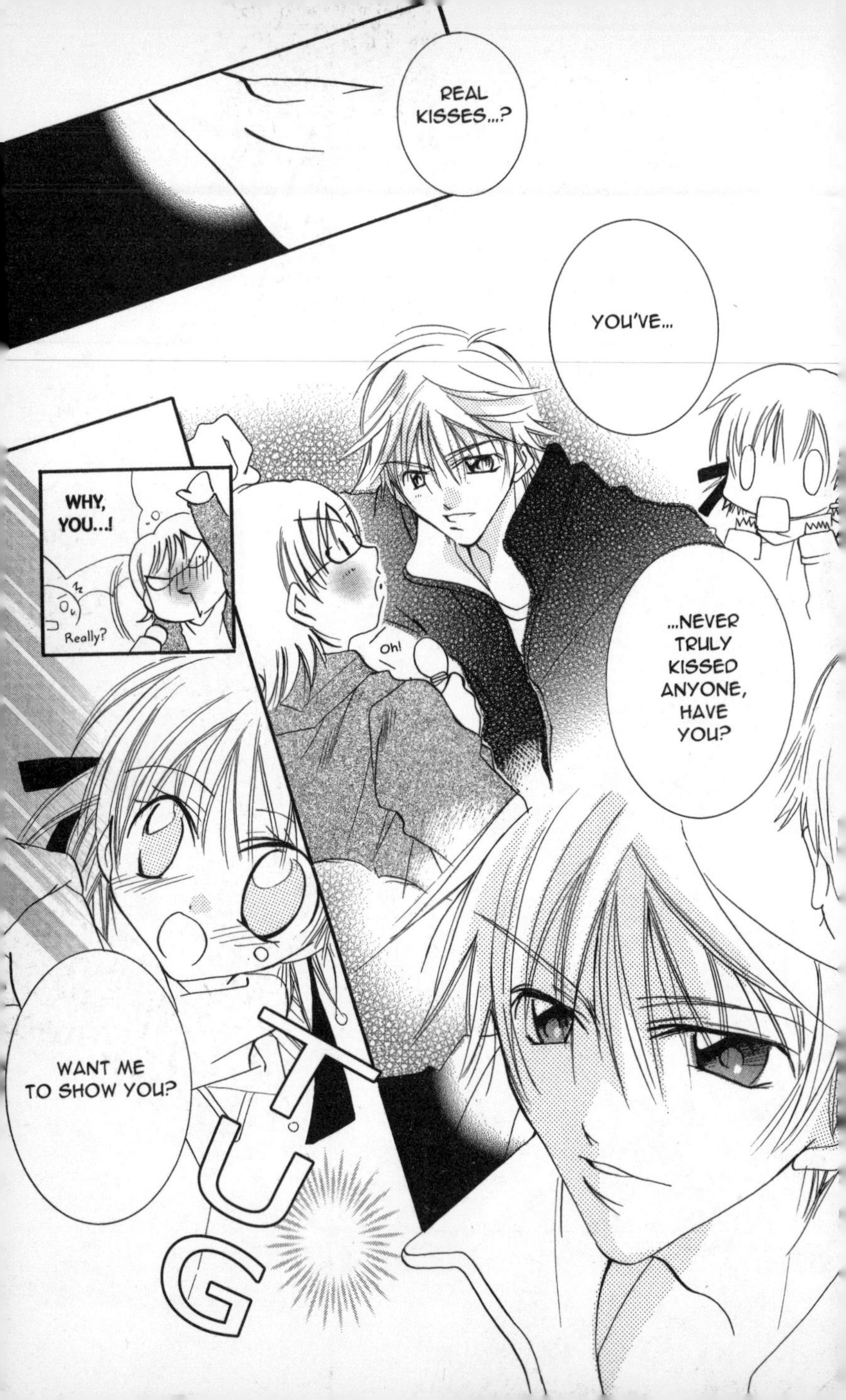
REAL KISSES...?
YOU'VE...
...NEVER TRULY KISSED ANYONE, HAVE YOU?
WHY, YOU...!
Really?
Oh!
WANT ME TO SHOW YOU?
TUG

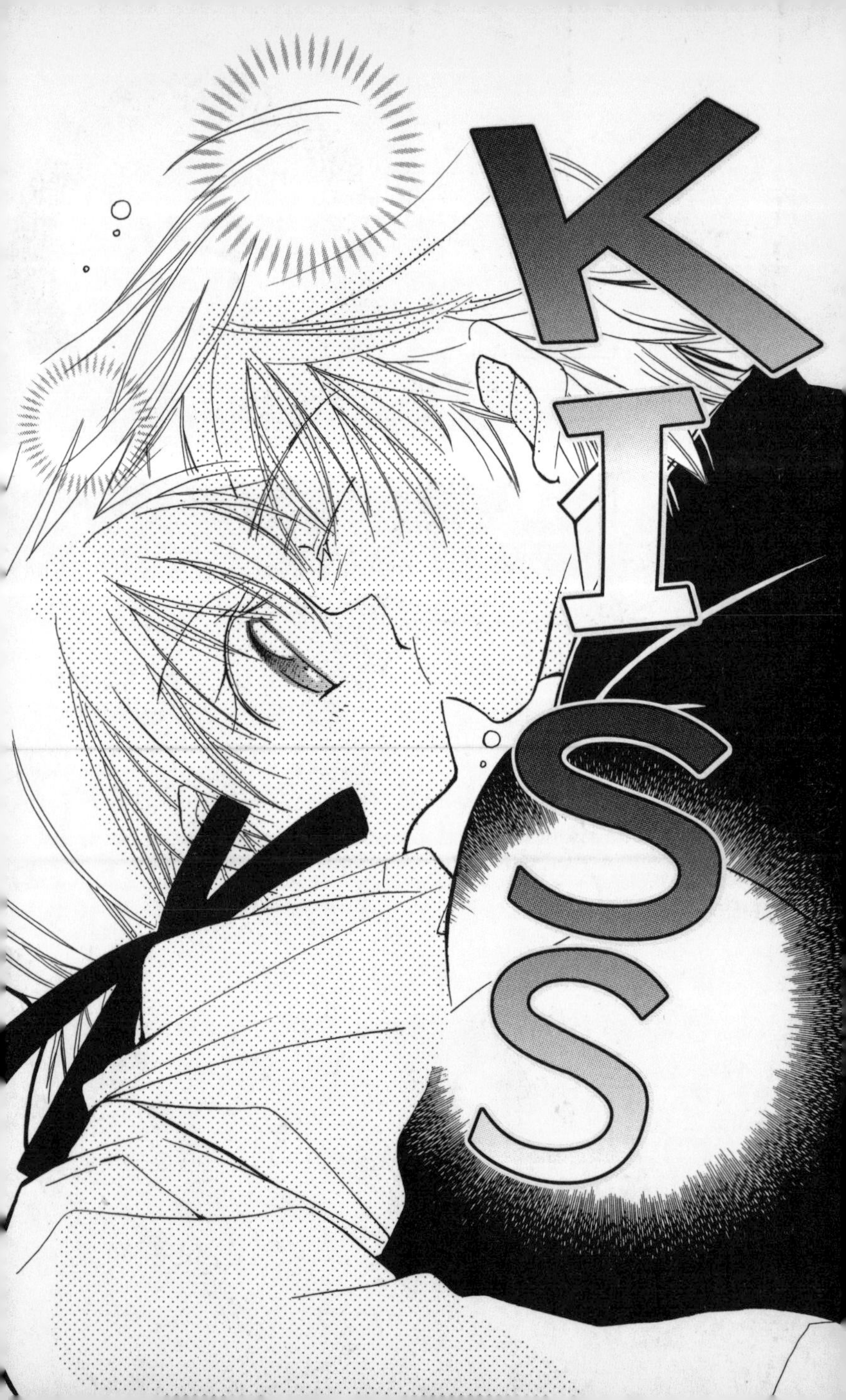
KISS

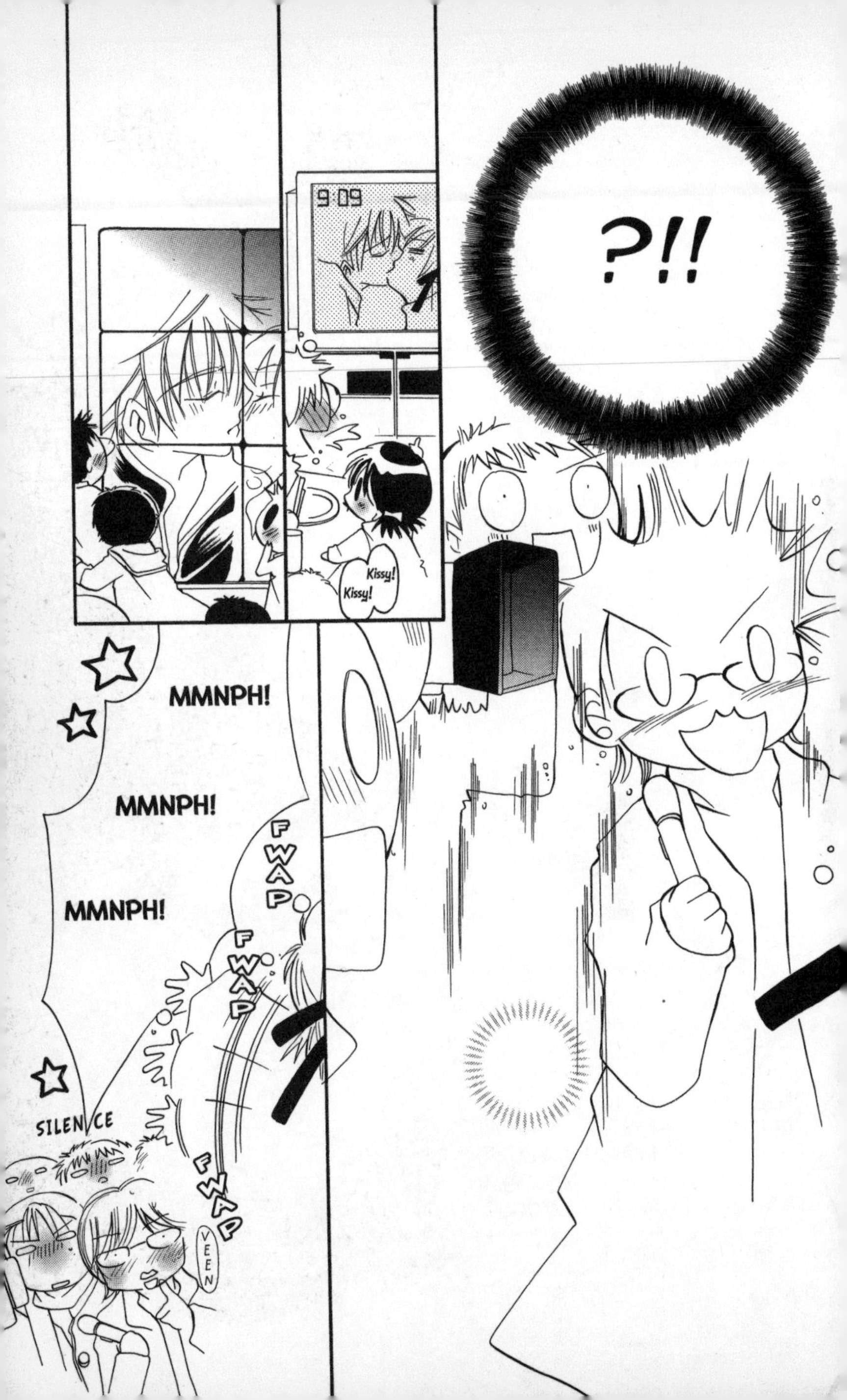
?!!
9:09
Kissy!
Kissy!
MMNPH!
MMNPH!
MMNPH!
FWAP
FWAP
FWAP
SILENCE
VEEN

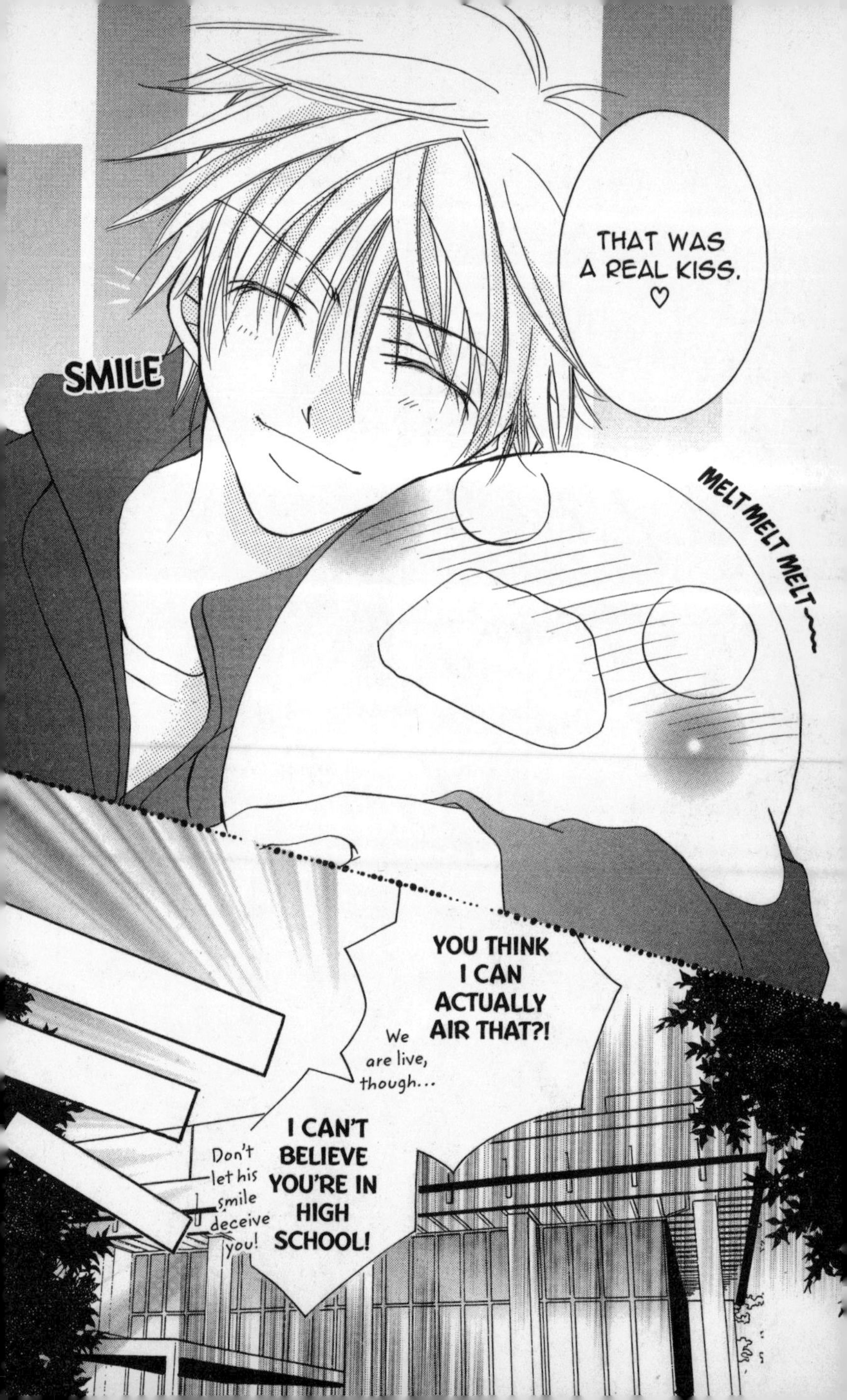
THAT WAS A REAL KISS. ♡
MELT MELT MELT~
SMILE
YOU THINK I CAN ACTUALLY AIR THAT?!
We are live, though...
I CAN'T BELIEVE YOU'RE IN HIGH SCHOOL!
Don't let his smile deceive you!

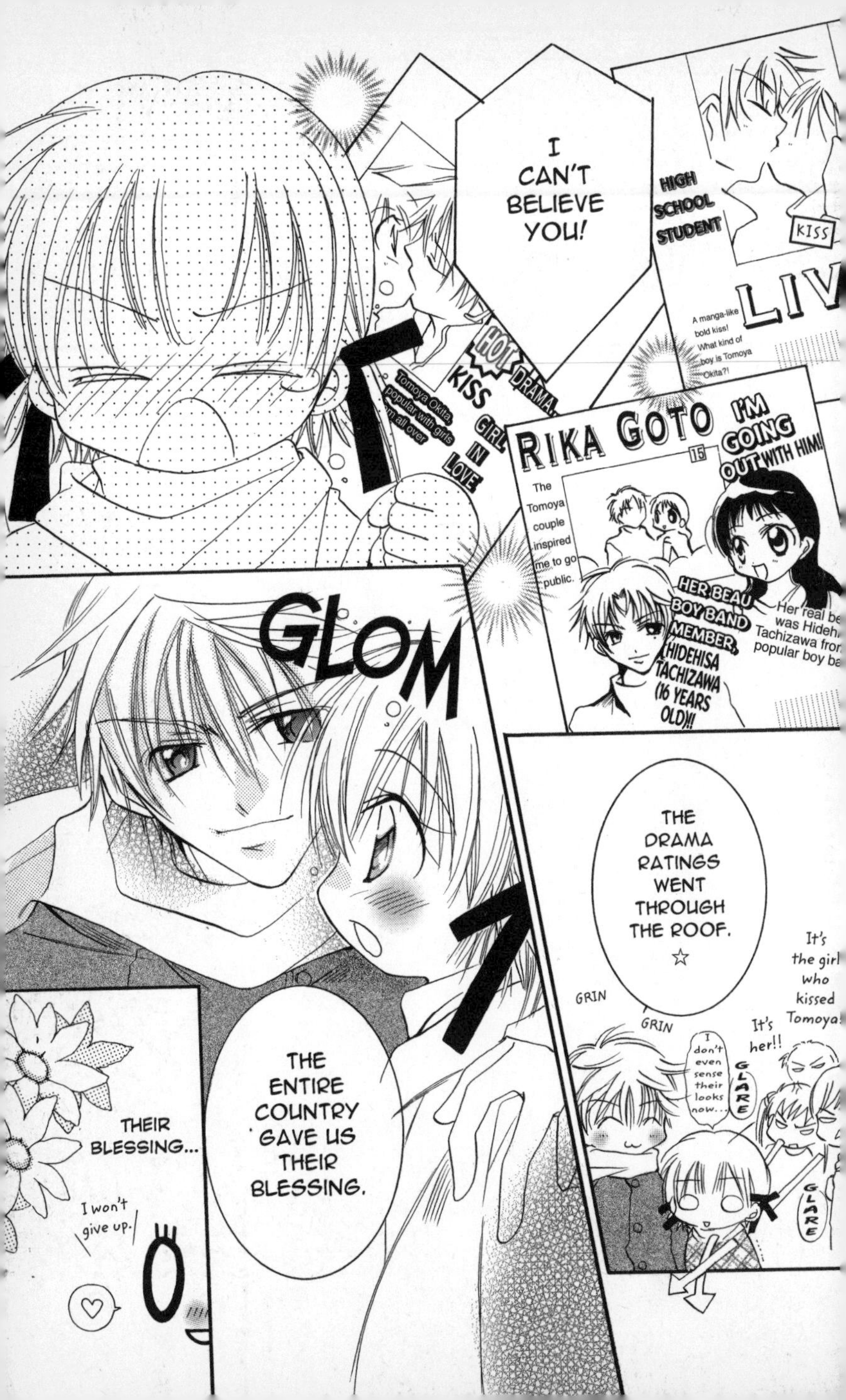
HIGH SCHOOL STUDENT
KISS
LIV
A manga-like bold kiss! What kind of boy is Tomoya Okita?!
HOT DRAMA,
KISS
GIRL IN LOVE
Tomoya Okita, popular with girls from all over
I CAN'T BELIEVE YOU!
RIKA GOTO
15
I'M GOING OUT WITH HIM!
The Tomoya couple inspired me to go public.
HER BEAU BOY BAND MEMBER, HIDEHISA TACHIZAWA (16 YEARS OLD)!!
Her real be was Hideh Tachizawa fro popular boy ba
THE DRAMA RATINGS WENT THROUGH THE ROOF. ☆
It's the girl who kissed Tomoya!
It's her!!
GRIN
GRIN
I don't even sense their looks now...
GLARE
GLARE
GLOM
THE ENTIRE COUNTRY GAVE US THEIR BLESSING.
THEIR BLESSING...
I won't give up.
♡

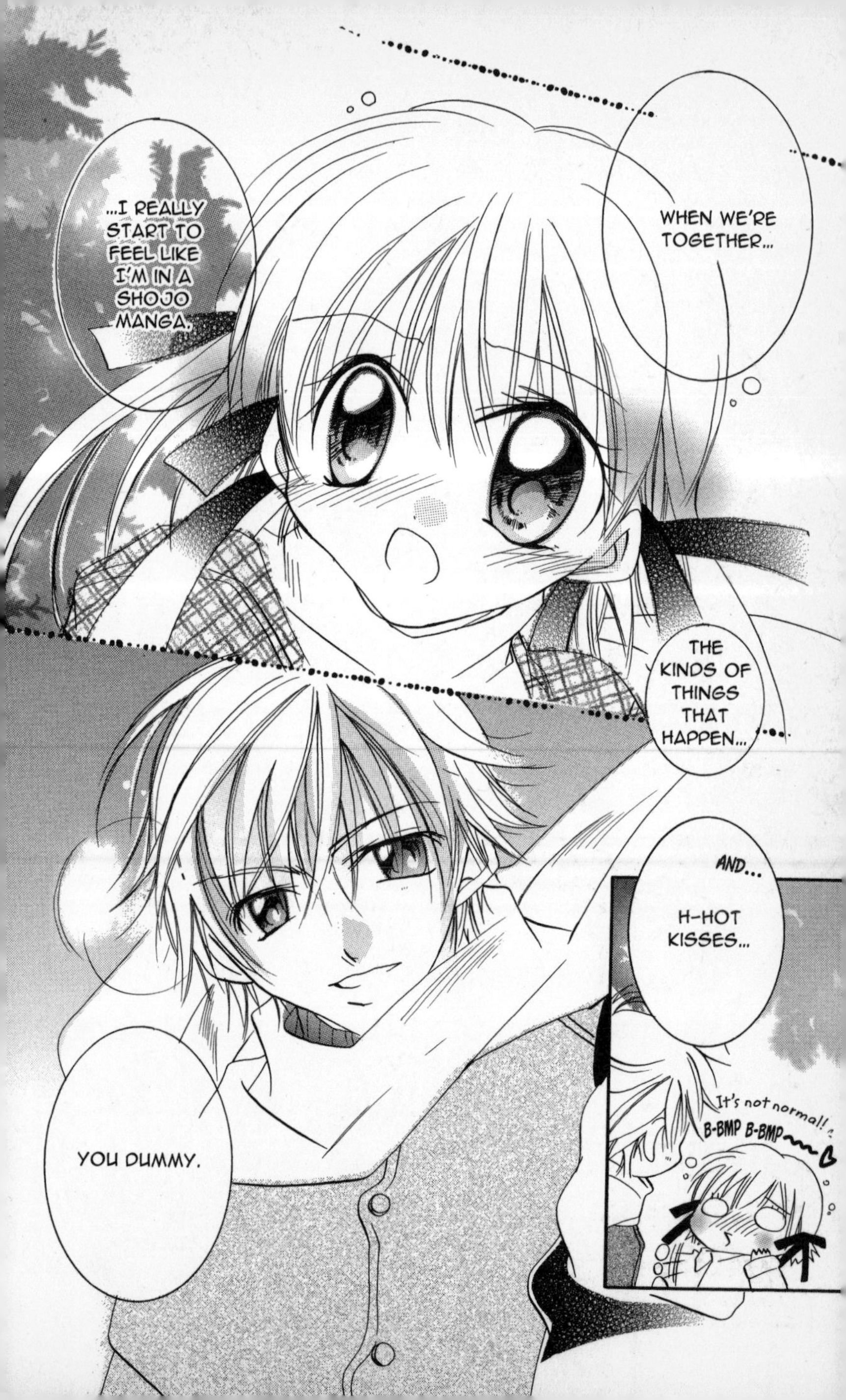
WHEN WE'RE TOGETHER...
...I REALLY START TO FEEL LIKE I'M IN A SHOJO MANGA.
THE KINDS OF THINGS THAT HAPPEN...
AND...
H-HOT KISSES...
It's not normal!
B-BMP B-BMP
YOU DUMMY.

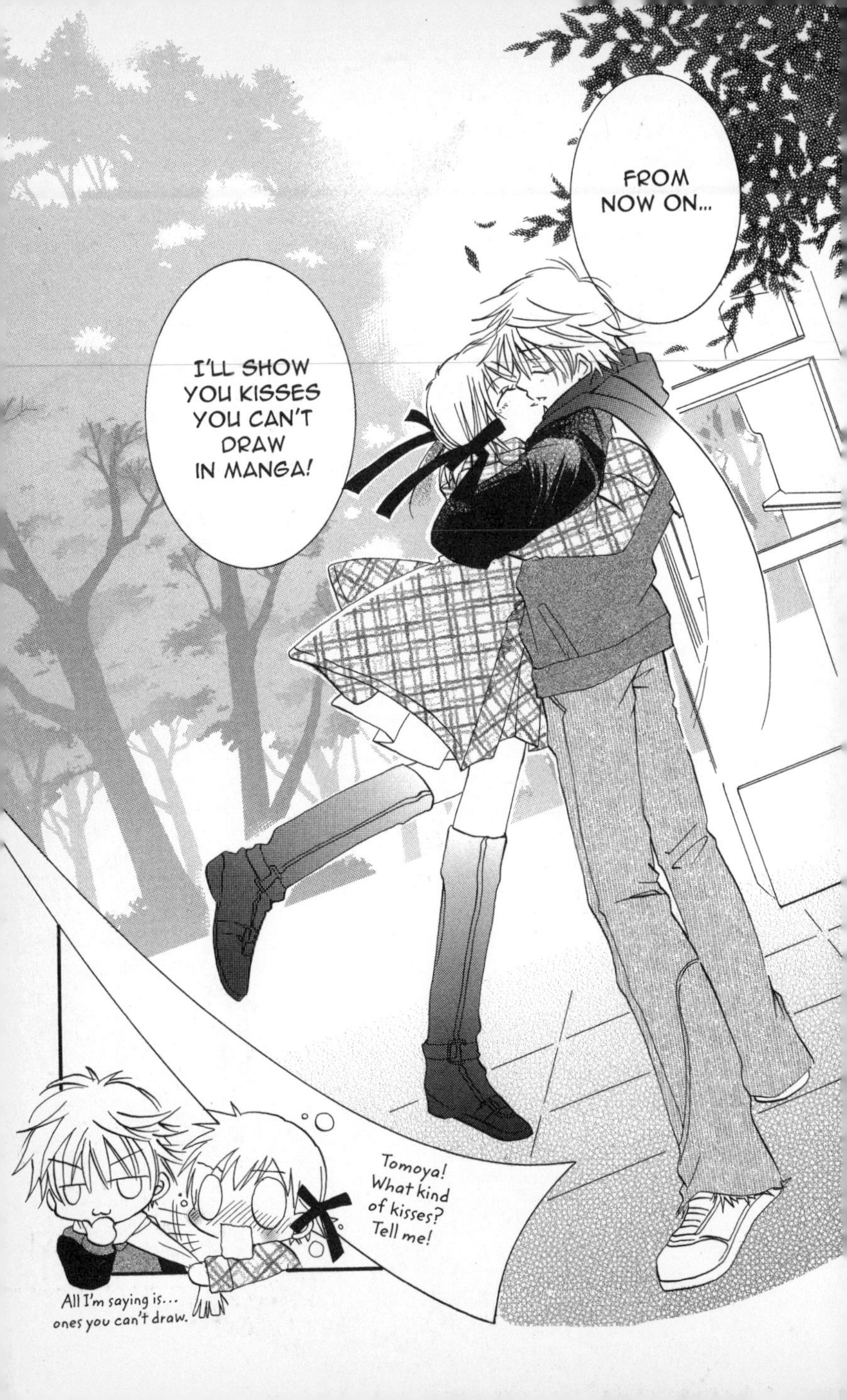
FROM NOW ON...
I'LL SHOW YOU KISSES YOU CAN'T DRAW IN MANGA!
Tomoya! What kind of kisses? Tell me!
All I'm saying is... ones you can't draw.

I wrote about art supplies and characters before, so now I'm going to answer some frequently asked questions.

Q. Why did you want to become a mangaka?

I've always loved to draw, and I would always be drawing on notebooks and scraps of paper. I didn't seriously consider becoming a mangaka until I graduated. I'm actually someone who submitted manga to the Ciao manga school.

Q. How can I improve my drawing?

If you find out, please let me know. I still practice every day. I'm still far from where I'd like to be. But I think you have to do sheer volume to really improve. Sounds like we've both got the same goal!

Q. I can't draw boys. Please give me some pointers.

You have to draw them with love. (←This is my tip.)
I think I over-love my boys. (This has nothing to do with whether or not I'm any good.)
But to give you an overview of a girl and a boy...

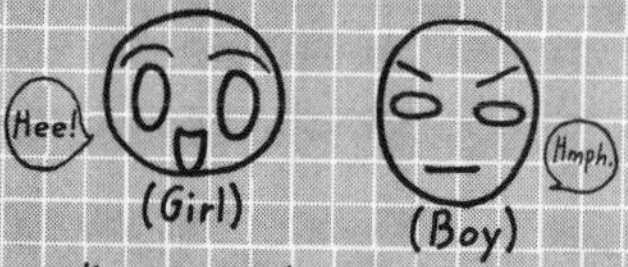
Hee!
(Girl)
Hmph.
(Boy)

← I think this is it.

Keep in mind that this is very rudimentary.
I think some boys have more feminine features and visa versa. Personality has a lot to do with facial features as well. But I think if you put these two figures out and asked which one the boy was, it would have to be the one on the right.

(Or you could say that Yamase is on the right.)

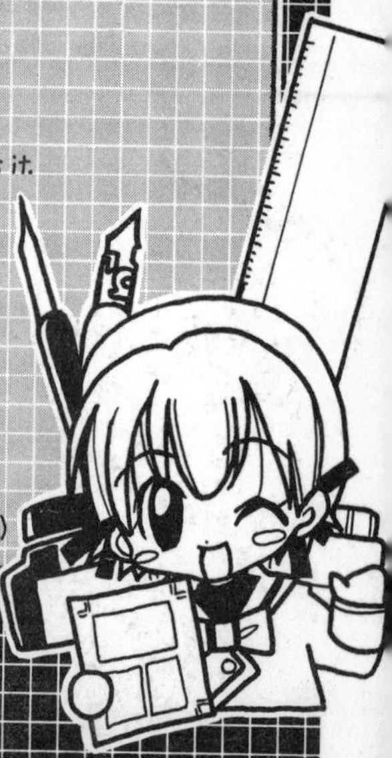

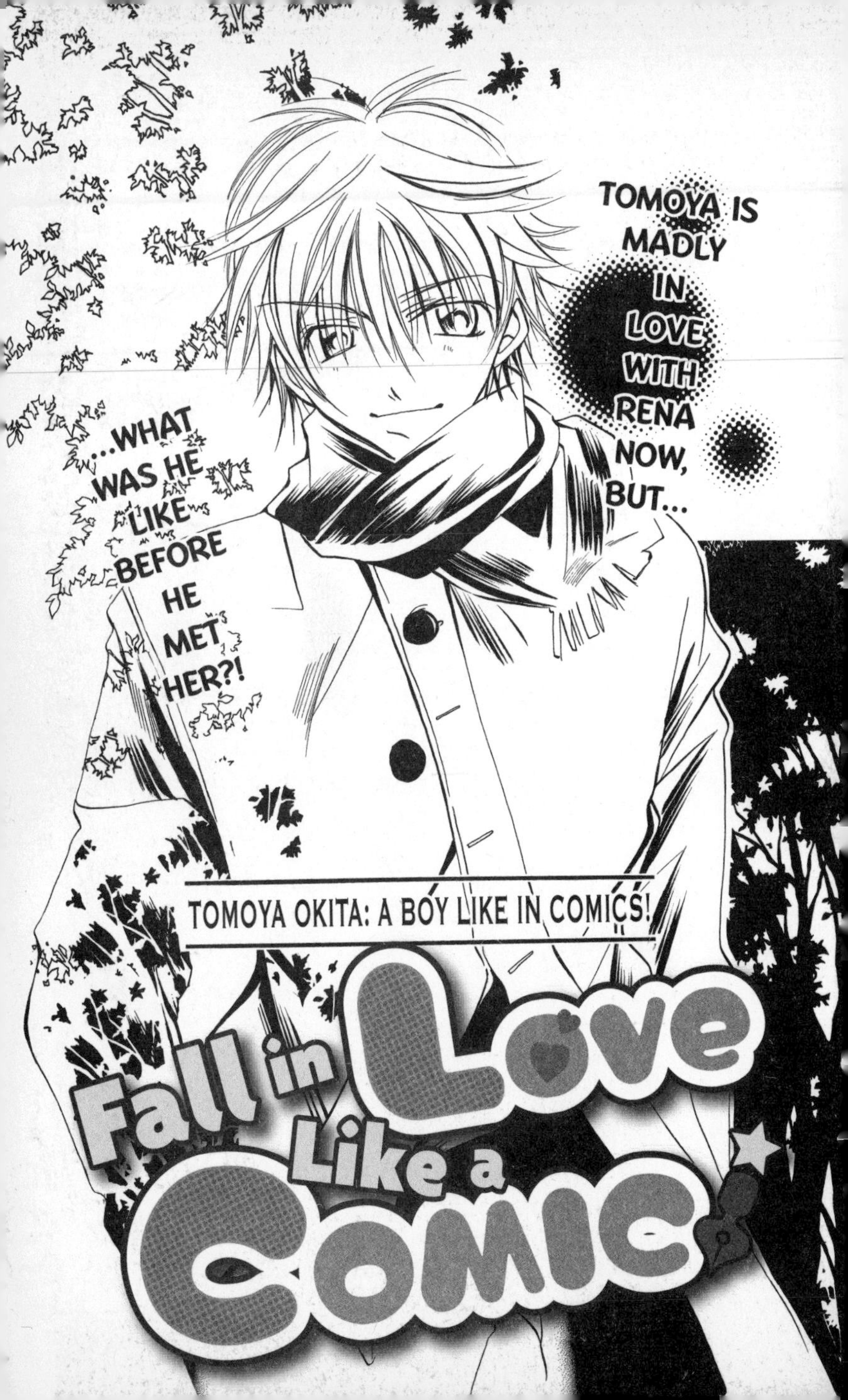
TOMOYA IS MADLY IN LOVE WITH RENA NOW, BUT...
...WHAT WAS HE LIKE BEFORE HE MET HER?!
TOMOYA OKITA: A BOY LIKE IN COMICS!
Fall in Love Like a Comic

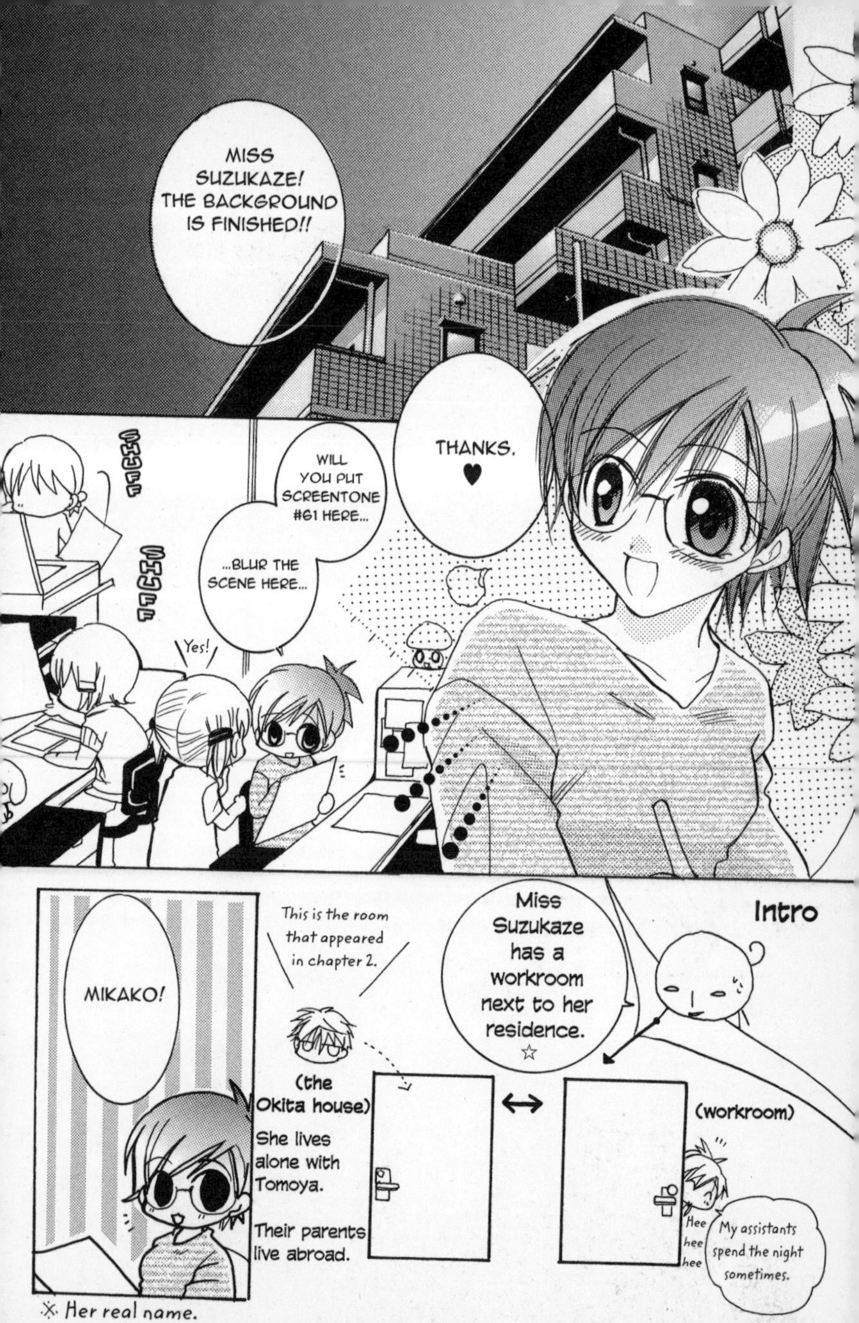
MISS SUZUKAZE! THE BACKGROUND IS FINISHED!!
THANKS. ♥
WILL YOU PUT SCREENTONE #61 HERE...
...BLUR THE SCENE HERE...
Yes!
SHUFF
SHUFF
Intro
Miss Suzukaze has a workroom next to her residence. ☆
This is the room that appeared in chapter 2.
(workroom)
Hee hee hee
My assistants spend the night sometimes.
(the Okita house)
She lives alone with Tomoya.
Their parents live abroad.
MIKAKO!

※ Her real name.

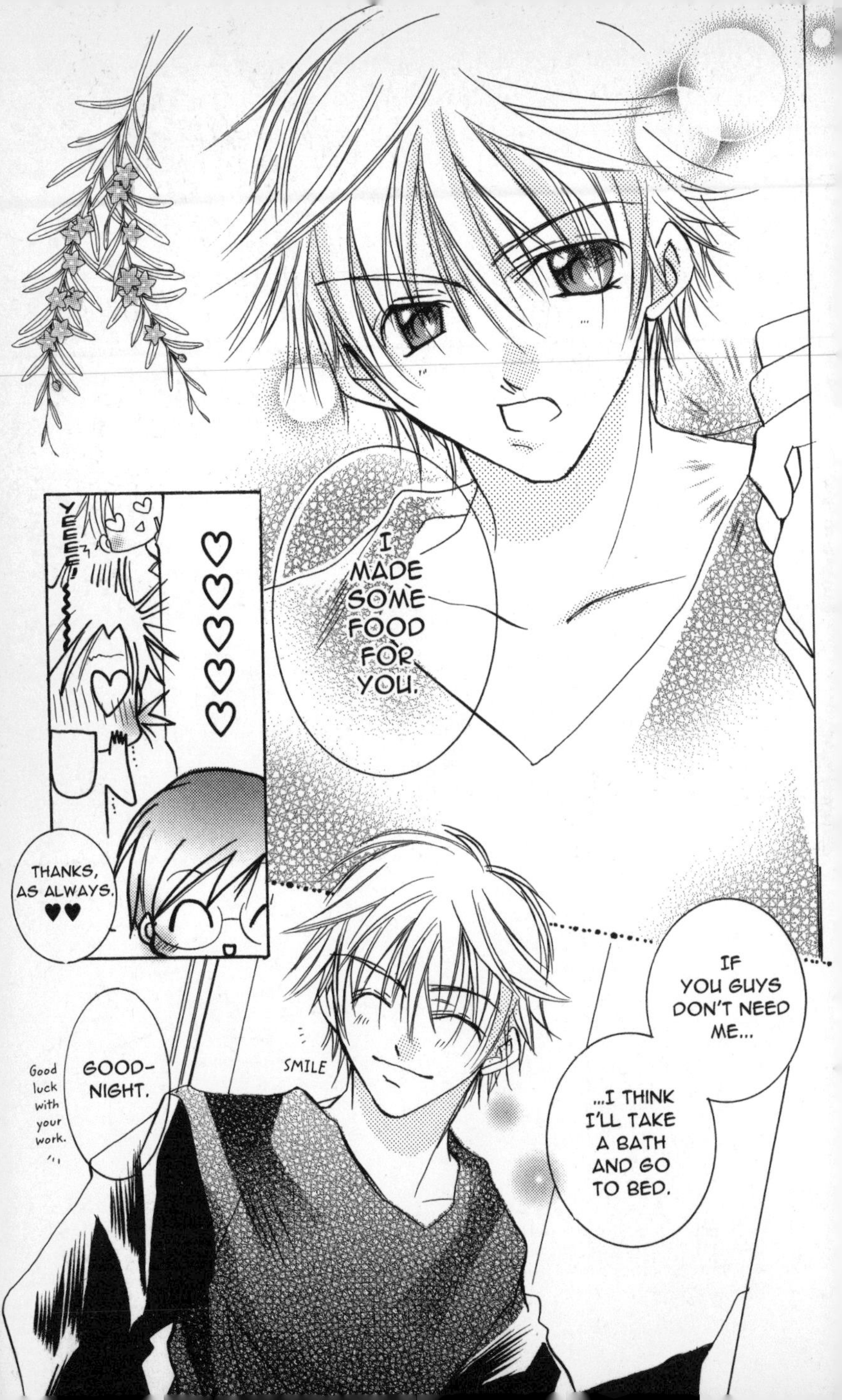
I MADE SOME FOOD FOR YOU.
YEEEE!
♥ ♥ ♥ ♥ ♥
THANKS, AS ALWAYS. ♥♥
IF YOU GUYS DON'T NEED ME...
...I THINK I'LL TAKE A BATH AND GO TO BED.
SMILE
GOOD-NIGHT.
Good luck with your work.

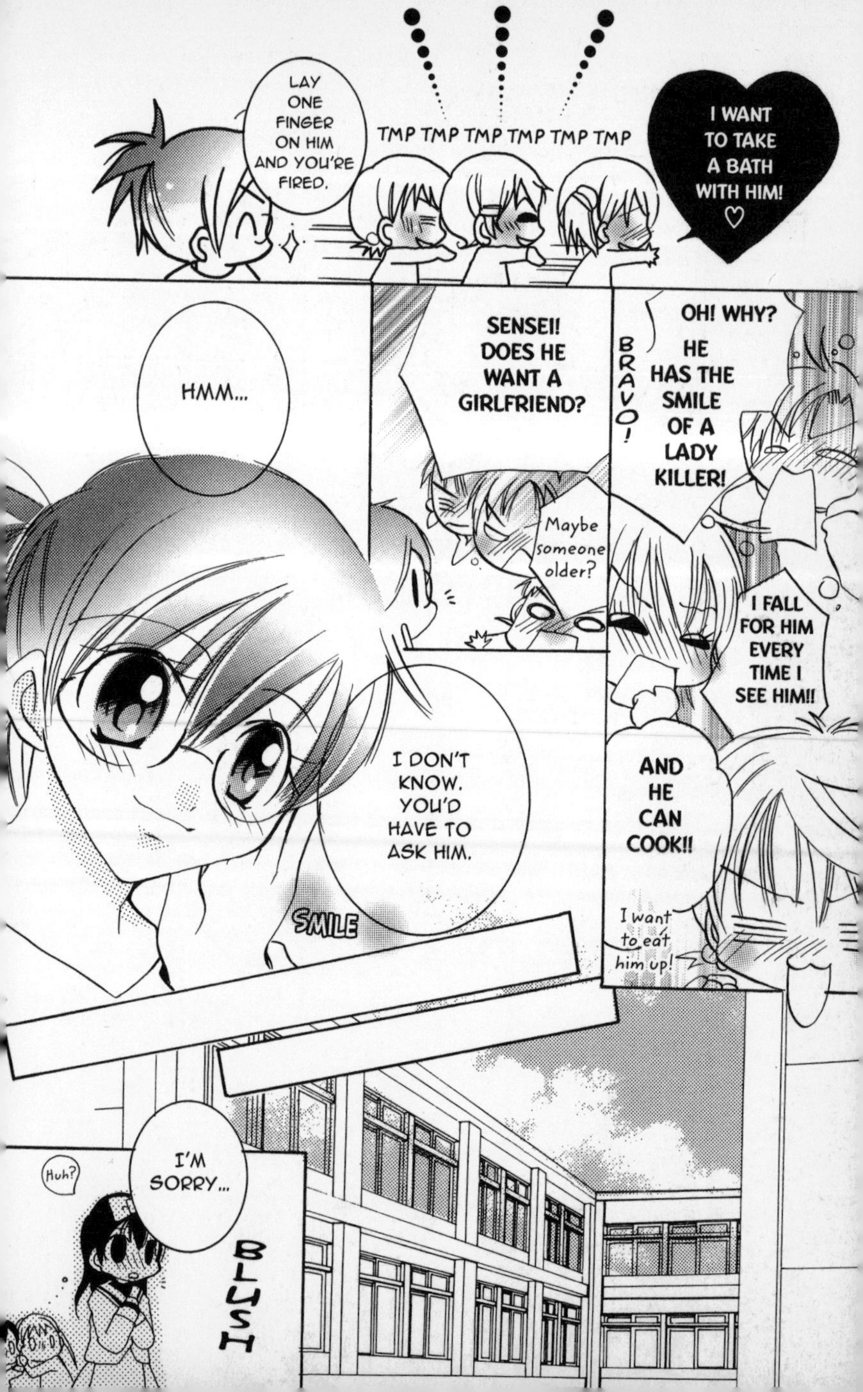
I WANT TO TAKE A BATH WITH HIM! ♡
TMP TMP TMP TMP TMP TMP
LAY ONE FINGER ON HIM AND YOU'RE FIRED.
OH! WHY?
HE HAS THE SMILE OF A LADY KILLER!
BRAVO!
I FALL FOR HIM EVERY TIME I SEE HIM!!
AND HE CAN COOK!!
I want to eat him up!
SENSEI! DOES HE WANT A GIRLFRIEND?
Maybe someone older?
HMM...
I DON'T KNOW. YOU'D HAVE TO ASK HIM.
SMILE
I'M SORRY...
Huh?
BLUSH

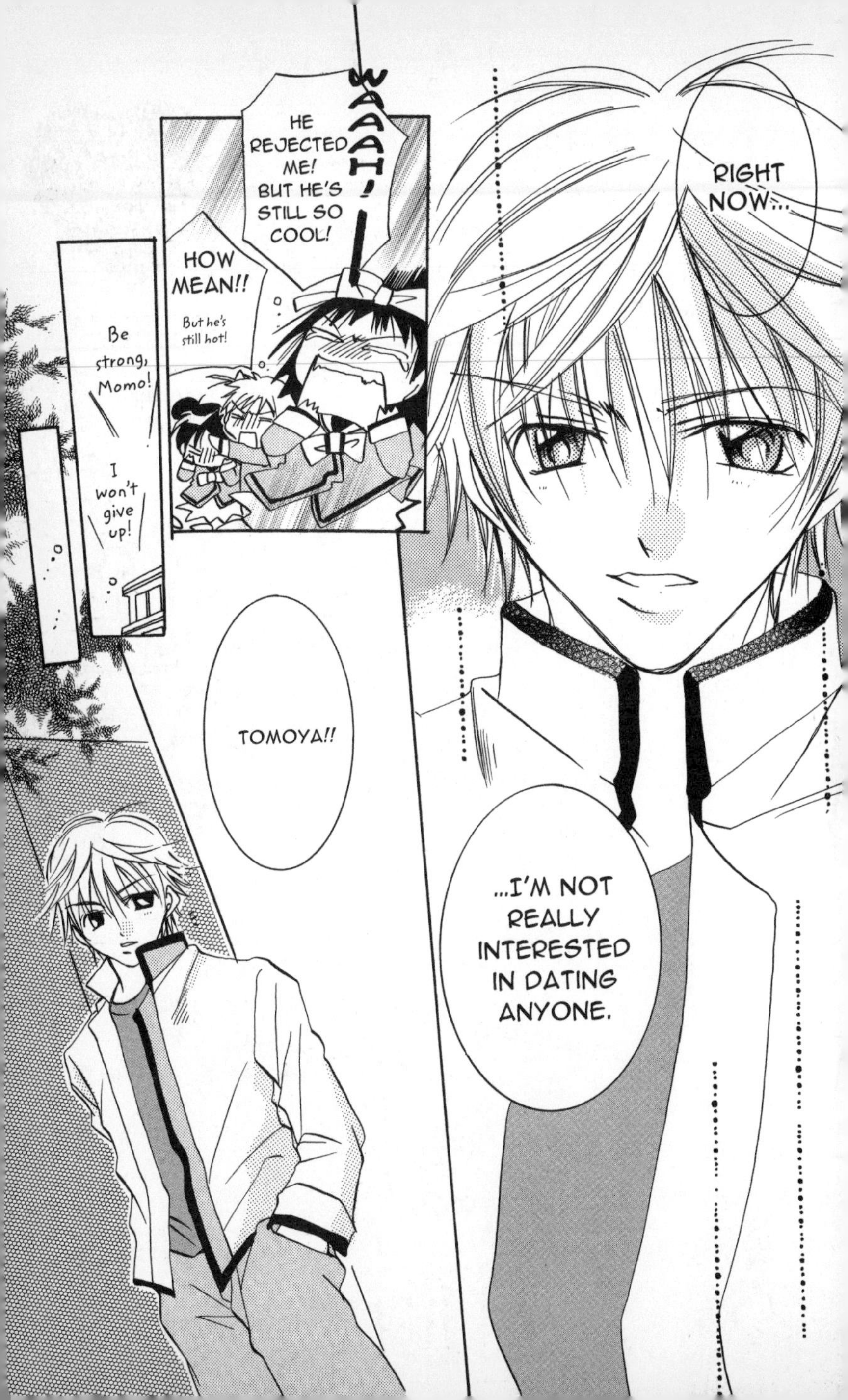
RIGHT NOW...
...I'M NOT REALLY INTERESTED IN DATING ANYONE.
WAAAAH!!
HE REJECTED ME! BUT HE'S STILL SO COOL!
HOW MEAN!!
But he's still hot!
Be strong, Momo!
I won't give up!
TOMOYA!!

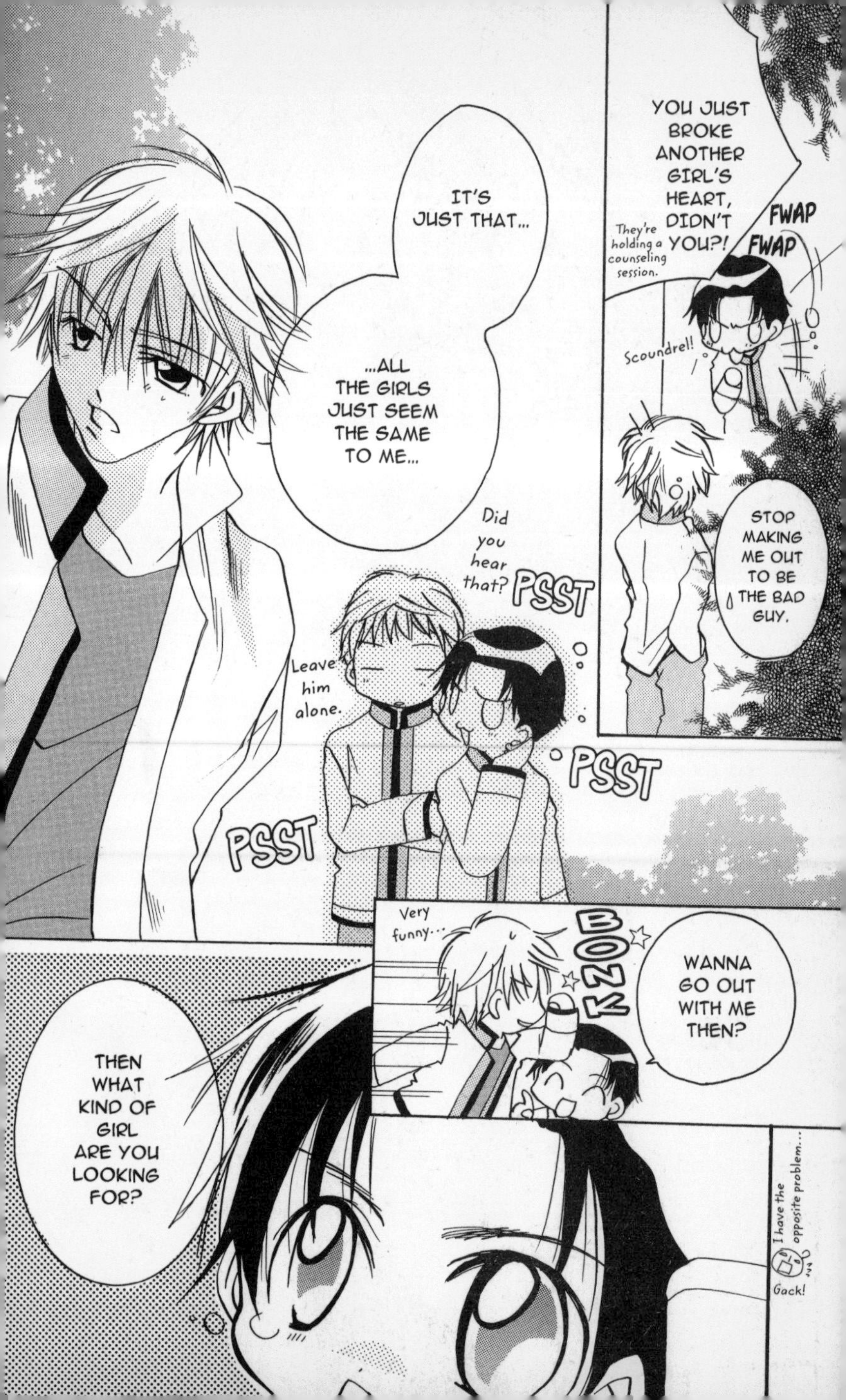
YOU JUST BROKE ANOTHER GIRL'S HEART, DIDN'T YOU?!
They're holding a counseling session.
FWAP
FWAP
Scoundrel!
STOP MAKING ME OUT TO BE THE BAD GUY.
IT'S JUST THAT...
...ALL THE GIRLS JUST SEEM THE SAME TO ME...
Did you hear that?
PSST
Leave him alone.
PSST
PSST
WANNA GO OUT WITH ME THEN?
BONK
Very funny...
THEN WHAT KIND OF GIRL ARE YOU LOOKING FOR?
I have the opposite problem...
Gack!

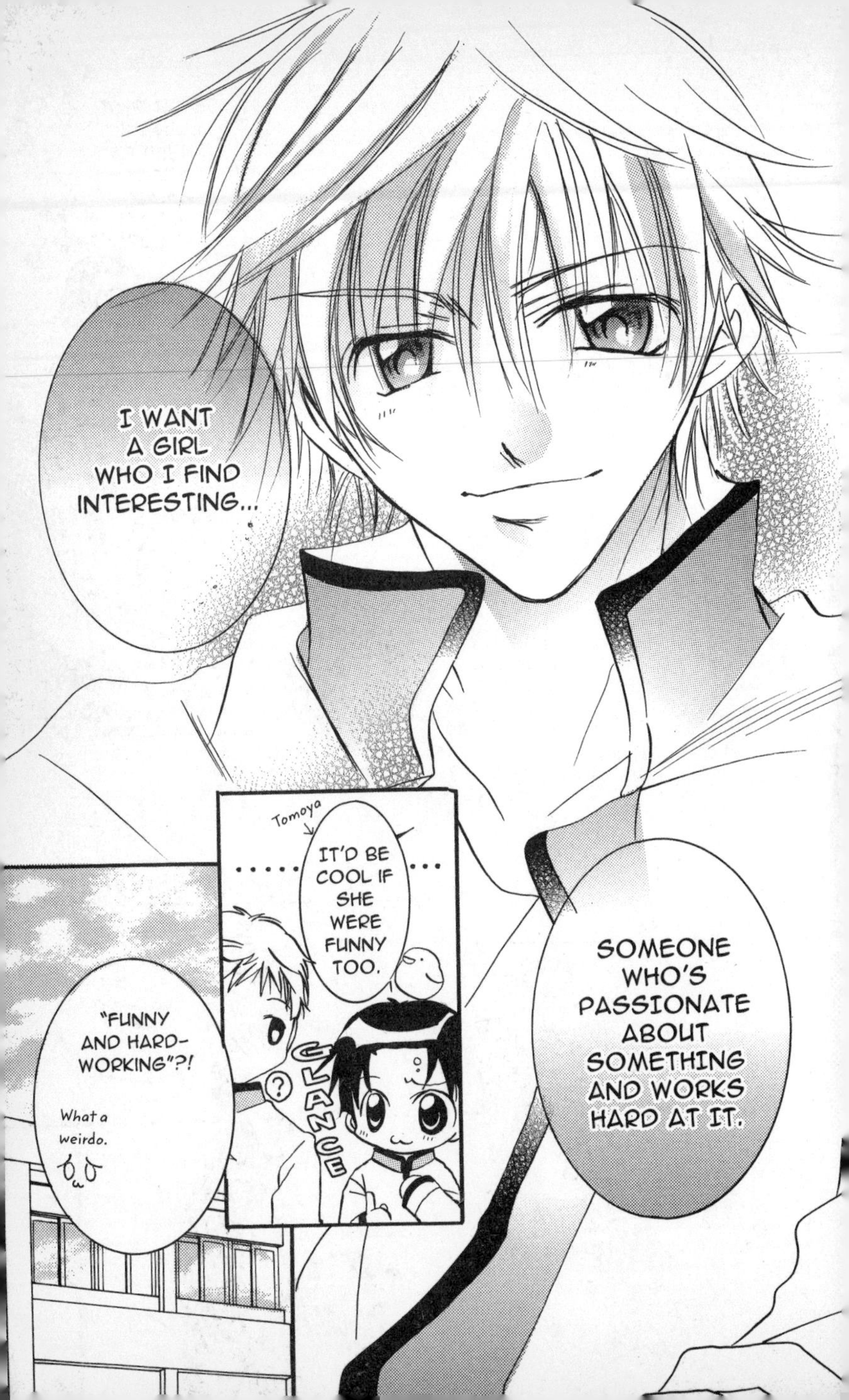

I WANT A GIRL WHO I FIND INTERESTING...
SOMEONE WHO'S PASSIONATE ABOUT SOMETHING AND WORKS HARD AT IT.
Tomoya
...... IT'D BE COOL IF SHE WERE FUNNY TOO. ...
GLANCE
?
"FUNNY AND HARD-WORKING"?!
What a weirdo.

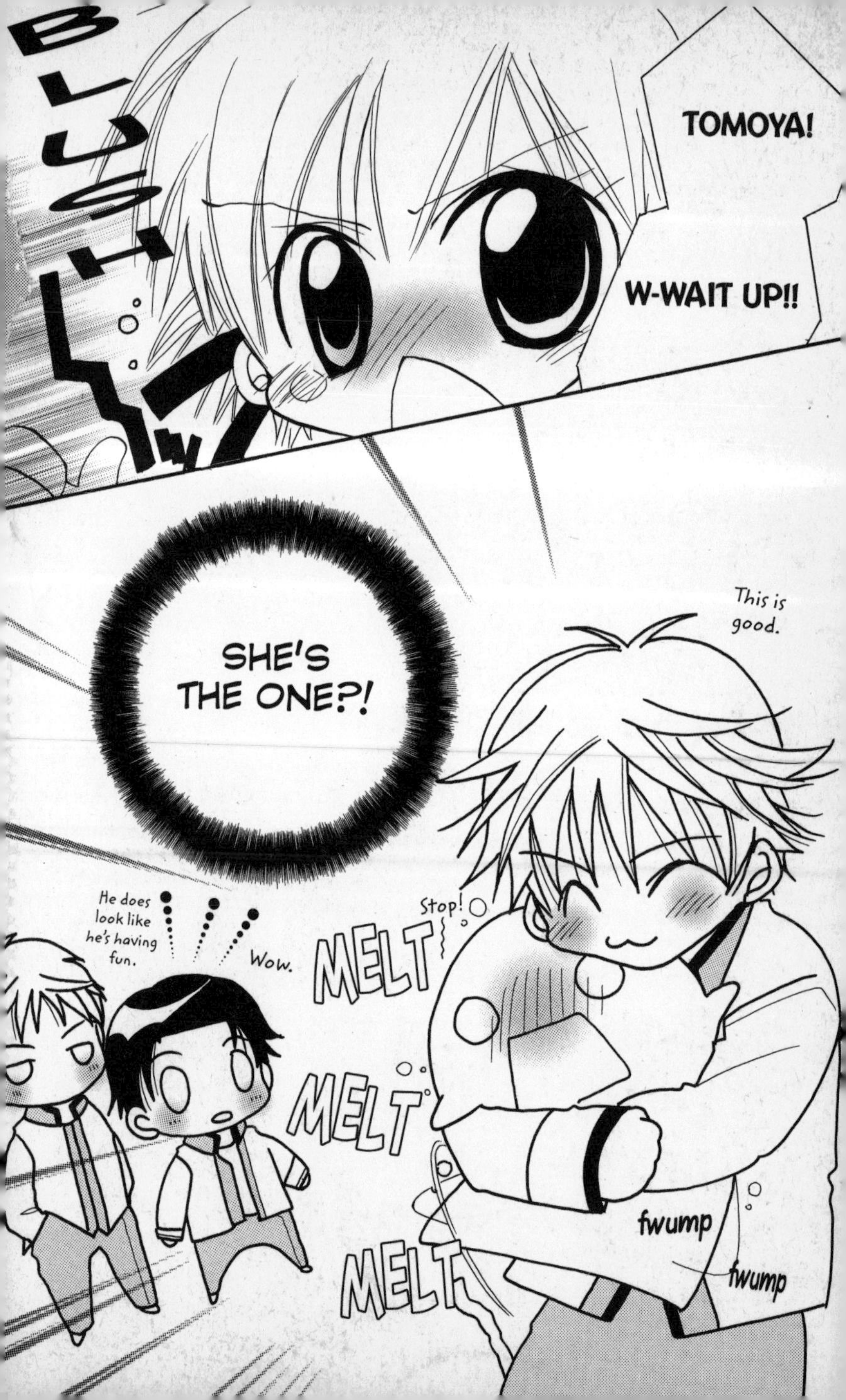
TOMOYA!
W-WAIT UP!!
BLUSH
SHE'S THE ONE?!
This is good.
Stop!
MELT
MELT
MELT
fwump
fwump
Wow.
He does look like he's having fun.

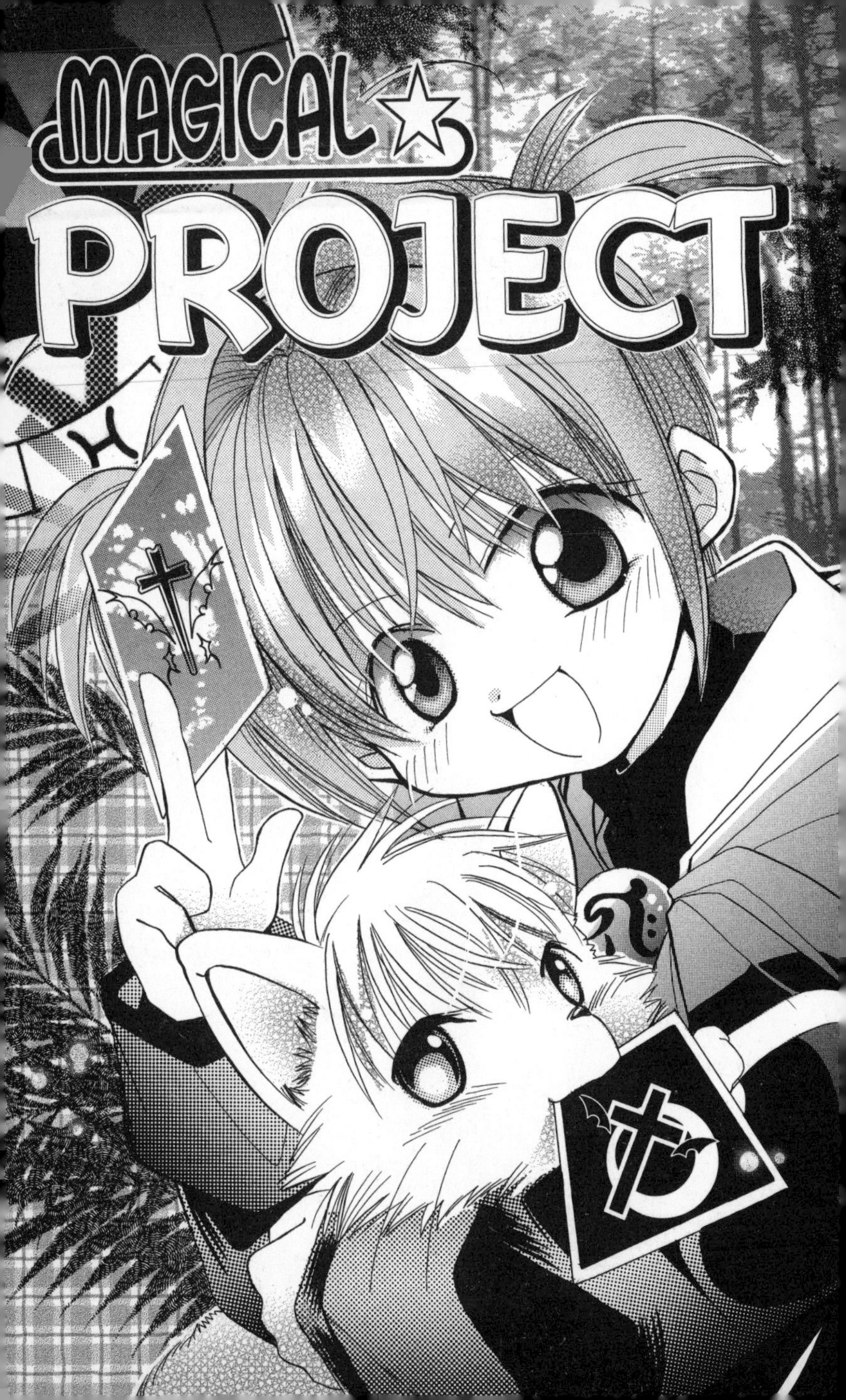
MAGICAL☆
PROJECT

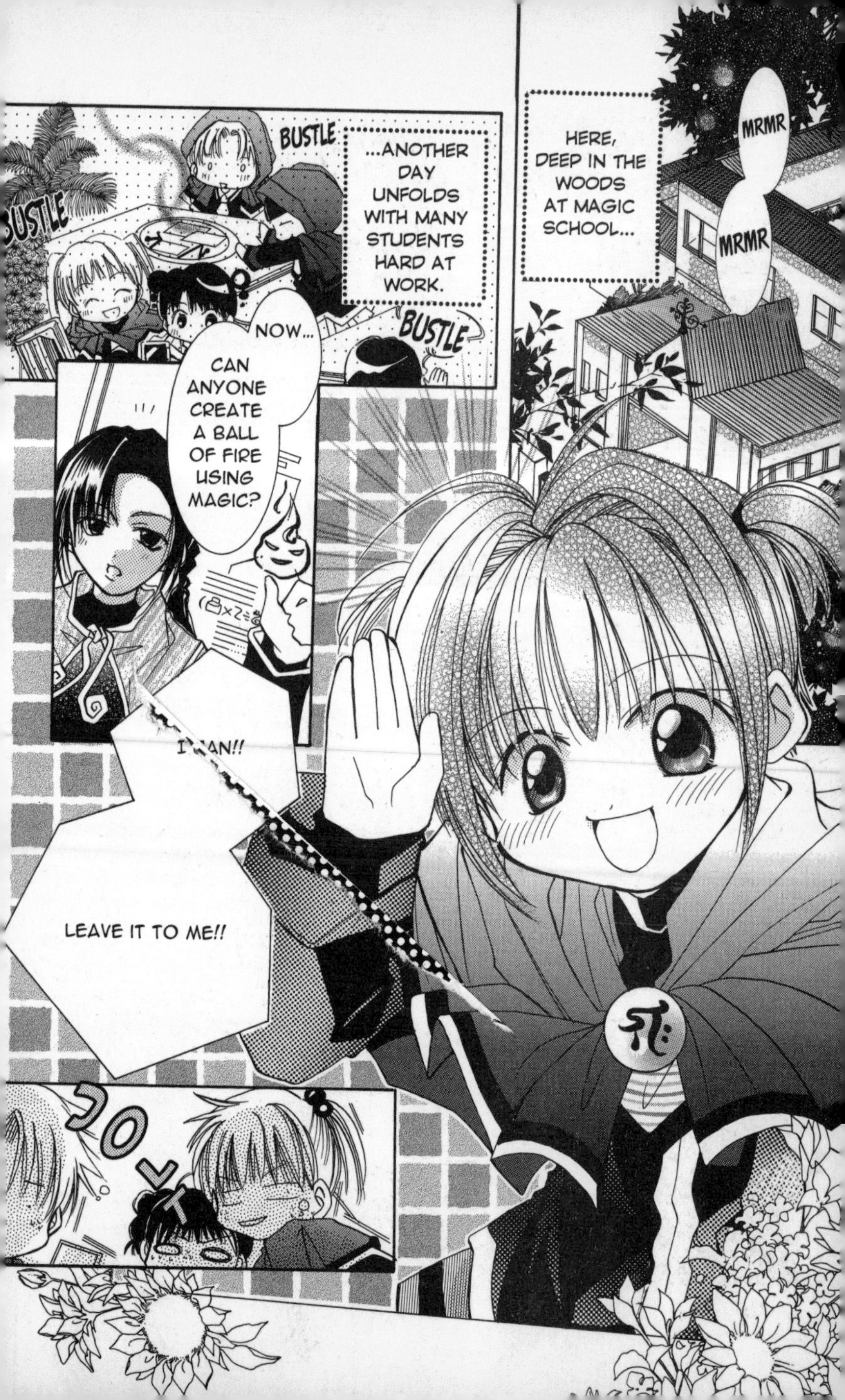
HERE, DEEP IN THE WOODS AT MAGIC SCHOOL...
MRMR
MRMR
...ANOTHER DAY UNFOLDS WITH MANY STUDENTS HARD AT WORK.
BUSTLE
BUSTLE
BUSTLE
NOW...
CAN ANYONE CREATE A BALL OF FIRE USING MAGIC?
I CAN!!
LEAVE IT TO ME!!

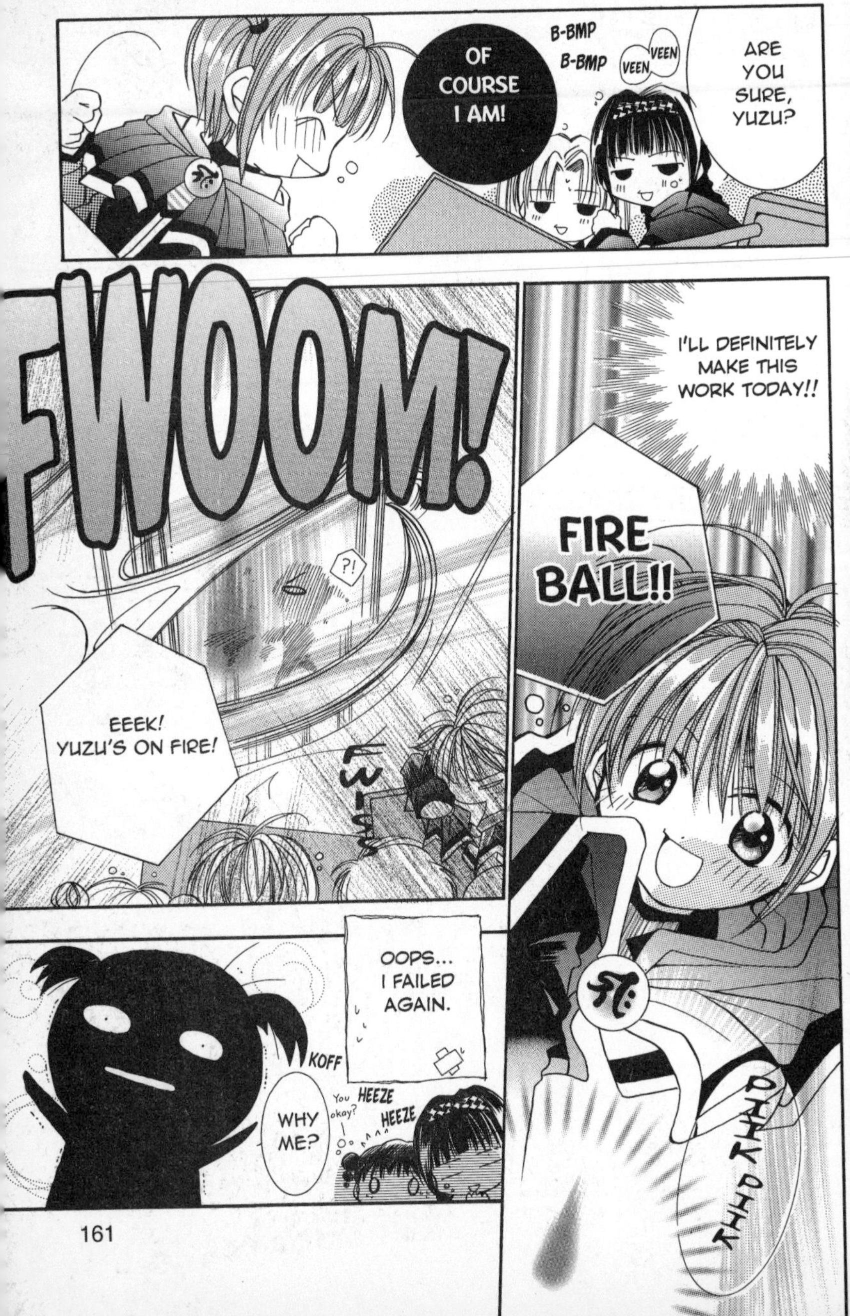
ARE YOU SURE, YUZU?
VEEN VEEN
B-BMP B-BMP
OF COURSE I AM!
I'LL DEFINITELY MAKE THIS WORK TODAY!!
FIRE BALL!!
FWOOM!
?!
EEEK! YUZU'S ON FIRE!
OOPS... I FAILED AGAIN.
HEEZE HEEZE
You okay?
WHY ME?
KOFF

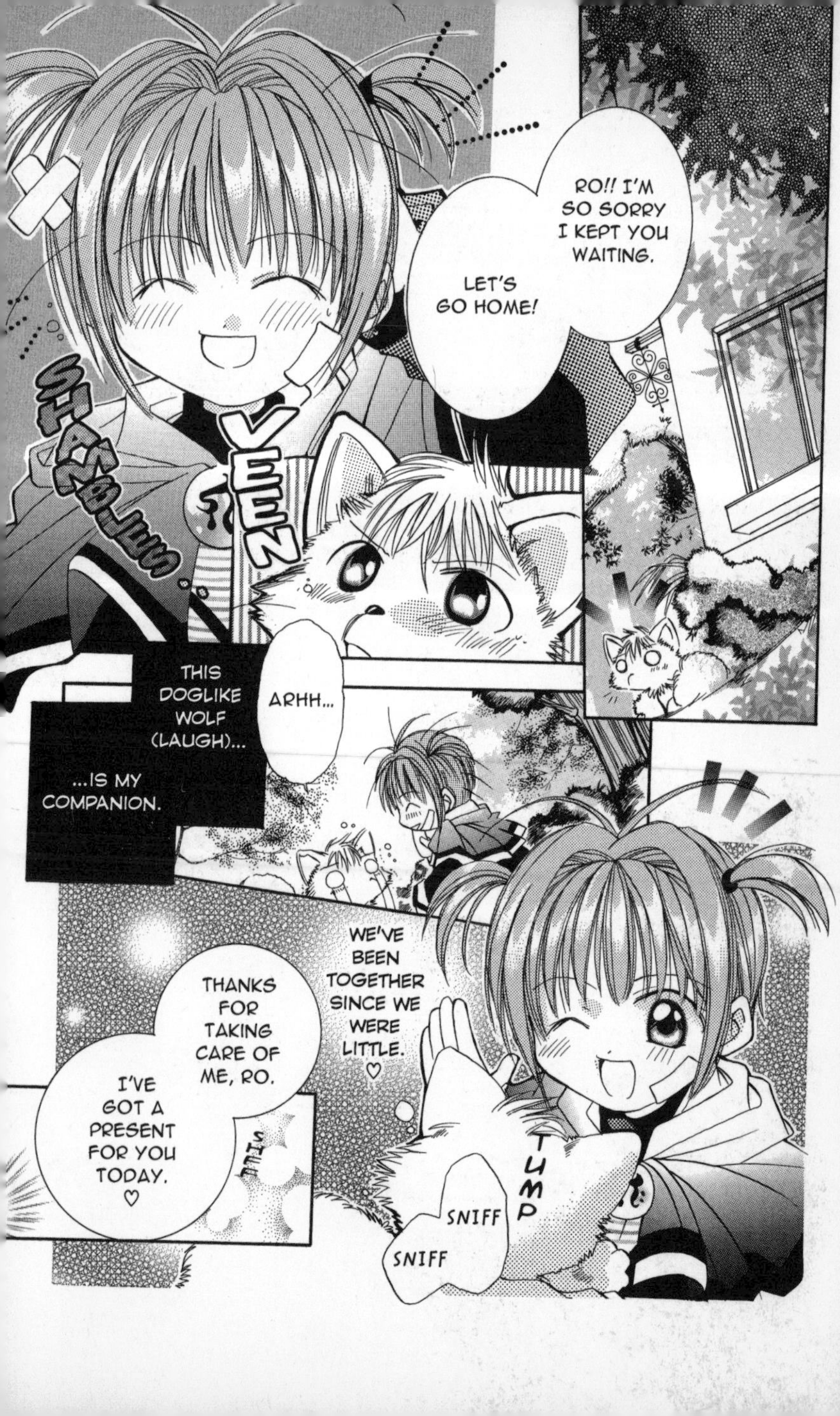
RO!! I'M SO SORRY I KEPT YOU WAITING.
LET'S GO HOME!
VEEN
SHAMBLES
ARHH...
THIS DOGLIKE WOLF (LAUGH)...
...IS MY COMPANION.
WE'VE BEEN TOGETHER SINCE WE WERE LITTLE. ♡
THANKS FOR TAKING CARE OF ME, RO.
I'VE GOT A PRESENT FOR YOU TODAY. ♡
TUMP
SNIFF
SNIFF
STILL

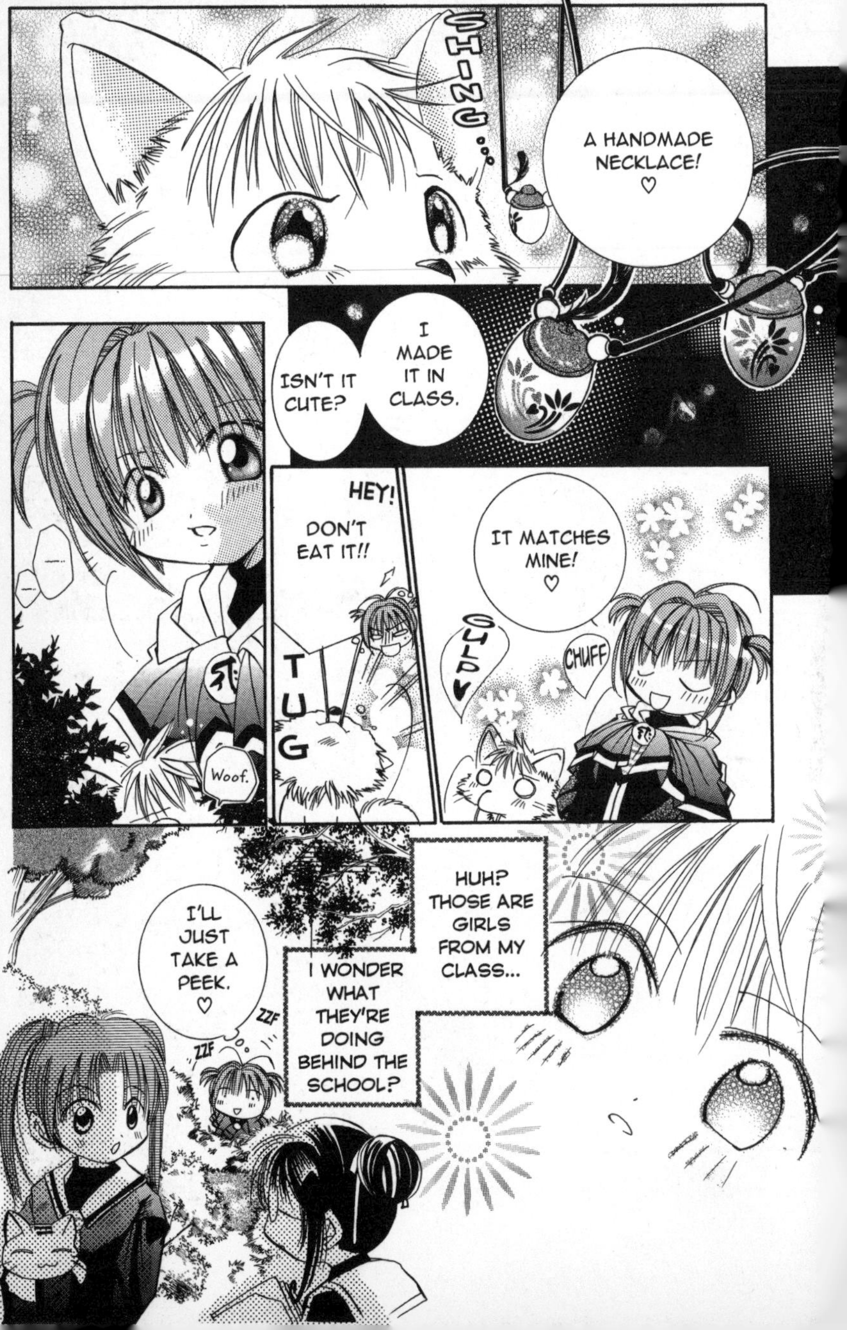
A HANDMADE NECKLACE! ♡
SHING...
I MADE IT IN CLASS.
ISN'T IT CUTE?
IT MATCHES MINE! ♡
CHUFF
GULP
HEY!
DON'T EAT IT!!
TUG
Woof.
HUH? THOSE ARE GIRLS FROM MY CLASS...
I WONDER WHAT THEY'RE DOING BEHIND THE SCHOOL?
I'LL JUST TAKE A PEEK. ♡
ZZF
ZZF

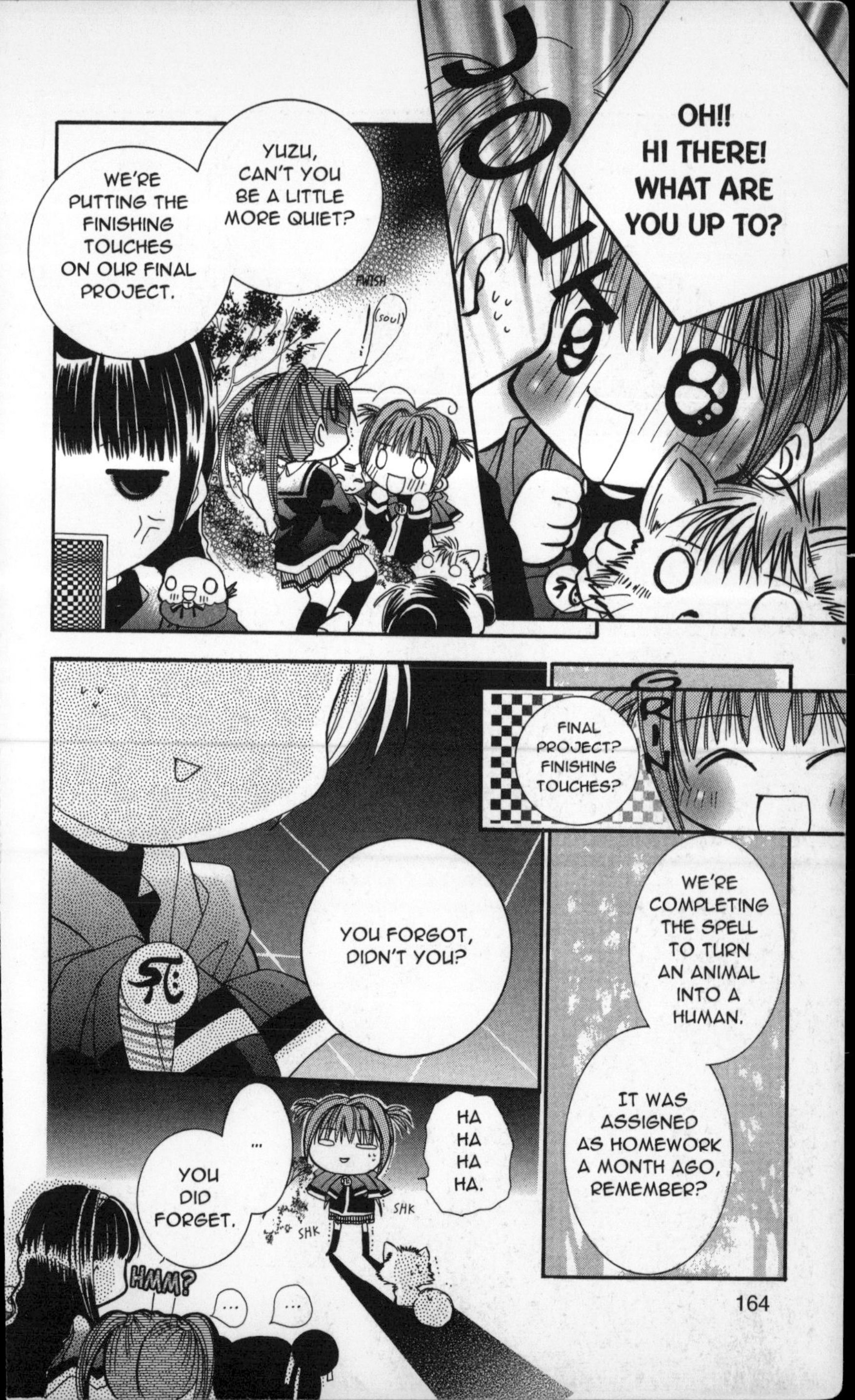
JOLT
OH!! HI THERE! WHAT ARE YOU UP TO?
YUZU, CAN'T YOU BE A LITTLE MORE QUIET?
WE'RE PUTTING THE FINISHING TOUCHES ON OUR FINAL PROJECT.
FWISH
(soul)
!
GRIN
FINAL PROJECT? FINISHING TOUCHES?
WE'RE COMPLETING THE SPELL TO TURN AN ANIMAL INTO A HUMAN.
IT WAS ASSIGNED AS HOMEWORK A MONTH AGO, REMEMBER?
YOU FORGOT, DIDN'T YOU?
HA HA HA HA.
SHK
SHK
... YOU DID FORGET.
HMM?
...
...

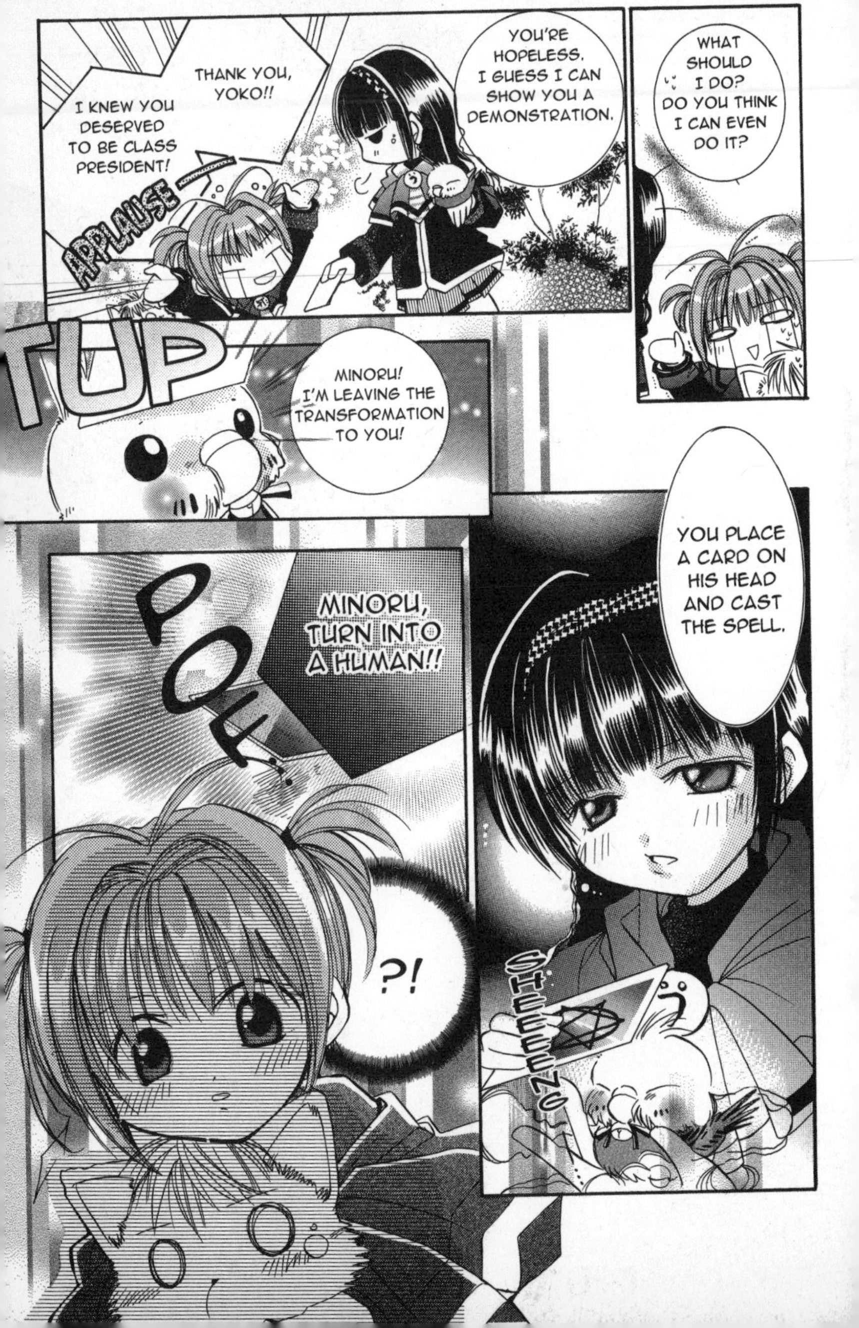
WHAT SHOULD I DO? DO YOU THINK I CAN EVEN DO IT?
YOU'RE HOPELESS. I GUESS I CAN SHOW YOU A DEMONSTRATION.
THANK YOU, YOKO!!
I KNEW YOU DESERVED TO BE CLASS PRESIDENT!
APPLAUSE
TUP
MINORU! I'M LEAVING THE TRANSFORMATION TO YOU!
YOU PLACE A CARD ON HIS HEAD AND CAST THE SPELL.
SHEEEENG
POOF
MINORU, TURN INTO A HUMAN!!
?!

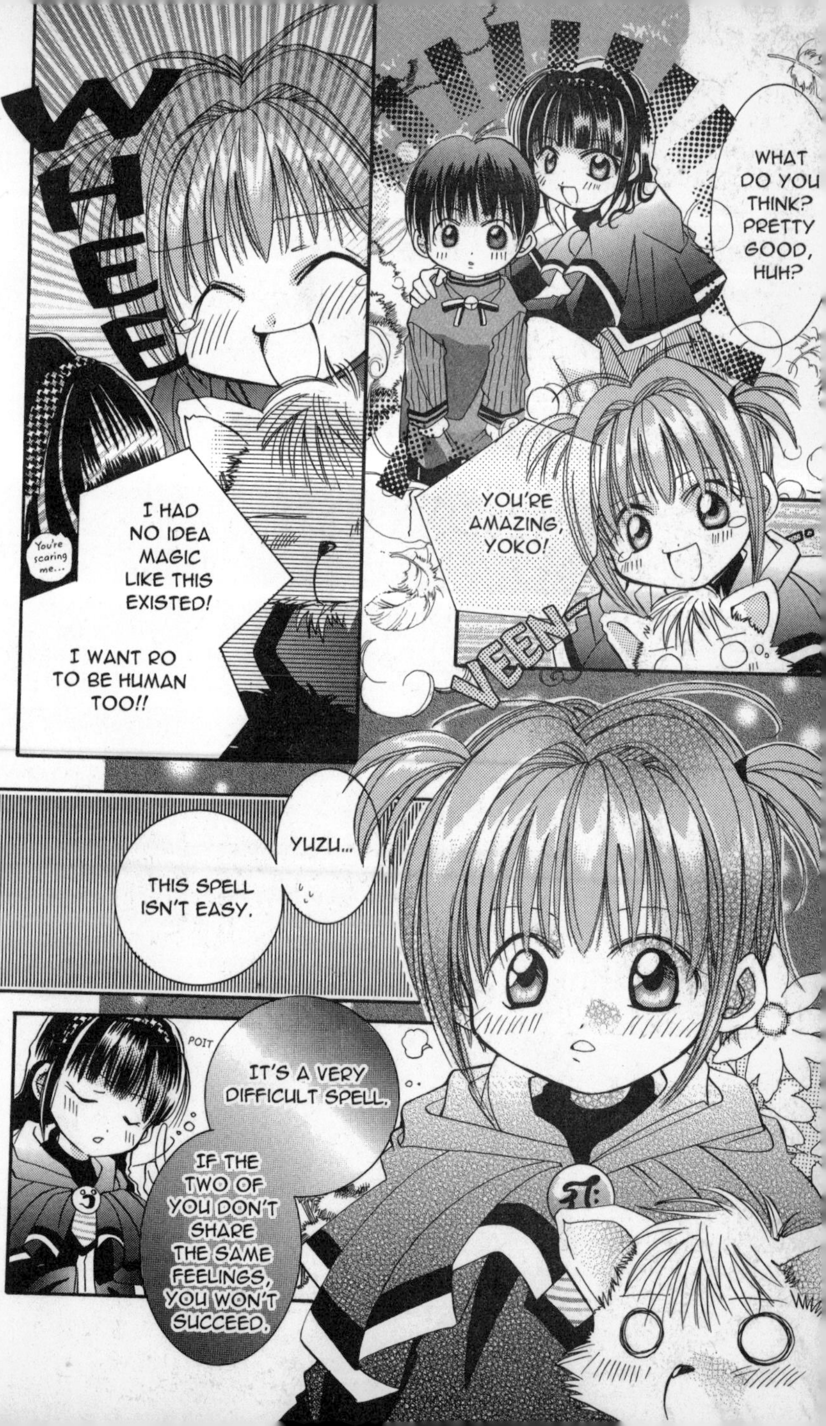
WHAT DO YOU THINK? PRETTY GOOD, HUH?
YOU'RE AMAZING, YOKO!
VEEN
WHEEE
I HAD NO IDEA MAGIC LIKE THIS EXISTED!
I WANT RO TO BE HUMAN TOO!!
You're scaring me...
YUZU...
THIS SPELL ISN'T EASY.
POIT
IT'S A VERY DIFFICULT SPELL.
IF THE TWO OF YOU DON'T SHARE THE SAME FEELINGS, YOU WON'T SUCCEED.

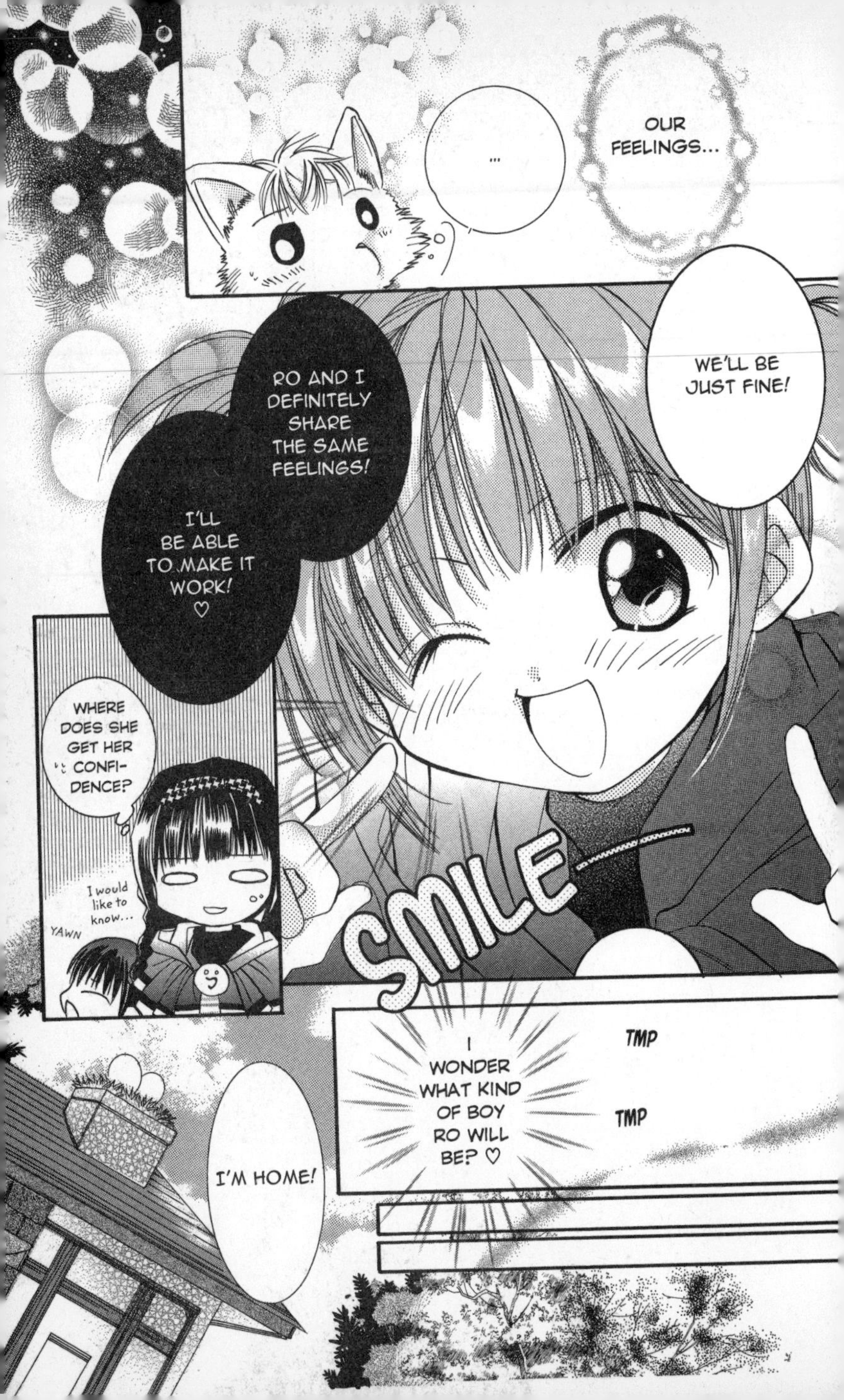
OUR FEELINGS...
...
WE'LL BE JUST FINE!
RO AND I DEFINITELY SHARE THE SAME FEELINGS!
I'LL BE ABLE TO MAKE IT WORK! ♡
SMILE
WHERE DOES SHE GET HER CONFIDENCE?
I would like to know...
YAWN
TMP
TMP
I WONDER WHAT KIND OF BOY RO WILL BE? ♡
I'M HOME!

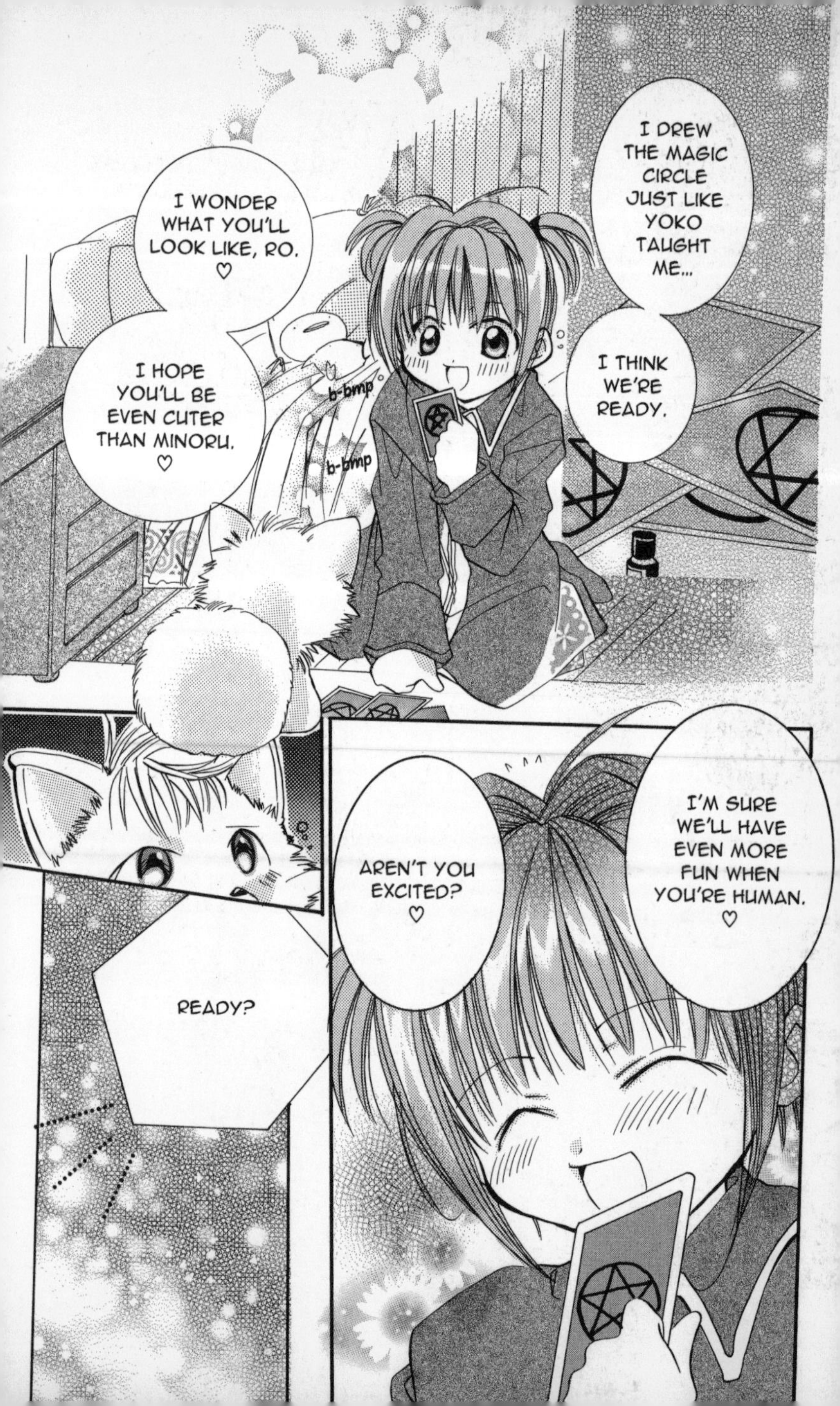
I DREW THE MAGIC CIRCLE JUST LIKE YOKO TAUGHT ME...
I THINK WE'RE READY.
I WONDER WHAT YOU'LL LOOK LIKE, RO. ♡
I HOPE YOU'LL BE EVEN CUTER THAN MINORU. ♡
b-bmp
b-bmp
I'M SURE WE'LL HAVE EVEN MORE FUN WHEN YOU'RE HUMAN. ♡
AREN'T YOU EXCITED? ♡
READY?

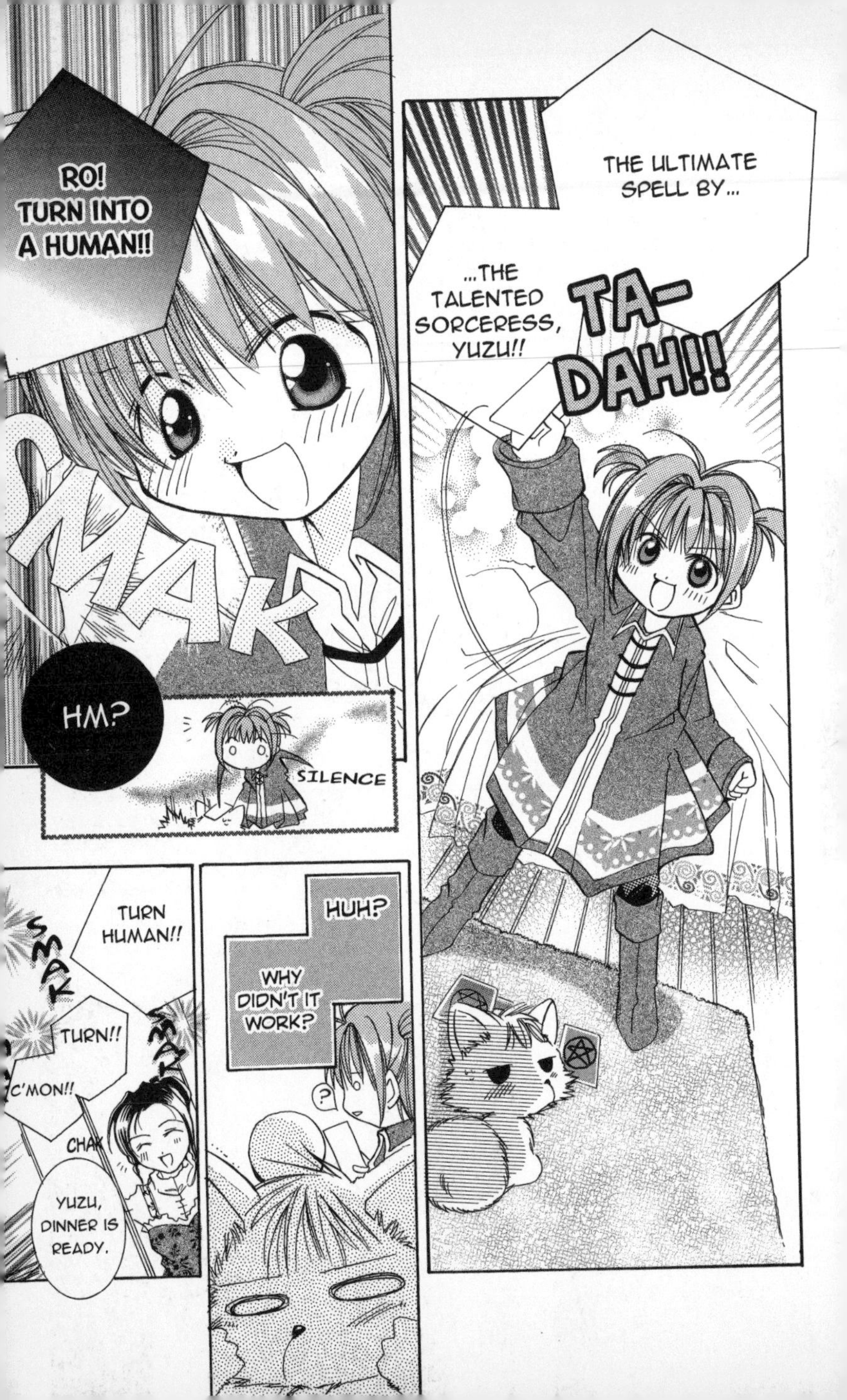
THE ULTIMATE SPELL BY...
...THE TALENTED SORCERESS, YUZU!!
TA-DAH!!
RO! TURN INTO A HUMAN!!
SMAK
HM?
SILENCE
HUH?
WHY DIDN'T IT WORK?
TURN HUMAN!!
SMAK
TURN!!
C'MON!!
CHAK
YUZU, DINNER IS READY.

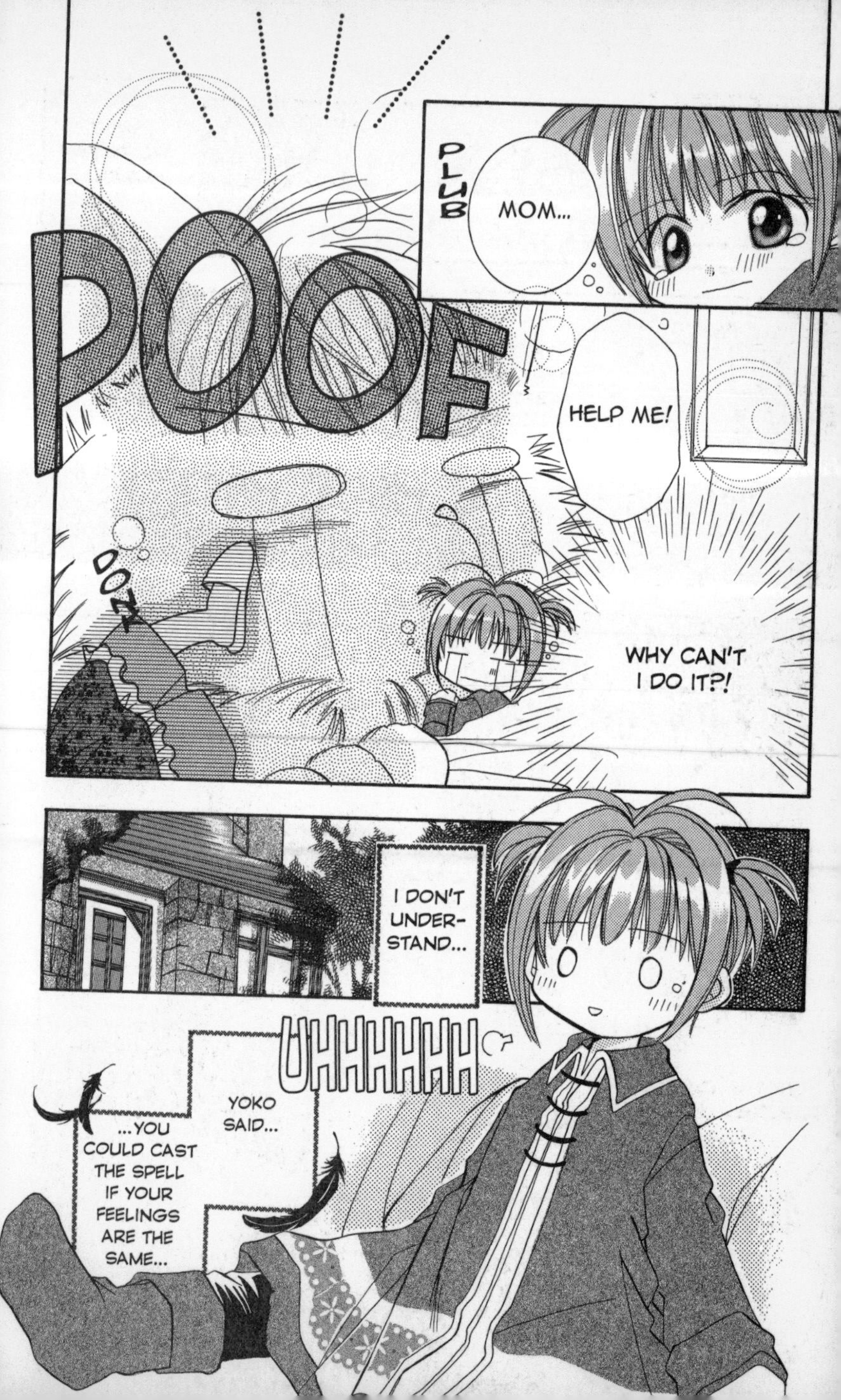
PLUB
MOM...
POOF
HELP ME!
WHY CAN'T I DO IT?!
DON
I DON'T UNDER-STAND...
UHHHHHH
YOKO SAID...
...YOU COULD CAST THE SPELL IF YOUR FEELINGS ARE THE SAME...

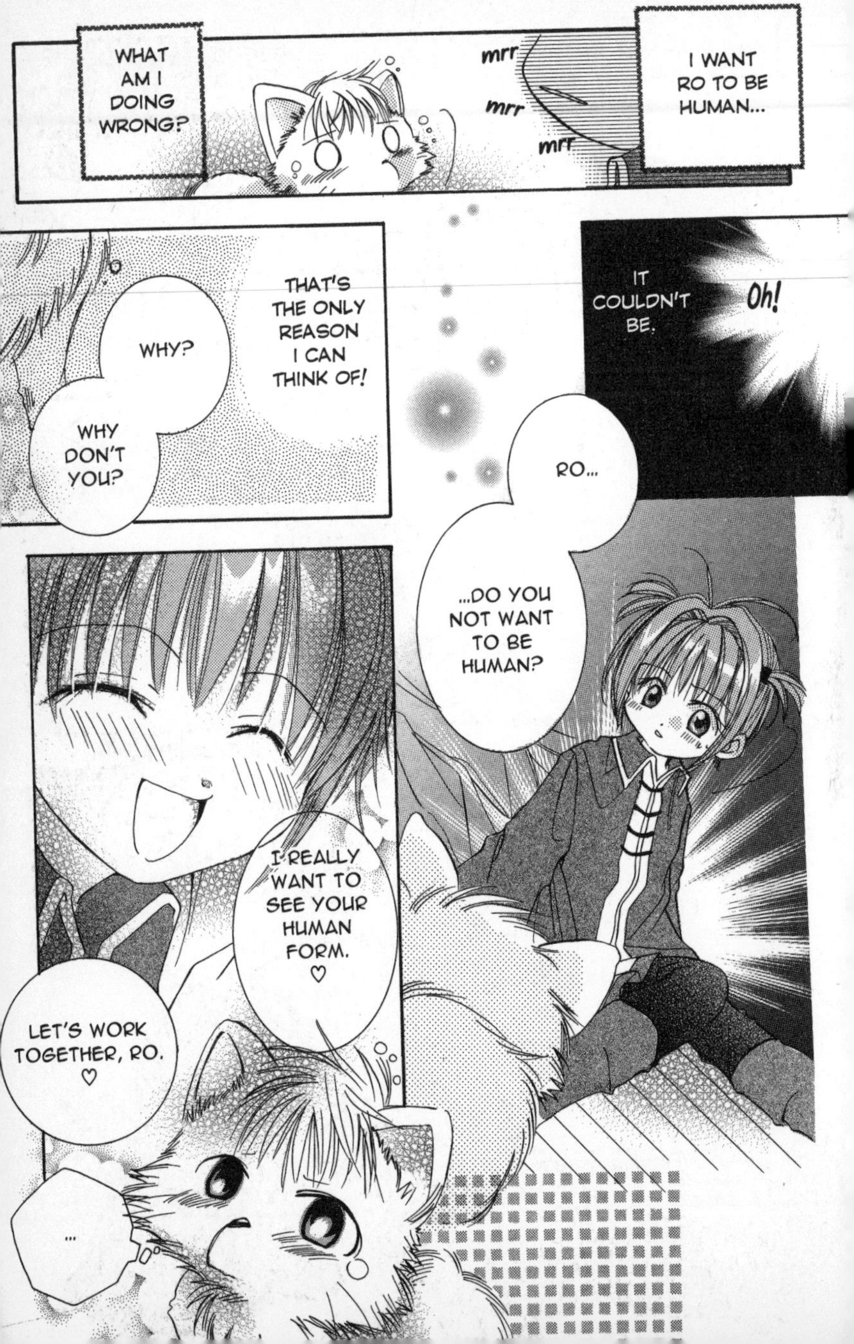
I WANT RO TO BE HUMAN...
mrr
mrr
mrr
WHAT AM I DOING WRONG?
IT COULDN'T BE.
Oh!
THAT'S THE ONLY REASON I CAN THINK OF!
WHY?
WHY DON'T YOU?
RO...
...DO YOU NOT WANT TO BE HUMAN?
I REALLY WANT TO SEE YOUR HUMAN FORM. ♡
LET'S WORK TOGETHER, RO. ♡
...

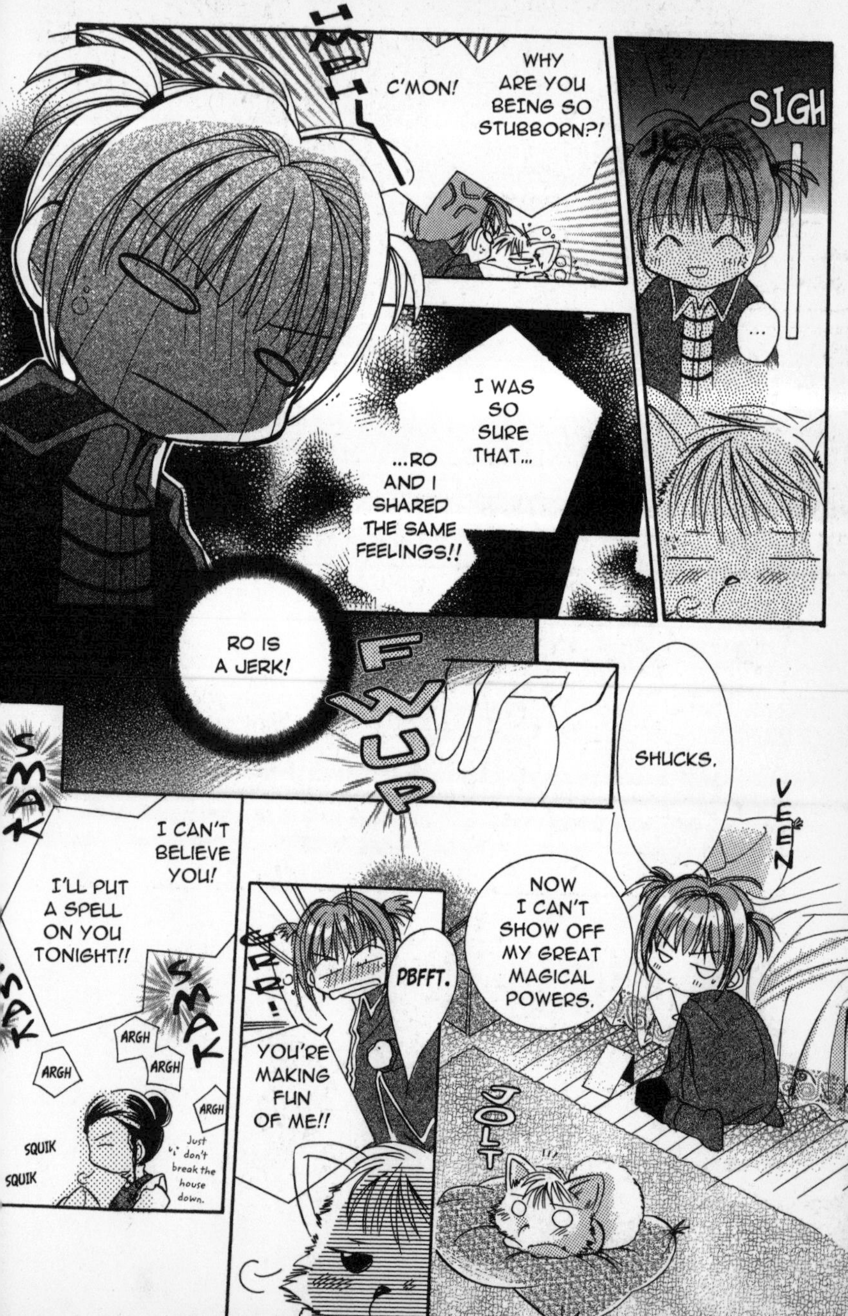
SIGH
...
WHY ARE YOU BEING SO STUBBORN?!
C'MON!
IRK
I WAS SO SURE THAT...
...RO AND I SHARED THE SAME FEELINGS!!
RO IS A JERK!
FWUP
SHUCKS.
VEEN
NOW I CAN'T SHOW OFF MY GREAT MAGICAL POWERS.
JOLT
PBFFT.
GRR!
YOU'RE MAKING FUN OF ME!!
I CAN'T BELIEVE YOU!
I'LL PUT A SPELL ON YOU TONIGHT!!
SMAK
SMAK
SMAK
ARGH
ARGH
ARGH
ARGH
Just don't break the house down.
SQUIK
SQUIK

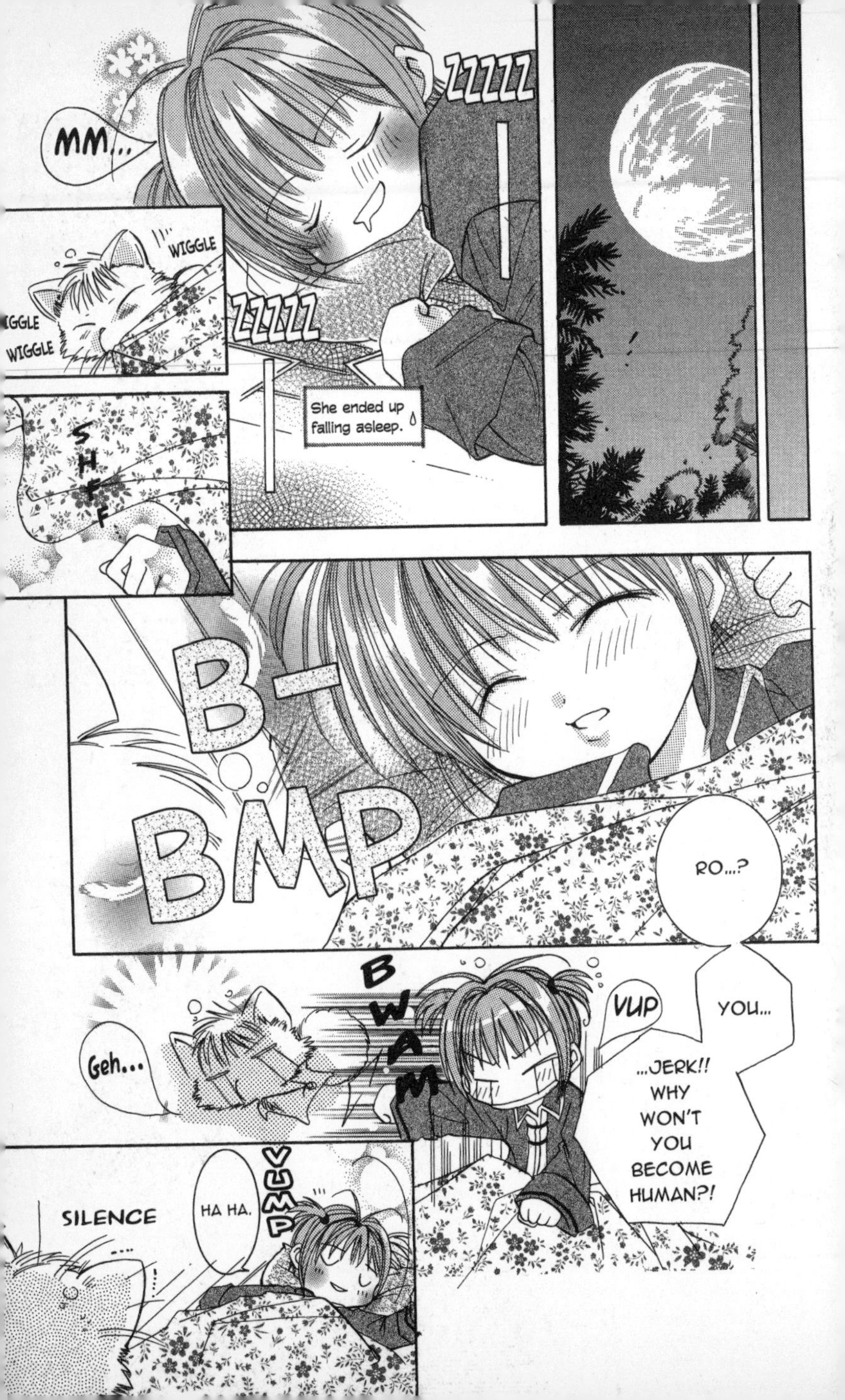
ZZZZZ
MM...
ZZZZZ
She ended up falling asleep.
WIGGLE
IGGLE
WIGGLE
SHFF
B-BMP
RO...?
YOU...
...JERK!! WHY WON'T YOU BECOME HUMAN?!
VUP
BWAM
Geh...
VUMP
HA HA.
SILENCE
...

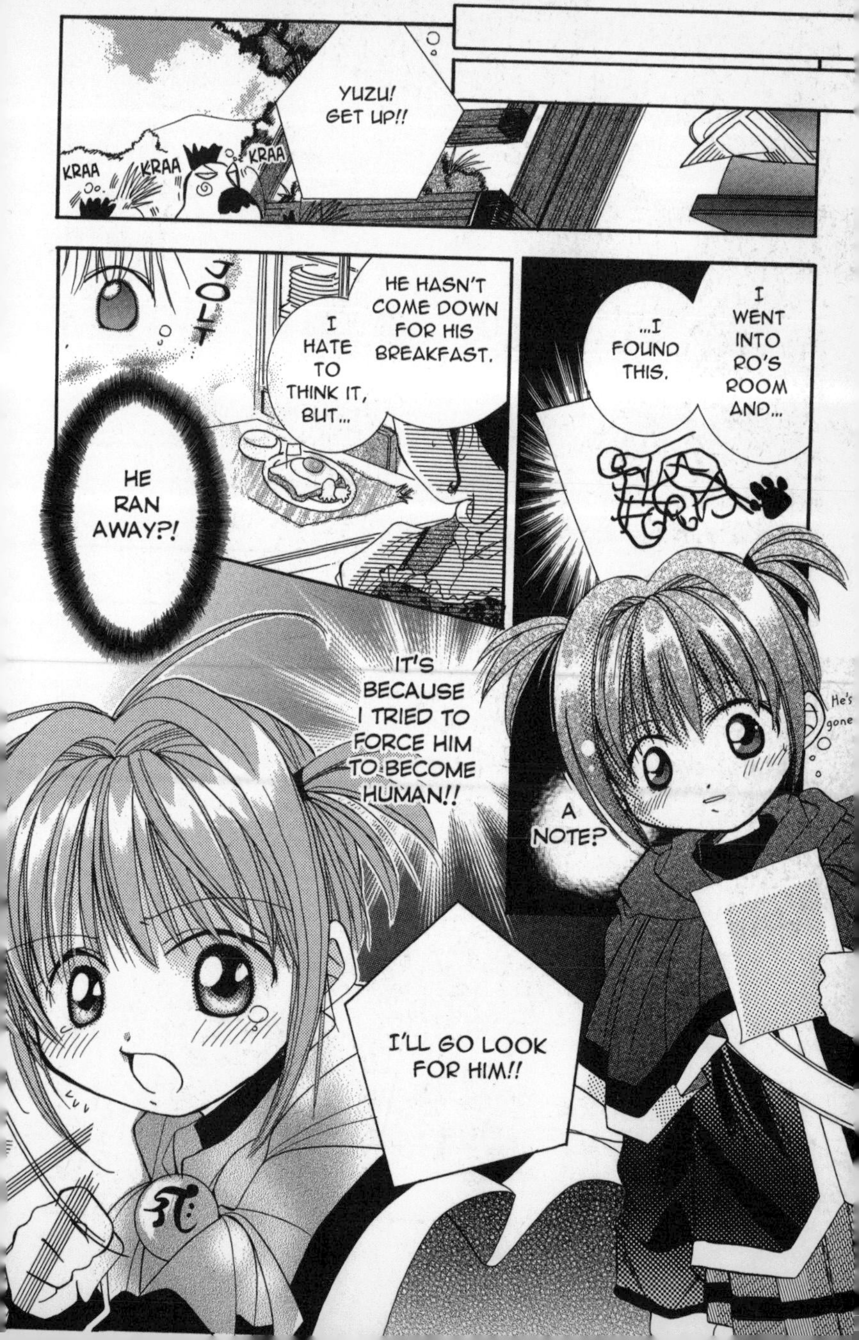
YUZU! GET UP!!
KRAA
KRAA
KRAA
I WENT INTO RO'S ROOM AND...
...I FOUND THIS.
He's gone
A NOTE?
HE HASN'T COME DOWN FOR HIS BREAKFAST.
I HATE TO THINK IT, BUT...
JOLT
HE RAN AWAY?!
IT'S BECAUSE I TRIED TO FORCE HIM TO BECOME HUMAN!!
I'LL GO LOOK FOR HIM!!

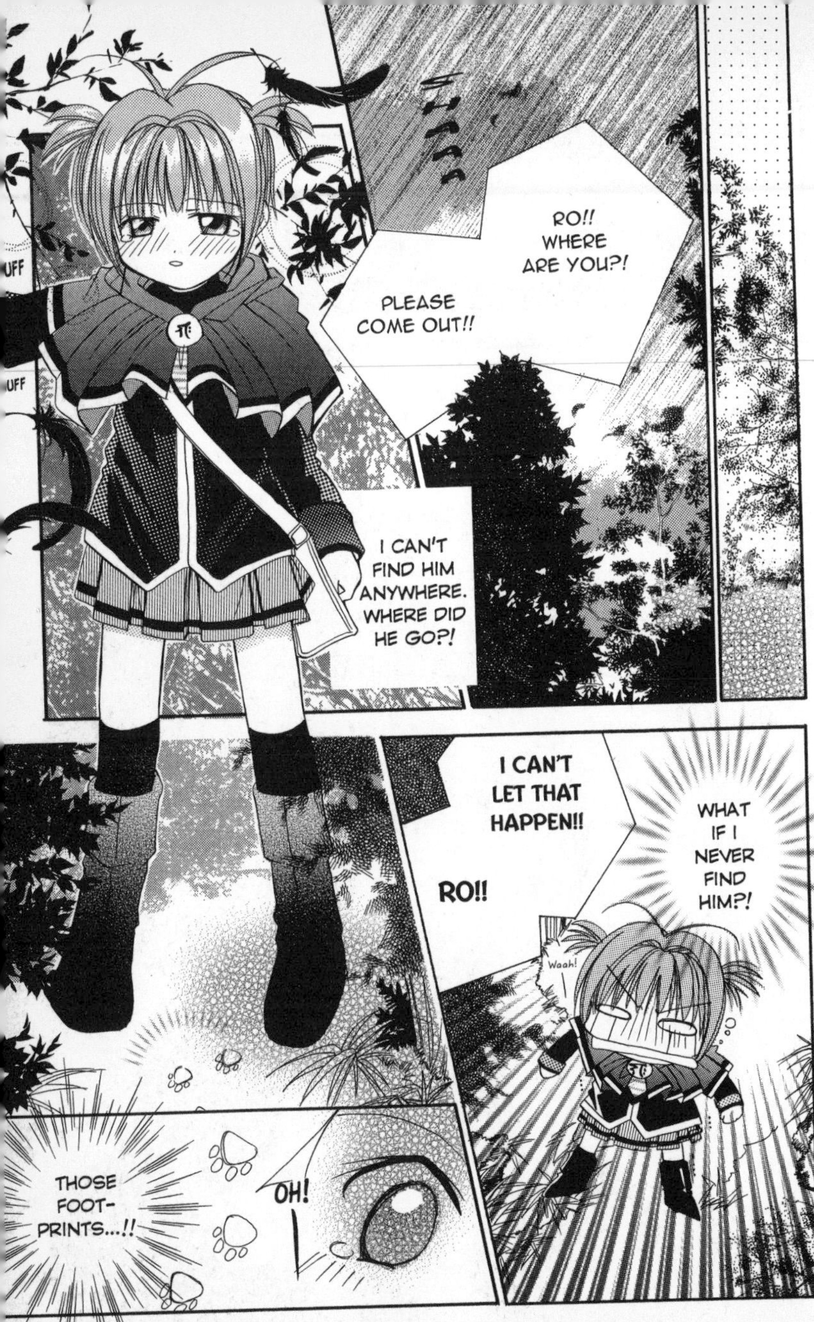
RO!! WHERE ARE YOU?!
PLEASE COME OUT!!
I CAN'T FIND HIM ANYWHERE. WHERE DID HE GO?!
WHAT IF I NEVER FIND HIM?!
Waah!
I CAN'T LET THAT HAPPEN!!
RO!!
OH!
THOSE FOOT-PRINTS...!!

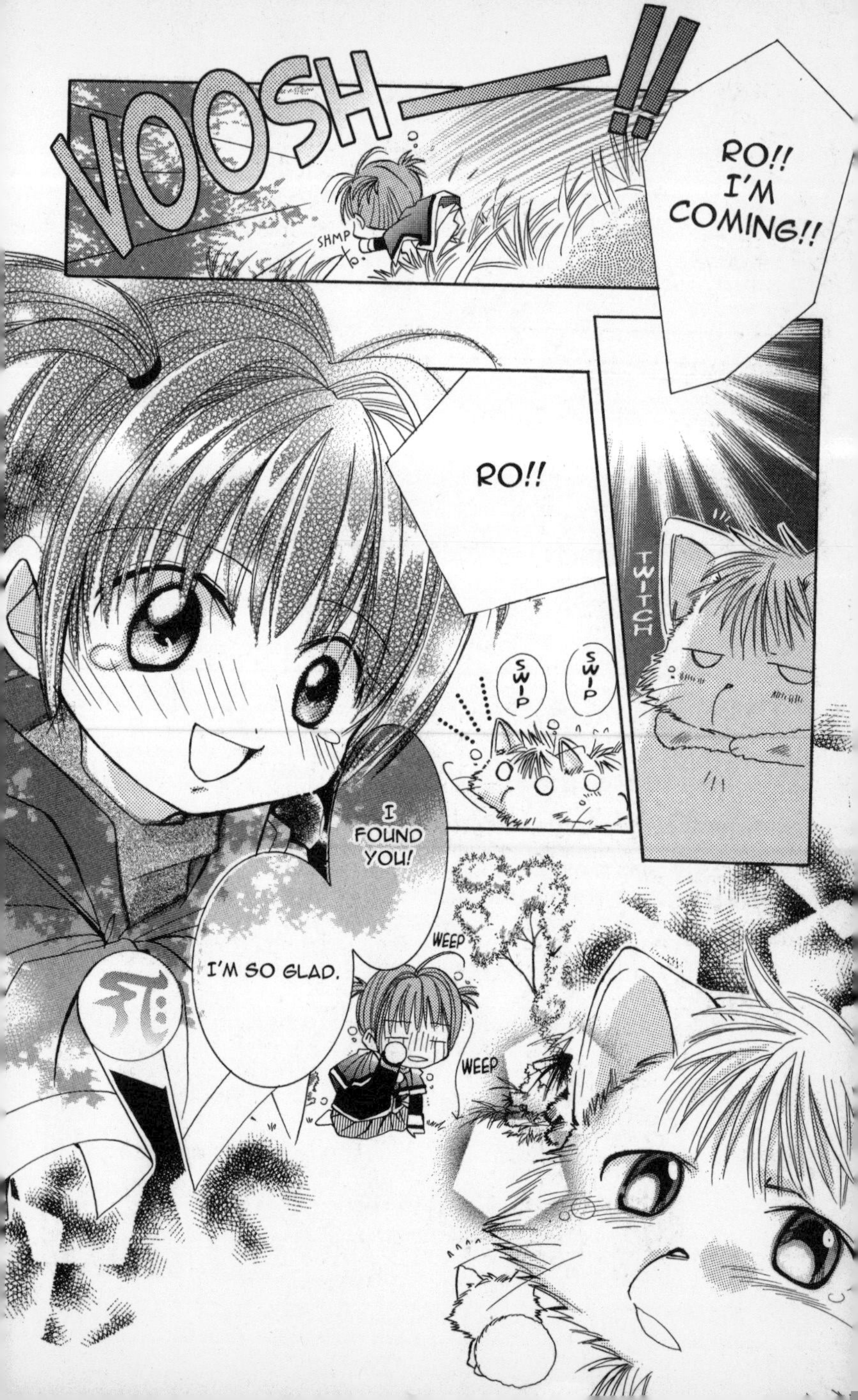
RO!! I'M COMING!!
VOOSH—!!
SHMP
TWITCH
RO!!
SWIP
SWIP
I FOUND YOU!
I'M SO GLAD.
WEEP
WEEP

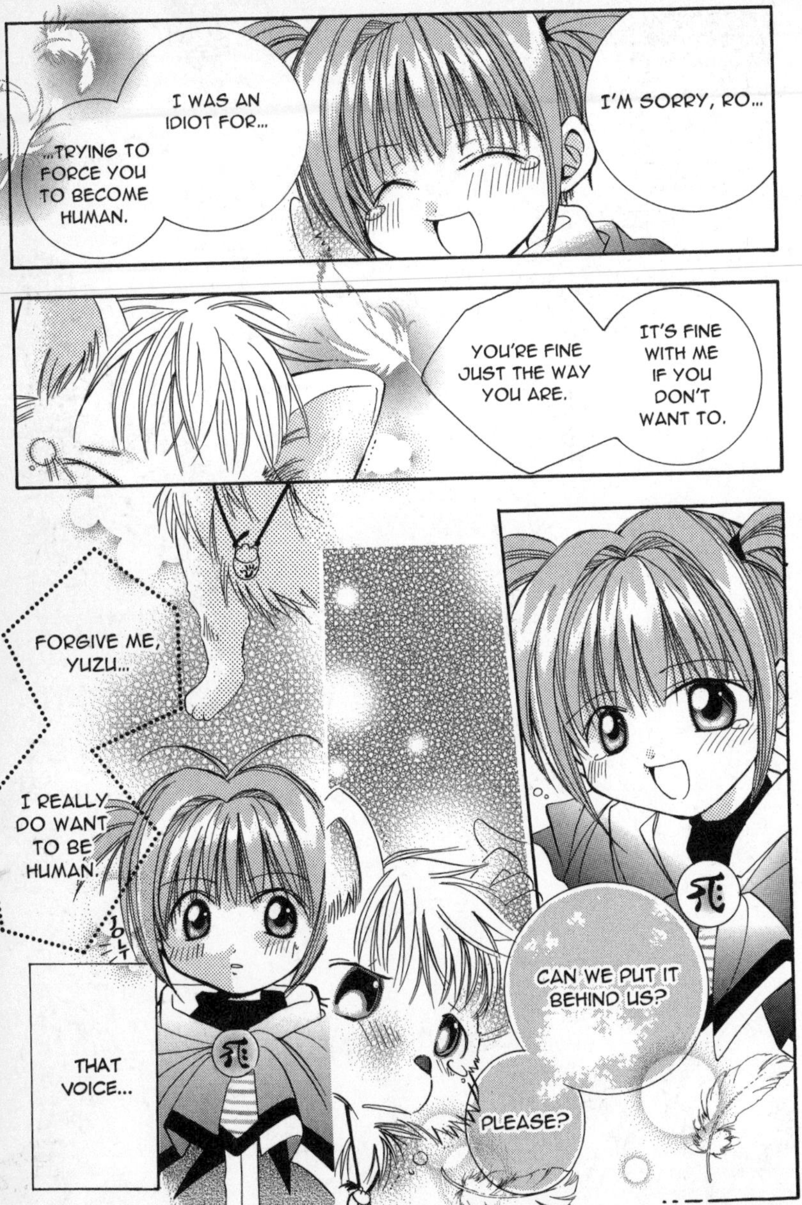
I'M SORRY, RO...
I WAS AN IDIOT FOR...
...TRYING TO FORCE YOU TO BECOME HUMAN.
IT'S FINE WITH ME IF YOU DON'T WANT TO.
YOU'RE FINE JUST THE WAY YOU ARE.
CAN WE PUT IT BEHIND US?
PLEASE?
FORGIVE ME, YUZU...
I REALLY DO WANT TO BE HUMAN.
JOLT
THAT VOICE...

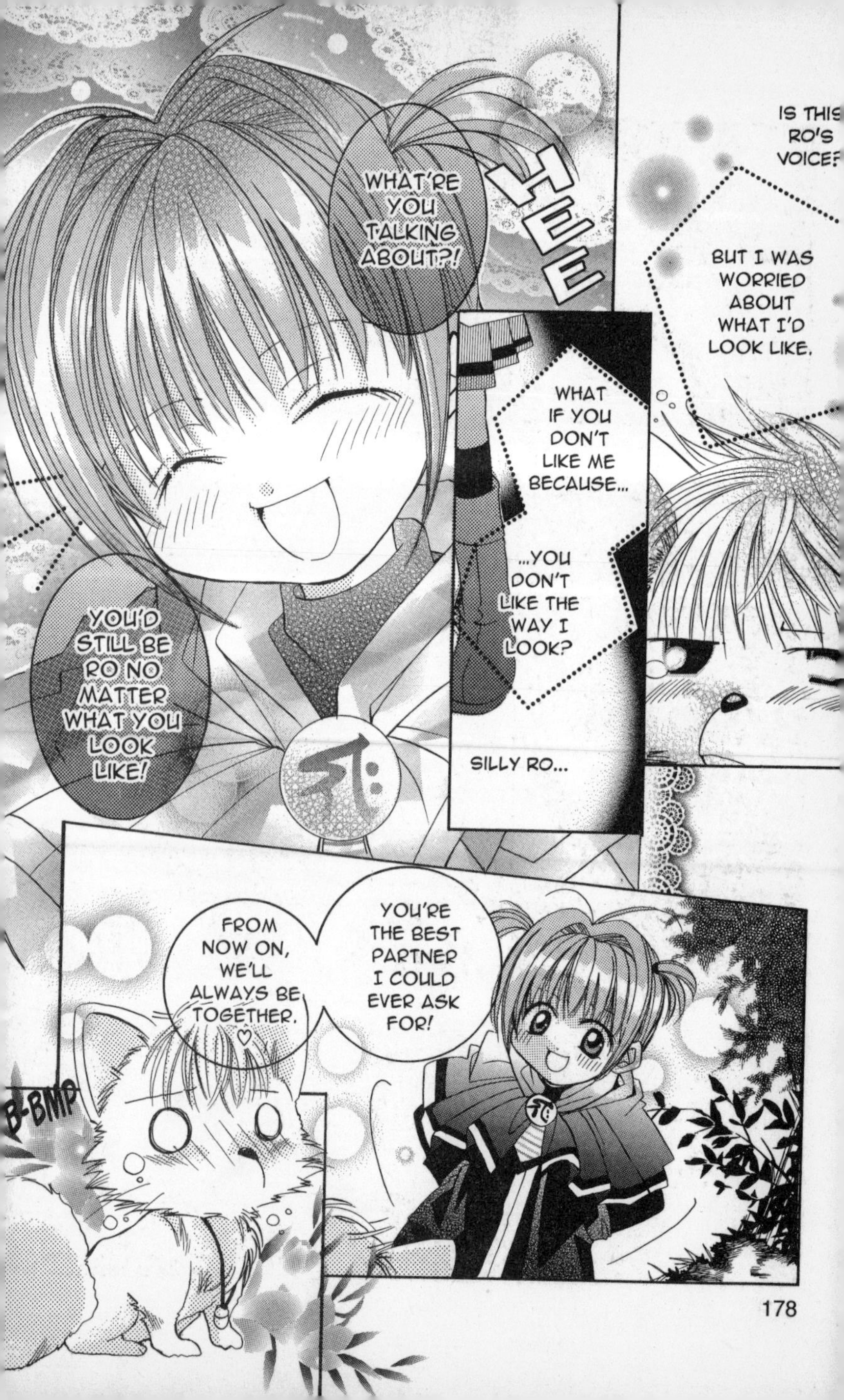
IS THIS RO'S VOICE?
BUT I WAS WORRIED ABOUT WHAT I'D LOOK LIKE.
WHAT IF YOU DON'T LIKE ME BECAUSE...
...YOU DON'T LIKE THE WAY I LOOK?
SILLY RO...
HEE
WHAT'RE YOU TALKING ABOUT?!
YOU'D STILL BE RO NO MATTER WHAT YOU LOOK LIKE!
YOU'RE THE BEST PARTNER I COULD EVER ASK FOR!
FROM NOW ON, WE'LL ALWAYS BE TOGETHER. ♡
B-BMP

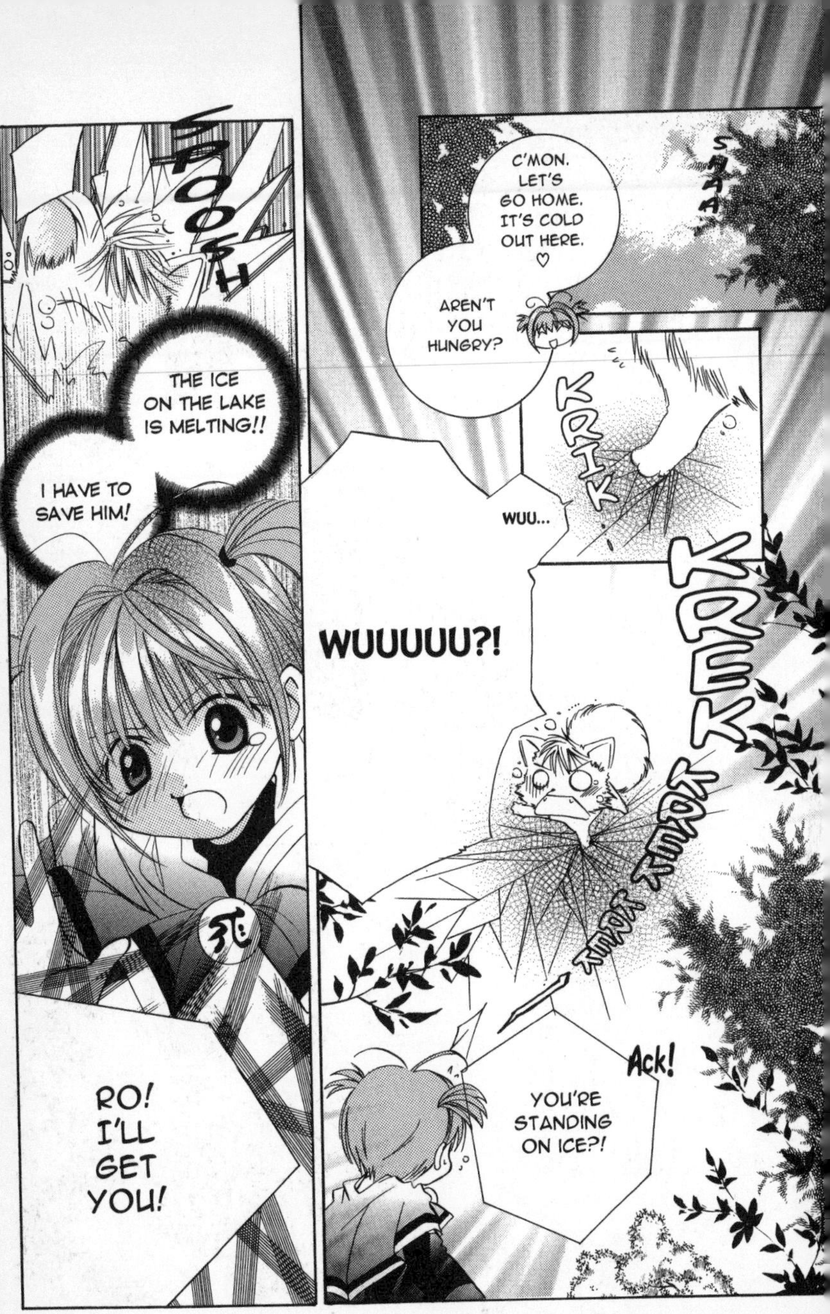
SHAA
C'MON. LET'S GO HOME. IT'S COLD OUT HERE. ♡
AREN'T YOU HUNGRY?
KRIK
WUU...
WUUUUU?!
KREK
Ack!
YOU'RE STANDING ON ICE?!
SPOOSH
THE ICE ON THE LAKE IS MELTING!!
I HAVE TO SAVE HIM!
RO! I'LL GET YOU!

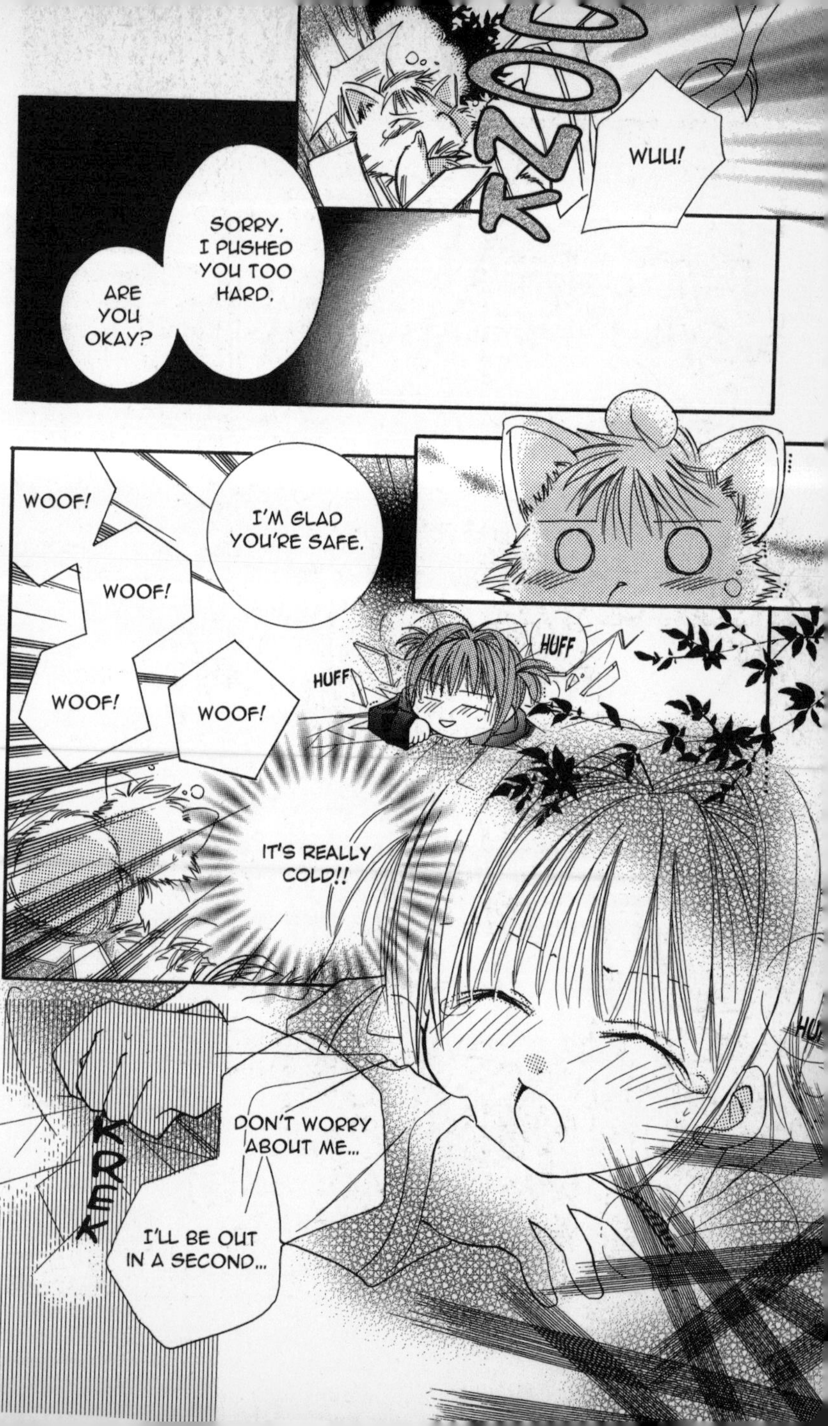
DONK
WUU!
SORRY. I PUSHED YOU TOO HARD.
ARE YOU OKAY?
I'M GLAD YOU'RE SAFE.
WOOF!
WOOF!
WOOF!
WOOF!
HUFF
HUFF
IT'S REALLY COLD!!
DON'T WORRY ABOUT ME...
I'LL BE OUT IN A SECOND...
KREK

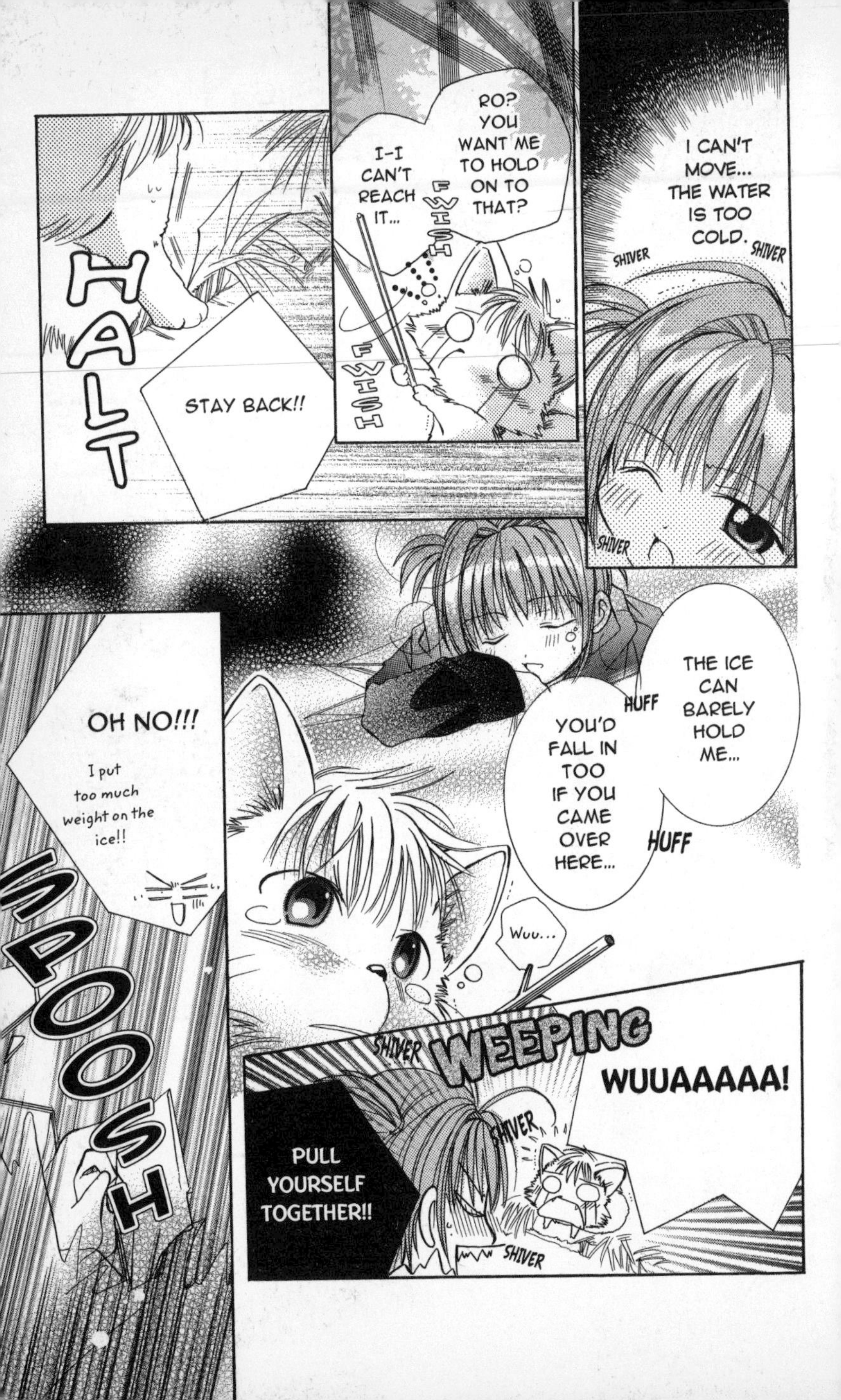
I CAN'T MOVE... THE WATER IS TOO COLD.
SHIVER
SHIVER
SHIVER
RO? YOU WANT ME TO HOLD ON TO THAT?
I-I CAN'T REACH IT...
FWISH
FWISH
STAY BACK!!
HALT
THE ICE CAN BARELY HOLD ME...
HUFF
YOU'D FALL IN TOO IF YOU CAME OVER HERE...
HUFF
Wuu...
WEEPING
WUUAAAAA!
SHIVER
SHIVER
PULL YOURSELF TOGETHER!!
SHIVER
OH NO!!!
I put too much weight on the ice!!
SWOOSH

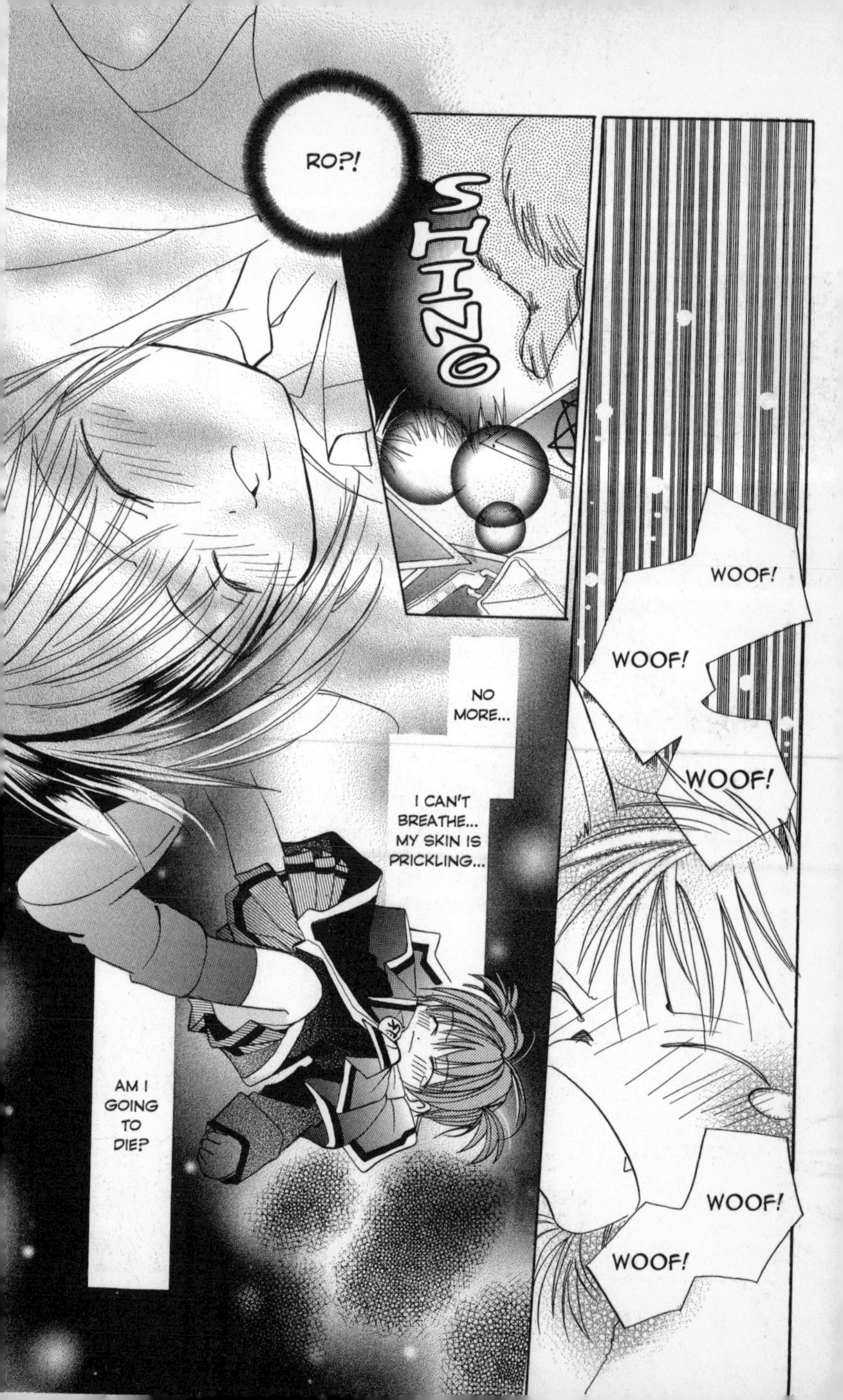
WOOF!
WOOF!
WOOF!
WOOF!
WOOF!
RO?!
SHING
NO MORE...
I CAN'T BREATHE... MY SKIN IS PRICKLING...
AM I GOING TO DIE?

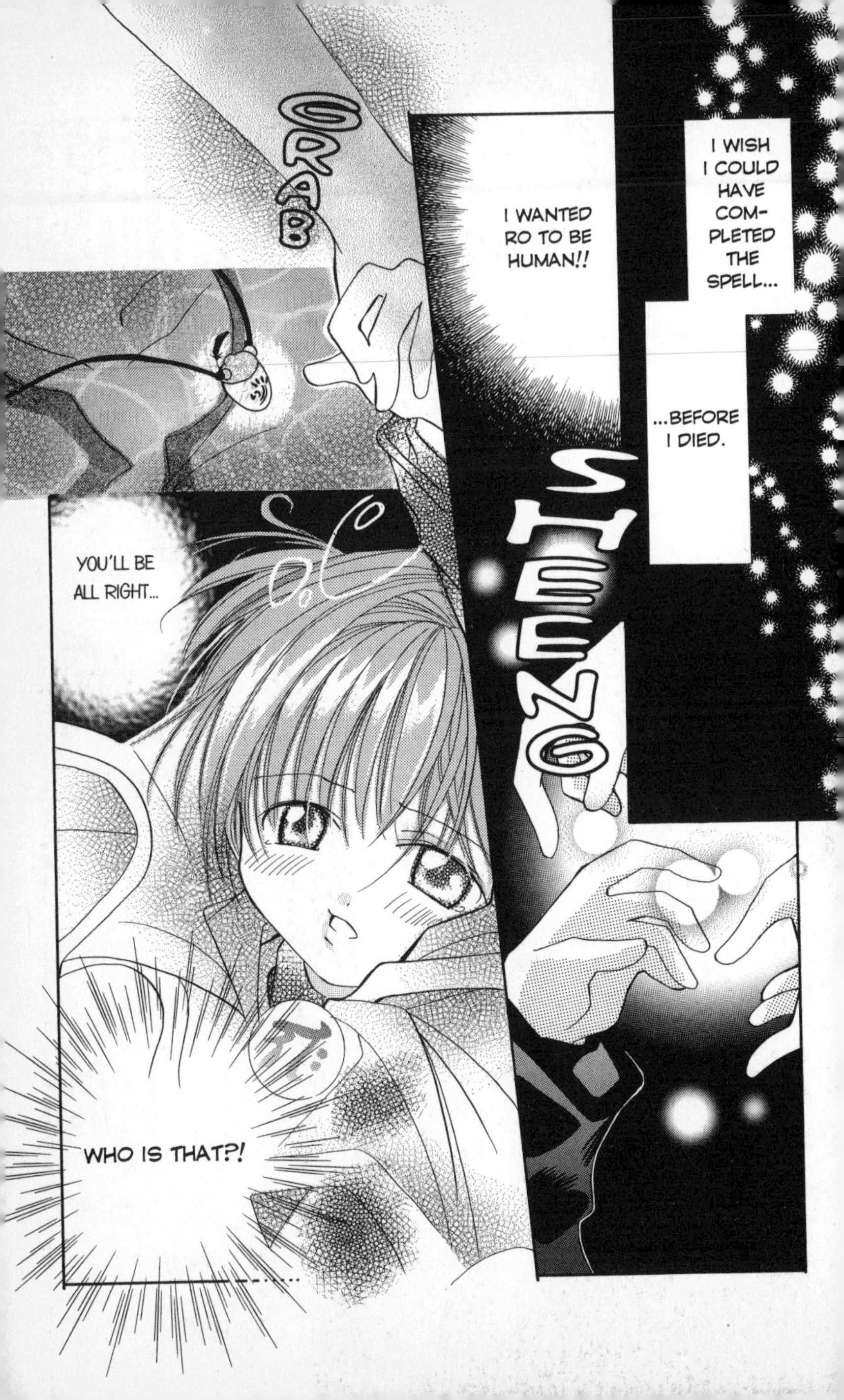
I WISH I COULD HAVE COMPLETED THE SPELL...
...BEFORE I DIED.
I WANTED RO TO BE HUMAN!!
GRAB
SHEENG
YOU'LL BE ALL RIGHT...
WHO IS THAT?!

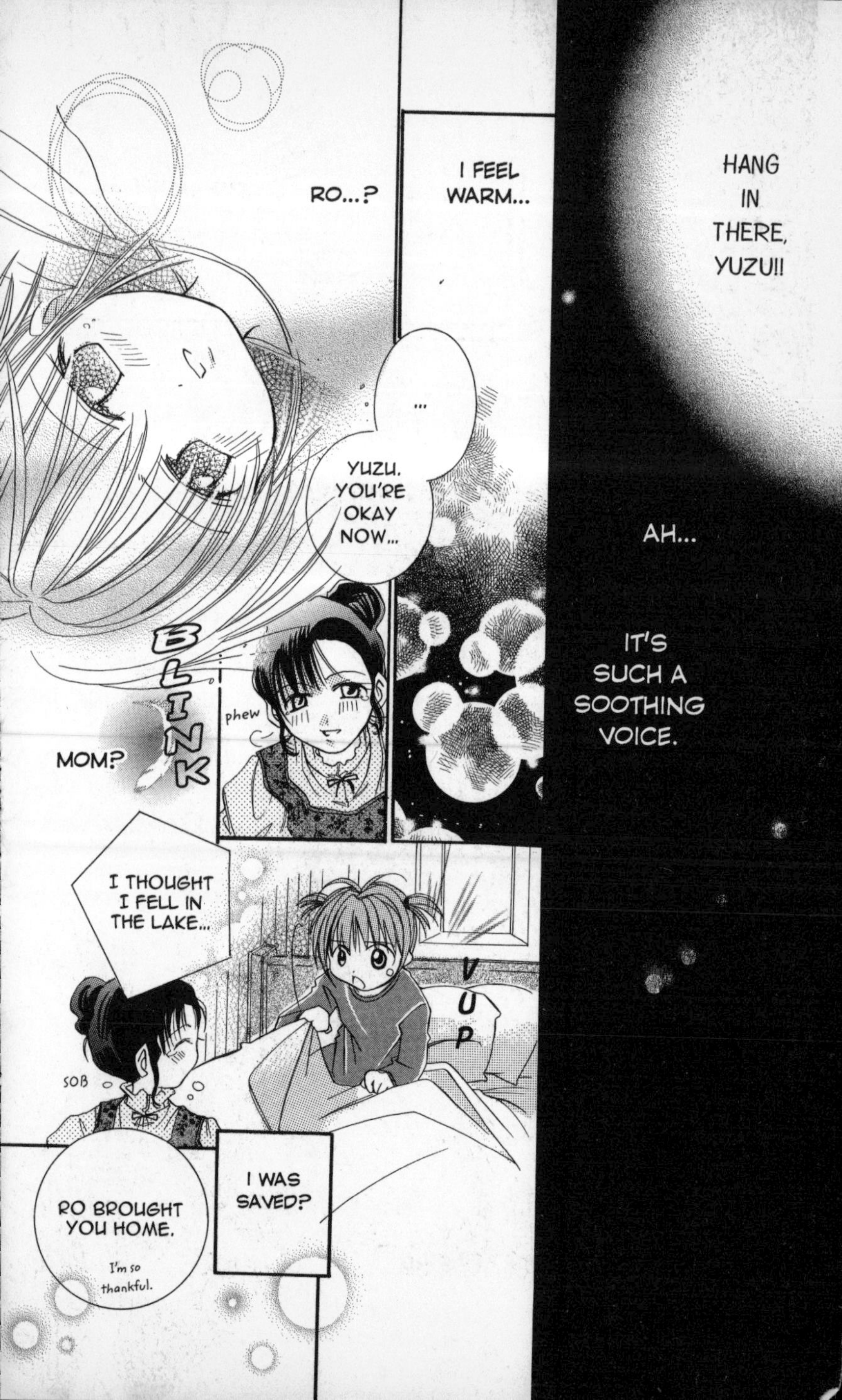
HANG IN THERE, YUZU!!
AH...
IT'S SUCH A SOOTHING VOICE.
I FEEL WARM...
RO...?
...
YUZU. YOU'RE OKAY NOW...
phew
BLINK
MOM?
I THOUGHT I FELL IN THE LAKE...
VUP
SOB
I WAS SAVED?
RO BROUGHT YOU HOME.
I'm so thankful.

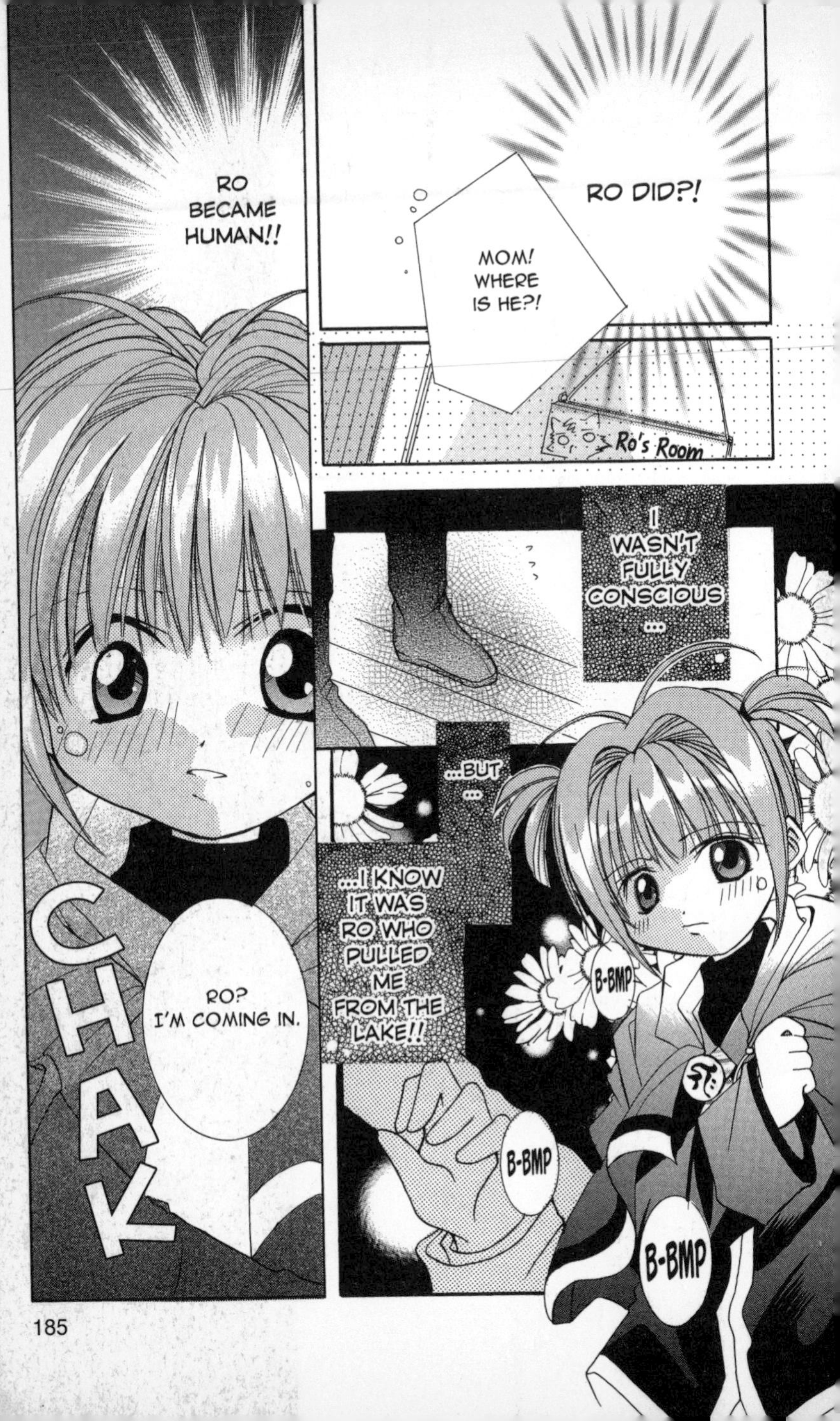
RO DID?!
MOM! WHERE IS HE?!
Ro's Room
I WASN'T FULLY CONSCIOUS...
...BUT...
...I KNOW IT WAS RO WHO PULLED ME FROM THE LAKE!!
B-BMP
B-BMP
B-BMP
RO BECAME HUMAN!!
RO? I'M COMING IN.
CHAK

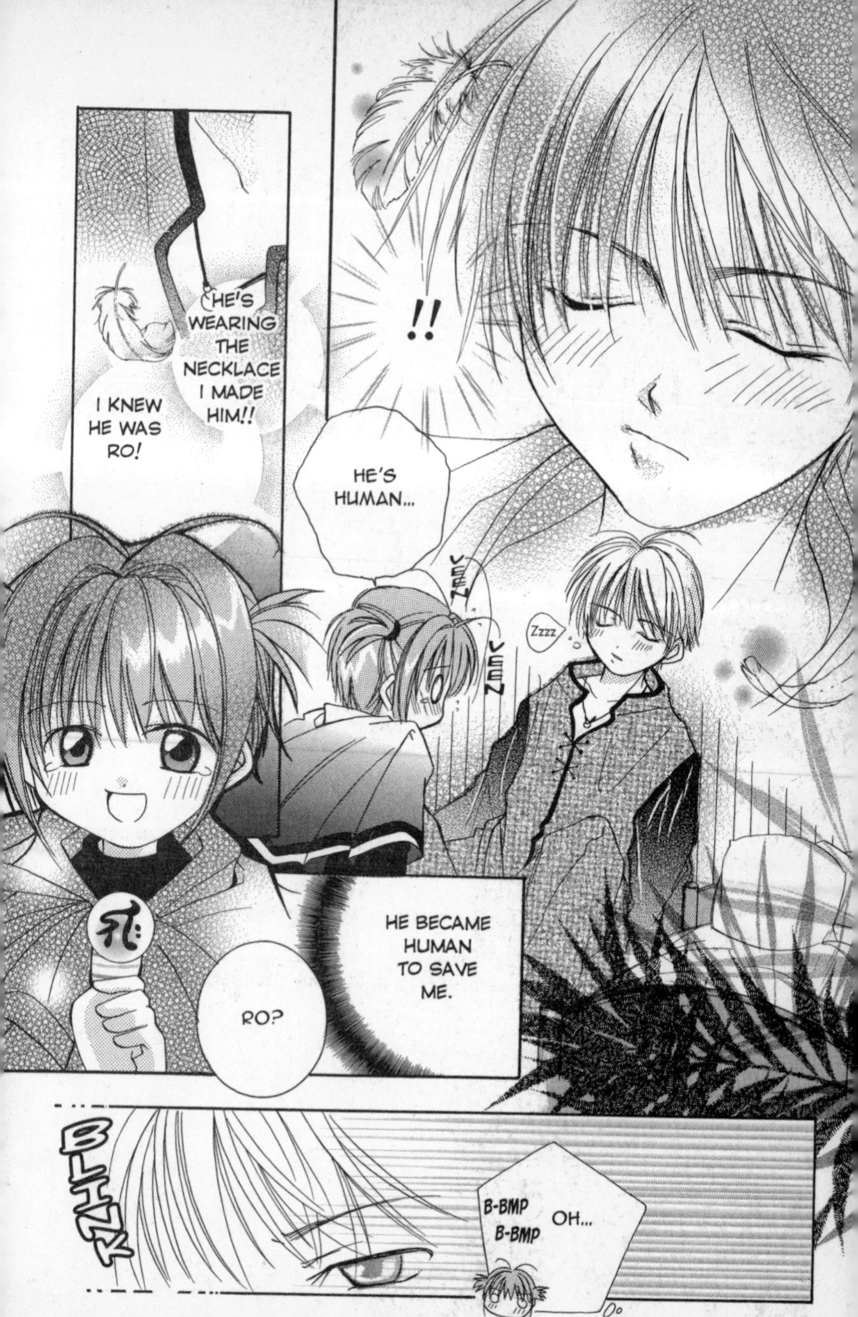
!!
HE'S HUMAN...
VEEN VEEN
Zzzz
HE'S WEARING THE NECKLACE I MADE HIM!!
I KNEW HE WAS RO!
HE BECAME HUMAN TO SAVE ME.
RO?
OH...
B-BMP B-BMP
BLINK

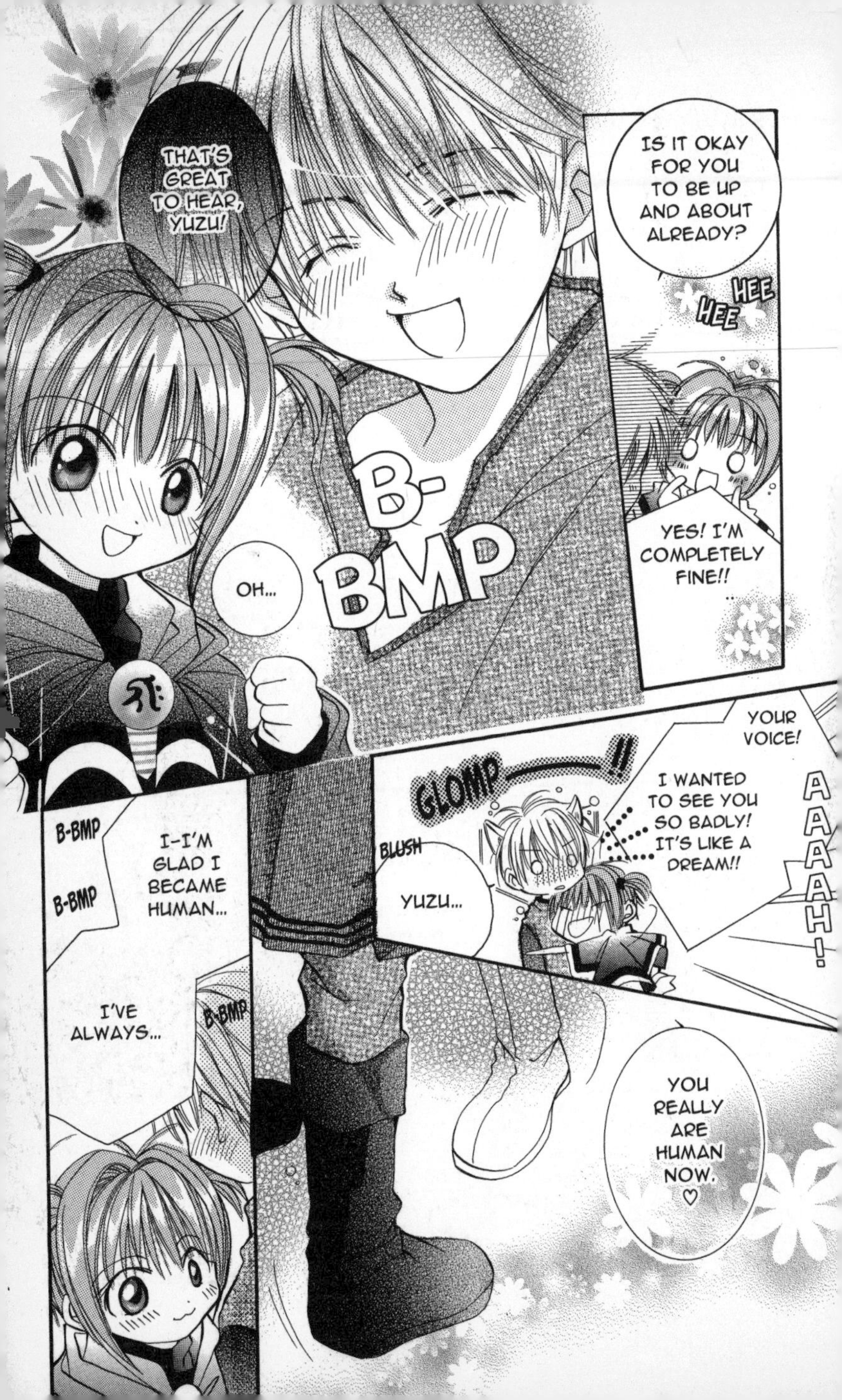
IS IT OKAY FOR YOU TO BE UP AND ABOUT ALREADY?
HEE HEE
YES! I'M COMPLETELY FINE!!
THAT'S GREAT TO HEAR, YUZU!
B-BMP
OH...
AAAAAH!
YOUR VOICE!
I WANTED TO SEE YOU SO BADLY! IT'S LIKE A DREAM!!
GLOMP—!!
BLUSH
YUZU...
YOU REALLY ARE HUMAN NOW. ♡
I-I'M GLAD I BECAME HUMAN...
B-BMP
B-BMP
I'VE ALWAYS...
B-BMP

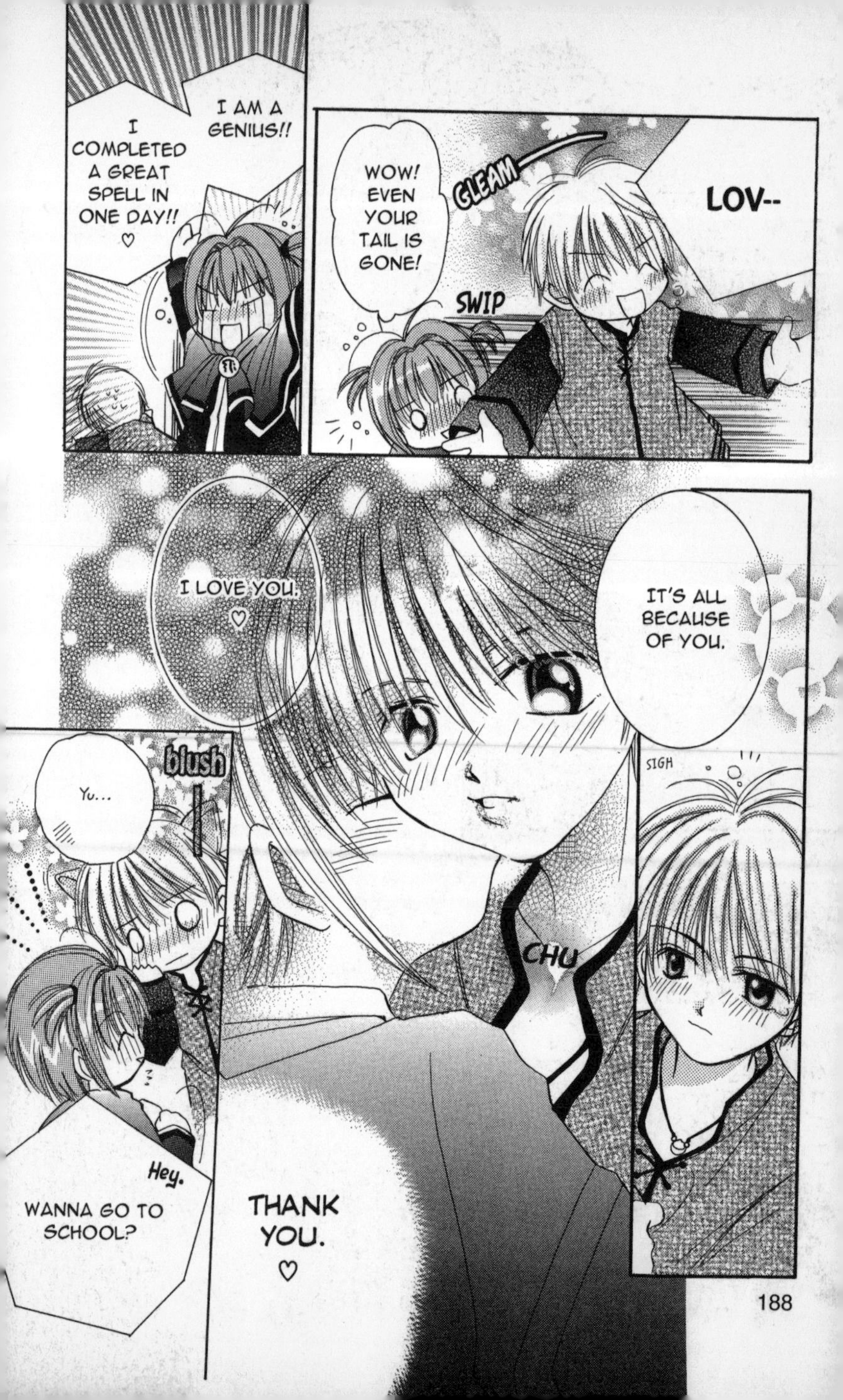
LOV--
GLEAM
WOW! EVEN YOUR TAIL IS GONE!
SWIP
I AM A GENIUS!!
I COMPLETED A GREAT SPELL IN ONE DAY!! ♡
IT'S ALL BECAUSE OF YOU.
SIGH
I LOVE YOU. ♡
CHU
THANK YOU. ♡
blush
Yu...
Hey.
WANNA GO TO SCHOOL?

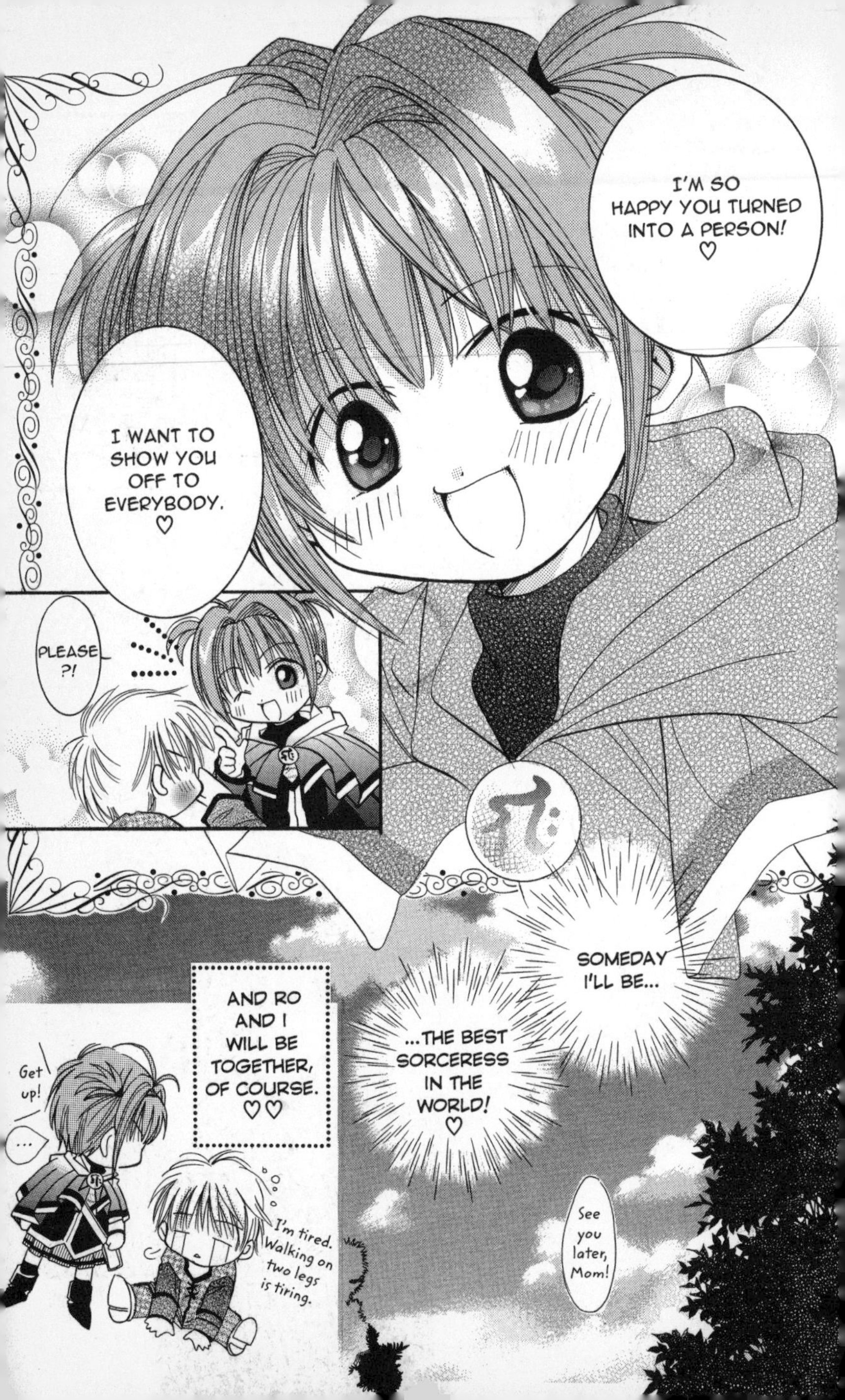
I'M SO HAPPY YOU TURNED INTO A PERSON! ♡
I WANT TO SHOW YOU OFF TO EVERYBODY. ♡
PLEASE?!
SOMEDAY I'LL BE...
...THE BEST SORCERESS IN THE WORLD! ♡
See you later, Mom!
AND RO AND I WILL BE TOGETHER, OF COURSE. ♡♡
Get up!
...
I'm tired. Walking on two legs is tiring.

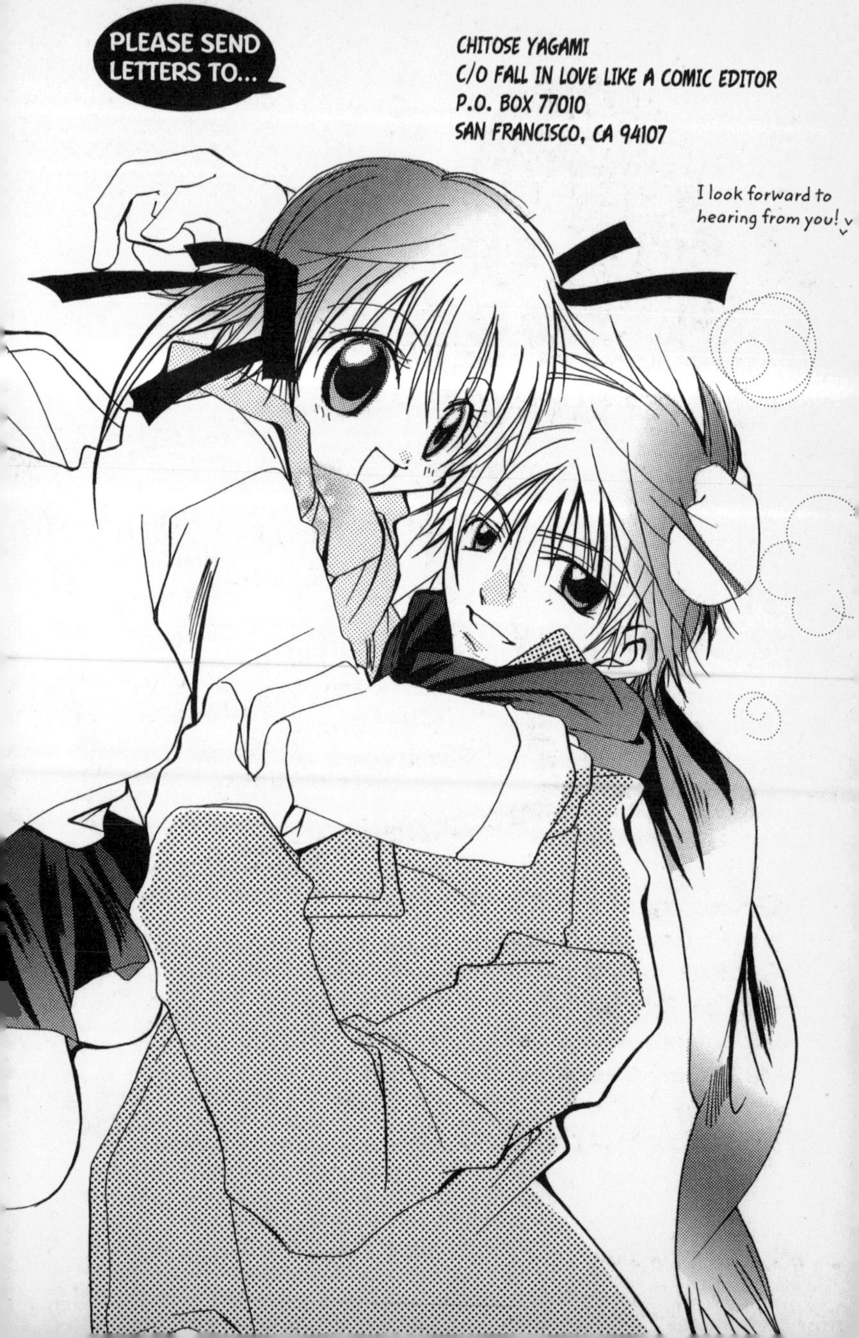
PLEASE SEND LETTERS TO...
CHITOSE YAGAMI
C/O FALL IN LOVE LIKE A COMIC EDITOR
P.O. BOX 77010
SAN FRANCISCO, CA 94107
I look forward to hearing from you!

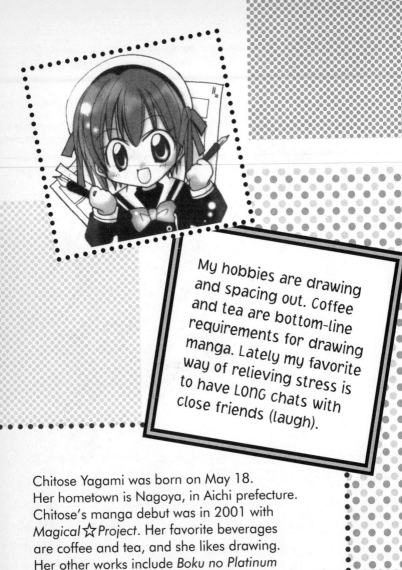

My hobbies are drawing and spacing out. Coffee and tea are bottom-line requirements for drawing manga. Lately my favorite way of relieving stress is to have LONG chats with close friends (laugh).

Chitose Yagami was born on May 18. Her hometown is Nagoya, in Aichi prefecture. Chitose's manga debut was in 2001 with *Magical ☆ Project*. Her favorite beverages are coffee and tea, and she likes drawing. Her other works include *Boku no Platinum Lady* (My Platinum Lady), *Kiss Kiss*, and *Ikenai Navigation* (Naughty Navigation).

Fall in Love Like a Comic
Vol. 1
The Shojo Beat Manga Edition

STORY & ART BY
CHITOSE YAGAMI

Translation & Adaptaton/Mai Ihara
Touch-up Art & Lettering/Elena Diaz
Design/Izumi Hirayama
Editor/Nancy Thistlethwaite

VP, Production/Alvin Lu
VP, Publishing Licensing/Rika Inouye
VP, Sales & Product Marketing/Gonzalo Ferreyra
VP, Creative/Linda Espinosa
Publisher/Hyoe Narita

MANGAMITAINAOKI SHITAI! by Chitose YAGAMI
© 2004 Chitose YAGAMI
All rights reserved.
Original Japanese edition published in 2002 by
Shogakukan Inc. Tokyo. The stories, characters and
incidents mentioned in this publication are entirely fictional.

Printed in Canada

Published by VIZ Media, LLC
P.O. Box 77064
San Francisco, CA 94107

Shojo Beat Manga Edition
10 9 8 7 6 5 4 3
First printing, October 2007
Third printing, February 2009

www.viz.com   store.viz.com

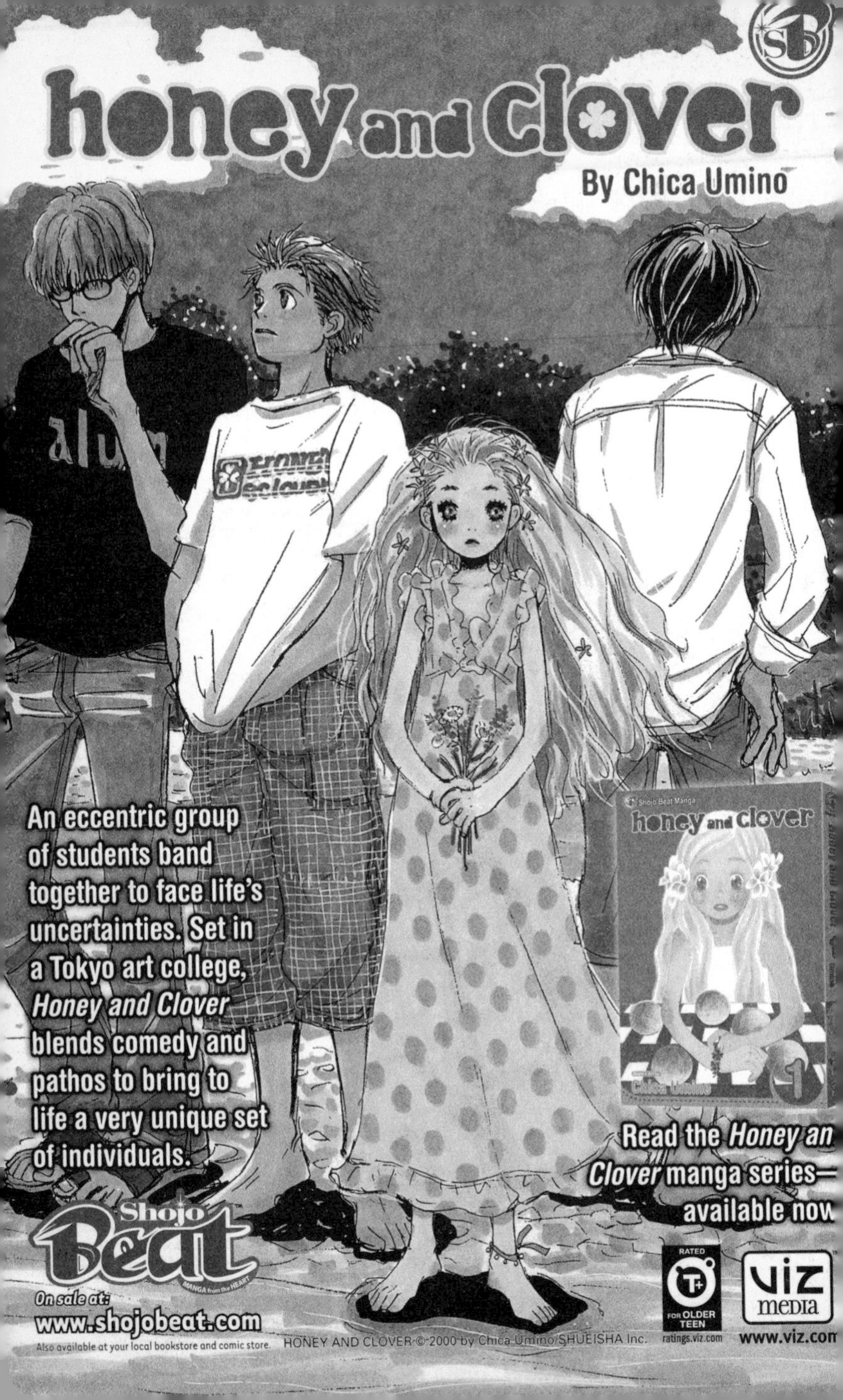

honey and clover
By Chica Umino
An eccentric group of students band together to face life's uncertainties. Set in a Tokyo art college, *Honey and Clover* blends comedy and pathos to bring to life a very unique set of individuals.
Shojo Beat Manga
honey and clover
1
Read the *Honey an* *Clover* manga series— available now
Shojo Beat
On sale at:
www.shojobeat.com
Also available at your local bookstore and comic store.
HONEY AND CLOVER © 2000 by Chica Umino/SHUEISHA Inc.
RATED T+ FOR OLDER TEEN
ratings.viz.com
viz media
www.viz.com

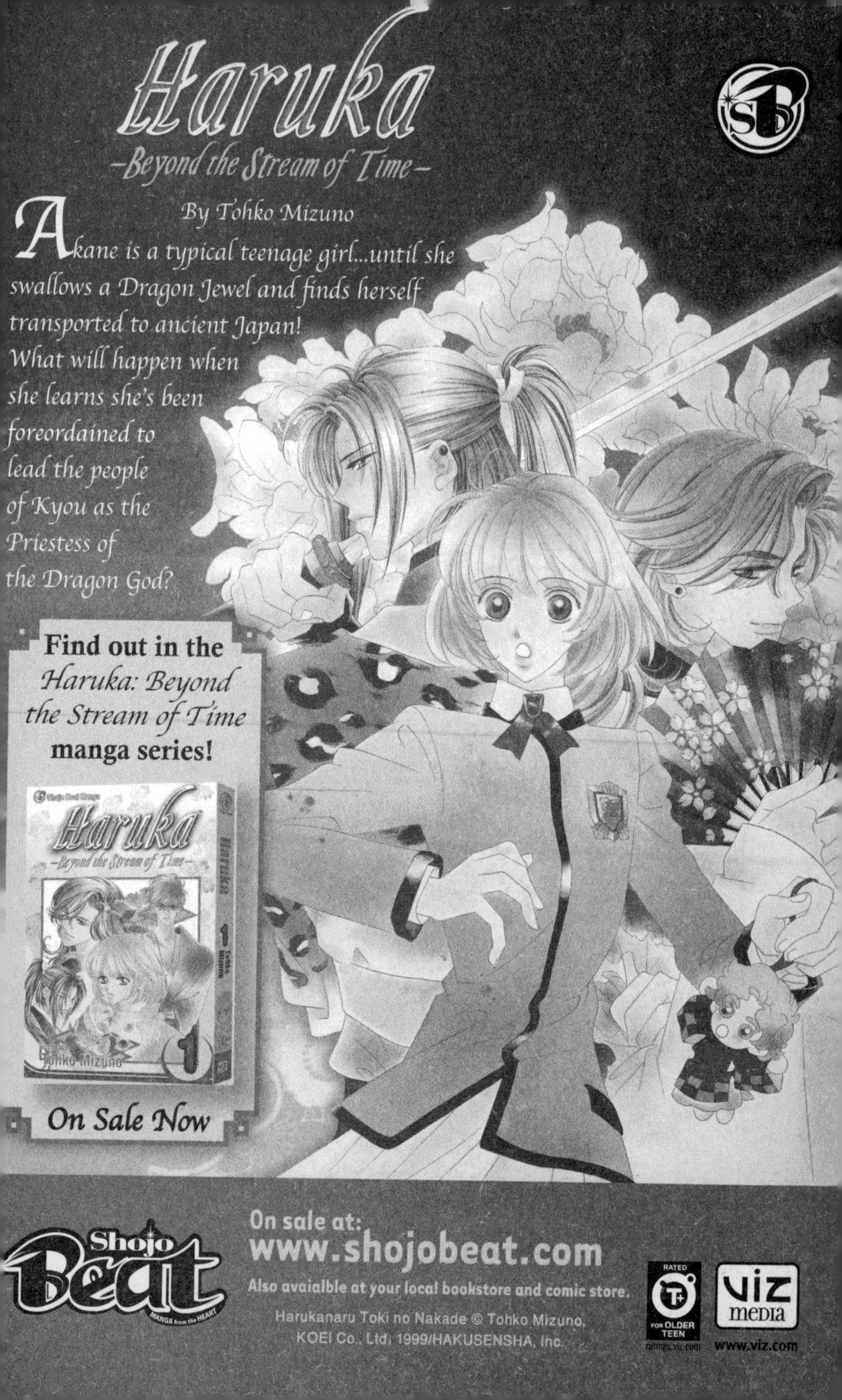
Haruka
-Beyond the Stream of Time-
By Tohko Mizuno
Akane is a typical teenage girl...until she swallows a Dragon Jewel and finds herself transported to ancient Japan! What will happen when she learns she's been foreordained to lead the people of Kyou as the Priestess of the Dragon God?
Find out in the Haruka: Beyond the Stream of Time manga series!
On Sale Now
Shojo Beat
MANGA from the HEART
On sale at:
www.shojobeat.com
Also avaialble at your local bookstore and comic store.
Harukanaru Toki no Nakade © Tohko Mizuno, KOEI Co., Ltd. 1999/HAKUSENSHA, Inc.
RATED T+ FOR OLDER TEEN
ratings.viz.com
VIZ media
www.viz.com

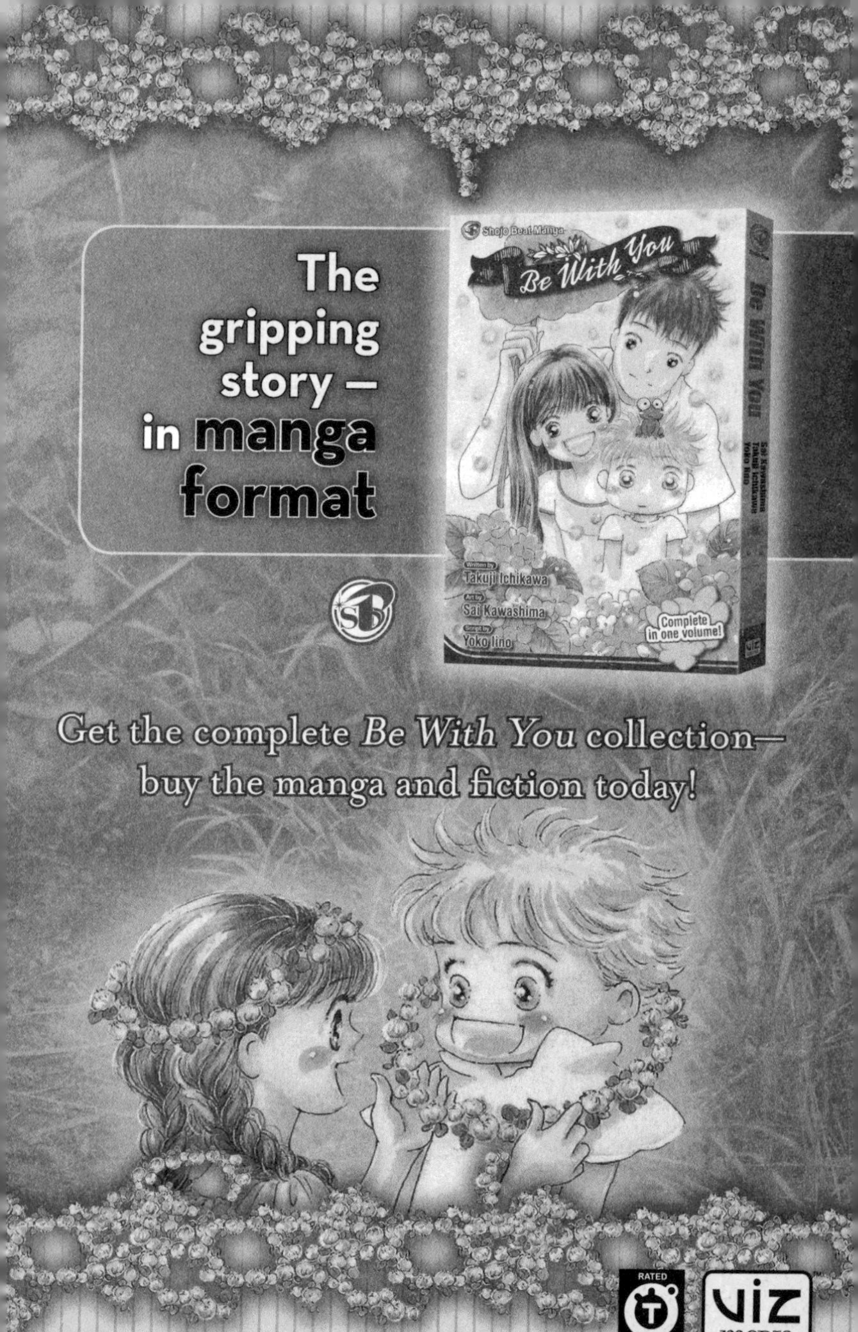

The gripping story — in manga format
Shojo Beat Manga
Be With You
Takuji Ichikawa
Sai Kawashima
Yoko Iino
Complete in one volume!
Get the complete Be With You collection— buy the manga and fiction today!
RATED T FOR TEEN
ratings.viz.com
VIZ MEDIA
www.viz.com

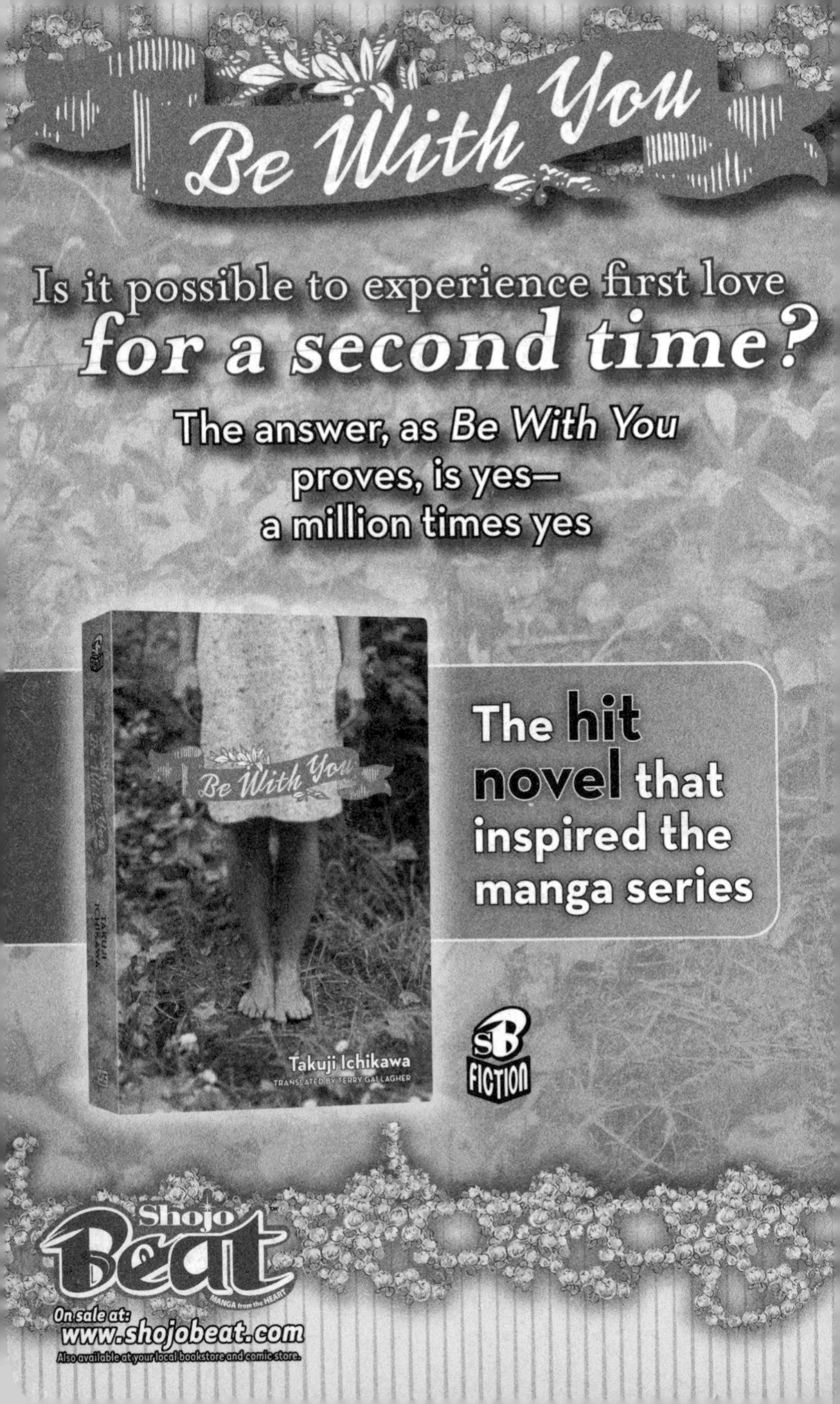
Be With You
Is it possible to experience first love
for a second time?
The answer, as Be With You
proves, is yes—
a million times yes
Be With You
Takuji Ichikawa
TRANSLATED BY TERRY GALLAGHER
The hit novel that inspired the manga series
SB FICTION
Shojo Beat
MANGA from the HEART
On sale at:
www.shojobeat.com
Also available at your local bookstore and comic store.

Tell us what you think about Shojo Beat Manga!

Our survey is now available online. Go to:

shojobeat.com/mangasurvey

Help us make our product offerings better!